Human Computer Interaction:
Issues and Challenges

Qiyang Chen
Montclair State University, USA

IDEA GROUP PUBLISHING
Hershey • London • Melbourne • Singapore

Acquisition Editor:	Mehdi Khosrowpour
Managing Editor:	Jan Travers
Development Editor:	Michele Rossi
Copy Editor:	Brenda Zboray Klinger
Typesetter:	Tamara Gillis
Cover Design:	Deb Andree
Printed at:	Sheridan Books

Published in the United States of America by
Idea Group Publishing
1331 E. Chocolate Avenue
Hershey PA 17033-1117
Tel: 717-533-8845
Fax: 717-533-8661
E-mail: cust@idea-group.com
Web site: http://www.idea-group.com

and in the United Kingdom by
Idea Group Publishing
3 Henrietta Street
Covent Garden
London WC2E 8LU
Tel: 44 20 7240 0856
Fax: 44 20 7379 3313
Web site: http://www.eurospan.co.uk

Library of Congress Cataloging-in-Publication Data

Human computer interaction : issues and challenges / Qiyang Chen [ed.].
    p. cm.
  Includes bibliographical references and index.
  ISBN 1-878289-91-8 (paper)
    1. Human-computer interaction. I. Chen, Qiyang, date.
QA76.9.H85 H858 2001
004'.01'9--dc21   00-054108

British Cataloguing in Publication Data
A Cataloguing in Publication record for this book is available from the British Library.

NEW from Idea Group Publishing

Human Computer Interaction:
Issues and Challenges

Table of Contents

Preface

Human-computer interaction (HCI) is a multi-disciplinary subject that involves information technology, computer science, psychology, library science, education, business and management, human factors, industrial engineering and ergonomics. As more and more peoples' life relate to interactions with computer systems, researchers, designers, managers and users have ever-stronger desires to understand the complexity, current situation and future development of HCI. This book will present a broad view of theoretical and practical issues in HCI to serve such desires. The goal of this book is to reflect the most current, primary issues regarding human-computer interactive systems. It emphasizes effective design, use and evaluation on computer interactive systems. It also intends to highlight the trend of HCI research, design and management at the turn of the century.

The effective HCI has been recognized as a very promising and challenging area for both research and applications. The objective of an interface is to adapt system responses to the user effectively in a complex computer-based task. In the context of human computer interaction, the relationship between a human and a computer involves many factors such as the computing environment, the nature of the tasks to be performed, as well as various characteristics of the users. The effectiveness of a human-computer interface system is influenced greatly by its ability to adapt to these factors.

This book contains fifteen chapters. They cover a variety of issues such as interface design and evaluation methodology, cognitive models and user models, health and ergonomic studies, empirical studies of user factors, intelligent agents, user interface prototyping, hypertext and virtual reality, and managerial issues in interface design.

The chapter by Drommi addresses the methodology that incorporates human behavior factors into the process of interface design. It emphasizes that the embedded process of interface design for human interactivity is essential for products that meet social and functional standards. The author discusses how the traditional process of software engineering embeds interface design as a task component. It shows that the interface design process has grown as a discipline and is beyond the single process within a larger scheme that may be lost on the priority list.

The chapter by Ambler describes the importance and the methodology of interface development that should be implemented within an organization's software development lifecycle. The author discusses a collection of techniques for each phase of software development, showing how user interface development can easily be integrated into the overall software process.

The chapter by Lowgren argues that an appropriate design perspective is better suited to meet the challenge than the traditional foundations of experimental psychology and information systems development. The author discusses the idea of interaction design and the issues of interactive systems with particular emphasis on their use qualities. The author also discusses a number of foundational concepts from contemporary design studies and interaction design perspective as well as their implications to software development and higher education.

There are four chapters in this book addressing the issues of applying agent technology to facilitate interactive systems. The chapter by Ayala addresses modeling of intelligent agents to support a learning environment through collaborative social interaction. The collaboration is based on the social construction of knowledge. The chapter includes a discussion on the requirements for modeling software agents for learning environments, as well as the use of AI techniques for their implementation. The HCI issues of group configuration and awareness based on learner modeling in web-based environments are also discussed.

The chapter by Park and Sugumaran focuses on the modeling phase of agent-oriented software life cycle. The authors present an approach for agent modeling consisting of *Agent Elicitation, Intra,* and *Inter Agent* modeling methods. *Agent Elicitation* deals with identifying and extracting agents from "classes" in the real world. *Intra Agent* modeling involves expressing agent characteristics such as goal, belief, plan and capability. *Inter Agent* modeling incorporates agent mobility and communication.

The chapter by Darbyshire and Lowry explores the application of agent technology to evolve an information system. In particular, the use of agents to evolve an educational subject management application is viewed in relation to an on-going project. The authors discuss the potential of agent technology to advance Web-based subject management courseware to a further evolutionary stage.

The chapter by Raisinghani, Klassen and Schkade provides an analytical review on software agents from a socio-technical viewpoint. This chapter presents some of the challenges of the current state of intelligent agent software technology. They include issues such as lack of standardization in mobile agents that may cause lack of ability of tracing identity and the security concerns related to limiting agent access rights.

The chapter by Chen and Norcio discusses the issues of user modeling and its role in adaptive human-computer interface. Particularly, it focuses on knowledge acquisition and representation in user modeling. The authors present several problems in traditional user modeling systems and suggest using neural network technology to address those problems.

The chapter by Sillince and Duska addresses the issue of how, in computer-mediated communication, an individual keeps in touch with what everybody else is doing. This issue is important to ensure team-workers to act proactively rather than to spend too much time on watching and listening passively. This chapter presents a cognitive model that provides a number of practical advantages for supporting the process of teamwork in computer-mediated environment.

The chapter by Chang and Jin presents a design to support the content-based information retrieval. A high-dimensional index structure based on the X-tree is developed to store and retrieve both color and shape feature vectors efficiently in an XML document retrieval system. The performance is evaluated in terms of system efficiency, such as retrieval time, insertion time, storage overhead, as well as system effectiveness, such as recall and precision measures.

The chapter by Lemahieu presents a hypermedia framework that is a structured approach to both data modeling and navigation, so as to overcome the problems of maintainability and user disorientation. The data model provides a hyperbase structure and an abundance of meta-information that facilitates implementation of an enhanced navigation paradigm. The author discusses this context-based navigation paradigm that builds upon the data model to reconcile navigational freedom with nested, dynamically created guided tours. The intended navigation mechanism functions as an "intelligent book" to provide a disoriented user with a sequential path as guidance.

The chapter by Lazar and Norcio presents a case study of user considerations in e-commerce transactions. The authors discuss the users' needs for functionality and usability of an interactive system for e-commerce transaction. Results of a study of over 150 users and the factors that influence their decision of purchase are presented and analyzed. This chapter is an example of current research on user satisfaction for e-commerce transactions.

The chapter by Ogata, Yano and Furugori describes an interactive system, PeCo-Mediator-II, to seek for capable cooperators with the chain of personal connections in a networked organization. It shows that this system helps gathering, exploring, and visualizing social networks in an organization. The experimental results show that the system facilitates users encounter cooperators and develop a new helpful relationship with the cooperators.

The chapter by Ron Purser discusses the possible social impact that Virtual Reality technology may have on society. This chapter examines two possible future scenarios for Virtual Reality technology, "VR1" versus "VR2." VR1 is shown to lead to further cultural fragmentation and pathologies of perception; whereas VR2 could evoke a cultural renaissance that stimulates social creativity and the evolution of consciousness.

The chapter by Lapeer, Chios, Linney and Alusi discusses the concepts of human-computer interaction in the context of computer-assisted surgical interventions, training and planning (CASPIT). This chapter presents some examples in commercial and academic applications in CASPIT. It also provides a case study on the ergonomic issues of computer-assisted ENT surgery using augmented reality (CAESAR).

Acknowledgment

The editor would like to acknowledge the help of all those involved in the review and collation process of the book, without whose support the project could not have been satisfactorily completed. A further special note of thanks goes also to all the staff at Idea Group Publishing, whose contributions throughout the whole process from inception of the initial idea to final publication have been invaluable. Most of the authors of chapters included in this also served as referees for articles written by other authors. Thanks go to all those who provided constructive and comprehensive reviews.

I would also like to thank Dr. Mehdi Khosrowpour whose enthusiasm motivated me to initially accept his invitation for taking on this project. Special thanks also go to the publishing team at Idea Group Publishing. In particular to Michele Rossi and Bill Breidenstine, who continuously prodded via e-mail for keeping the project on schedule and provided me with necessary information for organizing the chapters.

In closing, I wish to thank all of the authors for their insights and excellent contributions to this book. I also want to thank all of the people who assisted me in the reviewing process. In addition, this book would not have been possible without the ongoing professional support from Dr. Mehdi Khosrowpour and Jan Travers at Idea Group Publishing. Finally, I want to thank my mother, my wife and my daughter for their love and support throughout this project.

Qiyang Chen, Ph.D.
Associate Professor of MIS
Department of Information and Decision Sciences
School of Business
Montclair State University
Upper Montclair, NJ 07043, USA

Chapter I

Interface Design: An Embedded Process for Human Computer Interactivity

Antonio Drommi
University of Detroit Mercy, USA

INTRODUCTION

This chapter will address the issues of interface design and incorporation of human behavior factors into the design process. The traditional process engineering approach to software development embeds interface design as a task component. However, the interface design process has grown as a discipline and is beyond the single process within a larger scheme that may be lost on the priority list. The functionality and specifications for software developers tend to focus on the project and less on the product. In addition, bridging the gap of the design process to include global elements of the software is an issue for products that are internationally distributed. It is something that the computer industry must address and has been historically unsuccessful at doing. Incorporating human interactivity and screen design requires an understanding of the user and their behavior that is not part of the traditional tasks of most designers and programmers. This chapter presents the importance of human interactivity and interface design as an embedded process.

There are major strides towards interface design in the software process. The many approaches and theories guide the practitioner down a path that is normally practiced by graphic designers, artists, writers, psychologists, or marketing personnel. In many cases, the traditional software developer wears many hats plunging into a world of creativity and human behavior. These disciplines are not a natural path for developers who may began their career being computer savvy joining the ranks of the computer experts. Their successes have moved them up the ranks of the industry to lead many projects deemed for global markets.

Initially, many human factors did not play a major role in user interface design. Many of the interactive systems were products of manager decisions or it was implied for the product. Individuals involved in human behavior factors were brought into the projects in the middle or later in the project until they were no longer needed (Hix and Hartsen, 1993). Traditionally, designers have aimed at developing software products that meet the functional requirements of the application domain. We are moving into the direction of incorporating the behavioral domain of the user interaction developer that is responsible for class definitions, interaction design, and human factors engineering (Hix and Hartsen,

1993). Increasing interactivity is a major goal of every software design, which requires mirroring user behavior. The understanding and sensitivity of human nature is not an integral part of traditional approaches to the design process and the MIL-STD-1472C standard was developed by the military entitled "User-Computer Interfaces" to provide practitioners guidelines for interface design. The importance of this document lends itself to the discipline. However, graphical user interface and multimedia development guidelines focus on common sense practice of design. The literature and standards may not provide the developer with the skills of understanding human behavior and culture. We can only hope that the product developed meets the requirements intended for interactivity.

USER REQUIREMENTS

If we study the traditional waterfall approach to software development, we notice that design and development are used in a broader term that incorporates interface design within the development process. What we don't see in this model is whether interface design is actually a process. Nevertheless, interactivity for interface design is a norm and must be part of the process. The difficulty is designing products that can be ready for an audience to embrace. The audience can be a client for which the software is being developed or a target market for which the product to be adopted. Nevertheless, we don't know how the user of such products will react to the product. With that in mind, designers must develop requirements that reflect the intended user or target market. Therefore, communicating among the project team is essential. Interface design processes must be in the tasks of the project. However, what about interactivity and user reactions and adoption to the products? Project plans need to take stock of the fact that the behavior domain be part of the process. Several tasks may be performed concurrently. These are task analysis, user and audience analysis, market analysis, and cultural analysis. These tasks may seem broad, but are essential for designers who want to reach users expectations of the product.

The father of visual basic Alan Cooper says that design in terms of goals is usually derived from the programmer's point of view (Cooper, 1995). Cooper suggests that design should be directed toward more basic user goals such as *"to not look stupid or make any big mistakes"*. A front-end analysis is required to truly capture the essence of what is required of the product and not just examine problems in the application domain. It must also consider the factors that affect the human behavior elements. That requires getting into the mindset of the average user, a performance analyses term that describes a process to study what needs to be done (Rossett, 1999).

TASK ANALYSIS

Task analysis which is sometimes known as function analysis provides practitioners with the user tasks or functions that is required of the user. The user tasks are an important feature for investigating every element. Working with potential end users is an important component of the process. Collecting data and communicating with the user on their tasks or job functions paints a picture of their role during interactivity (Hackos and Redish, 1997). At this stage, the behavior or traits of the user begin to surface. The level of user skills is recorded to determine the adopting factor that reflects the user personality and skill level, knowledge, and experience (Galitz, 1997). While this task in this process is taking place, documentation on the user is building up to support some of the missing links of the human behavior domain. Software developers must take stock in this step of the process because it may be the only chance to gather this type of data. It's not enough to address the users perception for the product and interactivity based simply on tasks or functions that the software must provide. One could be mislead into designing an interface that reflects tasks that are required of the product. However, designers must look beyond the nature of what the product should do or provide for the end user. The difficulty of doing task analysis is the multiple variables that one must consider for the user such as the user environment.

ENVIRONMENT ANALYSIS

This task evaluates the environment where the user will use the product. Designers sometimes overlook the fact that interactivity and screen design must blend into the environment of the user. Human performance technologists look at organization performance levels. Where many problems of performance are a result of tools or resources. Tools and resources are required in the workplace and are considered essential for the day to day internal processes. A poor environment can block the success of skilled and motivated people (Rossett, 1999). No matter how important the software is as a tool, it does not guarantee efficiency and performance. A cause analysis may reveal that the users finds the software difficult to use or is difficult to work with in their environment. A possible intervention is ergonomics of redesigning the workspace to adapt to the computer workstation and the software. Making the tools that are used and compatible with the abilities of the person using the tool (Van Tiem, Moseley, and Dessinger, 2000). That is not an option for many clients, an expensive work space renovation is costly although it may be effective. Interface design is an intervention that can adapt to the environment of the user. If the environment is evaluated and considered in the design process, the software will provide the user a screen that contrast or blends with the workspace. Examples are cash register systems that are designed with screens that consider background and environment. Large touch screen buttons and numbers appeal to users that work in a fast paced environment. Restaurants have computers placed in areas of the restaurant where servers or managers interact. The systems are sometimes placed in areas that are close to customers. However, the restaurant lighting may be dimmed to provide their customers the elegance of fine dinning. The environment in this situation has created a problem for the user of the software on that system. Viewing the screen can be difficult and problematic, but with a redesigned screen with the dimmed lighting in consideration creates an interface that will work in that environment. It is necessary to control and measure the room illumination that will affect the visual threshold (Gordon, 1997). A physical change in the environment can change the meaning of the information users process (Mandel, 1997). One cannot stress an environment analysis before developing a screen. Conducting an environment analyses is important in order to create a software screen that will appeal and work in any environment. It is a difficult and tall task to consider and cannot be fulfilled without constructive criticism from end users, nevertheless, a designer must review and evaluate the environment to create an effective tool for interaction.

AUDIENCE ANALYSIS

Audience can be defined as the user of the software. System analysts generally provide information on job processes and description but sometimes leave out the human factor of the big picture. Many users are hired to work in positions that require them to use software tools but do not have the skill level to perform the job itself. As mentioned earlier human performance technologists may reveal the cause to be lack of skill or training and an intervention would be training or job aids. Another causal factor could be the interface the

Table 1

	Audience Checklist
Audience Factor	
Gender	How many males versus females. Female audience may perceive differently from a male audience.
Age group	Consider the age range of the users who will use the software. For example, children versus adults.
Skill level	Investigate the computer skill level and education of the user.
Work processes	Evaluate and study the task, work processes or function of the user.
Language and culture	Investigate the diversity of the audience. What is the common language and culture of the users?

user is working with. An interface designer has the opportunity to gather information about the user that programmers generally do not see. Asking questions about the users background and skill level is a practical solution to understanding the user. If you don't ask, you won't know. A needs assessment technique such as interviews is essential for gathering user data (Rossett, 1999). Users are diverse and most important they may not perceive things in the same way others do. Perception is an important factor. Perception is a combination of information available through the senses (Mandel, 1997). Understanding the perception of a user can be broken down into several essential areas. Table 1 is a checklist to consider when dealing with a user audience.

Table 1 provides a designer a quick checklist before beginning an audience analysis. There are many techniques for gathering information on an audience. Needs assessment techniques can uncover many pieces of the puzzle that will make up the mindset of the average user. Interviews, observation, surveys, and focus groups are a few techniques to consider (Rossett, 1987). The cost factor is time and the human resource to gather this type of information. However, doing right the first time can create the software on budget and on time. Not considering an audience analysis and referring audience information based on existing data may create a larger project, which may involve several prototypes before the audience accepts the software. The audience is the ultimate customer, getting buy-in from the customer is important. Most important get the buy-in from the management of the client. Decision makers should be part of the process and be aware of this task and the reasons for it. If management does not buy into the design process component, the design team is left with little to work on besides data and information the client provides them. Selling the process and the visual screen design is an important step for interface design.

DIVERSITY AND CULTURAL ELEMENTS

Culture can be anything. In the corporate world culture is viewed as the internal makeup and behavior of the masses within an organization. In a global environment, culture is language and perception. Culture can be viewed in context and context is everything. Language itself cannot be the only aspect of global culture. With the proliferation of web applications and e-commerce sites, interface design has become international. It is an exciting time for designers. However, gathering and evaluating cultural information on the cultural masses is a huge undertaking. Sociologist may provide some of the answers designers are looking for when designing for a global audience. However, each culture is different and perceives things differently. Table 1 lists culture and language as part of the audience analysis checklist. This checklist item is important if software or web sites are to reach the global masses. Design evolves from cultural attitudes and expectation towards tasks that are to be performed (Del Galdo, 1996). Thinking and designing globally must be included in the design process. However, cultural diversity can exist within an organization where companies and organizations employ many individuals of diverse cultures who may use the software that is to be developed. Cultural attitudes are difficult to determine for the designer and are rarely addressed in design (Del Galdo, 1996). Cultural diversity is a serous issue in interface design due to the fact that different cultural groups may react to features such as colors and screens design. Colors have cultural meaning to many; how does a designer factor color. The normal rule of thumb is to keep colors neutral and though there are millions of colors available, a designer only needs to use a few of them. When in doubt keep it neutral and simple and four colors per screen is a standard rule. The key is to research the cultural group before selecting colors and objects for the screen. The success of an international user interface is when a user can switch from one language to another and still know how to use the program (Mandel, 1997). The important issue to this component is to be cognizant of the potential diverse users of the software.

A FRAMEWORK OF INTERFACE DESIGN PROCESS

Interface design process is not necessarily part of the larger software development process. Design is a task of the process where the emphasis is to establish a design process that focus on screen design as a module of the larger software development process. Many models have been developed over the years that look at interface and GUI as a separate process. The models reflect their authors' perception of what designers should consider. Many models reflect the same components and issues, but have different graphical representation for designers to follow as a job aid. The traditional waterfall method incorporates a linear process of software development. However, with rapid prototyping in today's market, iterative processes are required. The traditional waterfall method lacks the iterative component. The components that will be introduced here are task and function analysis, audience analysis, cultural analysis, storyboard, customer evaluation and review, design, test and evaluation, implementation, formative, and summative evaluations. Figure 1 describes the processes of computer user interactive design process that would be embedded as part of the software development project. An iterative process can be part of the larger software engineering process. The analysis processes are generally included in the systems analysis stage of the software process, but could be added to include the interface design component. The prototype development implies an iterative process depending on the evaluation and usability testing of the software screen design. The designer must identify the areas of usability, which are critical of the interface such as rate of performance, error rate, GUI effectiveness (Redman-Pyle and Moore, 1995).

The process in Figure 1 is not linear, however represents an iterative opportunity for designers to revisit various steps if needed. Rapid design and prototyping is normal. The story board component will keep the cost of the project down with evaluation and buy-in of the design by the client or user. Each iterative process allows the designer the opportunity to focus on each specific component of the process. Evaluation by the client and the users is an integral part of the design's success. Including potential audience is an advantage and allows the audience or the user to be part of the process. It provides the user with a sense of ownership to the product. Formative evaluation comes in many forms such as customer surveys and interviews. For web-based applications, formative evaluation can be on-line and anonymous; however the information and data that is gathered of the functionality of the software is essential to its success. Web applications have a unique advantage of gathering data quickly for developers to test, redesign and implement to satisfy the users that

Figure 1: Interface Design Process

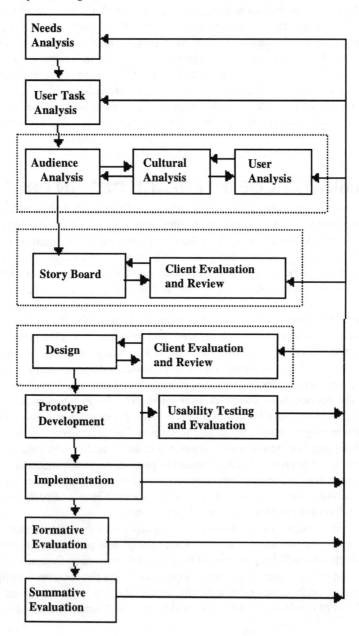

respond to the formative evaluation. There is no limit to the number of evaluations a designer should implement; the more data gathered the greater the success of the screen design. After a period, the product should undergo a summative evaluation to confirm the success of design with the users and clients. A summative evaluation is a final review of what the product and screen should be doing. It is not with out saying that further revisions won't occur, but summative evaluation signals the end of the project. However, software is dynamic in nature and it is always ongoing and usually requires revisions and changes.

DESIGN PRACTICES

Design practices are whatever the designer claims to be a best practice. Seasoned designers have learned that best practices evolve through success of their projects. To capture the essence of interface design today is to capture the human behavior aspects during the design process. Needs assessment is a major component which captures the human element of the interactivity component. The need of certain tasks and events for the software is difficult to determine. Documenting and evaluating each aspect of what the product is required to do is important; however what the product is supposed to do and what it will do in the context of screen design are two different things. Bridging the gap of "what" and "should" of the software is key to a needs assessment. Taking a page from performance technology, a needs assessment is a front-end technique that seeks opinion on the optimal feelings and solutions from users (Rossett, 1987). In many cases designers have little time to consider needs assessment. Simple interview and data collection may be the only needs assessment that a designer incorporates in the process. More sophisticated assessments techniques should be considered in order to keep the competitive edge. Working directly with the users provides a designer with a wealth of human factor information of how they think and react to certain stimuli. Focus groups are a practical way of gathering information about the attitudes and behavior of typical users that will use the software. Please remember that focus groups represent a sample of the audience that will use the software. It is difficult to determine exactly how users will react and interact with the screen. Behaviors are triggered by the screen and its objects. It is up to the designer to sample and develop metaphors that will stimulate the user. A needs assessment technique such as interviews and surveys can determine how people will react to these screen objects and events.

Figure 2 illustrates the merging of the application domain and behavior domain with their corresponding attributes. The intersection of the domains allows the process to merge both disciplines, ensuring a quality process for software, and interface development. As mentioned earlier in this chapter, the two domains must work hand in hand to ensure that interface design principles exist in a much larger software process.

A task analysis determines the workflow of the user. Performance issues that result from workflow can be remedied with a proper screen interface that will make user tasks simpler and intuitive. Analyzing every task and step of the user's tasks will determine the level of screen displays and functionality. How does an interface make life easier for a user? Chunking the tasks into multiple screens is one possibility for keeping the flow simpler and manageable. The motivation and behavior of the user will be positive resulting in the effective use of the product.

E-commerce sites are designed to sell products or services. Many sites are poorly designed with little thought of the user diversity. An example, students in my computer literacy course were asked to do an e-commerce exercise by shopping for an automobile on-line. They were to compare two vehicles from two different competitors. In their reports, they were to describe their experience as a user. Many enjoyed the experience but were

Figure2: Software Development and Interface Design Context Model

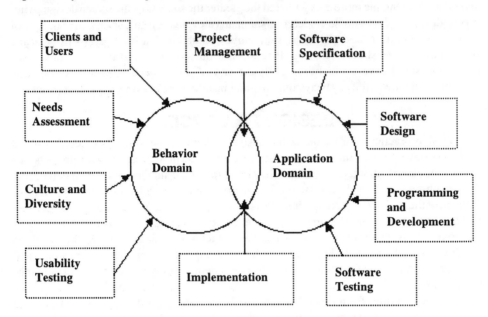

critical of the web sites. The majority felt the navigational components were not user friendly. Surprisingly, several of the women in this exercise were very critical and felt the sites were designed by male engineers that did not consider women automobile shoppers. The male portion of the class was indifferent to the look and feel of the sites. Though this was not a conclusive study, the exercise expressed reactions to the interface that were linked to gender attitudes. The interesting part about this exercise was that gender behavior was significant. Creating stereotypes will only defeat the purpose of the screen design. A designer must be compassion and cognizant of all aspects of human behavior. Gender is one of the most significant components along with race and culture. The only way a designer can be successful is to educate them on diversity and human behavior. The cultural diversity training is important as well as human perception theory.

PRODUCT OBJECTIVES

The objectives of the product may be documented by the client in a kickoff meeting, but the product make take on a new face in the end if the designer follows the design process. Product objectives must be determined in the early stages of the design processes. The decision makers of an organization may envision the product as a tool and resource that will improve performance levels. However, increasing performance via product specifications depicted in the application domain may not yield a product that will improve performance. The behavior domain will determine the product objectives and outcomes that incorporate humans who will perform the interactivity of tasks on the screen. During the user analysis stage, it is important to bring out the users expectations of the product. While incorporating their behavior and attitudes, the product objectives will come forward. The designer gathers all the objectives and strategies of the product and determines the strategies of each event that occurs on the interactive screen. Product strategies and objectives may seem related towards computer-based training product development. However, the human interactivity component of the screen and events occur as a result of the user interaction. It requires that the designer evaluates each objective and that it aligns them with the mission and goals of the organization or group that will use the software. All the variables of behavior and culture must be incorporated into the big picture of software development.

TRENDS OF INTERFACE DESIGN

The issues of trends in interface design leans towards rapid prototyping and cultural diversity. With the proliferation of e-commerce and Internet applications, it is understood that interface design is facing its biggest challenge in the global arena. Who will get it to market first and how? Rapid prototyping allows revisions to reach its target or test audience for evaluation. The issue of implementing a design process is essential for quality to withstand time. No rapid prototyping may result in products that skew from the original intentions. All steps of the process must be in place to encourage rapid prototyping. In figure 1 the design and evaluation iteration process allows room for rapid prototyping. A designer cannot produce a well-designed interface without checking with the users (Mandel, 1997). With the tools of development available today, design and rapid changes are common. It the context of this chapter the emphasis is maintaining the integrity of interface design during this process.

Cultural diversity is an essential element in interface design. The trend of incorporating or making screen interactivity politically correct has created an awareness for social correctness. Web site designs are scrutinized and evaluated based on objects and navigation, but have evolved to incorporate cultural diversity and sensitivity to those who would use these sites. The trend to incorporate the behavior domain and culture into software is a trend as long as designers are cognizant and compassion about designing for the intended users. If not, misunderstanding by the international user can result (Connelly, 1996). If the process is followed during the analysis stage and design stage, the product will conform to the cultural requirements.

CONCLUSION

The process of interface design in a larger context of software development has always existed. This chapter was designed to emphasize the embedded process of interface design for human interactivity that is essential for products that meet social and functional standards. The issue at stake is enforcing procedures and processes that incorporate the behavior domain into the product. However, with many products facing demands from clients to be completed and implemented, these products may miss the essential component that triggers the mindset of the user. How does a designer invest the time and resources into these processes? It's in the education of the designers to teach and discipline themselves into good practice. In the end, these practices will pay off. The measurement and evaluation of the users and clients will determine in the near future the gap of cultural diversity and human interactivity with the objectives of the product.

It is not enough to build and design without the human behavior factors of the product into the design process. As a thriving discipline the future of interface design professionals are endless. With Internet application and globally distributed software, designers have the world at their feet to create software that will intrigue and motivate people to use. It is not enough to be creative. Designers have to become culturally diverse and compassionate for the ultimate users. Getting to know the user and the interactivity is all in the process embedded in the software development cycle. In the end, it will be become a win-win situation for the designer and the user.

REFERENCES

Cooper, A. (1995), *About face- the essentials of user interface design*. Foster City, CA: IDG Books Worldwide Inc.

Connolly, J. (1996), Problems in designing the user interface for systems supporting international human-human communication. In Del Galdo, E., Nielsen, J., *International user interfaces*. New York, NY: John Wiley & Sons, Inc.

Del Galdo, E. M. (1996), Culture and design. In Del Galdo, E., Nielsen, J., *International user interfaces*. New York, NY: John Wiley & Sons, Inc.

Galitz, Wilbert O. (1997), *The essentials guide to user interface design: an introduction to GUI design principles and techniques*. New York, NY: John Wiley and sons, Inc.

Gordon, I.E., (1997), *The theories of visual perception*. West Sussex, England: John Wiley & Sons Ltd.

Hackos, J.T., Redish, J.C., (1998), *User and task analysis for interface design*. New York, NY: John Wiley & Sons, Inc.

Hix, D., Hartseon, H.R., (1993), *Developing user interfaces: ensuring usability through product & process*. New York, NY: John Wiley & Sons, Inc.

Mandel, T. (1997), *The elements of user interface design*. New York, NY: John Wiley and Sons, Inc.

Redmond-Pyle, D., Moore, A.(1995), *Graphical user interface design and evaluation (guide)-a practical process*. London, UK: Prentice Hall.

Rossett, A. (1999), *First things fast: a handbook for performance analysis*. San Francisco, CA: Jossey-Bass Pfeiffer.

Rossett, A. (1987), *Training needs assessment*. Englewood Cliffs, NJ: Educational Technolgy Publications.

Van Tiem, D.M., Moseley, J., Desinger, J. C. (2000). *Fundamentals of Performance Technology: A guide to Improving People, Process, and Performance*. International Society of Performance Improvement.

Chapter II

User Interface Development Throughout the System Development Lifecycle

Scott Ambler
Ronin International, USA

ABSTRACT

A fundamental reality of application development is that the user interface is the system to the users. Software development process should reflect this fact. When you ask how user interface development should be reflected within an software development lifecycle (SDLC), you quickly discover that it affects all aspects of software development from requirements through to system delivery. This chapter discusses how user interface development should be reflected in a mature software process and overviews a collection of techniques for each phase of software development, showing how user interface development can easily be integrated into the overall software process.

INTRODUCTION

What is a user interface (UI)? For this chapter a UI encompasses every aspect of a system that a user interacts with, works with, or uses. This includes the screens, browser pages, reports generated by the system. It also includes the documentation and training material, be it printed or electronic, that users work with to understand and/or learn the system. Furthermore, it includes any mechanisms to obtain help and/or support services for the system, either electronic or manual.

The UI is a primary aspect of a system: the UI defines how users interact with and how they perceive a system. Furthermore, the focus of users is primarily on the UI, not on other technical aspects such as the programming language used, the database technologies applied, or the network protocols used by the middleware strategy. To the users the UI is the system, a belief that Raskin (2000) shares when he states "users do not care what is inside the box, as long as the box does what they need done." The implication is that because the UI is of primary concern to the users of a system, the people that a system is built for, that the development approach taken by the builders of a system should reflect this fact. In other words, a modern software development process should include techniques and procedures required to effectively develop user interfaces.

Most modern software processes, including the *Unified Process* (Krutchen, 1999), the *OPEN Process* Graham, Henderson-Sellers, and Younessi, 1997), the *Object-Oriented Software Process* (Ambler, 1998b; Ambler, 1999), and even *eXtreme Programming (XP)* (Beck, 2000) all include the concepts of requirements engineering, analysis, design, implementation, testing, and delivery. So when should UI development issues be taken into consideration? Our industry has long had the concept of user interface design, yet is design the appropriate time to start UI development? Raskin (2000) believes not, pointing out that UI development should be started as early as the requirements phase. This belief also appears to be shared by Constantine and Lockwood (1999) with their inclusion of essential user interface prototyping as a key aspect of requirements definition, as well as by Wiegers (1999) with his inclusion of the identification of usability requirements and user interface prototyping as important requirements engineering techniques. A common principle of software development is that requirements should be analyzed to better understand them. Therefore, because there are UI aspects to the requirements process there must, therefore be UI aspects to analysis. It then follows that UI development must be an important aspect of design, a concept borne out by the plethora of excellent user interface design books on the market, as well as implementation. Finally, prototyping is always necessary to validate the design (Ambler, 2000).

It is clear that user interface development spans the entire software development process, from requirements through to delivery. In the following sections I overview proven UI development techniques for each phase of software development, including requirements, analysis, design, implementation, testing, and delivery. Although this is just a sampling of potential techniques that may be applied on a software development project the critical points to be made are that such techniques exist, and that they are often straightforward to introduce within an organization.

USER INTERFACE DEVELOPMENT AS PART OF REQUIREMENTS

Essential modeling is a fundamental aspect of usage-centered designs, an approach to software development that is detailed in the book *Software for Use* (Constantine and Lockwood, 1999). Essential models are intended to capture the essence of problems through technology-free, idealized, and abstract descriptions. The resulting design models are more flexible, leaving open more options and more readily accommodating changes in technology. Essential models are more robust than concrete representations, simply because they are more likely to remain valid in the face of both changing requirements and changes in the technology of implementation. Essential models of usage highlight purpose, what it is users are trying to accomplish, and why they are doing it. In short, essential models are ideal artifacts to capture the requirements for a system.

Essential UI prototyping, one aspect of essential modeling, is an important requirements engineering technique. An essential user interface prototype (Constantine and Lockwood, 1999; Ambler, 2000) is a low-fidelity model, or prototype, of the UI for a system. It represents the general ideas behind the UI, but not the exact details. Essential UI prototypes represent user interface requirements in a technology independent manner, just as essential use-case models do for behavioral requirements. An essential user interface prototype is effectively the initial state the beginning point of the user interface prototype for a system. It models user interface requirements, requirements that are evolved through analysis and design to result in the final user interface design for a system.

Two basic differences exist between essential UI prototyping and traditional UI prototyping. First, the goal is to focus on users and their usage of the system, not system features. This is one of the reasons designers want to perform essential use-case modeling and essential user interface prototyping in tandem: they each focus on usage. Second, the prototyping tools are simple, including whiteboards, flip-chart paper, and sticky notes. If a designer uses an HTML development tool to build a user interface prototype, then he or she immediately narrows the design space to the functionality supported within browsers. If a designer chooses a Java development environment, then he or she narrows the design space to Java, and if a designer chooses a Windows-based prototyping tool, he or she narrows the design space to whatever is supported on the Windows platform. At the earlier stage, designers should be focused on requirements, not design; therefore, people should be aware of the impact of using technology-specific prototyping tools.

So how to use sticky notes and flip-chart paper to create an essential user interface prototype? Let's start by defining several terms. A major user interface element represents a large-grained item, potentially a screen, HTML page, or report. A minor user interface element represents a small-grained item, typically widgets, such as user input fields, menu items, lists, or static text fields such as labels. When a team is creating an essential user interface prototype, it typically iterates between the following tasks:

1. **Explore system usage**. Your team will explore system usage via several means. First, you will likely work together on a whiteboard to discuss ideas, work on initial drawing together, and generally take advantage of the dynamic nature of whiteboards to come to an understanding quickly of the portion of the system you are discussing. For example, with the university system, you may gather around a whiteboard to make an initial drawing of what a university transcript would contain or what a seminar enrollment submission would contain. Second, essential use-case modeling (Constantine and Lockwood, 1999; Ambler, 2000) is an effective technique for understanding the behavioral requirements for the system and CRC models (Beck and Cunningham, 1989; Ambler, 2000) are an effective technique for understanding the domain concepts the system must support. As design progresses through the requirements analysis you will often work iteratively between essential use-case modeling, CRC modeling, and essential user-interface modeling.

2. **Model major user interface elements**. Major user interface elements, such as potential screens and reports, can be modeled using flip-chart paper. I say potential because whether something is a screen or printed report is a design decision a university transcript could be implemented as an HTML page that the users view by a browser, just like a paper report that is printed and mailed to students, or as an application screen. Each piece of flip-chart paper is given a name, such as "Student Transcript" or "Seminar Enrollment Request" and has the appropriate minor user interface elements added to it as needed. Pieces of flip-chart paper have several advantages: they can be taped to a wall; they are good for working in groups because they make it easier for everyone to see and interact; they are large enough so designers can put many smaller items such as sticky notes on them, which can be stored away between modeling sessions.

3. **Model minor user interface elements**. Minor UI elements, such as input fields, lists, and containers (minor UI elements that aggregate other minor UI elements) are

modeled using sticky notes. Constantine and Lockwood (1999) suggest using different color notes for different types of components, for example, bright colors (yellow or red) for active user interface elements such as input fields versus subdued colors (white or tan) for passive interface elements such as containers. Figure 1 depicts examples of several minor UI elements modeled using sticky notes. The "Student name" sticky is a container that includes four active elements: "First name," "Surname," "Initial(s)," and "Title." The other sticky represents a list of the seminars a student has taken or is currently enrolled in. Notice how each sticky has a name that describes its purpose, but not how it is implemented. You can look at the sticky and immediately know how it is used. On the bottom part of each sticky is a description of the UI element, indicating the type of UI element but, once again, not implying any given technology. For example, I have used terms such as "input field" and not "javax.swing.JtextArea." Even the student name container is described as a bounding box although, in practice, I typically don't bother to label containers. Different sizes of sticky notes are used, indicating the relative size of each UI element. Also notice how the relative order of the UI elements are indicated by the order of the sticky notes: a student's title comes before his/her first name, then come his/her initials and his/her surname. This ordering may change during design but, for now, it is close enough. Sometimes you identify a minor UI element that may not have a major UI element on which to place it. Don't worry. This is an iterative process, so attempt to identify an appropriate major UI element and continue. The very fact that sticky notes do not look like a real GUI widget is a constant visual reminder to the team that you are building an abstract model of the user interface and not the real thing. Each sticky note is, effectively, a placeholder that says you need something there, but you don't know yet the best way to implement it, so for now, you want to leave it open.

4. **Explore the usability of a user interface**. Highly usable systems are learnable; they enable user productivity; their use is easy to remember, and they are supportable. Ensuring system usability is discussed in Section 3.2.

5. **Explore the relationships between user interface elements.** The technique is to be called user interface-flow diagramming, the topic of the following Section 3.3.

Figure 1. Examples of minor user interface elements.

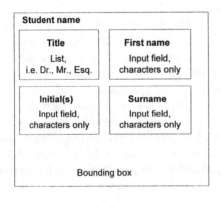

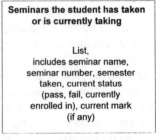

An Example Essential User Interface Model

Figure 2 depicts an essential user interface prototype (Ambler, 2000) for enrolling in a seminar. The outside box represents the flip-chart paper: you typically use one piece of flip-chart paper per major user interface element. The name of the major UI element, in this case "Enroll Student in Seminar," is typically written in one of the corners of the flip-chart paper. Notice how there are three containers, the three largest rectangles, none of which are marked as containers. Also notice how some minor UI elements are input fields, such as "Student Number" and "Student Name," whereas others are display only. "Student Name" is interesting because it is a bit of a cheat, listing four separate data elements on the one sticky note (compare this with the approach taken in Figure 1. I will often do this when I know some thing always come in a group and, when I think I will need the room, which, as you can see in Figure 2, I do. The "Professor" and "Enrollment Requester" hang off the edge of their container, something I did on purpose to show you that you do not have to get your essential user interface prototypes perfect. There are several "Requester" UI elements, for example, "Help Requester" and "Search Requester," indicating user interface elements that are often implemented as push buttons, function keys, or "hot key" combinations, such as CTRL-SHIFT-S. Many of the minor UI elements include detailed notes for how they are used, particularly the elements that support input and the requesters.

Figure 3 depicts a second example of an essential user interface prototype of a major UI element, in this case the student transcript. It is composed of several display-only minor UI elements, such as the name and address of the student. It also contains several elements pertaining to the current status of the student, including basic financial information, which could have been grouped together had the SMEs felt it necessary. Normally, when you build the actual transcript, perhaps as a printed report, you would use all the space available to you, although significant white space is left on the prototype. For example, the list of seminars could horizontally span the entire printed page, whereas this is not indicated in Figure 3. Sticky notes only come in certain sizes and are only meant to model the relative size and positioning of the minor UI elements. Notice how the seminar list in Figure 2 contains different information than the seminar list in Figure 3. This is because each list is used for a different purpose: in Figure 2, to determine which seminars are available, and in Figure 3, to indicate which seminars have been taken by a student. Occasionally, the result will be different informational content and a different purpose.

Figure 2. An essential user interface prototype to enroll a student in a seminar.

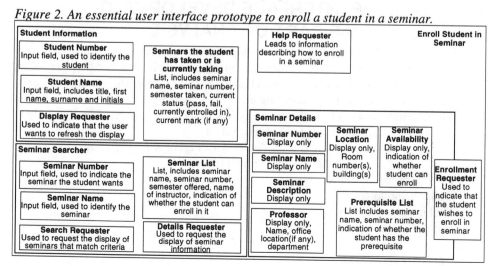

Figure 3. An essential user interface prototype for a student transcript.

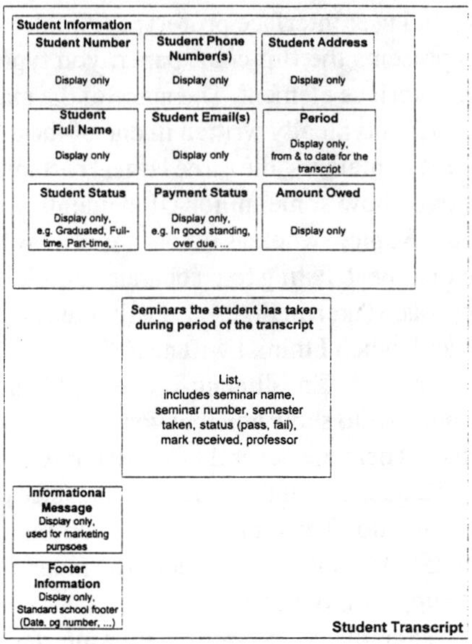

To be honest, I am jumping through hoops not indicating implementation decisions for the major user interface elements. The reality is well-known that the seminar enrollment prototype of Figure 2 is going to be implemented as either a screen or a browser page, so why not admit it? Furthermore, you know the student transcript prototype modeled in Figure 3 will be some sort of report because all the information is display only. Granted, it could be implemented as a printed report, as an electronic file, as a browser page, as a screen, or several of these. When a major user interface element contains one or more minor user interface elements that permit editing, then you know it's going to be a screen or a page. When it contains no editable elements, then it will be a report. If you are going to make a lot of "unnatural" efforts to ensure major user interface elements independent of implementation technology, then you may want to loosen up a bit and distinguish between reports and screens/pages.

USER INTERFACE DEVELOPMENT
AS PART OF ANALYSIS

User interface (UI) prototyping is an analysis technique in which users are actively involved in the mocking-up of the UI for a system. UI prototyping has two purposes: first, it is an analysis technique because it enables the designers to explore the problem space the system addresses. Second, UI prototyping enables the designers to explore the solution space of the system, at least from the point-of-view of its users, and provides a vehicle to communicate the possible UI design(s) of the system.

As shown in the activity diagram depicted in Figure 4 four high-level steps are iteratively performed during the UI prototyping process:
- Determine the user needs
- Build the prototype
- Evaluate the prototype
- Determine if the process is over.

Figure 4. The iterative steps of prototyping.

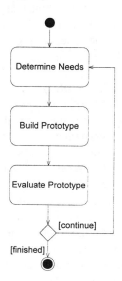

Determining the Needs of Users

User interface modeling moves from requirements definition into analysis at the point you decide to evolve all or part of your essential user interface prototype into a traditional UI prototype. This implies that you convert your hand-drawings, flip-chart paper, and sticky notes into something a little more substantial. You begin this process by making platform decisions. For example, do you intend to deploy the system so it runs in an Internet browser, as an application with a windows-based graphical user interface (GUI), as a cross-platform Java application, or as a mainframe-based set of "green screens?" Different platforms lead to different prototyping tools, for a browser-based application, you need to use an HTML-development tool; whereas a Java-based application would require a Java development tool and a different approach to the user interface design.

Building the Prototype

Using a prototyping tool or high-level language, you develop the screens, pages, and reports needed by users. The best advice during this stage of the process is not to invest a lot of time in making the code "good" because chances are high you will scrap large portions of the prototype code when portions or all of the prototype fail the evaluation. With the user interface platform selected, you can begin converting individual aspects of the essential UI prototype into traditional UI prototype. For example, with a browser-based platform, the major UI elements become HTML pages whereas, with a GUI platform, they would become windows or dialog boxes. Minor UI elements would become buttons, list boxes, custom list boxes, radio buttons, and so on as appropriate for the chosen platform.

Evaluating the Prototype

After a version of the UI prototype is built, it needs to be evaluated by the SMEs to verify it meets their needs. Three basic questions during an evaluation need to be addressed:
• What is good about the UI prototype?
• What is bad about the UI prototype?
• What is missing from the UI prototype?

Determining If the Process is Over

After evaluating the prototype, you may find that you need to scrap parts of it, modify parts, and even add brand-new parts. UI prototyping process will end when the evaluation process is no longer generating any new ideas or it is generating a small number of not-so-important ideas. Otherwise, back to step one.

Good Things to Understand About Prototyping

Constantine and Lockwood (1999) provide valuable insight into the process of user interface prototyping. First, you cannot make everything simple. Sometimes the software will be difficult to use because the problem it addresses is inherently difficult. Your goal is to make the user interface as easy as possible to use, not simplistic. Second, they differentiate between the concepts of WYSIWYG, "What You See Is What You Get," and WYSIWYN, ""What You See Is What You Need." Their point is a good user interface fulfills the needs of the people who work with it. It isn't loaded with a lot of interesting, but unnecessary, features. Third, consistency is important in a user interface. Inconsistent user interfaces lead to less usable software, more programming, and greater support and training costs. Fourth, small details can make or break a user interface. Have you ever used some software, and then discarded it for the product of a competitor because you didn't like the way it prints, saves files, or some other feature you simply found too annoying to use? Although the rest of the software may have been great, that vendor lost my business because a portion of its product's user interface was deficient.

Ensuring System Usability

An important issue to consider during both the analysis and design phases is usability. Why is usability important? First, by focusing on use and usability instead of on features or functionality, on users and their usage more than on user interfaces, the system can be turned into a better tool for the job that is smaller, simpler, and ultimately less expensive (Constantine and Lockwood, 1999). Second, the best systems give pleasure and satisfaction; they make people feel good about using them. Third, the harder a system is to use, the harder and more expensive it is to learn how to use and to support. Unusable features that are difficult to master lead to requests for changes, increasing future maintenance costs. Fourth, as users have grown accustomed to using computer applications, they have also grown less patient with them and, in particular, less patient with poorly designed software. The bar has been raised.

Constantine and Lockwood (1999) suggest five factors affect the usability of software:

1. **Access**. A system should be usable, without help or instruction, by a user who has knowledge and experience in the application domain, but no prior experience with the system.
2. **Efficacy**. A system should not interfere with or impede use by a skilled user who has substantial experience with the system.
3. **Progression**. A system should facilitate continuous advancement in knowledge, skill, and facility, and accommodate progressive change in use as the user gains experience with the system.
4. **Support**. A system should support the real work users are trying to accomplish by making it easier, simpler, faster, or more fun by making new things possible.
5. **Context**. A system should be suited to the real conditions and actual environment of the operational context in which it will be used and deployed.

User Interface-Flow Diagramming

To the users, the interface is the system. It is as simple as that. Designers should have some sort of diagram to model the user interface for the system. Essential user interface prototypes are an excellent means of documenting the requirements for a user interface. As discussed in Section 4, the user interface prototypes are great artifacts to develop user interface design. The problem with both of these techniques is one can quickly be bogged down in the details of the user interface and not see the bigger picture. Consequently, people often miss high-level relationships and interactions between the user interface elements of the application. User interface-flow diagrams (Ambler, 2000), also called interface-flow diagrams (Ambler, 1998a; Ambler, 1998b), windows navigation diagrams (Page-Jones, 2000), and context-navigation maps (Constantine and Lockwood, 1999), enable designer to model the high-level relationships between major user interface elements.

Figure 5 shows the start at a user interface-flow diagram for the university system. The Unified Modeling Language (Rumbaugh, Jacobson, and Booch, 1999), more commonly known as the UML, does not yet support user interface-flow diagrams. However, I have applied a combination of the notations for UML activity diagrams and UML collaboration diagrams in the example. The boxes represent major user interface elements, modeled as objects, and the arrows represent the possible flow between them, modeled as transitions in activity diagrams. For example, when you are on the main menu screen, you can use the "Enrollment Requestor" to take you to the "Enroll in Seminar" UI element. Once you are there, you can either go back to the main menu (going back is always assumed), go to the "Professor Information" UI element, or go to the "Seminar Information" UI element. The addition of these two major UI elements was the result of the SMEs decision to enable students to discover more information about the instructors teaching a seminar and the detailed information regarding prerequisites to a seminar.

Figure 5. Initial user interface-flow diagram for the university system.

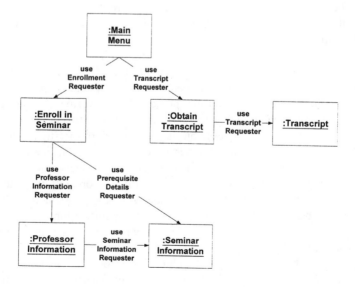

User interface-flow diagrams are typically used for one of two purposes. First, they are used to model the interactions that users have with the software, as defined in a single use case. For example, the use case enrolling a student in a seminar would refer to several UI elements and provide insight into how they are used. Based on this information one can develop a user interface-flow diagram that reflects the behavioral view of the single use case. Second, as shown in Figure 5, by combining all of the behavioral views into one diagram, it provides a high-level overview of the user interface for the application. The high-level overview approach, also referred to as the architectural approach, is preferred, because it helps to understand the complete user interface for a system.

USER INTERFACE DEVELOPMENT AS PART OF DESIGN

This section will discuss two important design issues, layering and improving user interface prototype.

Layering the Design

Layering is the concept of organizing the software design into layers/collections of classes or components that fulfill a common purpose, such as implementing a user interface or the business logic of the system. A class-type architecture (Ambler, 1998a; Ambler, 2000) provides a strategy for layering the classes of the software to distribute the functionality of software among classes. Furthermore, class-type architectures provide guidance as to what other types of classes a given type of class will interact with, and how that interaction will occur. This increases the extensibility, maintainability, and portability of the systems.

What are the qualities that make up good layers? First, designers should be able to make modifications to any given layer without affecting any other layers. This will help to make a system easy to extend and to maintain. Second, layers should be modularized. Designers should be able either to rewrite a layer or simply replace it and, as long as the interface remains the same, the rest of the system should not be affected. This will help to make increase the portability of software.

Figure 6 depicts a five-layer class-type architecture (Ambler, 2000) for the design of object-oriented software. As the name suggests, a user interface (UI) class implements the major UI elements of the system. The business behavior of the system is implemented by two layers: business/domain classes and controller/process classes. Business/domain classes implement the concepts pertinent to the business domain such as "student" or "seminar," focusing on the data aspects of the business objects plus behaviors specific to individual objects. Controller/process classes, on the other hand, implement business logic that involves collaborating with several business/domain classes or even other controller/process classes. Persistence classes encapsulate the capability to store, retrieve, and delete objects permanently without revealing details of the underlying storage technology. Finally, system classes provide operating-system-specific functionality for the applications, isolating the software from the operating system (OS) by wrapping OS-specific features, increasing the portability of the application.

Collaboration between classes is allowed within a layer, for example, UI classes can send messages to other UI classes and business/domain classes can send messages to other business/domain classes. Collaboration can also occur between classes in layers connected by arrows. As shown in Figure 6, user interface classes may send messages to business/

Figure 6. Layering system based on class types.

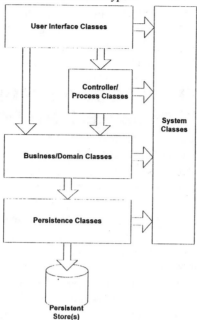

domain classes, but not to persistence classes. Business/domain classes may send messages to persistence classes, but not to user interface classes. By restricting the flow of messages to only one direction, the portability of your system can be improved by reducing the coupling between classes. For example, the business/domain classes do not rely on the user interface of the system, implying that the interface can be changed without affecting the underlying business logic.

A user interface class, often referred to as an interface class (Jacobson et al., 1992) or a boundary class (Jacobson, Booch, and Rumbaugh, 1999), is one that provides the capability for users to interact with the system. User interface classes typically define a graphical user interface for an application, although other interface styles, such as voice command or HTML, are also implemented via user-interface classes. A user interface class contains the code for the user interface part of an application. For example, a graphical user interface (GUI) will be implemented as a collection of menu, editing screen, and report classes. Do not lose sight of the fact that not all applications have GUIs, however. For example, integrated voice response (IVR) system using telephone technology are common, as are Internet-based approaches. Furthermore, by separating the user interface classes from the business/domain classes, designers can change the user interface flexibly. Consider the university where users currently interact with the system through an existing GUI application. It seems reasonable that people should also be able to interact with the system, perhaps find out information about seminars or even enroll in seminars over the phone or the Internet. To support these new access methods, designers should only have to add the appropriate user interface classes. Although this is a dramatic change in the way the university interacts with its customers (students), the fundamental business has not changed. Therefore, designers shouldn't have to change the business/domain classes. The point to be made here is the user interface for any given system can take on many possible forms, even though the underlying business is still the same.

Improving Your User Interface Prototype

During design process, interface prototyping effort continues and at the same time "cleans up" the overall design of the user interface. This clean-up effort focuses on applying common user-interface design principles and techniques, applying the organization's chosen user-interface design standards, and evolving a user-interface flow diagram.

USER INTERFACE DEVELOPMENT AS PART OF IMPLEMENTATION

User-interface implementation is a complex task, one that requires a wide range of skills to be successful. Constantine and Lockwood (1999) believe that most decisions regarding the design of the system's user interface, or affecting its usability, are made by ordinary developers. Although my advice to most project teams is to hire a user-interface design expert onto the team, the reality is few people are available with the appropriate development skillset. Therefore, it is important that all implementers have an understanding of the basics of user interface design. This section summarizes fundamental tips and techniques that I have found over the years to be of great value for developers involved with the implementation of a system's user interface.

1. **Consistency, consistency, consistency**. I believe the most important thing to do is to ensure the user interface works consistently. For instance, if users can double-click on items in one list and have something happen, then they should be able to double-click on items in any other list and have the same sort of thing happen. Put the buttons in consistent places on all windows, use the same wording in labels and messages, and use a consistent color scheme throughout. Consistency in user interface enables users to build an accurate mental model of the way it works, and accurate mental models lead to lower training and support costs.

2. **Set standards and stick to them**. The only way to ensure consistency within the application is to set user interface design standards, and then stick to them.

3. **Explain the rules**. Users need to know how to work with the application built for them. When an application works consistently, it means that the rules need to be explained only once. This is a lot easier than explaining in detail exactly how to use each feature in an application step-by-step.

4. **Support both novices and experts**. Consider the design of a library system within the university. Although a library-catalog metaphor might be appropriate for casual users of the system, students, it probably is not all that effective for expert users, librarians. Librarians are highly trained people who are able to use complex search systems to find information in the library. Therefore, a set of search screens designed for both types of users is necessary.

5. **Navigation between major user interface items is important**. If it is difficult to get from one screen to another, then users will quickly become frustrated and give up. When the flow between screens matches the flow of the work the user is trying to accomplish, then the application will make sense to users. Because different users work in different ways, the system needs to be flexible enough to support their various approaches. Interface-flow diagrams, described previously, should be developed help understanding of the flow of user interface.

6. **Navigation within a screen is important**. In Western societies, people read left to right and top to bottom. Because people are used to this, should you design screens that are also organized left to right and top to bottom when designing a user interface

for people from this culture? You want to organize navigation between widgets on the screen in a manner users will find familiar to them.

7. **Word your messages and labels appropriately**. The text you display on the screens is a primary source of information for users. If the text is worded poorly, then users will perceive interface poorly. Using full words and sentences, as opposed to abbreviations and codes, makes the text easier to understand. The messages should be worded positively, imply that the user is in control, and provide insight into how to use the application properly. For example, which message is more appealing "You have input the wrong information" or "An account number should be eight digits in length." Furthermore, the messages should be worded consistently and displayed in a consistent place on the screen. Although the messages, "The person's first name must be input" and "An account number should be input" are separately worded well, together they are inconsistent. In light of the first message, a better wording of the second message would be "The account number must be input" to make the two messages consistent.

8. **Understand the widgets**. Using the right widget for the right task helps to increase the consistency in the application. It also makes it easier to build the application in the first place. The only way to learn how to use widgets properly is to understand the user-interface standards and guidelines the organization has adopted.

9. **Look at other applications with a grain of salt**. Unless you know another application has been verified to follow the user interface-standards and guidelines of the organization, don't assume the application is doing things right. Although looking at the work of others to get ideas is always a good idea, until you know how to distinguish between good user interface design and bad user interface design, you must be careful. Too many developers make the mistake of imitating the user interface of poorly designed software.

10. **Use color appropriately**. Color should be used sparingly in the applications and, if it is used, a secondary indicator must be also used. The problem is that some users may be color-blind. Colors should be also used consistently to give a common look and feel throughout the application.

11. **Follow the contrast rule**. The best way to ensure good use of color is to follow the contrast rule: Use dark text on light backgrounds and light text on dark backgrounds. Reading blue text on a white background is easy, but reading blue text on a red background is difficult. The problem is not enough contrast exists between blue and red to make it easy to read; whereas there is a lot of contrast between blue and white.

12. **Align fields effectively (added text for index purposes only: field alignment)**. When a screen has more than one editing field, they should be organized in a way that is both visually appealing and efficient. The best way to do so is to left-justify edit fieldsæin other words, make the left-hand side of each edit field line up in a straight line, one over the other. The corresponding labels should be right-justified and placed immediately beside the field. This is a clean and efficient way to organize the fields on a screen.

13. **Expect users to make mistakes**. How many times have you accidentally deleted some text in one of your files or in the file itself? Were you able to recover from these mistakes or were you forced to redo hours, or even days, of work? User interface should able to recover from mistakes made by users.

14. **Justify data appropriately**. For columns of data, common practice is to right-justify integers, decimal align floating-point numbers, and to left-justify strings.

15. **Design should be intuitive**. In other words, if users don't know how to use the software, they should be able to determine how to use it by making educated guesses (Raskin, 1994). Even when the guesses are wrong, the system should provide reasonable results from which the users can readily understand and ideally learn.

16. **Don't create busy user interfaces**. Crowded screens are difficult to understand and, hence, are difficult to use. Experimental results (Mayhew, 1992) show that the overall density of the screen should not exceed 40 percent; whereas local density within groupings should not exceed 62 percent.

17. **Group things effectively**. Items that are logically connected should be grouped together on the screen to communicate they are connected; whereas items that have nothing to do with each other should be separated. Whitespace can be used between collections of items to group them.

USER INTERFACE DEVELOPMENT AS PART OF TESTING

If something is worth building, then it is surely worth validating. A user interface must be validated and tested. The *Full-Lifecycle Object-Oriented Testing (FLOOT)* methodology (Ambler, 1998a; Ambler, 2000) is a collection of testing techniques, including those applicable to UI-related artifacts, to verify and validate object-oriented software. The FLOOT lifecycle is depicted in Figure 7, indicating that a wide variety of techniques are available to you throughout all aspects of software development.

With respect to the UI-related artifacts described in this chapter, the following FLOOT techniques are applicable:

- Prototype walkthroughs
- User interface testing
- User acceptance testing
- Regression testing

Figure 7. The techniques of the Full Lifecycle Object-Oriented Testing (FLOOT) methodology.

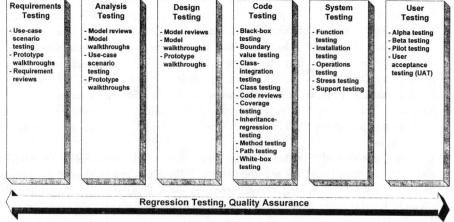

Prototype Walkthroughs

The basic idea of this technique is to use a collection of usage scenarios to walk through the UI prototype and validate that it is able to support those usage scenarios, and if it does not then the prototype needs to be updated appropriately. Usage scenarios are conceptually similar to use cases, although are still different. A use case describes the logic, including the basic and alternate courses of action, for a single cohesive task providing value to a user. On the other hand, a usage scenario describes a single path of logic through one or more use cases. A usage scenario could represent the basic course of action, the happy path, through a single use case, a combination of portions of the happy path replaced by the steps of one or more alternate paths through a single use case, or a path spanning several use cases.

The basic idea is that users pretend the prototype is the real application and try to use it to solve real business problems described by the scenarios. Granted, they need to use their imaginations to fill-in the functionality the application is missing (such as reading and writing objects from/to permanent storage) but, for the most part, this is a fairly straightforward process. The users sit down at the computer and begin to work through the use cases. The designers' job is to sit there and observe them, looking for places where the system is difficult to use or is missing features. In many ways, prototype walkthroughs are a lot like user acceptance tests, described in the following. The only difference is that designers are working with the prototype instead of the real system.

During a prototype walkthrough a facilitator typically leads a group of subject matter experts (SMEs) through the process of acting out the usage scenarios. The process starts by assigning major UI elements to each SME, the basic idea being that the SMEs take on the roles of the UI elements that they are given, describing how the user fulfills the appropriate step(s) of the usage scenario by interacting with a given UI element. To indicate which UI element is currently being used, a soft, spongy ball is held by the person with that element. Whenever a user would need to work with another UI element to fulfill the logic of the scenario, the SME currently holding the ball throws it to the holder of the required UI element. The ball helps the group to keep track of who is currently describing the business logic, and also helps to make the entire process a little more interesting.

User Interface Testing

User-interface testing is the verification that the UI follows the accepted standards chosen by the organization, and the UI meets the requirements defined for it. User-interface testing is often referred to as graphical user interface (GUI) testing, particularly when the target is a GUI. User-interface testing can be something as simple as verifying that the application "does the right thing" when subjected to a defined set of user interface events, such as keyboard input, or something as complex as a usability study where human-factors engineers verify that the software is intuitive and easy to use.

User-Acceptance Testing (UAT)

After system testing, the next step is for users to perform user-acceptance testing (UAT). UAT is a process in which users determine whether the application truly meets their needs. The people involved in the user-acceptance test should be the actual users of the system not their managers and not the vice presidents of the division they work for, but the people who will work daily with the application. Although users may need some training to gain the testing skills, actual users are the only people who are qualified to do user-acceptance testing.

Regression Testing

Regression testing is the act of ensuring that changes to an application have not adversely affected existing functionality. Have you ever made a small change to a program, and then put the program into production only to see it fail because the small change affected another part of the program you had completely forgotten about? Regression testing is all about avoiding problems like this. Regression testing is the first thing you should be thinking about when you begin the actual testing of your application (Ambler, 1999; Ambler, 2000). How angry would you get if you took your car into a garage to have a new stereo system installed only to discover afterward that the new stereo works, but the headlights do not? How angry do you think your users would get when a new release of an application no longer lets them fax information to other people because the new e-mail feature you just added has affected it somehow?

How to do regression testing? The quick answer is to run all previous test cases, including test cases developed for the types of testing described above, against the new version of your application. Although this sounds like a good idea, it often proves not to be realistic. First, part of, or even all of the design of the application may have to be changed. This means some of the previous test cases need to be changed. Second, if the changes truly affect only a component of the system, then potentially the test cases that affect this single component will be used. Although this approach is a little risky because the changes may have had a greater impact than what is expected, it does help to reduce both the time and cost of regression testing.

USER INTERFACE DEVELOPMENT AS PART OF DELIVERY

Aspects of user interface development affect the delivery of a system to its users. User documentation, often based on the use case models, is often written in parallel with system development and delivered to users at the same time as the system itself. How to deliver user documentation to users, physically in manuals or in electronic form, has an impact on how they use the documentation and therefore an impact on the overall user interface. Other pertinent issues include whether each user has a set of user documentation (if printed), whether a user is charged access fees for the documentation (for either printed or electronic documentation), as well as the actual design of the documentation itself.

User training, often a key aspect of system delivery, is obviously affected by the quality and style of the user interface of a system. The more natural the system, the more intuitive its user interface, the less training is required for users to learn how to work with it effectively. The training package/service that accompanies a system is part of its user interface, implying that the design and delivery of that training is an integral part of the overall system.

An important part of delivery is the implementation of the support environment, including the tools, documentation, and training of support staff. The manner in which a system is supported is part of its user interface; therefore once again aspects of a system's user interface are a factor in the delivery of a system.

FUTURE AND EMERGING TRENDS

It is clear that user interface development is an important part of the entire software development process. What isn't as clear is how to bring together standardization efforts such as the Unified Modeling Language (UML) and the Unified Process with user interface development practices. How do developers effectively apply the techniques of UML and user interface development together? How will the addition of UI development techniques to the Unified Process affect its implementation? How can the importance of UI techniques throughout the full system development lifecycle be communicated to practitioners? How will this affect the training and education of software professionals?

CONCLUSION

In this chapter I argued that user interface development techniques are applicable throughout the entire system development lifecycle (SDLC). I overviewed UI techniques such as essential user interface prototyping as part of requirements engineering, traditional user interface prototyping during analysis and design, development of the user interface itself during implementation, various techniques as part of testing testing, as well as training and documentation efforts that are applicable during system delivery. For the software process to truly reflect the needs of real-world development it must include user interface development as one of its integral aspects. It is time for both industry and academia to recognize this truth and act accordingly.

REFERENCES AND RECOMMENDED READING

Ambler, S.W. 1998a. *Building Object Applications That Work*. Cambridge, England: Cambridge University Press. http://www.ambysoft.com/buildingObjectApplications.html.

Ambler, S.W. 1998b. *Process Patterns: Building Large-Scale Systems Using Object Technology*. Cambridge, England: Cambridge University Press. http://www.ambysoft.com/processPatterns.html.

Ambler, S.W. 1999. *More Process Patterns: Delivering Large-Scale Systems Using Object Technology*. Cambridge, England: Cambridge University Press. http://www.ambysoft.com/moreProcessPatterns.html.

Ambler, S.W. (2000). *The Object Primer Second Edition: The Application Developer's Guide to Object Orientation*. Cambridge, England: Cambridge University Press. http://www.ambysoft.com/theObjectPrimer.html.

Ambler, S.W. & Constantine, L.L. (2000a). *The Unified Process Inception Phase*. Gilroy, CA: CMP Books. http://www.ambysoft.com/inceptionPhase.html.

Ambler, S.W. & Constantine, L.L. (2000b). *The Unified Process Elaboration Phase*. Gilroy, CA: CMP Books. http://www.ambysoft.com/elaborationPhase.html.

Ambler, S.W. & Constantine, L.L. (2000c). *The Unified Process Construction Phase*. Gilroy, CA: CMP Books. http://www.ambysoft.com/constructionPhase.html.

Beck, K. (2000). *Extreme Programming Explained—Embrace Change*. Reading, MA: Addison Wesley Longman, Inc.

Beck, K., and Cunningham, W. (1989). *A Laboratory for Teaching Object-Oriented Thinking*. New York: ACM Press. Proceedings of OOPSLA'89, 1-6.

Constantine, L. L. (1995). *Constantine on Peopleware*. Englewood Cliffs, NJ: Yourdon Press.

Constantine, L.L., and Lockwood, L. A. D. (1999). *Software For Use: A Practical Guide to the Models and Methods of Usage-Centered Design*. New York: ACM Press.

Graham, I., Henderson-Sellers, B., and Younessi, H. (1997). *The OPEN Process Specification*. New York: ACM Press Books.

Jacobson, I., Booch, G., & Rumbaugh, J., (1999). *The Unified Software Development Process*. Reading, MA: Addison Wesley Longman, Inc.

Jacobson, I., Christerson, M., Jonsson, P., and Overgaard, G. (1992). *Object-Oriented Software Engineering—A Use Case Driven Approach*. Wokingham, England: ACM Press.

Kruchten, P. (1999). *The Rational Unified Process: An Introduction*. Reading, MA: Addison Wesley Longman, Inc.

Maguire, S. (1994). *Debugging the Development Process*. Redmond, WA: Microsoft Press.

Mayhew, D.J. (1992). *Principles and Guidelines in Software User Interface Design*. Englewood Cliffs NJ: Prentice Hall.

McConnell, S. (1996). *Rapid Development: Taming Wild Software Schedules*. Redmond, WA: Microsoft Press.

Microsoft (1995). *The Windows Interface Guidelines for Software Design*. Redmond, WA: Microsoft Press.

Page-Jones, M. (1995). *What Every Programmer Should Know About Object-Oriented Design*. New York: Dorset House Publishing.

Page-Jones, M. (2000). *Fundamentals of Object-Oriented Design in UML*. New York: Dorset House Publishing.

Raskin, J. (1994). *Intuitive Equals Familiar*. Communications of the ACM, 37 (9), 17-18.

Raskin, J. (2000). *The Humane Interface: New Directions for Designing Interactive Systems*. Reading, MA: ACM Press.

Rumbaugh, J., Jacobson, I., and Booch, G., (1999). *The Unified Modeling Language Reference Manual*. Reading, MA: Addison Wesley Longman, Inc.

Vermeulen, A., Ambler, S.W., Bumgardner, G., Metz, E., Misfeldt, T., Shur, J., & Thompson, P. (2000). *The Elements of Java Style*. New York: Cambridge University Press.

Wiegers, K. (1999). *Software Requirements*. Redmond, WA: Microsoft Press.

Chapter III

From HCI to Interaction Design

Jonas Löwgren
Malmö University College, Sweden

The importance of the field we know as human-computer interaction grows as information technology increasingly becomes a pervasive part of everyday life. This chapter argues that a design perspective is better suited to meet the challenge than the traditional foundations of experimental psychology and information systems development. For professional software development, main implications include addressing the whole design task rather than merely the user interface, breaking monolithic processes into smaller steps, and recognizing that problem setting can never be separated from problem solving. The main implication for higher education is the notion of a design learning studio where constructive and reflective work are intertwined.

INTRODUCTION

The role of human-computer interaction in software development is unclear. This holds for professional practice as well as for the development of knowledge concerning appropriate and interesting applications of information technology to human and social contexts. It may be argued that the main emphasis of HCI has always been placed on identifying and understanding usability problems in task-oriented computer systems. This position is perhaps not the most appropriate one when the responsibility concerns use experiences in a constructive setting, where new artifacts and new use situations are developed. It is certainly not the only conceivable one.

In this chapter, I argue that concerns with use qualities of interactive systems are better addressed by viewing the work from a design perspective. The emerging discipline is called interaction design and defined as the shaping of interactive systems with particular emphasis on their use qualities. I introduce a number of foundational concepts from contemporary design studies and discuss the impact of an interaction design view on professional software development practice and higher education.

THE LANDSCAPE IS CHANGING

It is probably fair to say that the field of human-computer interaction still has its main strengths in improving user interfaces of task-oriented applications in work contexts. There are historical reasons for this bias, of course. When the field emerged (originally known as software psychology) in the 70s, computers were more or less only used for task-oriented applications in work contexts. Contemporary HCI carries this heritage in terms of, e.g., problem framing in research and education contexts, development methodologies with the emphasis on usability engineering and evaluation, academic prerequisites for HCI practice.

Example: The SIGCHI HCI curriculum. A slightly dated but still influential example is the recommended HCI curriculum developed by the ACM Special Interest Group on Computer-Human Interaction (ACM, 1992). It defines the contents of HCI quite generally as the nature of HCI, the use and context of computers, human characteristics, computer system and interface architecture, and development processes. However, the elaboration of the headings emphasizes descriptive models of human behavior and information processing and the optimization of human-machine fit for goal-oriented tasks. (End of example.)

History has shown rather conclusively that the integration of HCI in professional software development is not straightforward. One of the main issues is the HCI emphasis on evaluation of ideas, prototypes and artifacts. Empirical studies clearly illustrate the danger of antagonizing design and evaluation. (See, e.g., Näslund and Löwgren, 1999.) The surge of interest in usability labs in the early 90s, followed by a massive move to distributing HCI skills in development teams across organizations, is another example.

Other issues concerning HCI in professional software development include the "analyze without bias, then design" view of development processes that works poorly in practice; more on this below. It also favors incremental change (design based on fixing problems in the current state) over innovative leaps. One may even argue that the focus on user interfaces and measurable qualities—which is fully understandable given the academic heritage of the discipline and the industrial emphasis on requirement specifications—is actually harmful to the quality of the resulting product. These issues are discussed in some depth in (Löwgren, 1997).

The most significant change in the landscape of software development, however, is brought about by the rapid uptake of the World Wide Web. Suddenly, here is a whole new field of software design that calls for skillful crafting of use qualities. The majority reaction of the HCI community seems to be slight repurposing of existing methods and skill sets, in combination with advocacy for task-oriented perspectives on the "use" of the web. Some examples include Nielsen's (1995–2000) influential recommendations and the empirical studies by Spool and colleagues (1999).

Example: *An alternative perspective.* It is a useful exercise to compare the mainstream HCI approaches with other alternatives, such as the design-seductive-qualities perspective put forth by Khaslavsky and Shedroff (1999). Seductive means to have alluring or tempting qualities. A promise of extraordinary experiences is involved, as well as the qualities required to make good on the promise. Tetris is clearly a seductive game. People keep playing and developing a relationship that is something other than the simple fulfillment of task-related goals. And it is quite obvious that stunning graphics or beautiful visual design are not involved (at least in the original version from 1985 for the 9-inch Mac). Dynamic queries (Ahlberg et al., 1992) is another example of a seductive, albeit less well-known approach. The concept of turning boring old database queries inside out and shaping the data with your fingertips is immediately attractive and enticing to many people.

Khaslavsky and Shedroff describe seduction as a process of enticement (grabbing attention and making an emotional promise), relationship (making progress with small fulfillments and more promises. This step can continue for a long time) and fulfillment (fulfilling the final promises and ending the experience in a memorable and positive way). The checklist for identifying seductive qualities goes as follows. Ask yourself whether the product under scrutiny: Entices you by diverting your attention? Surprises you with something novel? Goes beyond obvious needs and expectations? Creates an instinctive emotional response? Espouses values and connects to personal goals? Makes inherent promises to fulfill these goals? Leads you to discover something deeper than you expected? Fulfills small promises related to your values and aspirations?

Enticement, surprise, emotional response and connection to personal goals are all beyond the scope of traditional HCI. However, it is my firm belief that these and other use qualities may be well as important for the use experience as the task efficiency and absence of usability problems.

There are two reasons why the current situation in use-oriented web design makes a good illustration of my point. First, it is a field where several enterprise cultures have equally strong claims. Some examples are advertising, broadcast media and graphic design. Apart from HCI and software engineering, most of the other players in the field of web design come from cultures where design as a creative activity has a strong tradition and is fairly well understood. This contrasts strongly with the cultural heritage of the HCI field. The difference is apparent, for example, in the recurring web designer/usability engineer split in recent job advertisements from web and new media companies.

Secondly, the web from the users' point of view is not a task-oriented application. It certainly has elements of task-oriented use, most notably the goal-directed location and retrieval of specific information. But it is also an entertainment arcade; a workshop for crafting and developing personal identity; a medium for everyday information-at-hand; a complex tangle of social arenas and relations; a shopping mall; and so on. Seductive qualities may be well as important as the efficiency of goal-directed information retrieval.

I would argue that these two traits of use-oriented web design are just as applicable in general interactive systems design. However, they are not as visible in other domains with the possible exceptions of multimedia (e.g., Hughes, 2000) and the games industry. Interactive systems design ought to involve the enterprise cultures mentioned above. Interactive systems can rarely be seen as purely task-oriented applications. The current standing of HCI in web design is the most illustrative example of a larger situation that may be anticipated across the field of interactive systems design. We may call it the development from HCI to interaction design.

From HCI to Interaction Design

The dissatisfaction with the role of HCI in software development is nothing new. In the course of the last ten years, several critics have voiced their concerns and suggested new foundations. Most of them approach the idea of viewing use-oriented software development as a design discipline, albeit in different ways. A few examples include Cohill's (1991) notion of an information architect, the collection by Winograd and colleagues (1996) where representatives of several design disciplines give their views on software design, and the work by Cooper (1999). The emerging perspective has increasingly been summarized under the label of interaction design. The term is still neither ubiquitous nor unambiguous. Some authors talk about software design, others of computer-related design. However, it is my impression that a growing majority has adopted the interaction design label.

"In the next fifty years, the increasing importance of designing spaces for human communication and interaction will lead to expansion in those aspects of computing that are focused on people, rather than machinery. The methods, skills and techniques concerning these human aspects are generally foreign to those of mainstream computer science, and it is likely that they will detach (at least partially) from their historical roots to create a new field of "interaction design." (Winograd, 1997).

Winograd discusses the emergence of interaction design from the foundations of computer science. This chapter is about another thread in the genealogy: from HCI to interaction design.

Let us consider the term itself: "interaction design". What does it mean to design interaction? First of all, the term clearly denotes a design activity. This should be understood as different from an analytical, evaluative or engineering activity, with connotations of constructive and creative work. It also points to new theoretical foundations in the interdisciplinary field of design studies.

Secondly, what does the "interaction" part refer to? The most obvious interpretation is the interaction between a user and a system. In this case, interaction design refers mainly to the shaping of interaction potentials in an interactive system. Indirectly, interaction design is also shaping the user to some extent, in the sense that the actual use is mediated by the (designed) artifacts. My own working definition is that

interaction design refers to the shaping of interactive systems with particular emphasis on their use qualities.

Further, it is implicitly understood that the aim of interaction design is to produce good use qualities. The point is, of course, that what is good depends on the design domain. Productivity tools are generally good if they support the users' professional goals without violating their personal goals, as Cooper (1999) puts it. This is the traditional domain of HCI theory and practice. But in the design of an interactive art installation, or a game, or a social communication device, or a program format for interactive TV, the term good has other meanings. Interaction design should recognize this variance and address it in a relativistic way; no single method or quality concept can be applied as a panacea or generalized insensitively.

The concept of use qualities is at the core of the interaction design field. An attempt to sketch its meaning is given below. Here, I will simply indicate the potential scope of the concept. The traditional quality criterion of HCI has been usability, mainly connoting task efficiency and absence of usability problems (a survey of the usability concept is given in Löwgren, 1995). Usability is strongly connected to the user interface, which is seen more or less as a separable layer mediating the transactions between user and system. Use qualities, on the other hand, comprise the whole system and the whole use situation. In the extreme case, this may entail structural, functional, emotional, aesthetical and ethical aspects of the use context. Interaction design cannot simplify and sidestep this complexity in a general way; rather, the appropriate tradeoffs and priorities must be addressed in every design situation anew. The examples below illustrate this for a few cases.

Why Bother with Interaction Design?

Changing the perspective on a discipline is hard work. It requires new professional roles, new curriculae, new literature, new arenas for professional and public discourse, and so on. There must be good reasons for any such proposal.

I can see several reasons for viewing use-oriented IT development as a design discipline, i.e., interaction design.

- We will get better products if we broaden our approach from user interfaces to use qualities.
- There is a chance to get out of the hampering design-evaluation dichotomy.

- The multidisciplinary nature of the discipline will be acknowledged, which increases the chances of employing appropriate skills in the development process.
- The interdisciplinary and well-established field of design studies opens up as an appropriate source of epistemological, ontological and methodological foundations.

Now, if we assume that it is relevant to facilitate the development from HCI to interaction design, the next question is what can be done. The rest of this chapter offers one attempt: an outline of new foundations for interaction design, based on contemporary design studies. I introduce a set of concepts that I find essential for understanding interaction design and then discuss their implications for software development practice and education.

NEW FOUNDATIONS FOR INTERACTION DESIGN

Perhaps the most important insight from design studies is that design should be viewed as practice, not as applied science. This does not mean that design is unfounded in knowledge. It does mean, however, that we must understand the foundations in a design context. The rest of this section addresses the following question: What kind of knowledge is required for interaction design, how is it acquired and how is it utilized?

A Repertoire of Exemplars

One of the main differences between skilled designers and novices is the repertoire of generative exemplars. An essential thread in a design process is the ongoing matching between the current understanding of the situation at hand and a set of possible solutions. This is consistent with the well-known finding that creativity is domain dependent (Smith et al., 2000). Empirical evidence (e.g., Stolterman, 1992; Lawson, 1997) shows that designers start thinking in terms of solutions already in the first contacts with the design situation. In the IT field, designers sometimes feel guilty of violating the honored "first-analyze-without-bias" principle. However, a more reasonable interpretation is that the principles of the field should yield to the nature of the design process.

Generative exemplars possessed by the designer are sometimes called formats (Lundequist and Ullmark, 1993). Synonyms or related terms include image (Alexander, 1979), primary generator (Darke, 1979) and concept (Lawson, 1994). The formats are clearly abstracted in some way beyond individual examples. This is necessary in order for them to be applicable in situations beyond the original one. Yet, they are specific enough to drive the expression of the designer's interpretation of the design situation in detailed design sketches.

A reasonable guess might be that the exact abstraction level and contents of the repertoire depends on the designer's individual style and aptitude. However, it is perfectly clear that designers lacking a substantial repertoire are significantly hampered in their ability to create appropriate and durable designs. "To the man who has only a hammer, the whole world looks like a nail."

Example: *Lack of generative exemplars.* A typical, albeit slightly dated example from our field is Nielsen's et al. study (1992) of IT designer cross-training at a time when graphical user interfaces were gradually becoming commonplace in business data processing. Professional IT designers possessed rich repertoires of dialogue-style user interfaces and many applied the same approaches also to object-oriented direct manipulation designs, leading to inappropriate and unusable solutions. Suggested remedies focused on the specific use qualities and interaction possibilities of graphical user interfaces, presented (of course) through exemplars and first-hand experience with systems from the new genre.

Use Qualities

Interaction design is concerned with shaping the use qualities of interactive systems. Hence, the repertoire of an interaction designer would be dominated by use-oriented exemplars. But if the exact characteristics of a repertoire are individual, would social construction and development of knowledge in that field be impossible? No, but I personally believe that the codification of specific exemplars is less than fruitful. The literature indicates that the current interest in patterns for software construction has been extended to comprise also use-oriented aspects. The main thrust of the work seems to be in the direction of capturing workplace patterns, involving interaction with information technology. The result, an interaction pattern language, is claimed to capture proven solutions to recurring design problems in a hierarchical structure from abstract to concrete issues (e.g., Borchers, 2000; Erickson, 2000). My emphasis is instead on developing the elements of a language, a product semantics of sorts, to address use qualities of interactive systems. Such elements cut across the field of specific solutions. They would make it possible to debate and develop the understanding of use qualities of specific exemplars, while allowing for individual variation in representing the actual exemplars.

Use qualities are connected to genres, which is a broader concept than the patterns mentioned above. The quality of user interface transparency, for instance, is generally held to be a good thing in HCI. I would agree that it is indeed essential for certain genres of productivity software, such as spreadsheet programs. On the other hand, the play experience of computer games sometimes hinges on the opacity of their user interfaces. Once the player cracks the code to break the interface open, the game is more or less over.

Examples of concepts I have found fruitful for discussing use qualities of interactive systems, and indirectly the formation of generative exemplars, are described in some detail in Löwgren and Stolterman (1998). For example, we find that the social action space is an essential quality of distributed, embedded information systems. Consider the case of automatic teller machines. It is certainly possible to analyze the user interaction with an ATM in terms of individual use properties. We can easily establish the importance of returning the card before the money (because premature task closure phenomena cause many users to take the money and leave the card behind if the reverse sequence is used). There are usability problems with ATMs due to the old-fashioned transaction architecture of the underlying infrastructure, potentially causing undue strain on the user's working memory and requiring unnecessary interaction steps. The ATM has been thoroughly usability tested for twenty years and most of the findings should be common knowledge.

The most interesting aspect of ATM technology, however, goes beyond the user interface of the machine. It is clear that it represents a new way of handling money in everyday life. Before ATMs were introduced, you had to plan your cash needs in advance in order to make appropriate withdrawals while the bank was open. Now, all you need to do is to make sure that you pass an ATM on your way to the restaurant.

The point is that ATMs, like any other product, are designed with the intention to change or facilitate change in the way people act. The ATM is a very clear example of how the social action space is designed. The intention is to change the activity patterns of bank customers from always coming into the bank to their performing simple tasks through machines. Cash cards, store cards, credit cards and web banking can be seen as extensions of the same phenomenon. The rationale for this intention may be economical (it is roughly five times more expensive for the bank to handle a manual transaction over the counter than to maintain a web self-service), or based on concerns for the bank clerks or the quality of customer service in the bank. The main point here is not why the social action space is

Figure 1. Snapshots of a web site navigation technique called Sens-A-Patch. One concept cluster at a time snaps to life as the cursor passes over its heading. Top frame shows the idle state. The illustrations are taken from www.animationenshus.eksjo.se.

changed, but rather that is changed significantly through what might appear as a straightforward technical intervention.

It is not difficult for the designer to change the social action spaces of the users. Any change in the man-made environment, any new artifact, brings with it some kind of the change in the social action space. The hard part is to predict the outcomes: the future social activities around the new artifact.

Example: *New spaces for social action.* A new intranet may be designed with the intention to facilitate internal communication in an organization in order to overcome entrenchment and hostility. As it turns out, the new artifact is instead used as a forum for intense and upsetting debate, where the employees anonymously voice unpleasant opinions about the organization and each other. This course of events may be good or bad, depending on the detailed context and the point of view, but it is certainly clear that the artifact plays a significant role in reshaping the activities in the organization. The social action space that is introduced was previously unthinkable, and apparently larger than the designers anticipated.

If the social action space around a distributed information artifact is made an explicit part of the design process and the ongoing quality assessment, the task becomes one of designing conceivable social environments. The chances increase that the result is satisfactory in the sense that it exhibits "good" use qualities. At the very least, a failure can be made into the raw material of further learning, since the relevant focus enables a fruitful understanding of the reasons behind the failure.

Another example of a pertinent use quality and its relation to a genre is the dynamic Gestalt of an interactive visualization. The genre in question comprises IT artifacts where the two (or three) dimensions of visual information presentation are combined with the temporal dimension of interactivity. Systems in this genre typically aim at facilitating rapid overview of large amounts of information, providing convenient access to detailed information, supporting the discovery of relevant relationships and making information-based decisions. An early and influential example of interactive visualization is the dynamic query technology developed by Ahlberg and colleagues that was mentioned earlier (Ahlberg et al., 1992). The genre is growing rapidly with the development of graphical technology and immersive spaces.

Interactive visualizations rely heavily on the temporal dimension. In order to start perceiving the whole, the Gestalt, the emergent properties of an interactive visualization, we have to experience it as a dynamic process. In short: we have to try it out. The user shapes the impression of the dynamic Gestalt in the interaction over time. Different possibilities and interaction paths are explored, and a general character emerges.

Example: *An interactive web site visualization.* Compare the screen shots in figure 1 with the interactive version found at www.animationenshus.eksjo.se. Note the differences between expectations formed by the screen shots and the experience of using the real thing.

The dynamic Gestalt of an IT artifact in general has several dimensions. The interaction has a temporal flow that can be calm and relaxing, or quick and responsive. It can also be stressful and jerky. Moreover, there is a dramatic structure to every dynamic process, going from introduction and presentation through performance to the resolution. The dramatic structure can also have different characteristics: predictable, inspiring, boring, obvious, or repetitive. The dynamic Gestalt provides the basis for understanding the relations between whole and parts, between figure and ground.

Assessing an interactive visualization concept without hands-on experience is more or less pointless. The emergent properties of the dynamic Gestalt are strong determinants of use quality in this genre. Does the dynamic interaction feel pliant and tightly coupled? Is there a meaningful whole with a beginning and an end?

In designing the dynamic Gestalt of an IT artifact, it is essential to understand the use context, including who the users are, what skills they have and how they regard their use. For instance, it would be a mistake to design a dynamic Gestalt where the user changes the character of an object with bold and powerful operations, if the users need to view their craft as the gentle shaping of a result through a flow of small incremental nudges. The Gestalt of an IT artifact always enters into an interplay with previous notions of the character of work (or play!) processes.

General Process Aspects

An inherent trait of the design process is the inevitable *intertwining of problem setting and problem solving.* J.C. Jones has put it best:

First, recognize that the 'right' requirements are in principle unknowable by users, customers and designers at the start. Devise the design process, and the formal agreement between designers and customers and users, to be sensitive to what is learnt by any of the parties as the design evolves. (Jones, 1984, p. 213)

This has several implications for interaction design. One is that there is no sequential order of first analysis, then creative work. Already the initial contacts with the design situation entail ideas on possible solutions. Sketching solution ideas is a way of putting questions to the design situation as much as a way of presenting a solution. In short, understanding the problem and solving the problem are two aspects of the same process: design.

A corollary is that design must be understood as exploring a potentially infinite space of possible solutions. The more ground covered during the explorations, the better. This means that it is a step forward, not a setback, to discover that an idea is inadequate. Such a discovery allows us to dismiss a point in the design space. If we can understand the reasons why the idea is inadequate, we can dismiss a whole region. Hence we narrow the field of further exploration. It also means that early phases in the design process should be directed towards non-committal sketches of many possible solutions. The dual tendencies of fixating on one idea and investing personal status in it must be overcome.

The explorative nature of the design process leads to questioning of the given and the implicitly assumed. To exaggerate mildly, when an engineer asks how to solve the given problem, a designer might ask why he/she should work on the problem based on his/her current understanding of it. The act of asking why reveals hidden and implicit assumptions; consequently, the problem might be redefined and the focus of attention moved to another level or field (cf. Jones, 1970).

Example: *Moving through levels.* A slightly exaggerated example, to make the point of level transitions clear:

- I need a PDA calendar. Can you recommend one?
- Why do you need a PDA calendar?
- Because I do, that's why!
- Seriously, why do you need a PDA calendar?
- Because I can't fit all my appointments into my paper calendar, and I still want something small that I can carry in my handbag.
- Maybe you should take a look at your work situation and see whether you can cut down on all your appointments.

Thus, the notion of design as exploration implies challenging and going beyond given limitations and hidden assumptions. A designer does not automatically accept the problem as stated, but assumes greater responsibility for examining it from different points of view. In short: the designer enters the role of an actor in a social context. This has implications for the relation to the customers, since they do not necessarily have answers to all the questions about assumptions. Ideally, the explorative questioning of givens and assumptions should include a critical examination of the assignment and the customer's view of the situation.

When viewed from a distance (or through the eyes of some methodologists), the design process might appear as a straight line through the *abstraction levels*: from abstract to concrete, from general to specific. It moves from vision through concept and sketches to a specification and finally a product. But if we move closer, we will discover a different structure. The line moves up and down the abstraction spectrum from very general thoughts on foundational principles to very specific work on a particular detail (see, e.g., the case study by Potts and Catledge, 1996, where the process is characterized as "non-monotonic" in the computer science sense of the word). The straight line is simply the average or the point of emphasis, which obviously moves from abstract to concrete in the course of the (successful) design process.

The movement up and down the abstraction spectrum can be understood as a picture of reflection-in-action and reflection-on-action (Schön, 1987). Surprises, breakdowns and questioning of assumptions can lead to experiments with new actions on other abstraction levels. It illustrates that design is not a logical deduction from a given situation to a singular solution but rather, as pointed out above, an exploration of a potentially unlimited space.

IMPLICATIONS

When taken seriously, the foundational concepts outlined above have significant implications for professional software development as well as interaction design education. I will outline the main issues here in the form of sketches for future practice and education in the field.

Professional Practice

Grudin (1991) distinguishes three categories of professional software development:

inhouse, product and contract development. This is a useful taxonomy because the conditions for use-oriented software development differ across the categories. Hence, it adds some precision to the discussion of design perspectives on professional development practice.

Inhouse development refers to a development situation where the users, clients and designers are found in the same organization. The conditions for explorative design are generally best in inhouse projects. There are several typical reasons for this: good and continuous access to users, more flexibility in terms of resource planning and, last but not least, less fixation on a delivery deadline. Many inhouse projects present examples of successful explorative design processes, ranging from Scandinavian participatory design projects in the 70s (see Bjerknes et al., 1987) to internal tool design in the games industry (Ahn, 2000).

Product development is initiated by the developing organization, typically oriented towards a customer market. The users making up the market are sometimes defined with high precision, sometimes more or less members of the general public.

There are no obstacles in principle to explorative design in product development settings. However, the historical roots of HCI seem to linger in that use-oriented software development is often relegated to user interface issues. The current collection of case studies by Dykstra-Erickson (2000) paints a rather bleak picture in this respect. She presents fourteen stories from professional HCI practitioners, thirteen of which working in product development settings. Most of the stories describe development methodologies addressing the full complexity of designing the use qualities of the whole product (including system concepts, ideas on user functionality, and so on). However, the specific examples the practitioners show of their work tell a slightly different story. I view eight of the thirteen, examples as pure user interface design work. The remaining five in my view illustrate a more suitable role for a professional interaction designer, oriented towards the wider concept of use qualities.

Example: *Addressing the whole design task.* One of the five positive examples in Dykstra-Erickson's collection (ibid., pp. 24-26) is the work on PlanetGirl.com, an online network for teen girls. The work is driven by a strong vision of the audience's needs and wants, which permeates every aspect of development from editorial to production, sales, marketing and operations. And, of course, the user interface design which is said to be the best-distributed skill in the company. In her description of how the focus on the target audience informs development, Nancie Martin does not distinguish between editorial content, user interface features, technical implementation and iterative user testing. "For girls and women ... it's what you can do with [the technology] that matters."

It is, of course, possible to explain the user interface bias of the presented case studies in several ways. It might be the case that constraints on the presentation format made the practitioners choose user interface examples even though they are not representative for the bulk of their work. Another possibility is that the marketing and product lead functions of the development companies, who are presumably responsible for the deeper design issues that the HCI professionals did not address, are stocked with skilled concept designers and interaction designers. But if the correct interpretation is a remaining tendency in product development to equate use qualities with usability and user interfaces, I would argue that we have a potential problem. As I have indicated above, the separation between user interface and system services is artificial from a use-quality point of view and leads to organizational difficulties.

An obvious recommendation is to bring concept design and interface design together with product strategy and marketing, and adapt suitable field methods from the rich catalog of feasibility and assessment methods developed within HCI, CSCW and information systems. That would make it possible to explore the space of consumer wants and needs by means of interaction design methods for concept generation, expression and assessment.

Contract development refers to the situation where a client hires a developer to create a specialized system for the client's use. This is the traditional setting in information systems development where the client is an organization and the developer is an IT consultant. Most contract development models are based on the assumption that it is possible to first analyze what to build, then build it. The extreme case is represented by supposedly exhaustive requirement specifications, detailing the what but not the how of the future product (including usability requirements). Such analysis-design splits are typically induced by the business agreements surrounding the design work (Näslund and Löwgren, 1999).

The view above, that problem setting and problem solving proceed jointly throughout the design process, obviously question the traditional contract development models. Are there alternatives that deal with the nature of the design process in a better way?

An obvious improvement is to break the development process into smaller steps, where decisions concerning design direction, delivery time and cost are re-evaluated at each step.

Example: *Linné Data.* A more fine-grained development process was implemented in the IT consultancy Linné Data (now Cell Networks) of Gothenburg, Sweden, and the main experience is that the role of the client changes. One of the central tasks of the design process facilitators becomes to help the clients realize that they are not paying a fixed amount of money for a piece of software. Rather, they are entering a process of change and development where they discover strengths, weaknesses and futures of their own enterprises together with the designers as the development project proceeds. The clients are responsible for the direction, time and cost decisions at each milestone, which means that they must invest more effort and commitment in the project than in more traditional development models.

A consequence of breaking up the development process is also the reduced importance of the final delivery object. Facilitating change and development processes in the client organizations is typically a more long-term relation for the designer. This might suggest that models like the above are best suited for inhouse development; however, Linné Data and some other Swedish consultancies managed to build successful long-term relations also with external clients.

The notion of interaction design as a creative process partly based on individual repertoires clashes with traditional contract development practices in at least three respects. First, the qualities of style and domain understanding could become important when a client is looking for interaction designers. This suggests portfolio-based tender submissions and possibly design competitions similar to architecture competitions.

Secondly, and quite generally across Grudin's categories, the goal of software development methods in the development organization cannot be to make people interchangeable. Field studies of large projects invariably point to the importance of the "super-designer" role. This refers to a project member who is either appointed or simply undertakes the responsibility to carry and disseminate the vision for the interaction design (e.g., Poltrock and Grudin, 1994). The point is that design project dynamics work against interchangeable people, even if it is an implicit aim of the methodology in use. Methods and techniques should rather be seen as tools for communication and coordination. The difference may be subtle, but it is clearly there. For one thing, an appropriate design method would not implicitly assume that careful adherence to the method steps is enough to ensure an adequate result. Instead, it would insist that the results of all the steps are documented in order for the designer to make her reasoning explicit and available to her colleagues.

Thirdly, by acknowledging the individual nature of creative work we approach a possible conflict in that the strong emphasis on explicit briefs and user needs might clash with the individual designer's self-centered explorations of the design space. Hughes (2000) explains the apparently paradoxical but quite common coexistence of satisfied users and self-centered designers by the trust in the designer and their domain expertise, the pleasure involved for the users in viewing the designer taking risks, and the sense of quality that enables users to react intuitively to good or bad use experiences.

Interaction Design Education

From the educational point of view, the main implication of the foundations outlined above is an educational setting that strikes the middle ground between HCI-as-applied-science and design-as-vocational-training. In other words, a **design learning studio** similar to what Schön (1987) calls a reflective practicum where the doing and the reflection upon the doing are both facilitated. Passive knowledge and active knowing are balanced through the integration of constructive and reflective work (cf. Heylighen et al., 1999). Pedagogical forms must be found where the students learn to design appropriate IT artifacts and develop knowledge through reflection and articulation in an arena of ongoing critical discourse.

This middle ground lies between two extremes (some might say caricatures). On one side, there is classical HCI where design is the question of applying findings of experimental science. The focus is to a great extent on evaluation methods and on avoiding mistakes in the form of usability problems. Generalized design guidelines largely take the place of generative design exemplars; systematic methodology often consists of some variation of the analyze-then-design ideal; the pedagogical forms occasionally subordinate constructive design work to evaluation exercises and internalization of scientific findings.

The other extreme is the "silent" design schools, where the students develop excellent vocational skills but all isolated. It is probably safe to say that traditional fine arts and craft schools have emphasized the skilled execution at the expense of reflection, articulation and the development of transferable knowledge. This practice is increasingly criticized for its lack of critical analysis and articulation work (e.g., Friedman, 1997).

Example: *An interaction design curriculum.* The Interaction Design programme at the School of Arts and Communication, Malmö University, Sweden, is an attempt to find the middle ground where students can develop generative skills as well as a sense of use quality, a design language, a reflective and articulated stance. I describe it briefly below, mainly in order to illustrate the role of "classical HCI" in a larger interaction design curriculum.

Interaction Design is a two-year, masters-level programme with portfolio and interview admission for students with a bachelor's degree in a relevant subject or corresponding professional experience.[1] It is built around a studio where the students work individually or in groups on large and small design tasks. The tasks are never set with a clear problem statement, but rather through introductions to interesting ideas and open issues by experts in the field to be studied. The students explore the field, delimit a manageable problem, develop solution concepts, assess them empirically and theoretically and finally present their results. The role of the teacher is mainly that of the advisor or studio master, normally taking her point of departure for didactical discourse from the point in the design process that the student has reached. Student work is supported with three advisors, one each from the fields of information technology, media studies, and art and design. This structure reflects the topical integration of the whole school. Dealing with the sometimes contradictory standpoints of the three advisors helps the students discover the importance of articulated reasons for design decisions.

The first semester of year one is devoted to Research topics, currently space and virtuality; IT and learning; narrativity; information complexity and overflow; digital arts. Each of the topics is explored in a project of two to three weeks. A course on Use quality assessment runs in parallel with the studio projects, covering assessment methods ranging from cognitive ergonomics to public social use aspects. The aim is for the students to apply the assessment methods to their ongoing studio work. The second semester addresses Professional contexts, with projects drawn from partners outside academia. The use quality assessment course continues.

Year two is mainly devoted to a large individual interaction design project of the student's own choice. It is supervised by an expert in the field the student has chosen to concentrate upon. During the first semester, a course on Design as knowledge construction is integrated with the individual projects. It covers issues of design epistemology and ontology. The individual project ends midway into the second semester. It is followed by a course on IT criticism, where the students explore the role of the critic in other design disciplines and experiment with similar roles within the field of interaction design. The programme then ends with a collaborative production where the students present their second-year work in a format that they are free to jointly choose and develop.

The curriculum is designed to interweave constructive and reflective work. This principle operates both in the small (teachers acting as studio advisors, prompting articulation and questioning of the material at hand) and in the large (reflective courses integrated with constructive studio work). Compared with traditional HCI education, the main differences seem to be:

- the broader scope of the design task—including all use-oriented aspects of IT rather then merely the "user interface";
- the emphasis on studying and working with exemplars from a variety of domains in order to build up a rich repertoire;
- the emphasis on constructive work on the level of design concepts.

CONCLUSIONS

I have argued in favor of a design perspective on the shaping of use qualities in interactive systems. By introducing a few concepts from contemporary design studies, I constructed an outline of a discipline that may be called interaction design. Implications for professional software development practice include:

- addressing the whole design task rather than merely the user interface;
- breaking monolithic processes into smaller steps;
- recognizing that problem setting can never be separated from problem solving.

The main implication for higher education is the notion of a design learning studio where constructive and reflective work are intertwined.

It must be noted that interaction design is concerned with shaping the use qualities of interactive systems. In the full picture of software development, many other qualities are obviously relevant. Reliability and maintainability are obvious examples of technical qualities. Similarly, there are economical qualities to be addressed. The role of the interaction designer in a full-scale development organization is still very much an open question. Currently, the answer seems to be worked out on an individual basis. It is probably fair to say that software development has a long way to go before it can be considered a design discipline in practice.

I pointed out above that changing the perspective on a discipline entails hard work. However, my personal conviction is that it is worth it.

ACKNOWLEDGMENTS

I am grateful to my friend and colleague Erik Stolterman. Much of the material in the chapter has grown from our collaboration. Jörn Nilsson, my teammate in running the Interaction Design programme, has contributed immensely to the quality of the students' learning. Phil Agre, Mikael Ericsson, David Erixon, Stefan Holmlid and Matthew Holloway contributed to the design of the programme in the early and crucial stages.

Last but not least, I am grateful to the Interaction Design students for demonstrating the value of the concept by their progress. Their accomplishments have surpassed my expectations by far.

NOTES

1. Some relevant subjects include informatics, computer science, arts, graphic design, cognitive science and ethnology. This reflects the necessarily multidisciplinary nature of the interaction design field.

REFERENCES

ACM (1992). Curriculum for human-computer interaction. ACM Special Interest Group on Computer-Human Interaction (SIGCHI) Curriculum Development Group. <http://www.acm.org/sigchi/cdg>, accessed August 9, 2000.

Ahlberg, C., Williamson, C., Shneiderman, B. (1992). Dynamic queries for information exploration: An implementation and evaluation. *Human Factors in Computing Systems (CHI '92 Proceedings)*, pp. 619-626. New York: ACM Press.

Ahn, E. (2000). In Dykstra-Erickson (2000), *interactions* vii(2):16-19.

Alexander, C. (1979). *The timeless way of building.* New York: Oxford University Press.

Bjerknes, G., Ehn, P. and Kyng, M. (eds, 1987). *Computers and democracy: A Scandinavian challenge.* Aldershot, England: Avebury.

Borchers, J. (2000). CHI meets PLoP: An interaction patterns workshop. *SIGCHI Bulletin* 32(1):9-12.

Cohill, A. (1991). Information architecture and the design process. In Karat, J. (ed.) *Taking software design seriously*, pp. 95-113. Boston: Academic Press.

Cooper, A. (1999). *The inmates are running the asylum.* Indianapolis, Ind.: Sams.

Darke, J. (1979). The primary generator and the design process. *Design studies* 1:36-44.

Dykstra-Erickson, E. (2000). An insider's view of interface design. *interactions* vii(2):7-86.

Erickson, T. (2000). The interaction design patterns home page. <http://www.pliant.org/personal/Tom_Erickson/InteractionPatterns.html>, accessed May 12, 2000.

Friedman, K. (1997). Design science and design education. In McGrory, P. (ed) *The challenge of complexity*, pp. 54-72. Helsinki: University of Art and Design UIAH.

Grudin, J. (1991). Interactive systems: Bridging the gap between developers and users. *IEEE Computer*, 59-69. April 1991.

Heylighen, A., Neuckermans, H., Bouwen, J. (1999). Walking on a thin line—Between passive knowledge and active knowing of components and concepts in architectural design. *Design Studies* 20:211-235.

Hughes, B. (2000). *Dust or magic: Secrets of successful multimedia design.* Harlow, England: Addison-Wesley.

Jones, J.C. (1970). *Design methods: Seeds of human futures.* New York: Van Nostrand Reinhold.

Jones, J.C. (1984). Continuous design and redesign. In Jones, J.C. *Essays in design.* Chichester: John Wiley.

Khaslavsky, J., Shedroff, N. (1999). Understanding the seductive experience. *Communications of the ACM* 42(5):45-49.

Lawson, B. (1994). *Design in mind.* London: Butterworth Architecture.

Lawson, B. (1997). *How designers think, 3rd ed.* Oxford: Architectural Press.

Lundequist, J., Ullmark, P. (1993). Conceptual, constituent and consolidatory phases— New concepts for the design of industrial buildings. In Törnqvist, A. and Ullmark, P. (eds.) *Appropriate architecture: Workplace design in post-industrial society,* pp. 85-90. IACTH 1993:1, Chalmers University of Technology, Gothenburg, Sweden.

Löwgren, J. (1995). Perspectives on usability. Lecture Notes LiTH-IDA-R-95-23, Dept. of Computer Science, Linköping University, Sweden. <http://www.animationenshus.eksjo.se/Jonas.Lowgren/Download/r-95-23.pdf>

Löwgren, J. (1997). Design for use quality in professional software development. In *Proc. 2nd Conf. European Academy of Design,* Stockholm, April 1997. http://www.svid.se/ead-programme.htm.

Löwgren, J., Stolterman, E. (1998). Developing IT design ability through repertoires and contextual product semantics. *Digital Creativity* 9(4):223-237.

Nielsen, J. et al. (1992). Teaching experienced developers to design graphical user interfaces. In *Human Factors in Computing Systems (CHI '92 Proceedings),* pp. 557-564. New York: ACM Press.

Nielsen, J. (1995-2000). The alertbox: Current issues in web usability. <http://www.useit.com/alertbox>, accessed May 12, 2000.

Näslund, T., Löwgren, J. (1999). Usability inspection in contract-based systems development—A contextual assessment. *J. Systems and Software* 45:233-240.

Poltrock, S., Grudin, J. (1994). Organizational obstacles to interface design and development: Two participant-observer studies. *ACM Trans. Computer-Human Interaction* 1(1):52-80.

Potts, C., Catledge, L. (1996). Collaborative conceptual design: A large software project case study. *Computer Supported Cooperative Work: The Journal of Collaborative Computing* 5:415-445.

Schön, D. (1987). *Educating the reflective practitioner.* San Francisco: Jossey-Bass.

Smith, D. et al. (2000). Prepare your mind for creativity. *Communications of the ACM* 43(7):111-116.

Spool, J. et al. (1999). *Web site usability: A designer's guide.* San Francisco: Morgan Kaufmann Publishers.

Stolterman, E. (1992). How system designers think about design and methods: Some reflections based on an interview study. *Scand. J. Information Systems* 4:137-150.

Winograd, T. (1997). From computing machinery to interaction design. In Denning, P., Metcalfe, R. (eds.) *Beyond calculation: The next fifty years of computing,* pp. 149-162. New York: Copernicus.

Winograd, T. et al. (eds., 1996). *Bringing design to software.* Reading, Mass.: Addison-Wesley.

Chapter IV

Intelligent Agents Supporting the Social Construction of Knowledge in a Learning Environment

Gerardo Ayala
Research Center of Information and Automation Technologies, Mexico

INTRODUCTION

For a virtual community, learning is a distributed and collaborative process based on the active interaction among its members, sharing and constructing knowledge. In a collaborative learning environment learning advances through collaborative social interaction and the *social construction of knowledge* (Brown, 1989). In the area of artificial intelligence applied to education (Ayala, 1998b), research has been focused on the modeling of intelligent agents for CSCL (Computer-Supported Collaborative Learning) environments (Ayala, 1998a) and internet-based learning communities (Lin, 1995), (Wolf, 1996), (Bos, 1996). Currently, there is an increasing interest in applying these methodologies from the perspective of *lifelong learning* (Dunlap, 1999), (Fischer, 2000), (Ayala, 2000).

The chapter focuses on the modeling of software agents that present the performance and functionality needed for supporting collaborative learning, where collaboration is based on the social construction of knowledge, implementing the theory of knowledge creation by Nonaka and Takeuchi (1995). The chapter includes a discussion on the requirements for modeling software agents for learning environments, as well as the use of AI techniques for their implementation. The HCI issues of group configuration and awareness based on learner modeling in web-based environments are also discussed.

The chapter is organized as follows. The next section introduces the area of collaborative learning environments, as the context of this work, discussing the problem of effective collaboration in CSCL environments and the field of lifelong learning. The fundamentals of the theory of social construction of knowledge, background of our research, are presented. Following this, the chapter includes the discussion of intelligent agents for learning environments, presenting the basic aspects of learner-agent interaction and the characteristics of software agents in collaborative learning environments. The project CASSIEL (Computer Assisted Intelligent Environment for Learning) is introduced. This project includes the development of three intelligent agents modeled in order to support collaboration from the perspective of social construction of knowledge in a web-based community: a *user agent*, a *facilitator agent* and an *information agent*. The user agent and its functionality in learner modeling and group configuration are topics discussed. A facilitator agent, that assists the learner in her/his participation in the social construction of knowledge in the community, is presented. Assistance in locating resources in the community's web is done by an information agent is discussed a general view of the role of the CASSIEL agents in the social construction of knowledge is provided. Finally some implementation issues are presented.

COLLABORATIVE LEARNING ENVIRONMENTS

Learning is not only a way to know about our society, after all it is a way of becoming a productive member in it. We should not consider learning only as the acquisition of knowledge structures, but also as an attitude of active participation of the learner in a community of practice (Lave, 1991). Learning means social participation in a particular environment, not only in the mind of an individual.

From the perspective of situated learning (Brown, 1989), learning is considered a process of becoming a member of a community of practice. Situated cognition proposes the shift from Intelligent Tutoring Systems, where the system communicates the represented domain knowledge to the students, to environments where the computer is a tool that facilitates collaborative work (Clancey, 1991). For a collaborative learning environment learning is not just a condition for membership, but an *evolving* form of membership. It is a process of *enculturation*, where the learner participates in order to enter a community of practice and its corresponding culture, using the community knowledge in real situations as the practitioners do.

Collaborative learning, sometimes also called cooperative learning, has been defined as the instructional strategies which depend on the interaction of persons that help each other and which have some reciprocal influence. In a collaborative learning environment the learners become able to participate in a community of practice, working with the other members as they create their own models of the domain. Collaborative learning allows the progress of the knowledge of the group members and the solution of problems that would not be possible without a group effort. Through collaboration learners reflect, present and discuss their ideas and misconceptions.

The application of techniques from computer-supported cooperative work (CSCW) to collaborative learning gave birth to networked collaborative learning environments (Collis, 1994; O'Malley, 1994). A computer supported collaborative learning environment must provide a virtual space where learners, based on the experience of old-timers, propose the situations and knowledge to be practiced in a distributed community. There is not a generally accepted definition of the term computer-supported collaborative learning or CSCL. I would like to define it as:

> the use of the computer as a mediational device that helps the learners to communicate, cooperate and collaborate through a network, providing assistance in their coordination and the construction and application of knowledge, becoming active members in a virtual community.

A CSCL environment implies the support needed in the development of the following basic skills by the participants:

a) Communication and cooperation skills.

b) Creation of new knowledge and its application.

c) Management of requirements and available knowledge resources.
d) Influencing others to learn.
e) Questioning, reflection and discussion.
f) Responsibility of their own learning by determining the skills they need and how and where they can acquire them.
g) Learning at their own speed and in their own way, *anytime, anywhere*.

Lifelong Learning

Currently there is an increasing interest in the development of information technologies that support lifelong learning (Ayala, 2000), (Fischer, 2000) (Dunlop, 1999). Lifelong learning is more than training. It is a habit to be acquired by people and implies multiple learning opportunities like self-directed learning, learning on demand, collaborative learning and organizational learning (Fischer, 2000). Longworth (1996) presents a detailed description of the area of lifelong learning from the educational and social perspectives.

Dunlap (1999) has proposed a Web-based Support System (WPSS) based on generative and intentional learning methodologies, which promote the development of metacognitive and self-directed learning skills, considered necessary for lifelong learning activities. *Generative learning* considers that the learner has to take responsibility of her/his own learning, being an active agent creating knowledge in an organized manner in her/his community. *Intentional learning* implies a learner who determines her/his learning goals, being aware of her/his own learning and progress.

Effective Collaboration in CSCL Environments

One of the main issues in CSCL environments is to find strategies and mechanisms to promote effective collaboration in the community. Effective collaboration implies taking into account two factors: the appropriate configuration of the learning group and the awareness of knowledge and activities in the community.

By the term *effective collaboration* we refer to the situation when a learner can learn from others while she/he performs a task which demands the application of knowledge elements believed to be learned by other learners, and which are also related to those knowledge elements already acquired by her/him (Ayala, 1997). In general terms, the basic characteristics of an appropriate group for collaborative learning are its heterogeneity and small size (Bannon, 1994) Group configuration in the CASSIEL learning environment will be discussed in section 6.4.

There has been some research work on the support and maintenance of awareness for the creation of opportunities in collaborative learning environments (Gutwin, 1995). A collaborative learning environment must allow realistic possibilities for effective collaboration and, therefore, opportunities for learning in a group. Learners work together by sharing a virtual workspace and being aware of the knowledge and actions of the members of the learning group. Gutwin at al. (1995) have defined the term workspace awareness as the up-to-the-minute knowledge a learner requires about the interactions of other group members with the shared workspace. This concept is considered critical for collaborative learning. Workspace awareness is maintained by getting information the learners' locations, intentions, actions, and history with the communication of roles, capabilities and tasks of the learners in the group. A CSCL environment implies four types of awareness:

a) Social awareness

Based on the communication of the roles and capabilities of the learners.

b) Task awareness

Based on the relations between the capabilities of the learners and a given task (situation) where knowledge elements have been applied successfully.

c) Concept awareness

Related to the concepts of feasibility and relevance of knowledge, since it implies how a task fits with the knowledge already acquired by the learner and what knowledge is needed to be practiced in order to accomplish a task. It is also concerned with the reflection of the learner about her/his current level with respect to the group members.

d) Workspace awareness

Communication about who are the learners, where are they, what are they doing in the common task, which constructions and commitments they have made and what have they done.

Communities of Practice

Communities of practice are considered incubators of intellectual capital in leading edge organizations. They are virtual communities of reflective practice where knowledge is applied. A community of practice evolves by the knowledge progress of its members and reproduces itself with the transformation of newcomers into old-timers by practical and collaborative activities.

The issues to consider when designing an environment that allows the production, transformation and reproduction of a community of practice are the following:

a) The access of learners to their activities.

b) The distribution of knowledgeable skills.

c) The segmentation, distribution and coordination of activities.

d) The conflicts, interests, common meanings and interpretation of knowledge.

e) The motivation of all the participants.

f) The legitimacy of participation within a community.

g) The transparency of technology, social relations and forms of activity.

SOCIAL CONSTRUCTION OF KNOWLEDGE

For a learning environment the continuous social construction of knowledge is not a specialized activity, but a way of being in a community. With the increasing use of the Internet in education there is a necessity in the development of software for collaborative learning that allows the *social construction of knowledge* (Barret, 1992) in a virtual community, where learners interact with resources at anytime from anywhere.

The theoretical foundation of knowledge construction in CASSIEL comes from the work of Nonaka and Takeuchi (1995). This theory has been applied for learning organizations (Morabito, 1999) and, in general terms, proposes that knowledge in an organization is constructed through the phases of *socialization, externalization, combination* and *internalization*.

a) Socialization

Interaction among participants in the community. The learner provides and has access to *new ideas* and viewpoints concerning the application of knowledge in an industrial or academic context.

b) Externalization

Formalization and organization of socialized ideas and viewpoints for their presentation and discussion in the community. Some ideas are justified during their discussion in the community and become *shared beliefs*.

c) Combination

Discovering relations between the shared beliefs and the established knowledge in the community. Those validated beliefs are then considered *new knowledge* in the group.

d) Internalization

Promoting the *application* of the new established knowledge by the members in the community.

From this perspective, *knowledge is justified true belief.* The individual's personal ideas, once socialized, formalized and externalized, are socially justified, becoming shared beliefs, which once validated are transformed into knowledge in the community. In this approach, knowledge comes from the individual participant to the group and then from such community to their members.

INTELLIGENT AGENTS FOR LEARNING ENVIRONMENTS

The term *agent* has been used in diverse ways. When in AI we refer to the term *agent* we mean an entity that functions *continuously and autonomously* (with a degree of autonomy) in an environment in which other agents exist. The term *autonomy* means that the agent's activities do not require constant guidance and not direct instructions from the user.

In order to determine if a piece of software is one an agent depends on if it can be viewed as having a *mental state.* According to Shoham (1993), what makes any software component an agent is the fact that one has chosen to analyze and control it in mental terms. From this perspective, an agent is an entity whose mental state consists of components like *capabilities*, *beliefs* and *commitments*. In general terms, an intelligent agent is considered a system which behavior is determined by reasoning based on these attitudes (Wooldridge, 1999).

In GRACILE (Ayala, 1998a) we developed a CSCL environment based on two kinds of intelligent agents: domain agents and mediator agents, modeled based on ideas from distributed artificial intelligence. The domain agents are able to assist the learners in the application of domain knowledge elements. In order to support the collaboration between learners each mediator agent constructs and maintains a learner model represented as a set of beliefs about the capabilities, commitments, intentions and learning opportunities of its learner.

Learner-Agent Interaction

In order to model the interaction between the agent and the learner we have considered the following:

1) The learner should not instruct the agents. The user agent has a degree of autonomy and makes decisions based on its beliefs about its user (learner model).
2) The learner controls the agent by making requests to it.
3) The agent always presents to the learner what it is doing.

There are important aspects concerning the interaction between the agents and the learner. Learners must be comfortable with the actions performed by the agents through a feeling of understanding and confidence in them. Taking into account the human-agent interaction proposed by Norman (1994), our agents have been designed on the following guidelines:

a) Supporting understanding

The learner should be able to ask why does the agent propose an activity related to a knowledge resource. The agent must provide clear explanations of its behavior.

b) Supporting confidence

The agents work on the learner's behalf, promoting her/his knowledge progress, providing possibilities of effective collaboration and learning in the community. The technical requirements for acceptability are based on the support for the collaborative learning environment (robustness). The social requirements for acceptability of the agent's actions imply two basic ideas. First, the agent shows the learner those actions that have been taken on her/his behalf, especially in the case of a creation of commitments and requests to other agents and learners in the network. Second, the agent does not make commitments or send requests or refusals without the permission of the learner.

c) Feeling of control

The learner must feel in control of the agents. The agent must be faithful to the learners' requests. In the determination of what knowledge resources the learner should interact with, the agent proposes the resources, but the learner has the final word in the decision of her/his learning activities.

d) Realistic expectations

The agent does not propose a learning activity if it believes that the learner is unable to participate successfully or that nobody can assist her/him to accomplish it.

e) Adaptive behavior

The interaction between agent and learner is based on a *learner model*, which is a representation of the agent's beliefs about the learner's interests, intentions, capabilities and preferences.

f) Transparency

The complex processes of learner modeling and cooperation between agents, must be transparent to the learner. The agent must only inform the commitments and activities to and from other agents and learners in the community.

Software Agents and Collaborative Learning

There have been proposals including intelligent agents in web based collaborative learning environments. Norrie and Gaines (1995) have introduced the Learning Web as a distributed intelligent learning environment, introducing an agent-based collaborative learning system.

In the Learning Web software agents are able to make intelligent decisions based on the content of their knowledge base and the messages they receive. An interface agent learns from the user's actions, working as an intelligent assistant, while a tutor agent provides scaffolding to the learner, progressively removing it as the learner internalizes the knowledge. Although not explicitly presented, it is clear that these agents require a model of the learner in order to perform their tasks.

With CASSIEL we propose that intelligent agents in CSCL environments must make intelligent decisions concerning the construction knowledge in the community and the promotion of collaboration possibilities in the group based on their beliefs about the learner's capabilities, commitments and intentions.

CASSIEL

At the Universidad de las Américas-Puebla we have been developing CASSIEL

(Computer Assisted Intelligent Environment for Learning) as a prototype for a lifelong learning environment (Ayala, 2000). CASSIEL contributes with a new approach of agent-based learning environments designed to promote and support lifelong learning.

Collaboration in a lifelong learning environment is essential because learners construct knowledge by externalizing, sharing and integrating new ideas (justified beliefs) into prior knowledge (Bos, 1996).

Our community of practice is formed by computer science academic members such as students and researchers, as well as novices and experts working in the IT industry. Every year IT companies expend a lot of time and resources in training programs in order to make the employees able to face and perform appropriately, according to the current hardware and software technologies and the applications the clients demands. Software companies in Mexico are planning to increase their human resources during the next years, and the training cost is considered to become very high. On the other hand, the university is not totally aware of the requirements of industry and develops academic programs sometimes more related to research projects than to the requirements of the companies where the graduate students will work.

The members in our community need to be aware of what is going on in the area from the perspectives of industry, academy and research. Each one provides information and knowledge from her/his perspective:

University students

Need to be aware of:
- Graduate courses at the university.
- Research projects at the university.
- Human resources required by the software company.
- Development projects at the software company.

Provide information and knowledge about their:
- Areas of interest and capabilities.
- Research interests.
- Intentions of interns at the software company.
- Intentions of professional development.

Professionals at the software company

Need to be aware of:
- Continuing education courses.
- Graduate courses at the university.
- Researchers who provide consulting services.
- Research fields.
- Research projects at the university.
- Capacities of the students.
- Intentions of students about interns at the software company.

Provide information and knowledge about their:
- Training requirements.
- Human resources requirements.
- Development projects.

Researchers at the university

Need to be aware of:

- Development projects of the software company as a framework reference for their research.
- Training requirements from the software company.
- Consulting requirements from the software company.

Provide information and knowledge about their:

- Research projects and proposals (development of new technologies).
- Consulting services.

The research issues in the CASSIEL project are:

1. Determine the software components and functionality needed for a lifelong learning environment, and implement them for a learning community in the area of information technologies, formed by university teachers, researchers, students and software industry professionals.
2. Support the social construction of knowledge in a virtual community, assisting the learner in the organization and presentation of her/his beliefs and knowledge to the community (supporting generative learning).
3. Assist the distance learner in the location of information and knowledge considered relevant for her/him in the web according to her/his interests and learning attitudes.
4. Determine the information needed in a learner model for lifelong learning used in order to assist the learner in the construction of her/his learning plan (supporting intentional learning), and her/his participation in discussion groups considered of her/his interest.

Three intelligent agents for learning environments have been modeled and implemented in CASSIEL:

a) A *user agent* that supports collaboration and adaptability, maintaining a user model and assisting the learner in the configuration of discussion groups.
b) A *facilitator agent* that assists in the organization of ideas, information and knowledge to be provided by the users to the community.
c) An *information agent* that supports awareness and the location of relevant information.

THE USER AGENT

The user agent cooperates with other user agents in the network sharing the information of their learner models. Based on the information of the learner models the user agent can make an autonomous configuration of discussion groups and construct a proposal for the learning plan of its learner, considering her/his interests as well as the demands and capabilities of the community members. It promotes collaboration and provides adaptability.

The user agent constructs and maintains a learner model. Based on the information from their learner models and the messages from other agents, the user agents are able to determine the collaboration and learning possibilities of the learners in the group and promote tasks of mutual interest.

The model of the user agent is defined in terms of its beliefs, commitments and capabilities.

User agent beliefs:
- Learner model (desires, intentions, capabilities and interests of its user).
- Learning plan of its user.
- Learner commitments to other members.
- Groups where the learner participates.

User agent commitments:
- Send information about its learner model to other user agents.
- Ask other participants to register in a proposed group.

User agent capabilities:
- Updates the stereotype learning plan (default learning plan).
- Shows and negotiates the learning plan to/with its user.
- Shows the information of the participants of a given group.
- Revises the learner model.
- Configures a group proposal.
- Sends invitations for group registration to other learners.

Conditions for collaboration

In order to support awareness in a web-based collaborative learning environment, the software agents must allow the communication of commitments, interests and capabilities of the learners, who are considered as active agents in the collaborative learning process.

Collaboration in a group is based on the communication of the capabilities of its members, the construction of knowledge in the community and the assistance that the learners can get from other learners and interacting with the knowledge resources distributed in the network. While the information agent in CASSIEL assists the user to locate knowledge resources in the community web, the user agent keeps the awareness and the conditions of collaboration by allowing the communication of:

1. Desires. The learners can be aware of the requirements and proposals for participation in a common task or project.
2. Commitments. The learners can be aware of the intentions of each other.
3. Capabilities. The learners will be aware of who would be able to assist them in a given topic.
4. Interests. The learners are informed of changes and new material in those frequently visited nodes by them in the community web.
5. Learner's ego development phase. The web proposed material to interact with is sorted according to her/his learning attitudes and navigation strategies.

The user agents construct a learner model which is considered necessary in order to create collaboration possibilities in the group. The learner model, as a specific case of modeling of an agent, is represented as a set of beliefs (Self, 1992) that the respective software agent holds about the learner's desires, intentions, capabilities and interests.

Learner modeling

The satisfaction of the learning needs and demands of each individual is the essence of web based learning environments. We consider adaptability to the learner an important issue. The user agent in CASSIEL facilitates the adaptability and the collaboration of learners by constructing and maintaining a learner model. Together with the information agent, the user agent cooperates in monitoring the user actions, maintaining the learner model.

Generally speaking, the learner model is considered as *a set of beliefs held by the system about the learner* (Self, 1992). For an Intelligent Tutoring System learner modeling has been considered as a cognitive diagnosis process, where the computer system infers the learner's knowledge by analyzing her/his behavior (Dillenbourg, 1992).

In CSCL environments the issue of learner modeling has been already discussed (Ayala, 1996). In CLARE, a CSCL environment that facilitates knowledge construction from research papers (Wang, 1994), learners work on the construction of a group knowledge base by the processes of knowledge summarization, evaluation, argumentation and integration. CLARE includes a representation of the group's knowledge base, but not of an individual learner model.

In GRACILE (Ayala, 1996) we present our approach in learner modeling for CSCL environments, where learner models provide the information needed in order to support awareness and promote opportunities of relevant collaboration and learning in a networked community of practice. We propose that the role of the learner model in CSCL environments should not be to support tutoring or diagnosis, but to enhance awareness and the relevant collaboration between learners.

The learner models of the participants provide the user agents with the information they need in order to support the coordination and effective collaboration in the group. For the purpose of establishing a complete communication of interests, commitments and capabilities in the group, all learner models in the community must be freely accessible to the learners at any time, via the user agents. This is important since learners can locate their level with regard to the others in the group, and become aware of the capabilities of those more advanced learners.

Learner modeling is a process of belief revision since the learner model is a set of beliefs the agent has about the learner. Since a change in a belief is a function of the reasons why it is held, a belief must be related to its justification (Self, 1992). The process of learner modeling is implemented based on AI techniques of belief revision (Russell, 1995). The learner model includes the following beliefs, generated or removed by a set of production rules:

1. *Desires*. Inferred from the learners' personal requirements and proposals for participation in a common task or project.
2. *Intentions*. Inferred from the learners' commitments to participate in projects or cooperate with members of the community.
3. *Capabilities*. Inferred from the learners' fields of expertise and qualifications.
4. *Interests*. Inferred from the learners' most visited web nodes.
5. *Ego development phase*. Inferred from the learners' navigation strategies in the community web.

It is known that a lifelong learner presents three phases of ego development (Fales, 1989) which represent different learning and collaborative attitudes. These phases represent the degree of maturity of the lifelong learner:

a) *Conformist*: The conformist learner is mainly looking for social acceptance, making relations of her/his learning plan to the progress of her/his peers, and associates new material to existing popular knowledge resources in the community.
b) *Conscientious*: The conscientious learner looks more for self evaluated standards, interpersonal interaction, learning goals consistent with self expectations and making reflection and introspection for future goal identification.
c) *Autonomous*: The autonomous learner presents more autonomy and independence, tolerance to ambiguity and self directed learning.

The information agent also makes decisions based on the learner model, assisting the user in the navigation through the community web.

Assistance Constructing the Learning plan

A necessary task for the learner in a web-based learning environment is to construct her/his personal *learning plan*. Research results indicate that adults spend about 500 hours a year at major learning efforts. In 73% of the reported cases learning is planned by the learner her/himself (Tough, 1989). In CASSIEL a learning plan is represented by a network of web nodes to be visited and commented by the learner. The links between nodes represent the cognitive relations of part-of, generalization, analogy and refinement. This knowledge representation is based on the implementation of genetic epistemology ideas in learning environments (Goldstein, 1982). Each node in the learning plan contains information about:

1. Demands of the software company, from current *desires* of the participating company employees.
2. Research topics, from *interests* and *capabilities* of participating researchers.
3. Student *interests*.
4. Related knowledge, via part-of, generalization, analogy or refinement links.

The initial proposal of a learning plan by the user agent to the new user of the environment is a *stereotype learning plan*. This "typical" learning plan is continuously updated based on the changes in the learning plans of the community members. This is done through the cooperation of the user agents whenever they report changes in the learning plan of their users.

Figure1 shows the user agent assisting the learner in constructing her/his learning plan, presenting each topic or resource (web node) in the community as well as those resources

Figure 1. The user agent assists the learner in constructing her/his learning plan.

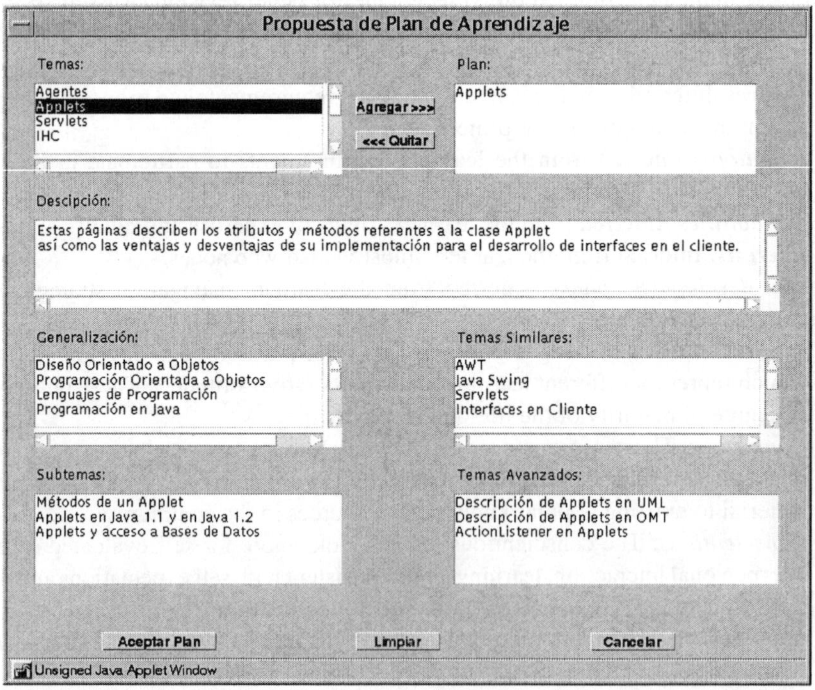

related to it by generalization, part-of (sub topics), analogy (similar topics) or refinement (advanced topics) relations.

In figure 1 the user agent presents a list of topics referred to knowledge resources (*Temas* in Spanish). Once the learner selects one of them, he/she can add (*agregar*) or remove (*quitar*) it from her/his plan. A description of the topic is presented, together with the list of general topics, (*Generalización* list) analog topics (Temas Similares list) included topics (*Subtemas* list) and refinements (*Temas Avanzados* list).

Assistance in Group Configuration

Effective collaboration in CSCL implies an appropriate learning group and an intelligent task distribution based on the relations among the knowledge resources available in the community web.

In GRACILE (Ayala, 1997) effective collaboration in a CSCL environment was implemented with software agents that help the learners to navigate through the domain knowledge and to take advantage of the interactions with each other, working in heterogeneous learning groups. The results obtained from several simulations of the interaction of our user agents in diverse types of groups provided us with guidelines for the group selection for CSCL environments where effective collaboration is possible, as well as conclusions concerning the definition of learning groups for these type of educational systems. We found that the best group was that group where: a) the learner with the higher level played the role of *leader* (autonomous), b) the learner with a high-middle level played a *conservative* role (conformist), c) the low-middle level learner tried to increase its scope by selecting its task by *relevance* (conscientious*)*, and d) the low-level student played the role of *follower* selecting tasks where the rest of the group has already successfully worked (Ayala, 1997).

Figure 2. The user agent proposes the creation of a discussion group, considering the interests and capabilities of the community

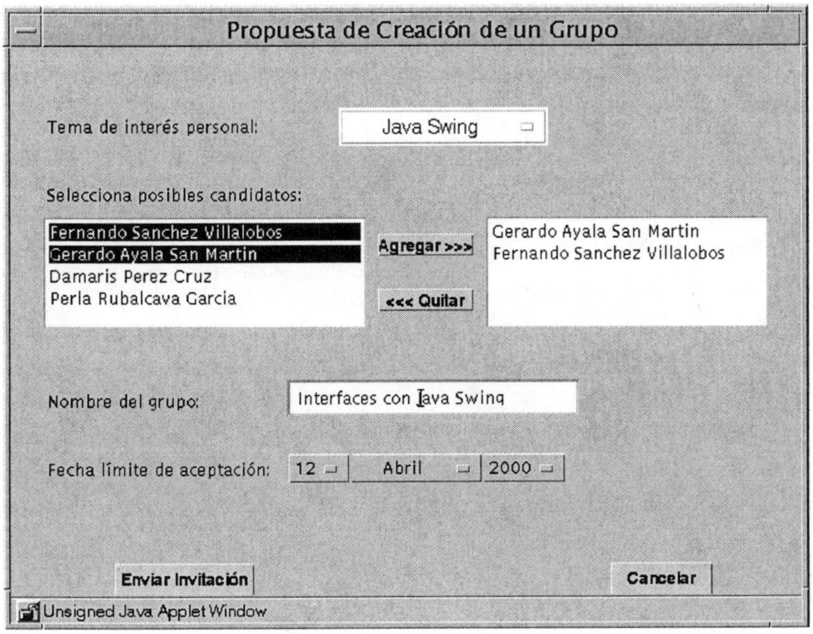

In CASSIEL the user agents *cooperate* in order to determine appropriate groups for effective collaboration by exchanging information of their learner models. Then, considering the desires, intentions, interests and capabilities of the other members in the community the user agent proposes the creation of a discussion group to its user. The interface includes the definition of deadline for the selected potential members of this group to answer the call for participation (see figure 2). The user agent proposes the creation or a group of interest in the topic of Java Swing, indicating the user the candidates to conform it. This list is constructed according to the learner models of the community participants. The user selects the participants, provides a name and a deadline for registration. The user agent will send an e-mail to each one of the selected members of the community, informing them the group creation proposal and keeps track of their answers until the deadline defined.

Once the learner participates in one or more groups, the user agent also assists her/him in the creation of commitments to members of the discussion groups. A commitment may refer to her/his participation in a virtual session (chat) or in an asynchronous discussion (e-mail). In figure 3 the user agent helps the establishment of a commitment. The user selects a topic to discuss (*Manejador de Bases de Datos Oracle*), selects a discussion group (*Bases de Datos Distribuídas*) and indicates the points to be discussed, selecting that the discussion will be a chat session (*Cita*).

THE FACILITATOR AGENT

In a CSCL environment the learner must work as an active agent being a member of a group that makes her/him have enough collaboration and learning possibilities, being motivated with the experience of social knowledge construction.

The facilitator agent assists the learner in the organization of knowledge provided by her/him. This refers to web resources or relations between them. The facilitator agent also assists the learner in providing her/his ideas and *beliefs* (comments and recommendations) to the community, providing assistance for organizing ideas, justifying beliefs and relate them with data and knowledge established in the community, using knowledge representation techniques.

Figure 3. The user agent assists the learner in establishing a commitment with the members of a discussion group.

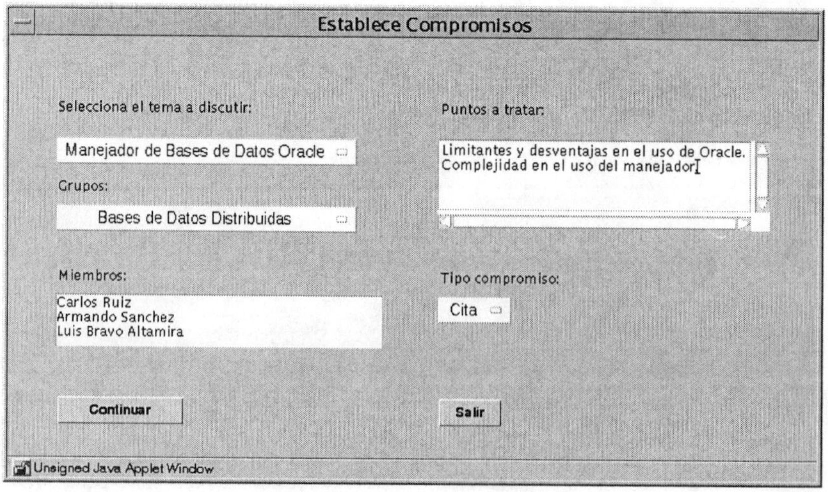

The approach adopted in CASSIEL for knowledge construction in constructive web-based learning environments is the development of new documents linked to previous ones, by the learners (Wolf, 1996). In CASSIEL relationships among knowledge resources create a web of associations where the information of the relations constitutes the "semantics" of the web (generalization, analogy, refinement and part-of). In this way the web becomes a higher-order abstraction of knowledge which makes it possible to make implicit knowledge structures explicit (Carlson, 1992).

The facilitator agent assists the learner in her/his active participation in the social construction of knowledge in the community by:

1. Providing the URLs of web nodes considered relevant to all (socialization), relating them by cognitive relations of part-of, generalization, analogy and refinement (combination).

2. Including her/his beliefs (comments and recommendations) about a web node (appearing as related comments to the site), or by indicating the justification of beliefs based on additional information (externalization).

3. Validating those justified beliefs about web nodes presented by other members of the community, providing comments and cognitive relations to other nodes (combination).

An interface of the facilitator agent where the learner is assisted in the organization of material in the community web is shown in figure 4. In this case the user is selecting the resource *Agentes Inteligentes* en Java, include some comments and establishes a part-of (*parte-de*) relation with the more general *Agentes* resource.

The model of the facilitator agent is also defined in terms of its beliefs, commitments and capabilities:

Facilitator agent beliefs:

- Knowledge resources web (cognitive relations between community web nodes).
  Facilitator agent commitments

- Notify new knowledge resources, comments and recommendations provided by its user to the community members.

Figure 4. A learner is assisted by the facilitator agent in organizing web based material.

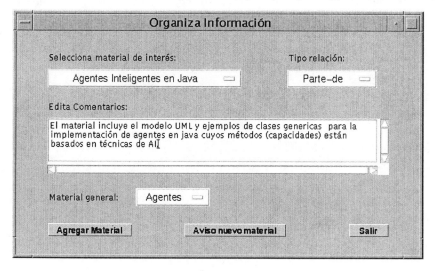

Facilitator agent capabilities
- Assist the learner in adding a knowledge resource.
- Assist the learner in adding comments and recommendations about a knowledge resource.
- Organize a knowledge resource provided by the learner in the community web by using the generalization, analogy, refinement and part-of relations.

THE INFORMATION AGENT

The information agent in CASSIEL is designed to guide the participants in the location of knowledge and information. The information agent autonomously navigates through the community web sites in order to provide information about new and updated material believed to be of the interest of the learner. It intelligently searches in the Internet, allowing the easy location of relevant information and knowledge. It also navigates through the community web nodes looking for information based on a request from its learner. A request to the information agent consists of a selection or input of a keyword. The initial web nodes for the search requested by the learner are obtained from her/his interests according to its learner model.

The strategy of navigation of the information agent through the web nodes is based on AI techniques of heuristic search, being a variation of best-first search (Russell, 1995). The search results are URLs and titles of web sites. The agent presents them sorted by *relevance* (quantity of related content-based on the topic of interest in the html file) by *popularity* (frequency of visit by the community members) or by *newness* (promoting new web sites or web sites that have been updated since her/his last visit), according to the agents beliefs about the learner's ego development phase. For a learner believed conformist the results are presented by popularity. They are presented by relevance for the learner believed in the conscientious phase, and by newness to the learner believed already autonomous (see figure 5).

The information agent keeps its learner aware of new web nodes, as well as recent modifications in nodes visited by her/him. The agent autonomously starts a travel through

Figure 5. The information agent presents the results of its navigation in the community web, showing the sites sorted by popularity, relevance or newness.

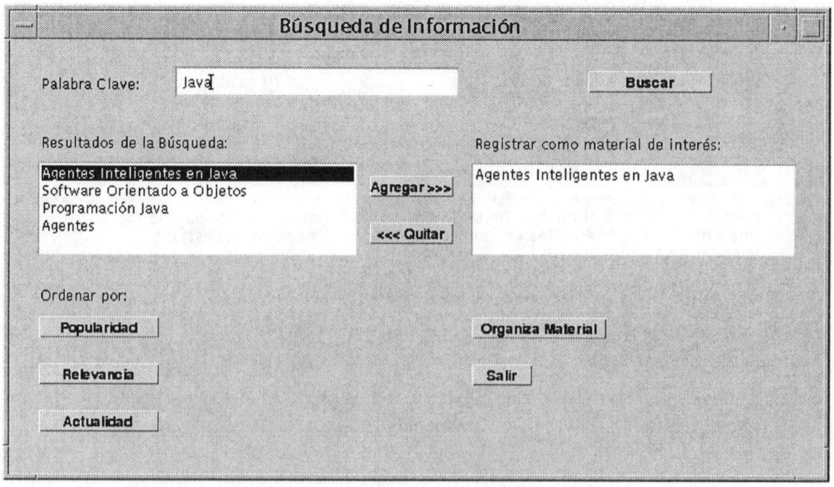

the corresponding web servers, checking the time of the last update of those web nodes believed of the interest of the user, and notifies her/him any updating that occurred after her/his last visit to that web resource.

The information agent also notifies the learner about the new comments and links provided by the community members via their facilitator agents concerning a knowledge resource (an educational material, a research project or a development at the software company).

Figure 5 presents an example of interaction with the information agent. The user requests a search with the keyword (*palabra clave*) Java. The agent presents the results (*resultados de la búsqueda*) which may be sorted by popularity (*popularidad*), relevance (*relevancia*) or newness (*actualidad*) and included as resources of her/his interest (i.e. *Agentes Inteligentes en Java*).

The beliefs, commitments and capabilities of the information agent are:
Information agent beliefs
- Learner model (desires, intentions, interests and ego development phase).
Information agent commitments
- Visit and analyze a community web resource.
- Inform the learner about updated material believed of her/his interest.
- Inform the learner about new material believed of her/his interest.
Information agent capabilities
- Search for new information in the community web believed of the interest of the learner.
- Navigate the community web-based on a request (keyword).
- Navigate the community web starting from those sites of interest.
- Show a knowledge resource list as the result of a search in the web.
- Sort a knowledge resource list by popularity.
- Sort a knowledge resource list by relevance.
- Sort a knowledge resource list by newness.

SOCIAL CONSTRUCTION
OF KNOWLEDGE IN CASSIEL

For a learning environment the continuous social construction of knowledge is not a specialized activity, but a way of being in a community, which represents a culture that consists of ideas, beliefs and knowledge shared by its members.

Our virtual community, seen as a learning organization, should be able to transform data and information into knowledge, and thereby increase its adaptive capacity.

Based on the knowledge creation theory of Nonaka and Takeuchi (1995) we consider the construction of knowledge in CASSIEL as a process of four steps:
1. Knowledge socialization
   The user agent assists the learner in the knowledge socialization phase by proposing the configuration of groups for discussion, dialogue and collective reflection of ideas with those members believed to share common interests with her/him. The user agent keeps social awareness by communicating the capabilities, interests, desires and intentions of its learner.
2. Knowledge externalization
   The information agent provides material from which the user can comment, relate and express her/his ideas in a more formal way. The facilitator agent assists in the

Figure 6. Roles played by the CASSIEL agents in the social construction of knowledge.

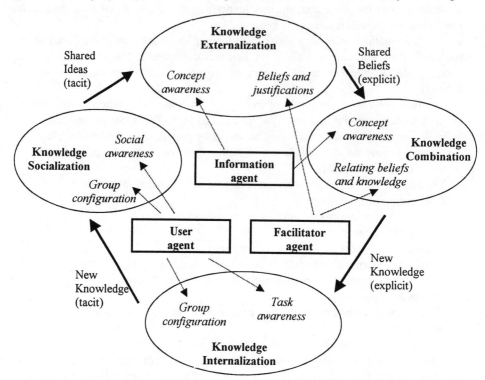

express her/his ideas in a more formal way. The facilitator agent assists in the formalization and sharing of the beliefs (justified ideas) of each member within the community. In this way the beliefs of a learner are shared within the community in the form of comments associated to knowledge resources in the community web. This keeps concept awareness in the community.

3. Knowledge combination

The facilitator agent assists the user in her/his active participation validating her/his socially justified beliefs based on existing knowledge in the community, relating them by cognitive relations of part-of, generalization, analogy and refinement. The information agent assists the user in this phase by providing information resources referred to existing knowledge in the community. This keeps concept awareness, by allowing the relation of knowledge already established in the community.

4. Knowledge internalization

Knowledge internalization implies learning by doing. The members put into practice the knowledge of the community, converting the explicit new knowledge created by the community into implicit personal knowledge, by applying it. The user agent supports this phase by assisting in the configuration of working groups and the communication among them. It keeps task awareness in the community.

A general view of the participation of the agents in the process is presented in Figure 6.

IMPLEMENTATION ISSUES

The modeling of the intelligent agents in CASSIEL was done following the Unified Modeling Language (UML) (Booch, 1999). Each agent has been modeled as a concurrent object (thread) with its correspondent attributes, representing the corresponding beliefs and commitments of the agent. The methods represent the capabilities of communication, cooperation, belief revision, navigation and knowledge relation. CASSIEL is implemented in 100% pure Java as a set of platform independent software components. The AI methods of each agent were implemented in Java as well (Bigus, 1998). By now the interfaces of CASSIEL are implemented as Java applets under a Web browser (Communicator or Explorer, versions 4.0 required), and have communication to an Informix DBMS via the corresponding JDBC driver. We are migrating the interfaces to implement them as html files generated by servlets.

We are now working on the implementation of CASSIEL for its release in order to establish a lifelong learning environment with participants from the computer science people at the Universidad de las Américas-Puebla and a software company. The Universidad de las Américas-Puebla is considered one of the most prestigious academic institutions in the area of computer science in Mexico and is committed to strengthen ties with a local software company which develops products for the world market. We hope that CASSIEL will establish a channel that keeps our university and the software company updated in the dynamic changes they face and aware of their knowledge and requirements.

CONCLUSIONS

In our knowledge society we learners need information technologies that assists us to maintain a learning plan and to be aware of the demands and opportunities in our global community in order to keep our competitive advantage as individuals and organizations. In this context, we have presented a framework for web-based environments that support lifelong learning based on agent and AI technologies according to the requirements that these environments present.

In this active learning environment, the CASSIEL software agents support awareness of capabilities, commitments and intentions of the community members, providing easy access to knowledge resources, assisting in the social construction of knowledge (socialization, externalization, combination and internalization) by the participants.

We believe that CASSIEL proposes an agent-based learning environment advancing towards the development of lifelong learning environments that promote our competitive advantage as individuals and organizations.

ACKNOWLEDGMENTS

The project has been supported by the Red de Desarrollo e Investigación en Informática (REDII) of the CONACYT, National Council of Science and Technology, Mexico. The author would like to thank Arlette Hernández, Alfredo Ocádiz and Perla Rubalcava for their valuable work in the CASSIEL project.

REFERENCES

Ayala, G. and Yano, Y. (1996) Learner models for supporting awareness and collaboration in a CSCL environment. Intelligent Tutoring Systems. *Proceedings of the conference*

ITS96, Montreal, Canada, Lecture Notes in Computer Science 1086, Claude Frasson, Gilles Gauthier and Alan Lesgold (Eds.), Springer Verlag, 158-167.

Ayala, G. & Yano, Y. (1997) Evaluating the performance of agents that support the effective collaboration of learners in a CSCL environment, *IEICE Transactions on Information and Systems*, Special Issue on Educational Systems Using Multimedia and Communication Technology, February 97, Vol.E80-D, No.2, 35-46.

Ayala, G. & Yano, Y. (1998) A collaborative learning environment based on intelligent agents, *Expert Systems with Applications*, 14, 129-137.

Ayala, G. (1998) *Current trends of artificial intelligence in education.* Gerardo Ayala (Ed.), Workshop Proceedings, 4th World Congress on Expert Systems, ITESM, Mexico City, Mexico.

Ayala, G. & Hernández, (2000). CASIEL: modeling intelligent agents for a lifelong learning environment, *MICAI2000: Advances in Artificial Intelligence,* Lecture Notes in Artificial Intelligence 1793, Springer Verlag, 741-747.

Bannon, L. J. (1994) Issues in computer supported collaborative learning, *Computer Supported Collaborative Learning*, Claire O'Malley (Ed.), Springer Verlag, 267-281.

Barret, E. (1992) *Sociomedia: multimedia, hypermedia, and the social construction of knowledge*, Barret, E. (ed.), MIT Press.

Bigus, J. P. & Bigus, J. (1998) *Constructing intelligent agents with java*, John Wiley & Sons, New York.

Booch, G., Rumbaugh, J. & Jacobson, I. (1999) *The unified modeling language user guide*, Addison Wesley.

Bos, E. S., Kikstra, A. and Morgan, C. M. (1996) Multiple levels of use of the web as a learning tool. *Proceedings of the ED-TELECOM 96, World Conference on Educational Telecommunications*, Boston, USA, Patricia Carlson and Filia Makedo (Eds.). AACE, 31 - 36.

Brown, J. S., Collins, A. and Duguid, P (1989) Situated cognition and the culture of learning. *Educ. Researcher* 18 (1) 32 - 42.

Carlson, P. A. (1992) Varieties of virtual: expanded metaphors for computer-mediated learning, in *Sociomedia: Multimedia, HyperMedia, and the Social Construction of Knowledge*, Barret, E. (ed.), MIT Press, 53-77.

Clancey, W. J. (1991) Invited speaker: Bill Clancey, in *AICOM* Vol. 4 No. 1 March 1991, 4 - 10.

Collis, B. A. (1994). Collaborative learning and CSCW: research perspectives for interworked educational environments, in *Lessons from Learning*, R. Lewis and P. Mendelsohn, (eds.), IFIP Transactions A-46, Elsevier Science B. V, North-Holland, 81-104.

Dillenbourg, P. & Self, J. (1992). A framework for learner modelling, *Interactive Learning Environments*, Vol. 2, Issue (2), 111-137.

Dunlap J. C. (1999) Revisiting the web-based performance support systems for lifelong learning: learner-centered resource development tool. *Proceedings of ED-MEDIA99, World Conference on Educational Multimedia, Hypermedia and Telecommunications*, Seattle, USA, Betty Collis and Ron Oliver (Eds.) AACE, 1140-1145.

Fales, A. W. (1989) Lifespan learning development. *Lifelong Education for Adults*, Colin J. Titmus (Ed.) Pergamon Press, 183-187.

Fischer, G. (2000) Lifelong learning—more than training, in special issue on IntelligentSystems/Tools in Training and Life-long Learning, *International Journal of Continuing Engineering Education and Life-Long Learning* (Richiiro Mizoguchi and Piet Kommers, Eds.), (in press).

Goldstein, I. P. (1982) The genetic graph: a representation for the evolution of procedural knowledge, *Intelligent Tutoring Systems*, D. Sleeman and J. S. Brown (Eds.) Academic Press, 51-77.

Gutwin, C. Stark, G. & Greenberg, S. (1995). Support for workspace awareness in educational groupware, *Proceedings of CSCL '95*, Indiana University, http://www-cscl95.indiana.edu/cscl95/ gutwin.html.

Lin, X. and Hmelo, C. E. (1995) design and development of technology supported learning communities. *Proceedings of ICCE 95, International Conference on Computers in Education*, Singapore, AACE, David Jonassen and Gordon McCalla (Eds.), 519 - 526.

Longworth, N. and Davies, W. K. (1996) *Lifelong learning*. Kogan Page, London.

Morabito, J., Sack, I. & Bhate, A. (1999) *Organization modeling: innovative architectures for the 21st century*, Prentice Hall PTR, Upper Sadle River, NJ.

Nonaka, I. & Takeuchi, H. (1995) *The knowledge creating company*, Oxford University Press, Oxford.

Norrie, D. H. and Gaines, B. R. (1995). The learning web: a system view and agent-oriented model, *International Journal of Educational Communications*, Vol. 1 No. 1, 23-41.

O'Malley, C. (1994). Designing computer support for collaborative learning, *Computer Supported Collaborative Learning*, Claire O'Malley, (Ed.), Springer Verlag, 283-297.

Russell, A. J. and Norvig, P (1995) *Artificial intelligence: a modern approach*. Prentice Hall, New Jersey.

Self, J. (1992). Computational viewpoints, *Knowledge Negotiation*, Moyse, R. & Elsom-Cook, M. (Eds.), Academic Press, 21-40.

Shoham, Y. (1993). Agent-oriented programming, *Artificial intelligence 60*, 51-92.

Tough, A. M. (1989) Self-directed learning: concepts and practice. *Lifelong education for adults*, Colin J. Titmus (Ed.) Pergamon Press, 256-260.

Wang, D. and Johnson, P. (1994). Experiences with CLARE: a computer-supported collaborative learning environment, *International Journal of Human-Computer Studies*, No. 41, 841-879.

Wolf, K. D. (1996) Analyzing the process of learning in a web-based community of learners. *Proceedings of the ED-TELECOM 96, World Conference on Educational Telecommunications*, Boston, USA, Patricia Carlson and Filia Makedo (Eds.). AACE, 337-342.

Wooldridge, M. (1999) Intelligent agents. *Multi-agent systems: a modern approach to distributed artificial intelligence*, Gerhard Weiss (Ed.) MIT Press, 27-77.

Chapter V

A Modeling Methodology for Intelligent Agents: An Electronic Commerce Application

Sooyong Park
Sogang University, Korea

Vijayan Sugumaran
Oakland University, USA

ABSTRACT

The unprecedented growth of the internet and web-based applications has necessitated the deployment of intelligent agents to facilitate some of the tedious and time-consuming activities on the Web. Consequently, there is an increasing demand for agent-oriented systems, which are soon becoming large and complex. To support a systematic development of such systems, an agent-oriented software development methodology is necessary. This chapter focuses on the modeling phase of agent-oriented software life cycle and, presents an approach for agent modeling consisting of Agent Elicitation, Intra, and Inter Agent modeling methods. Agent Elicitation deals with identifying and extracting agents from "classes" in the real world. Intra Agent Modeling involves expressing agent characteristics such as goal, belief, plan and capability, whereas, Inter Agent modeling incorporates agent mobility and communication.

INTRODUCTION

As web-based applications get large and complex, sophisticated technologies are needed to support and execute heterogeneous and distributed applications. To manage this complexity, intelligent agent technology is beginning to be employed as part of the solution in various web applications (Wooldridge, 1999). Since its introduction in the AI community, agent technology has permeated to various application domains as simple as e-mail filtering, to as complex as Air-traffic Control (Jennings, 1998). Recently, in distributed and heterogeneous environments such as Electronic Commerce (EC) applications, intelligent agents are increasingly being utilized to perform various tasks.

Since agents are used in many application areas, a systematic approach that is grounded within the software engineering paradigm is highly important for the development of agent-oriented software. However, there has not been enough research on this subject in the Software Engineering Community.

The fundamental question is how to model software in an agent-oriented paradigm, similar to object-oriented paradigm, which utilizes procedural and data abstractions. To facilitate the design and development of agent-based systems, higher levels of abstractions are necessary to accurately model the flexible, dynamic, and autonomous problem solving characteristics of agents. Some of the agent behaviors may be application domain specific, while others are domain independent. This triggers several research questions such as how best to analyze and model the problem domain in order to facilitate agent-oriented software development, how to identify potential agents within the problem domain, how to model the internal and external behaviors of agents, the inter agent communication and cooperative problem solving, and agent mobility. Our research has been motivated by the above mentioned questions and attempts to develop an agent modeling methodology that facilitates capturing the domain independent and domain dependent aspects of agents. This chapter focuses on the initial phase of agent-oriented software development which includes: a) domain analysis – problem domain modeling as well as agent identification, and b) agent modeling consisting of intra agent and inter agent modeling.

We assume that the real world consists of agents and objects, and an agent is similar to an active object (Jennings, 1998) or a distributed object (Schroeder, 1999). In our agent-oriented process model, we obtain objects from problem domain analysis using UML (Unified Modeling Language) (Harmon, 1998; Selic, 1998), then, extract and create agents from these objects using agent selection rules. Typically, the agent modeling activity consists of two parts: intra agent modeling and inter agent modeling. The former focuses on agent's attributes and behaviors resulting in an "Intra Agent Model," whereas, the latter concentrates on agent communication (message exchanges) and mobility, yielding an "Inter Agent Model."

The remainder of the chapter is organized as follows. Section 2 briefly discusses agent characteristics and modeling methods. Section 3 describes the first two phases of our lifecycle model, namely, domain analysis and agent modeling. Specifically, the UML based problem domain analysis, as well as the agent elicitation process based on Agent Selection Rules are described. This section also discusses the intra agent and inter agent modeling. We have applied our approach to a simple agent-based application in the electronic commerce domain, which is presented in section 4. We have also developed a proof-of-concept prototype to demonstrate the feasibility of our approach using the Zeus agent building toolkit (BT, 1998), which is discussed in section 5. Section 6 provides summary and future research.

AGENT PROPERTIES AND AGENT MODELING METHODS

The concept of agent was introduced by John McCarthy in the mid-1950's and established by Oliver G. Selfridge several years later (Kay, 1984). In the early years, though many researchers investigated different aspects of the agent technology, it was still not considered as mainstream research within the AI community. However, since the late 80's, there has been a resurgence of interest in agent technology, and currently we are seeing a proliferation of agent-based applications, particularly on the Web.

Though several characteristics of agents have been discussed in the literature (Jennings, 1998; Nwana, 1996), we have concluded that the following three properties are essential to an agent in our modeling approach.

Autonomy – an agent can make decisions about what to do based on its own state, without the direct intervention of humans.

Adaptation – an agent can perceive its environment and respond to changes in the environment in a timely fashion.

Cooperation – an agent can interact with other agents through a particular agent-communication language and typically has the ability to engage in collaborative activities to achieve its goal.

Much of the agent modeling work reported in the literature has been in the context of conceptualization of complex systems that make use of Agents. Rao-Georgeff's BDI (Belief-Desire-Intention) model (Rao, 1991) is regarded as one of the relatively successful Agent models. Based on this BDI model, Kinny proposed a design methodology to develop MAS (Multi Agent System) extending OMT (Kinny, 1996). He proposed two main views of BDI agent modeling: internal and external view. These views incorporate typical Object-Oriented (OO) concepts such as Abstraction, Inheritance and Modularity. Burmeister (1996) describes an Agent-Oriented (AO) methodology which also extends OO techniques and generates an agent model, an organizational model and a cooperation model. Recently, Falchuk and Karmouch proposed a modeling methodology called Visual Agent Modeling (Falchuk, 1998) which incorporates the mobility and communication between agents. They define various elements of an agent's active environment, such as agent, server, data, document, etc., with 26 icons. With the help of their Iconic Modeling Tool (IMT), users can visualize and model mobile agents and their itineraries. While their visual modeling approach focuses on the agent environment and the interaction between agents, it fails to adequately support the modeling of the internal aspects and behavior of the agents.

Some of the agent modeling methods mentioned above use object-oriented analysis and design techniques for modeling agents. While the OO techniques may be a good starting point, they are incapable of distinguishing between objects and agents. Consequently, there is lack of definite classification scheme for agent artifacts and object artifacts in the systems analysis procedure. To model static agents and mobile agents in a multi agent environment, a unified modeling method is needed. Therefore, our research presents a new agent oriented modeling methodology, which is an integrated and unified modeling approach.

AGENT - ORIENTED MODELING METHOD

In proposing an agent-oriented approach to modeling a real world application domain, we assume that agents in that domain have the following characteristics:

- Objects and agents can co-exist, and have mutual relationships.
- An active object can be regarded as an agent (Jennings, 1998).
- Agents act asynchronously.
- Interactions among agents take place through message exchanging.

Based on the above assumptions, we propose an agent-oriented modeling process, as depicted in Figure 1. This modeling process consists of the following four steps: (a) UML based Problem Domain Analysis, (b) Agent Elicitation, (c) Intra Agent Modeling, and (d) Inter Agent Modeling. UML based Object-Oriented Analysis Method is used for the problem domain analysis. Since the utility of UML has been extensively validated in different industries, the UML based approach will provide an objective view of the domain in the early stages of Agent Elicitation. It also provides a deep understanding of the problem domain with static and dynamic aspects of the system. After analyzing the problem domain, objects that can be "agentified," as well as the agents that need to be added are determined by agent selection rules, shown in Table 1. These objects and agents that are derived from the domain analysis are assimilated and represented in an Agent-Class diagram. This diagram depicts the relationships between the various objects and agents. Once agents are identified, their internal characteristics are captured in the intra-agent modeling step. The inter-agent modeling step involves developing the agent mobility model, as well as the agent communication model.

Problem Domain Analysis with UML

For the problem domain analysis, the UML based approach is used. With UML (Harmon, 1998; Selic, 1998), not only static, but also dynamic aspects of the system can be analyzed and agent elicitation can be conducted. Diagrams used in problem domain analysis are represented below.

1. Use Case Diagram: A use case diagram shows a set of use cases and actors and their relationships. It supports the behavior of a system by modeling static aspects of a system.
2. Sequence Diagram: Sequence diagram shows interactions, consisting of a set of objects and their relationships, emphasizing the time ordering of messages. It models dynamic aspects of a system.
3. Class Diagram: Class diagram shows a set of classes, interfaces, and collaborations and their relationships. It addresses the static design view of a system, showing a collection of declarative elements.
4. Activity Diagram: Activity diagram shows the flow from activity to activity. Activities ultimately result in an action, which is made up of executable atomic computations that result in a change in state of the system, or the return of a value. It is used to depict dynamic aspects of a system in terms of its functions.

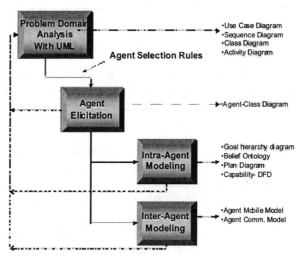

Figure 1. Agent-Oriented Modeling Process

Table 1. Agent Selection Rules

1. Autonomy
   1.1 Does it need internal knowledge?
   1.2 Does it make decisions by itself?
   1.3 Can it be tolerant of unexpected, or wrong inputs?

2. Adaptation
   2.1 Does it need internal knowledge?
   2.2 Is its knowledge updated continuously?
   2.3 Does it interact with external entities?

3. Cooperation
   3.1 Does it interact with external entities?
       3.1.1 Does it operate cooperatively?
       3.1.2 Is it operated in multi-threaded style?

Table 2. Agent Meta Rules

---

1. If the agent has autonomy, adaptation, and cooperation, it is called a "smart agent".
2. If the agent has adaptation and cooperation, it is called a "collaborative learning agent".
3. If the agent has autonomy and cooperation, it is called a "collaborative agent".
4. If the agent has autonomy and adaptation, it is called an "interface agent".

Agent Elicitation

With the consideration of static and dynamic aspects of a system, objects that need to be "agentified" are determined by applying Agent Selection Rules.

Each rule is closely related to the agent's characteristics. To represent the relationships among agent's attributes, we define meta-rules (shown in Table 2). Nwana (1996) suggests that agents can be classified into four groups: smart agent, collaborative learning agent, collaborative agent, and interface agent. Elicited agents are also classified as mobile agents and general agents (stationary agent), based on the mobility of agents. Agents derived using agent selection rules, as well as the objects remaining in the Class diagram, are consolidated and represented in the Agent-Class diagram.

Agent-Class Diagram

Based on the assumption that objects and agents can exist together in the real world, the Agent-Class diagram shows the relationships among agents and objects in the target problem domain. The notion we use in expressing the different elements within the Agent-Class diagram is shown below:

Element

- $\bigcirc_A$: Agent without mobility

- $\bigcirc_M$: Mobile agent

Class: Established classes
Relation

- Cooperation (—O—): shows the relationships between agents, meaning that cooperation is needed among them.
- Employ ((E)): shows the relationships between agents and classes, meaning that agents can use established classes

The Agent-Class diagram expresses agent's internal characteristics goal, belief, plan, and capability as its attributes.

IntraAgent Modeling

The Intra agent modeling approach proposed in our methodology is based on the BDI model (Rao, 1991) and Reticular Agent Mental Models (Thomas, 1993) proposed by Thomas. We propose that the internals of an agent consist of the following four parts, namely, goal, belief, plan, and capability. Figure 2 shows an abstract view of the Intra agent model, which basically comprises of the above-mentioned components.

Goal Model

Goal is an ultimate objective of an agent to be achieved. In KAOS (Dardenne, 1993)s approach, goals are identified in the problem domain analysis. A goal can be expressed as Pattern_of_Goal [objective], and it can be categorized into five groups: Achieve, Cease, Maintain, Avoid, and Optimize. The goal hierarchy diagram shows co-operation among agents corresponding to each goal, depending upon the goal structure. The notations used in the goal hierarchy diagram are given below:

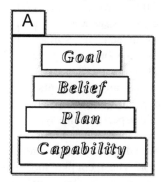

Figure 2. Abstract view of Intra agent model

Element
- Nonfunctional Goal: an objective achieved by the entire system
- Operationalizable Goal: a functional objective achieved by agents

Relation
- AND (**A**): Every sub-goal should be satisfied to achieve the parent goal
- OR (**A**): One or more sub-goals should be satisfied to achieve the parent goal
- Conflict (—): shows whether a particular goal conflicts with other goals

Each goal is treated as a hierarchy so that it can be divided into several sub-goals. These goals and sub-goals can be mapped to one or more agents based on the relationship among agents. Thus, the goals and sub-goals shown in the goal hierarchy are accomplished based on how agents cooperate with one another.

Belief Model

Belief is considered to be data that an agent already possesses. It contains information about the environment and the agent itself. This data should be updated if necessary. This information is used to establish the agent's knowledge base, or Ontology, which can be built using Ontolingua (Gruber, 1993) or KIF (Knowledge Interchange Format) (UMBC Lab for AIT).

The rules that determine what kind of information goes into different ontologies are listed below.

1. Ontology that can be established in the early stage
   - Information about Protocol or ACL (Agent Communication Language) for inter agent communication.
2. Ontologies that need to be updated continuously
   - Attributes and operations in the Class diagram.
   - Messages among objects in the Sequence diagram.
   - Agent's information that needs to be built as a knowledge base.

Each ontology can be represented using XML according to SHOE (Heflin, 1999). For each ontology, there is an ontology ID, its categories and the relationships among them.

Plan Model

Plan shows agent's behavior to achieve a goal. It focuses on the changes in an agent's behavior as time goes on and shows the messages exchanged among agents. Based on the analysis of the dynamic aspects of the sys-

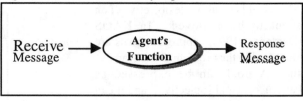

Figure 3. *General Form of Agent's*

tem, each agent can determine its own behavior, based on its goal and beliefs. Agent Plan Sequence diagram, which extends an established Sequence diagram, represents an agent's behavior. The agent plan model uses the following primitives:

- Mobile(Goal[Objective]): the agent with its goal tends to migrate to other domains
- Update(Belief[Type_of_ontology]): the agent updates its ontology corresponding to its information
- employ: the agent uses classes
- msg[message_context]: message that is exchanged between agents

Capability Model

An agent's capability model shows the set of operations that it can perform. It explains the agent's internal changes from inputs and outputs. The agent capabilities are represented using a DFD (Data Flow Diagram) as shown in Figure 3.

Inter-Agent Modeling

Agent's mobility and exchange of messages among agents in multi-agent systems are modeled in the Intra agent modeling process. This results in two different types of models: Agent Mobility Model and Agent Communication Model.

Agent Mobility Model

The Agent Mobility Model shows how an agent migrates to perform a specific task. It also shows mechanisms that determine the destination that the mobile agent migrates to, i.e., the basis of mobile agent migration and which host the agent will move to. Since we cannot tell how the agent decides its destination from the external viewpoint, agent's internal view (the mental state) is needed to know the agent's decision mechanism.

Agent Communication Model

The Agent Communication Model shows exchanging of messages among agents based on Sequence Diagram. The difference between Sequence Diagram and Agent Communication Diagram is the "subject" of communication. A Sequence Diagram shows the messages among agents and objects, while the Agent Communication diagram shows the communication among agents.

This model has two parts: external view and internal view of agent communication. The external view shows how a stationary agent communicates with mobile agent, and the internal view shows which process within the agent is needed to exchange messages. To generate messages, the result value from agent's operation and the given goal are entered as inputs. These inputs generate the messages for the communication by agent's internal processing routine.

AN EXAMPLE FROM ELECTRONIC COMMERCE (EC) DOMAIN

In this section, we apply our modeling approach to the electronic commerce domain. We start with the explanation of the problem domain and a sample scenario and show how we apply our agent modeling methodology to generate an agent-based solution for this problem.

Problem Scenario

Let us consider a very simple electronic commerce application in which the user is attempting to purchase a component. Let us also assume that in this EC application domain, there are four servers connected to a network. Two hosts are operating on Windows 98, one on Windows NT, and one on Solaris. Each host has a database that contains information regarding products and components of a PC. We employ mobile agents to help us find the best information regarding PCs and its components and then place an order and carry out a transaction. Figure 4 depicts an abstract view of the whole system. The details of a particular scenario in which the user interacts with agents to specify what he/she wants and then places an order based on the information gathered by the agents is shown in Table 3.

UML based Agent Elicitation

In applying our modeling approach, we first perform the EC problem domain analysis, which results in a Use Case Diagram, Sequence Diagram, Class Diagram, and an Activity Diagram. Then we apply the Agent Selection Rules to identify and extract relevant agents. Finally, we produce Agent-Class Diagram for our example scenario.

Use Case Diagram

There are four actors in our example: a) the user who enters the information, b) the company which has the actual product, c) company's databases which have the information about the products, and d) the bank which can check the user validation. There are also three use cases, namely, Display use case that captures the communication with customers, Search use case that finds the informa-

Figure 4. System Diagram for Problem Domain

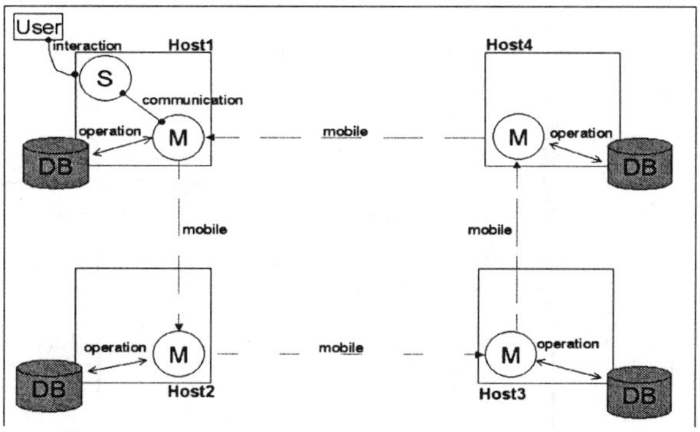

Table 3. Sample Problem Scenario

A User intends to purchase components of a PC through the Internet. The user enters the name of the component, to an Agent. Agent migrates to search for the information related to that item. Agent compares the information obtained from different sources. Agent sends the information to the user and asks whether to place an order for that item. If the user wants to order, Agent processes the transaction.

Figure 5. Use Case Diagram Applied to the Example Domain

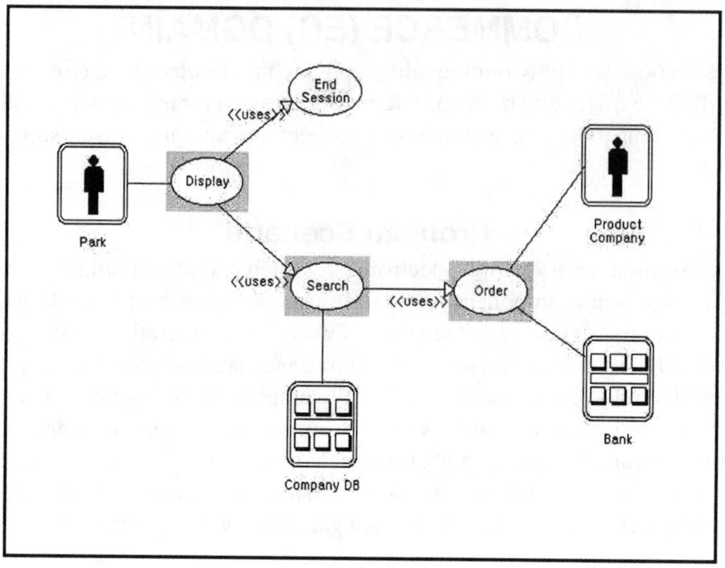

tion about products, and Order use case that processes the order. Figure 5 shows the Use Case diagram applicable to our Example Domain. This system communicates with the user, searches for the product that the user wants, and orders the best product for the user.

Sequence Diagram

For each use case, we produce a Sequence Diagram. Figure 6 shows the Sequence Diagram related to the Search use case, which performs the main tasks. In this diagram, five

Figure 6. Sequence Diagram applied to example domain

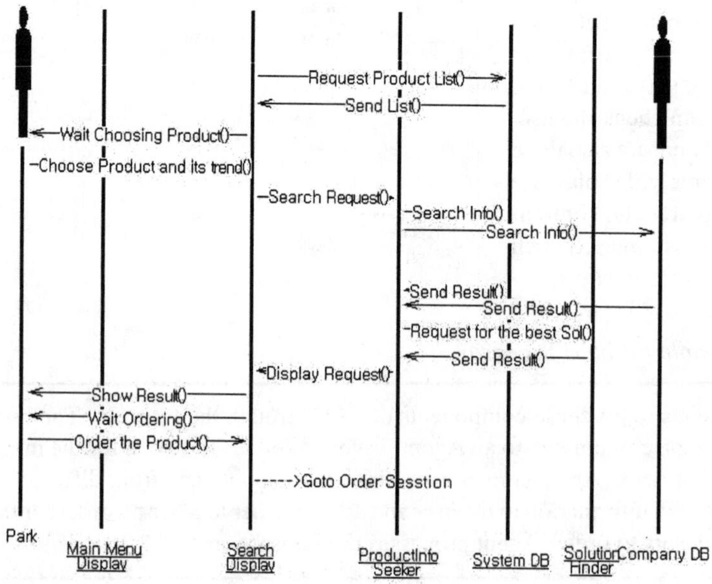

Figure 7. Class Diagram(top) and Activity Diagram(bottom) Applied to Example Domain

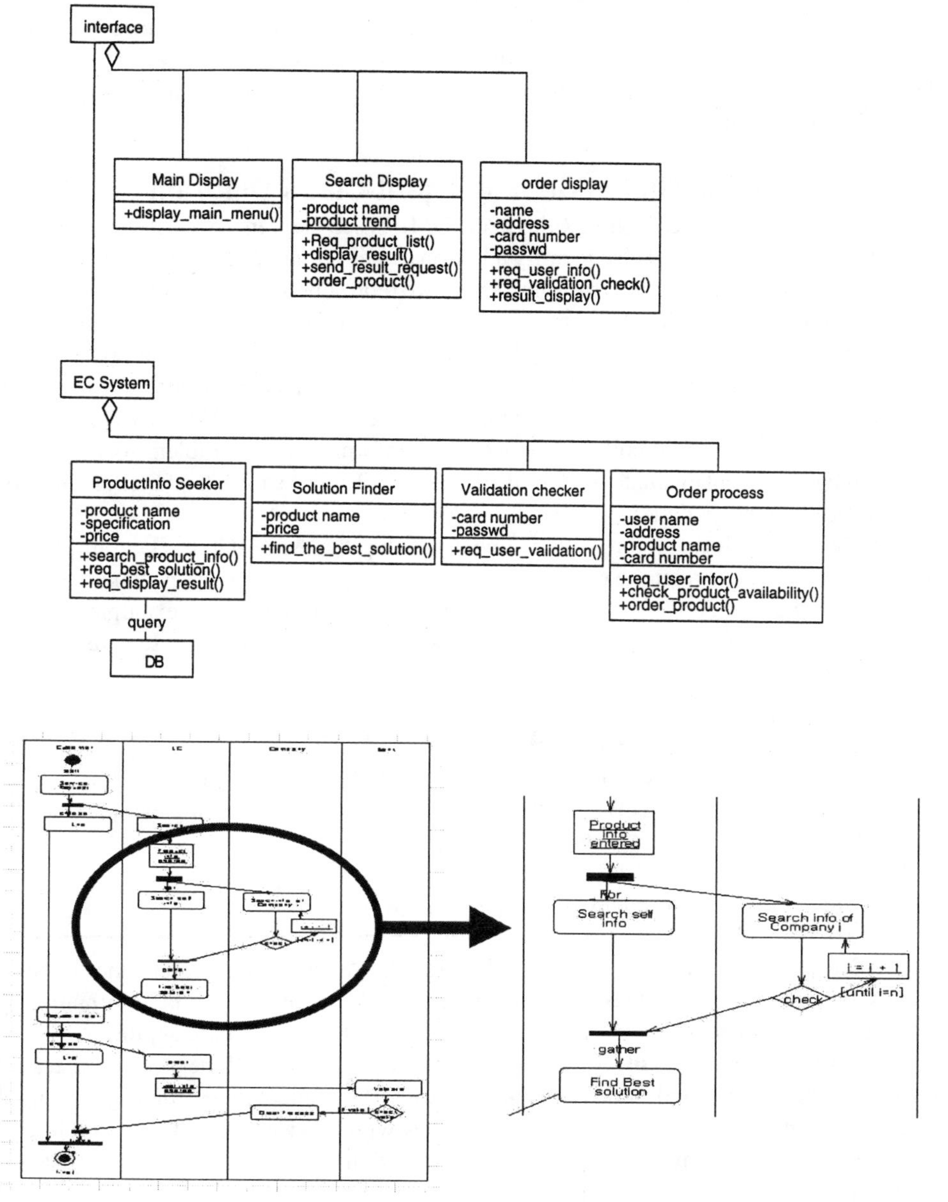

classes are produced; Main Menu Display, Search Display, ProductInfo Seeker, System DB, and Solution Finder. Each class passes messages to other classes. For example, ProductInfo Seeker class gets the message, Search Request(), processes some events to satisfy the request message, and sends back the result to the Search Display class.

Class Diagram and Activity Diagram

The Class and Activity Diagrams are generated by extracting objects from Use Case Diagram and Sequence Diagram. The static and dynamic aspects of objects are represented by the attributes and operations of the object. Figure 7 shows the Class Diagram (top) and Activity Diagram (bottom) applied to our example domain. In the Class Diagram, there are nine classes for our problem domain and EC system class consists of four classes by way of aggregation. Each class has attributes and operations, showing their roles. The Activity Diagram shows how to search for information and find the best solution, and focuses on the dynamic aspect of the classes.

Agent Elicitation and Agent-Class Diagram

By applying Agent Selection Rules to the UML based diagrams, we determine objects that can be "agentified" and also identify additional agents that need to be added. If one or more classes contribute towards the same agent, we represent them in one group. From the Class Diagram and Activity Diagram for the current EC application shown in Figure 7, we derive three Agents (Interface Agent, Product Info Seeker Agent, and Solution Finder Agent) and one additional agent (Coordinator Agent). The Interface Agent is responsible for facilitating the interaction between human and agents as well as between agents. The Product Info Seeker Agent collects the necessary information for problem solving. The Solution Finder Agent evaluates different alternatives. Table 4 shows the functionalities of each of these agents in detail.

Based on the identified agents, we next develop the Agent-Class Diagram, which shows how the agents relate to each other and what other classes that they make use of in carrying out their tasks. Figure 8 shows the Agent-Class Diagram for our example domain. The Product Info Seeker Agent is indicated with the notation to represent its mobile characteristics.

Intra Agent Modeling

In this section we present the modeling of the internals of the agent, namely, the Intra Agent modeling process. This step involves capturing and representing the goal, belief, plan, and capabilities of the agents.

Table 4. Elicited Agents based on Agent Selection Rules

Interface Agent: Communicating with the user, the Agent understands his/her intentions and exchanges messages with Product Info Seeker Agent to get the information. It has autonomy and adaptation as its attributes (Rule 1.1, 1.3, 2.3 are applied).

Product Info Seeker Agent: As performing the main formation of the product, checks the user validation, and processes the ordering. This agent does multi-threading operations in the environments and it cooperates with other agents. It is the mobile, collaborative agent that has autonomy and cooperation (Rule 1.1, 3.1(3.1.1, 3.1.2) are applied).

Coordinator Agent: Perceiving the external environments, if there are any changes, the agent should update its internal knowledge and provide the route that informs the next mobile place to the Product Info Seeker agent. This is the newly created smart agent that helps to perform agent's mobility efficiently, having autonomy, adaptation and cooperation (Rule 1.2, 2.1, 2.2, 3.1.1 are applied).

Solution Finder Agent: From the information that Product Info Seeker Agent has found, Solution Finder Agent determines the best result. It is the collaborative agent that has autonomy and adaptation (Rule 1.1, 1.2, 3.1.1 are applied).

Figure 8. Agent-Class Diagram for the Example Domain

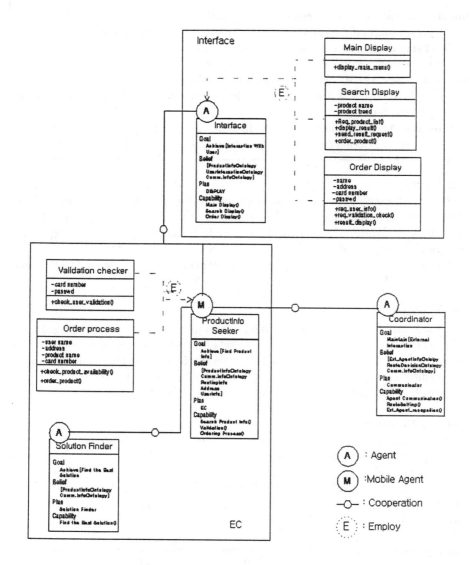

Goal Modeling

Every agent has a goal and performs one or more tasks to achieve its goal. In our Example Domain, the four agents that we have identified have their own set of goals, as shown in Table 5.

To achieve its goal, each agent has several sub-goals that should be satisfied. Figure 9 shows the Goal-hierarchy diagram for the current EC application, which shows the relationships among goals and their sub-goals. For example, the ProductInfoSeeker Agent has the goal, *Achieve SearchProductInfo*, and several sub-goals, such as *Maintain WellformedSearchPath* and *Maintain SearchProductInfo*.

Table 5. Goal Modeling of Each Agent

Interface Agent: Achieve[Interaction With User]
- It serves successful results to the user, interacting with him/her efficiently

Product Info Seeker Agent: Achieve[Find Product Info]
- It searches the product information successfully

Solution Finder Agent: Achieve[Find the Best Solution]
- It finds out the best one from the product information that Product Info Seeker Agent has found

Coordinator Agent: Maintain [External Interaction]
- It perceives external environment and maintains its information

Belief Modeling

Based on the ontology decision rules mentioned in the previous section, Table 6 shows the ontologies established for our problem domain. For example, the "Product Info Seeker Agent" uses ProductInfoOntology and CommunicationOntology. In addition, it has RoutingInfo, UserInfo and Address as the basic belief information.

Furthermore, these ontologies can be represented in XML according to SHOE. Table 7 shows the UserInteractionOntology representation by XML.

Plan Modeling

As indicated earlier, an agent's Plan represents its behavior to achieve the goal. For example, Figure 10 shows the plan characteristic of "Product Info Seeker Agent," which specifies message exchanges among agents from the Interaction Diagram. This agent moves to different locations in search of the product information. It also employs several classes, such as Validation Checker and Order Process to achieve its goal.

Capability Modeling

Agent's capability represents operations that are needed for achieving its goal. Figure 11 shows the capability model for "Product Info Seeker Agent," using the DFD notation. This agent has three capabilities, namely, "Search Product Info()," "Validation()," and "Ordering Process()." To add more details to the "Search Product Info()" capability, it can be further decomposed into three sub-capabilities, i.e., "Communication," "Migrate & Search," and "Send Info to Solution Finder Agent."

Figure 9. Goal Hierarchy Diagram applied to Example Domain

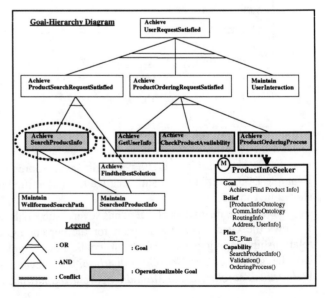

Table 6. Ontology and its decision rules

ProductInfoOntology: It is the overall knowledge for the user to choose the product. The product kind and its trend are established as ontology (Attributes of the Search Display class are applied).

UserInteractionOntology: To understand user's input about ordering process, user information such as name, address, credit card number, and etc. is established as ontology (Attributes of the Order Process class are applied).

CommunicationOntology: When agents need to cooperate one another, protocol or ACL (Agent Communication Language) are established as ontology (Requested operations of classes are applied).

ExternalAgentInfoOntology: The overall knowledge to perceive the external environments is established as ontology (Interacting messages in Sequence diagram are applied).

RouteDecisionOntology: The knowledge about the route, which needs for moving to other databases, is established as ontology (Interacting messages in Sequence diagram are applied).

Table 7. UserInteractionOntology Representation by XML

```
<ONTOLOGY ID="UserInteractionOntology" VERSION="1.0">
<DEF-CATEGORY NAME="Actor"  ISA="base.SHOEEntity">
<DEF-CATEGORY NAME="Card"  ISA="base.SHOEEntity">
<DEF-CATEGORY NAME="Company"       ISA="Actor">
<DEF-CATEGORY NAME="User"  ISA="Actor">

<DEF-CATEGORY NAME="UserName" ISA="User">
<DEF-CATEGORY NAME="UserAddr" ISA="User">

<DEF-CATEGORY NAME="Master" ISA="Card">
<DEF-CATEGORY NAME="Visa" ISA="Card">
<DEF-CATEGORY NAME="Express" ISA="Card">

<DEF-CATEGORY NAME="CardNumber" ISA="Master, Visa, Express">
<DEF-CATEGORY NAME="IssueDate" ISA="Master, Visa, Express">
<DEF-CATEGORY NAME="ExpDate" ISA="Master, Visa, Express">

<DEF-RELATION NAME="Issue">
<DEF-ARG POS="1" TYPE="Company">
<DEF-ARG POS="2" TYPE="Card">
</DEF-RELATION>

<DEF-RELATION NAME="Hold">
<DEF-ARG POS="1" TYPE="User">
<DEF-ARG POS="2" TYPE="Card">
</DEF-RELATION>
```

Figure 10. Plan Sequence Diagram of ProductInfoSeeker Agent

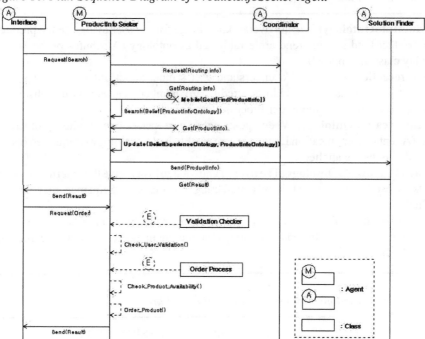

Inter Agent Modeling

In this section we present the Inter Agent modeling process for the EC problem domain under discussion. This process consists of agent mobility modeling, which includes strategies for agent migration, as well as agent communication modeling, which captures the dynamics of message exchanging between agents.

Agent Mobility Modeling

The Agent Mobility Model shows how an agent migrates to perform a task and the criteria that determine the destination for the mobile agent. Figure 12 shows the "Product Info Seeker" agent's migration mechanism applied to our example domain. An abstract view of the agent's internal processing to determine when and where to migrate next is shown in the lower half of the diagram (under the bar) shown in Figure 12. This corresponds to the agent's decision mechanism for the next destination. Based on G1 (the previous goal) and IOE (Information of Environment) as inputs, Decision Making State brings forth G2 (the next goal) and next address as outputs. IOE has all information about agent's state. For instance, IOE informs you where Mobile Agent is, how Mobile Agent processes its task, etc. If G1 is equal to G2, the previous goal is the same as the next one and the given task is finished. If not, G2 is the sub-goal of G1 and Mobile Agent should process G2 (the next goal). The mobile agent sends the search results from the databases back to the Coordinator Agent.

Agent Communication Modeling

The Agent Communication Model shows message exchanges between agents. It shows which agent communicates with what other agents, and which message format is used

Figure 11. Capability Model of ProductInfoSeeker Agent

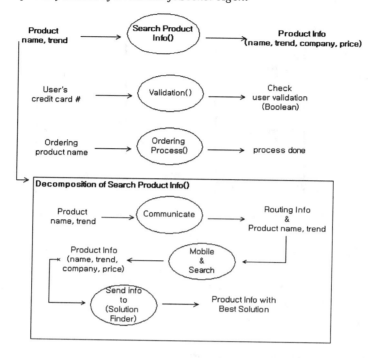

for the communication. Figure 13 shows the Agent Communication Model specific to our example domain.

Generally, to generate a message, the results from an agent's operation, as well as the current goal are used as inputs. These communication messages are generated by the agent's internal processing routine. Typically, a message consists of three parameters, namely, sender_address (sender's address), receiver_address (receiver's address), and message content.

PROTOTYPE IMPLEMENTATION

This section briefly illustrates how our approach has been implemented using ZEUS, an agent building toolkit developed by British Telecom Labs [6]REF _Ref492722036 \h **Error! Bookmark not defined**. For reasons of brevity, we omit some details and focus on the user interface aspect of the system and provide a general flavor of the implementation.

The main user interface window comprises of three panels (see Figure 14). The top panel of the window shows the advertisement logo for this implementation. The middle panel of the window contains a text area that displays information to users depending upon what actions are being taken by the system. For example, if an agent is interacting with another agent, the messages being exchanged are displayed in the middle part. The bottom panel of the window is the control panel where the user can initiate certain tasks and get the status of various actions. This portion also shows the results of execution. This panel also contains two tabs, one labeled "Inventory" and the other called "Buy Item". In this e-commerce application, the "inventory" tab is used to see what items have been acquired so far. The user can explicitly initiate the buying process for an item by clicking on the "buy item" tab and then selecting that item. The user can also specify different parameters for that purchase.

Figure 12. Agent Mobile Model applied to problem domain

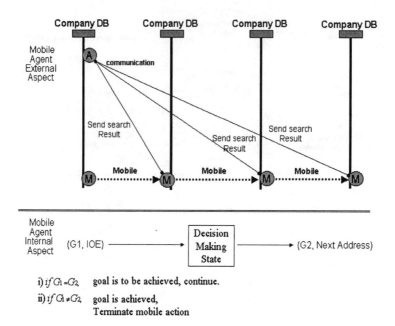

i) *if* $G_1 = G_2$ goal is to be achieved, continue.

ii) *if* $G_1 \neq G_2$ goal is achieved,
Terminate mobile action

In our current implementation scenario, there are four sellers of computer systems, two for Windows98, one for Windows NT, and one for Solaris systems. They are distributed over a network and have common items to sell, namely, monitors, mouses, speakers, and keyboards. The price and profit rates are different for each seller.

Now, we briefly present a sample interaction with the system based on the problem scenario outlined in Table 3. When the user starts the system, first, the user interface (UI) window is launched, which is shown in Figure 14a. This UI window shows the three panels described above. Since the user has not initiated any purchasing process, the middle panel shows that the ProductInfoSeeker agent is waiting for instructions. In the bottom panel, the inventory tab is open, and it shows that there are no items currently on hand. It also shows that the user has $10,000 at his or her disposal to purchase different items.

The user starts the purchase of an item by clicking on the "buy item" tab. The bottom panel now displays two buttons labeled "Choose" and "Seeking." It also contains slots for specifying the item to be purchased, maximum offer price, and a time deadline (as shown in Figure 14b). When the user clicks on the "Choose" button, the system displays another panel, which contains a list of items that can be purchased and the user can select one or more of these items. This panel is shown in Figure 15a. For example, if the user selects the Monitor entity from this panel, the item to trade slot in the buy item panel is automatically filled in as Monitor. The items to be purchased (displayed in Figure 15a) are derived from the EC-ontology. The user can now specify the maximum offer price and the time allotted for this purchase by typing in the values in the appropriate slots. Then, the user clicks on the "Seeking" button to start the purchasing process. The time-grain is also used for agent synchronization.

Once the purchase is initiated, the ProductInfoSeeker agent starts gathering information about computer monitors and the negotiation process starts. The SolutionFinder agent

Figure 13. Agent Communication Model applied to problem domain

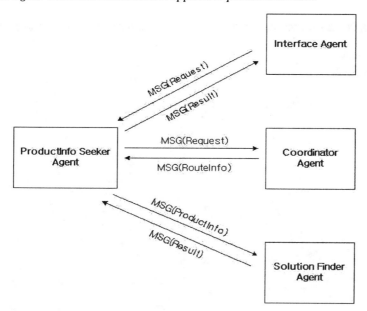

evaluates different proposals from the sellers and eventually the purchase is carried out through the Coordinator agent. Part of the message exchange between agents during the negotiation and purchase activity is shown in Figures 14b and 15b.

Once the purchase activity is completed, the user is notified and the results are viewed by clicking on the "Inventory" tab. In this specific example, a monitor has been purchased from "NTHost," and after payment, the user is left with $9884.01, as indicated in Figure 15b.

SUMMARY AND FUTURE RESEARCH

We have presented an agent modeling methodology that is essential for developing agent-based software. The major activities in our agent modeling methodology are Agent Elicitation, Intra and Inter Agent Modeling. Prior to the agent modeling process, the application domain is analyzed and modeled using the UML approach. From the UML-based domain model, we suggest criterias on how to select objects that should be agentified and produce an Agent-Class Diagram. This diagram describes the static parts of a system, as well as cooperation among agents. In Intra Agent modeling, we capture the internals of an Agent. The Goal-hierarchy diagram represents cooperation relationships among agents corresponding to each goal. Belief modeling in our methodology provides classification criteria on what knowledge should be established as ontology. Plan Sequence Diagram is used to describe changes in Agent's behavior and DFD is used to represent agent's capabilities. In Inter Agent Modeling, we model agent mobility and communication. We have demonstrated the feasibility of our modeling methodology by applying it to a small e-commerce example.

In our approach, we build each model as a module and map them to agent architecture: Belief model is built as a knowledge base so that it has information about the system

14a. User Interface Window and Processing   Figure 14b. User CommFigure
Window

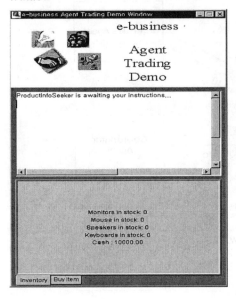
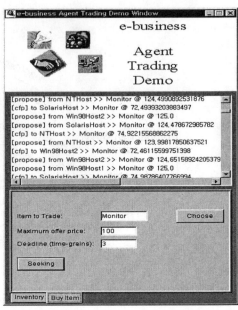

Figure 15a. Purchase Items defined in EC-   *Figure 15b. Purchase Execution Results*
Ontology

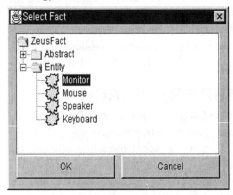
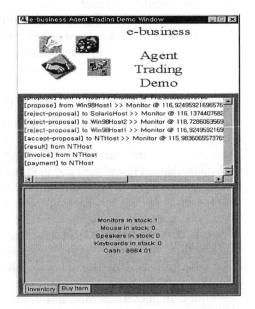

environment and the agent itself. Plan model is built as a control module, which manages agent tasks to achieve its goal. Capability model is built as a "methods" module that executes the agent functions. Communication model and mobility model are also built as control module that manages message exchanges and mobility. Finally, Goal model is used for the validation and test module so that each module can be checked whether it can achieve the goal or not.

While we have developed an overall agent modeling methodology, much work remains to be done. It is necessary to evaluate the efficiency of agent modeling method and the appropriateness of agent selection rules. We are also investigating the applicability of Goal-oriented modeling method to our approach. This is based on the concept that systems are constructed with some goals in mind and each agent performs its task actively to achieve the goal. From the problem scenario, goals are elicited and relationships between goals are defined. Based on these goal relationships, we can derive a goal model which can augment agent selection rules.

REFERENCES

British Telecommunication plc. The ZEUS Agent Building Toolkit 1998, http://www.labs.bt.com/projects/agents/.

Burmeister, Birgit. Models and methodology for agent-oriented analysis and design. In K Fischer, Ed., *Working Notes of the KI'96 Workshop on Agent-Oriented Programming and Distributed Sytstems*, 1996. DFKI Document D-96-06.

Dardenne, A. Van Lamsweerde and S. Fickas (1993). Goal-directed Requirements Acquisition. *Science of Computer Programming*, 20, 3-50, 1993.

Falchuk, Benjamin and Ahmed Karmouch (1998). Visual Modeling for Agent-Based Applications. *IEEE computer*, December 1998.

Gruber, T. R. (1993). A Translation Approach to Portable Ontologies. *Knowledge Acquisition*, 5(2), 199-220, 1993.

Harmon, P. and M. Watson (1998). *Understanding UML: The Developers Guide*. Morgan Kaufmann Publishers, 1998.

Heflin, Jeff Heflin, James Hendler, and Sean Luke (1999). A Knowledge Representation Language for Internet Applications. Technical Report CS-TR-4078(UMIACS TR-99-71).

Jennings, N. R. Jennings, K. P. Sycara, and M. Wooldridge (1998). A Roadmap of Agent Research and Development. *International Journal of Autonomous Agents and Multi-Agent Systems*, 1(1), 7-36.

Kay, , A. (1984). Computer Software, *Scientific American* 251(3), 53-59.

Kinny, D., M. Georgeff, and A. Rao (1996). A methodology and modelling technique for systems of BDI agents. In W. Van de Velde and J. W. Perram, Ed., *Agents Breaking Away: Proceedings of the Seventh European Workshop on Modelling Autonomous Agents in a Multi-Agent World MAAMAW'96, (LNAI Volume 1038)*. Springer-Verlag: Heidelberg, Germany, 56-71.

Nwana, H. S. (1996). Software Agents: An Overview. *The Knowledge Engineering Review*, 11(3), 205-244.

Rao, A. Rao and M. Georgeff (1991). Modeling rational agents within a BDI-architecture. In R. Fikes and E. Sandewall, Ed., *Proceedings of Knowledge representation and reasoning (KR&R-91)*. Morgan Kaufmann Publishers: San Mateo, CA, 473-484.

Schroeder, M. (1999). Are Distributed objects agents? In Position Papers of *International Bi-Conference Workshop on Agent-Oriented Information Systems (AOIS'99)*, 1999.

Selic, B. Selic and J. Rumbaugh (1998). *Using UML for Modeling Complex Real-Time Systems*.

Thomas, S. R.(1993). *PLACA, An Agent Oriented Programming Language*. PhD Dissertation, Stanford University.

UMBC lab for AIT] UMBC Lab for Advanced Information Technology, KIF (Knowledge Interchange Format), http:// www.cs.umbc.edu/kse/kif/.

Wooldridge, M., N. R. Jennings, and D. Kinny (1999). A Methodology for Agent-Oriented Analysis and Design. In *Proceedings of the Third International Conference on Autonomous Agents (Agents 99)*, Seattle, WA, 69-76.

Chapter VI

Courseware and Its Possible Evolution through the Use of Agent Technology

Paul Darbyshire and Glenn Lowry
Victoria University of Technology, Australia

ABSTRACT

This chapter explores the potential for the application of agent technology to evolve an information system. In particular, the use of agents to evolve an educational subject management application is viewed in relation to an on-going project. Such software forms part of a courseware information system currently in use, and being further developed at Victoria University. Agent software is an emerging technology that has its roots in artificial intelligence research. With the recent proliferation of "agent" applications in areas such as e-commerce and Internet marketing, many agent applications fall squarely in the domain of Information Systems. Although there is little consensus at present regarding the nature and capabilities of software agents, agent technology may have the potential to advance Web-based subject management courseware to a further evolutionary stage.

INTRODUCTION

The term *"courseware"* is a relatively recent term that is used to describe the comprehensive software available to manage many aspects of the educational delivery process. The software that preceded what we regard as modern courseware had many names: Computer-Aided Instruction (CAI); Computer-Managed Instruction (CMI); Computer-Aided Learning (CAL); Computer-Managed Learning (CML); on-line teaching and learning and more recently Web-Based Learning (WBL) (Darbyshire and Wenn, 1996). However, the World Wide Web technology we now use as the platform for courseware, and the sophistication of the software have reached a stage of maturity that courseware products are attracting academics in greater numbers than ever before. Of course there are other factors driving this migration, including the rationalization of education as an economic activity.

The increased sophistication of courseware has evolved over many years by the addition of improved functionality. This evolutionary process has been largely driven in the past few years by advances in the technological environment, which is consistent with Lehman's observations of the evolutionary process (Lehman, 1982). The development of the Web has led to Web-based courseware which offers flexibility previously unavailable in many areas of delivery and management (Darbyshire and Wenn, 1998). However, as a commercially available *Information System*, courseware products as a whole may have enabled the *substitution* of computer power for manual human effort in many aspects, but have not yet progressed as far down the evolutionary path as they might given today's technology. There are some excellent commercial products available, such as, *TopClass*, *Learning Space*, *Virtual-U*, *WebCT*, *Web Course in a Box*, *CourseInfo* and *First Class*. Landon (Landon, 1988) provides an on-line comparative analysis of fourteen courseware products, including those just mentioned; however, they have thus far not enabled us to alleviate the need for conscious human control at all times.

If we view the development of courseware products as an evolutionary process, then it is interesting to pause and ask the questions, "*How have courseware systems evolved*" and "*How might courseware systems evolve in future*". Of course future directions will depend on available technology at the time, but we can pose some directions for this evolution based on emerging technologies. *Agent technology* may provide the means by which courseware can "*evolve*" and anticipate and assume many of the functions that humans must now initiate.

While agent technology holds considerable promise, it is still in an embryonic stage. Despite this, a broad range of organizations and disciplines are researching and pursuing software advances through agent technology. The Web provides a good architectural framework for the development of agents because it facilitates many of the characteristics of agent software such as *mobility* and *communication*. Given the existing base of courseware information systems and the functionality they provide, agents can be used to evolve these systems by supporting development based on a predictive model rather than simply relying on traditional incremental improvements.

It should be noted that some excellent work is already being undertaken in the area of Intelligent Tutoring Systems (ITS) (Ottmann and Tomek, 1998). However, we are particulary interested in viewing courseware from the perspective of the academic as the stakeholder (Darbyshire, 1999; Darbyshire and Wenn, 1999). With this perspective, the subject administration and management functionality of such systems take on more importance and indeed become the focus of the research described in this chapter.

In the following sections the notion of *information system evolution* is explored and some definitions for *evolutionary stage* (based in part on the work of Lehman and Belady (Lehman and Belady, 1985)) are introduced. Some background material on agents is provided and in particular the notion of *autonomous agents* which expands on the base idea of agency. The use of autonomous agents to enable evolution of course management software is then explored, and finally, a detailed description of the application of autonomous agents to an on-going courseware project is given.

INFORMATION SYSTEMS EVOLUTION

The early work on software evolution began in the late 1960's and early 1970's with much of the work credited to Lehman, Belady, Boehm and a few others whose names appear in the early literature. One of the earlier papers to seriously discuss software evolution as applying to individual artificial systems was written by Gerald Weinberg (Weinberg, 1970). Weinberg drew an analogy between program evolution and that of the natural evolution of living organisms proposed by Charles Darwin. However, the first recognition of the intrinsic evolutionary nature of software was by Belady and Lehman (Belady and Lehman, 1971; Lehman and Belady, 1985).

The term *software* is often used as a surrogate for *program*. However, in our context software is much more than just a program, with the term subsuming the entire program development process. The study of Information Systems has led to the term *information system* being used in place of *software*. The FRICSO report (IFIP, 1998), uses the term *"Computerized Information Sub-System" (CISS)*. A CISS is a computer-based implementation of a *model* from a *domain* (IFIP, 1998), and we use this term in place of the traditional *"software"*.

Although the evolution of CISS's is an accepted fact, most of the relevant papers, (and indeed the appropriate disciplines), are concerned with the micro-management of the evolutionary process itself, (Lehman, 1981; Mills, 1980; Oman and Lewis, 1990; Sommerville, 1989; Zachman, 1987). This is understandable given the financial and human resources devoted to this evolutionary process (or maintenance) (Boehm, 1976; Brooks, 1974). However, in order to view the larger picture or to reason about the evolutionary process, we need to develop a *meta-level* understanding of the evolutionary progression. With such an understanding, we are then perhaps in a better position to conceptualize and direct the overall evolutionary process.

For instance, if we somehow plot the functionality of a CISS as a function of time (or even version number), then we can view the overall evolution (in the traditional sense) as an increasing trend in functionality as in Figure 1. If we take any two points on our plot, then it is interesting to ask, *what is the quantitative difference between these two versions*? Is one definitely more *evolved* than the other, or is the difference only an increase in similar functionality? In other words, can we divide the time-line in Figure 1 into evolutionary stages (a stage may include many versions), where as the evolution of a CISS progresses over time, it passes through discrete stages which can be quantified? We have defined two evolutionary stages for a CISS in the following paragraphs. These definitions were formulated in part based on earlier work of Lehman and Belady (Lehman and Belady, 1985) and Parker and Benson (Parker and Benson, 1988).

We view a CISS as being in the *First Evolutionary Stage* (FES) while it is implemented from a specification of a model which contains no predictive elements. This means that the model of implementation is not based on any predictive views on the domain's information system. Parker and Benson's *Substitutive* and *Complementary* Information Technology applications would correspond to this stage of development (Parker and Benson, 1988), as would the *S* and *P* type systems from Lehman's *SPE* classification (Lehman, 1982). A representation of this evolutionary state is shown in Figure 2.

Figure 1. CISS plot of functionality vs. time

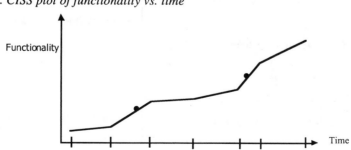

Figure 2. First evolutionary stage

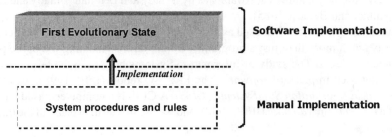

CISS applications in this stage of evolution are typically a computerized implementation of an existing set of manual procedures and rules, with organizations initially tending to implement these types of systems (Ostwald, 1996). Another characteristic of a CISS at this stage is that of their interaction metaphor, *direct-manipulation*. In this metaphor, the user is required to personally initiate all tasks and monitor all events (Schneiderman, 1983). While all systems continually evolve through maintenance and version releases governed by some life-cycle model, they may not necessarily progress to a higher stage of evolution (as we have defined it). Adding more functionality to such a system may lead to traditional generational evolution, but functionality that does not feedback to substantially improve the underlying model is basically, "more of the same". In other words, if this new functionality can be realized easily in the underlying domain (manual system), then the new version still satisfies our definition of being in the first evolutionary state.

In contrast, we classify a CISS as being in the *Second Evolutionary Stage* (SES) when it is implemented from a model that cannot have a realization in the underlying information system. By having a model which cannot have a realization in the underlying information system, the CISS has functionality which cannot be implemented manually (either for physical or practical reasons). We believe that a CISS in this stage would represent an evolutionary jump from the first stage, as its model is either based on a pre-existing first stage model, or it could be implemented directly from an initial predictive model. This is depicted in Figure 3.

Once a CISS is implemented, the tangible benefits that manifest themselves often lead to a realization of what may now be possible with the CISS in place. The development of a model for improved functionality that relies on the existence of an already implemented CISS leads to an evolutionary progression to the second stage and the benefit acceleration

Figure 3. Second evolutionary stage

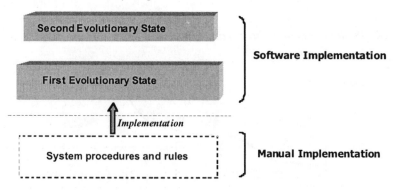

implied by Parker and Benson (Parker and Benson, 1988). It is possible that a CISS may be implemented directly in the second evolutionary state, but this would require an initial predictive model, which would be based on the underlying information system as it would be with a CISS already implemented. The *E* type systems of Lehman's *SPE* classification (Lehman, 1982) and the *innovative* applications of Parker and Benson (Parker and Benson, 1988) would correspond to this state.

It should be stated that not all CISS's will evolve to this second evolutionary stage, nor need they, to be useful members of an organizational information system. One of the main characteristics envisaged of a CISS at this stage is a move to an interaction metaphor of *indirect-manipulation*, in which the system will serve as a surrogate for human operation and direction (Maes, 1995). Instead of user-initiated interaction via commands and direct manipulation, the user engages in a cooperative process with the computer where both may initiate communication, monitor events, and perform tasks. Usually this type of functionality is built into a CISS after many generational life-cycles, when new functionality becomes reliant on previous functionality.

Given our definitions of evolutionary stages, how can we evolve software from the first to the second stage of evolution as we have defined it? What type of approaches might lead to this second evolutionary stage? The emerging field of *Agent Technology* holds much promise in this respect, and it is this approach that we have taken with the research described later in this chapter. The following sections provide some background on this often misunderstood technology.

Table 1 **Some agent descriptions**

Type	Description
Mobile	Agent processes capable of roaming wide area networks such as the WWW, and interacting with foreign hosts, gathering information on behalf of its owner
Interface	Agents that support and provide assistance, typically to a user learning to use a particular application or perform a specific task
Autonomous	Agents that can operate independently of any user, can sense its environment and react to it
Internet/Information	There agents help manage the vast amount of information in wide area networks like the Internet
Deliberative	One that possesses an explicitly represented, symbolic model of the world, and in which decisions are made via symbolic reasoning
Reactive	Agents that act using a stimulus/response type of behavior by responding to the present state of their environment
Intelligent	Agents that can perform reasoning functions and possess knowledge and obligation
Static	Antithesis of mobile agents, remain stationary on one server
Collaborative	Agents that cooperate with other agents in the performance of specific tasks
Smart	Agents that are not necessarily intelligent but possess more than one of the characteristics above: eg autonomy, learning ability, etc.

SOFTWARE AGENTS

No universally acknowledged definition of a software *agent* is currently available; however, this can be readily forgiven as even the 'experts' cannot agree on a definition for an agent (Nwana, 1996; Wooldridge & Jennings, 1995). Agent software is an emerging technology which promises to be many things to many people; however, the technology is still in an embryonic stage. Despite this the range of organizations and disciplines researching and pursuing agent technology is broad. The term '*agent*' is being increasingly used by computer researchers, software developers and even the average computer user, yet when pressed, many would be unable to give a satisfactory explanation of just what an agent really is.

Agent technology emerged from the field of AI research; so often the term '*Intelligent Agent*' is used. However, agents need not be intelligent, and in fact most people do not need '*smart agents*' (Nwana, 1996). Other adjectives often used with agents are: *interface, autonomous, mobile, Internet, information* and *reactive*. The term 'agent' can be thought of as an umbrella under which many software applications may fall, but is in danger of becoming a *noise* term due to over use (Wooldridge and Jennings, 1995). Many agents are currently characterized by descriptive terms that accompany them, for example intelligent, smart, autonomous. Table 1 contains a brief descriptive definition of these common agent types. Some of these definitions will be given elsewhere in this chapter, but they are placed here in Table 1 for completeness.

What makes agents different from standard software is the characteristics that agents must possess in order to be termed agents. There are a number of classification schemes that can be used to type-cast existing agents. They include *mobile* or *static, deliberative* or *reactive*, but Nwana (Nwana, 1996) classifies agents according to primary attributes which agents should exhibit, illustrated in Figure 4. The three primary attributes are *cooperation, learning* and *autonomy*. These attributes are laid out as intersecting circles in Figure 4, and to be classified as an agent, software must exhibit characteristics from any of the intersecting areas.

Nwana uses the diagram in Figure 4 to to derive four types of agents: *Collaborative, Interface, Collaborative Learning* and *Smart* agents. However, Nwana recognizes that the categories in the diagram are not definitive, and agents can also be classified by their roles and so adds to that list *Mobile, Information/Internet, Reactive* and *Hybrid* agents.

Wooldridge (Wooldridge & Jennings, 1995), takes a more formal approach to the definition of agent, falling back to the more specific meanings from AI researchers. However, he notes that as the AI community cannot agree on the question of *What is Intelligence?*, a less formal definition may be needed to include many software applications being developed by researchers in related fields. To this end, Wooldridge introduces the notions of *weak* and *strong* agency.

Strong agency takes on the specific meaning from AI research, implying that agents must exhibit men-

Figure 4. Nwana's Classification

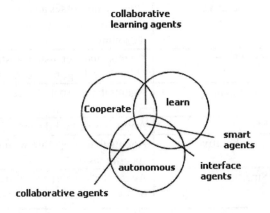

talistic notions such as knowledge, belief, intention and obligation, with some researchers considering emotional characteristics as a requirement. If this definition of agent is strictly adhered to, many software applications claiming to use agent technology would be rejected as such.

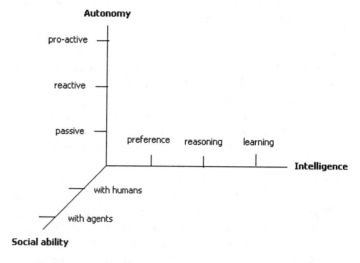

Figure 5. 3D-Space model of agency

In the weak notion of agency, the term agent can be applied to software that exhibits the following characteristics:

- Autonomy: agents operate without direct human intervention and have some control over their actions and internal state.
- Social Ability: agents interact with other agents and humans through some defined protocol.
- Reactivity: agents can perceive their environment and can respond to it in a timely fashion.
- Pro-activeness: agents do not just respond to the environment, but can take a proactive role and exhibit some goal-oriented behaviour.

The definitions of Nwana and Wooldridge above are not wholly incompatible. They do identify common characteristics that agents should exhibit, but most of the agent types identified by Nwana would come under Wooldridge's weak-agent classification. Other researchers have also identified the characteristics of *autonomy*, *cooperation*, *intelligence*, *reactivity* and *pro-activity*. Gilbert *et al* (Gilbert and al., 1995) provide a model where the degree of agency can be crudely measured by an agent's position in a three-dimensional space relative to a 3-D axis. This model has been refined (anonymous, 1999) using the three dimensions of Intelligence, Autonomy and Social Ability defined from the list above. This model is shown in Figure 5.

In order to qualify as an agent in this model, software must exhibit at least the minimal characteristics in each dimension. That is, it must be able to communicate with the user, allow users to specify preferences, and be able to work out for itself how to accomplish tasks assigned to it. While this model may not be ideal, it does provide for a more simplistic definition based on the common agent characteristics identified by a number of researches.

AUTONOMOUS AGENTS

One of the important characteristics of agents just identified is that of *autonomy*. Agents do not have to be intelligent, indeed after forty years of trying to build knowledge based agents, researchers have still not been able to build a base of common sense information that intelligent agents may need to operate within their environment (Maes,

1995). Until truly smart agents are feasible and commercially viable, it is the degree of autonomy that agents exhibit which will determine their usefulness to many users.

The interaction metaphor for user interaction with a computer that is dominant in most CISS's is direct manipulation (Maes, 1994). As previously discussed, with this metaphor the user is required to initiate all tasks directly and monitor all events. This metaphor will have to change in order for users to make more efficient use of computer systems. Autonomous agents can be particularly useful in implementing the complimentary interaction metaphor called indirect manipulation (Maes, 1994). With indirect manipulation, the user works together with a software agent where both may initiate tasks and monitor events.

These types of agents will take on the role of personal assistants to help users perform tasks and in time may learn to become more effective. We can see this type of software already in existence. For example, the sub-routines in word processors that automatically check for spelling as you type and sometimes offer suggestions for the completion of words based on what was previously typed. Some of these also automatically capitalize words at the beginning of sentences. While some of these software examples may not exactly fall under our previous definitions of agent, they are small examples of the types of autonomy and cooperation that agents, and particularly autonomous agents will play in future. Autonomous agents have the potential to radically alter the way we work, but this will begin to appear in commercially available products as an evolutionary process rather than a revolutionary one (Nwana, 1996).

Franklin further refines our thinking about agents by writing that:

An **autonomous agent** is a system situated within and part of an environment that senses that environment and acts on it, over time, in pursuit of its own agenda and so as to effect what it senses in the future (Franklin and Graesser, 1996).

In addition to the emphasis on autonomy, autonomous agents have a sense of temporal continuity in that they persist over time. Most software programs are invoked, perform their tasks, and then finish. For example a payroll program may be invoked once a week to perform its payroll run, but would fail the test of agency as its output would not normally affect what the payroll program would sense the following week. The payroll program does not persist beyond the completion of its task. An autonomous agent on the other hand would continue to persist and monitor/effect a portion of its environment according to its specific task.

Franklin and Graesser also propose an initial taxonomy of autonomous agents based on biological models (Franklin and Graesser, 1996), and this is shown in Figure 6. Further classifications of agents may be obtained by adding a list of features of the agent. For example, mobile, information, planning and learning can be used.

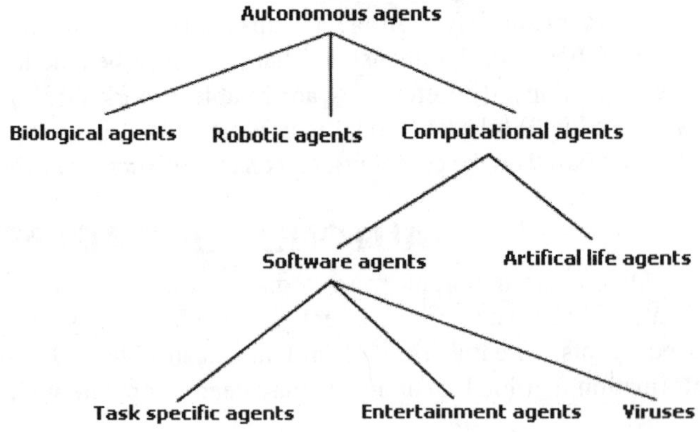

Some of the more recent notable applications for agents, and in particular, autonomous agents, include e-commerce, Web

Figure 6. An initial taxonomy of autonomous agents

marketing and Internet search agents. What these applications have in common of course is the Web. It seems that with the many types of Web-based software being developed, the Web provides a good architectural framework for the development of agents. Partly this is due to the fact that the Web facilitates many of the characteristics of agent software just discussed, eg. mobility and communication.

AGENTS AND THE WEB

Many agents (or software masquerading as agents) have been developed for use on the Web in recent years. Some examples of these are (Nwana, 1996; Weiss, 1999):

- *BarginFinder:* which compares prices and shops from Internet stores for CDs
- *Jasper:* works on behalf of a user or community to store and retrieve useful information on the WWW
- *Internet Softbot:* infers which internet facilities to use under given circumstances from high-level search requests
- *Webwatcher:* An Internet spider which searches and indexes the Web[1].

These examples are typical of the types of tasks assigned to agents operating on the Web; however, there has been so many developed in the last few years that they have been termed *Information/Internet agents*. The reason for the term Information is that these agents have access to at least one and usually many more sources of information. Most of these agents have come about because of the demand for tools to help manage the enormous growth of information available on the Web. The majority of the Internet agents to date are static and not mobile (Nwana, 1996), but there has been much interest generated in mobile agents in the last two years.

Another reason that we can expect to see growth of Internet agents in the future is that the Web provides a fertile framework in which to place agents. Recall that in order to be an agent, software must exhibit minimal characteristics as indicated in Figure 5. Some of these characteristics are *mobility*, *social ability* and *intelligence*. The infrastructure of the Web provides a mechanism for most of an agent's required characteristics to be realized. Agents can implement mobility and communication requirements by using standard Internet protocols. The global infiltration of the Web also helps ensure that infrastructure is mostly in place, providing worldwide connectivity.

Given the number of applications being either currently built for, or being ported to the Web, the conditions are right for a dramatic increase in the number agents designed to operate in the Web environment. Additionally, with the development of Web-based courseware, the way now lies open for the application of agent technology to Web-based educational software development.

AGENTS AND COURSEWARE EVOLUTION

Since the development of the Web in the early 1990s the development of Web based courseware gained momentum as the new paradigm became available for CAL and CML developers. As we mentioned in the introductory section, there are now some very good commercial and non-commercial courseware products that allow delivery of educational material and performance of administrative functions via the Web. But what stage of evolution are these systems in?

While there are some specific examples of highly evolved intelligent Web based educational systems, for example PROPA (Case et al.,), because of the lead time in development and developmental costs, such systems are few and far between (Cheikes,

1995). Also, ITS developers have been largely unable to incorporate commercial, 'off-the-shelf' software (Cheikes, 1995). Thus, the bulk of commercially available systems are still bound by the '*direct manipulation*' interaction metaphor and can be deemed to be in the first stage of evolution.

If a courseware product, which is a CISS from the educational domain, is currently in the first evolutionary stage of development, we must now ask the following question. *What can we now do with our CISS in place, that could not be performed (or not easily performed) previously?* If from this we can identify further functionality for incorporation into our CISS, then this development would represent the transition to the second evolutionary stage for courseware. Of course, such an evolutionary transition need not take place if the stakeholders are satisfied with the CISS and desire no further functionality.

If we view our CISS with the Learner as the major stakeholder some possible SES improvements can be envisioned for Web-based courseware. These include:

- Monitoring of student study patterns;
- Monitoring of student learning processes;
- Presenting tailored study material to students based on performance history;
- Personalized, helpful on-line hints based on current session Web navigation.

Does the above list does represent valid SES improvements? Although such functionality could be realized in the underlying Information System (manually), it would be impractical and cost inefficient. However, if software could be constructed to realize this functionality, then our CISS would be based on a model that couldn't be realized in the underlying domain manually, albeit for practical efficiencies. These SES improvements may be achieved through the use of Web-based autonomous agents operating on the Internet.

Recent agent technology makes many of the above enhancements feasible; whereas, without agents, the delivery of some of the above enhancements would be difficult at best. In fact, Cheikes (Cheikes, 1995), outlines an agent-based architecture for ITS's which could facilitate the implementation of such functionality and discusses the benefits of using agents (Cheikes, Major, Murray, and Bloom, 1995). Ritter and Koedinger (Ritter and Koedinger, 1995) also discuss tutoring agents. In both cases, the focus of the research is on the functionality achievable for the Learner as stakeholder and not on the overall evolutionary result.

The above examples target the learner as the major stakeholder to benefit from these possible SES improvements. Our research takes the approach of targeting the Instructor as

Figure 7. CISS development with the Learner as the stakeholder

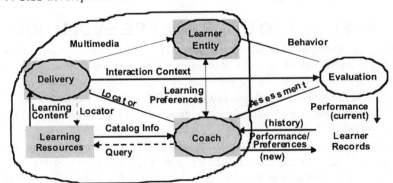

the major stakeholder. Thus, the emphasis for functionality and development is diverted from one area of our CISS to another. For example, if we consider the LTSA component model (Darbyshire and Wenn, 1999; IEEE, 2000), which is an abstraction of the CISS components present in a Learning Technology System, then Figure 7 shows the area for functional development with the Learner as the stakeholder.

Conversely, Figure 8 shows the area for functional development with the Instructor as the stakeholder. By changing stakeholders, we only shift developmental efforts within the CISS. Using agent technology to evolve our CISS is just as valid when the development of functionality is concentrated in different areas. In either case, if the result is a system based on a model which cannot be realized in the underlying IS domain, then we have evolved our CISS.

With the Instructor as the stakeholder, we see the primary focus as being on the *subject management* aspects of the CISS. We can define subject management as *"those tasks of subject delivery that do not play a part in the instructional role, and whose functions are directed towards the control, administration and testing of the learning process.* This is a slight variation of the definition for Computer-Managed Learning offered by Stanford and Cook (Stanford and Cook, 1987). Some possible second tier improvements for the subject management component include:

- Monitoring of assignment submission patterns by individual students;
- Notifying the subject lecturer of late assignment submission;
- Generating reminders of assignment due dates based on past late submission patterns
- Arranging personalized meeting times for individual students based on performance.

This functionality can be achieved with agent technology, but will this evolve the CISS as we have defined it? It is possible to realize the above functionality in the underlying IS that academics already work in. In fact, most academics probably perform some (or all) of the functions already. But as class sizes increase and other factors combine to increase workloads, many of these functions become impractical for lack of funding and time. It is in this environment that agent technology can begin to take on some of these previously human-based tasks and work cooperatively with their human counterpart (Maes, 1994).

The following section describes in detail aspects of an on-going research project to evolve a Web-based educational CISS using agent technology.

PROJECT DESCRIPTION

Over the past three and a half years we have implemented a Web-based subject

Figure 8. CISS development with the Instructor as the stakeholder

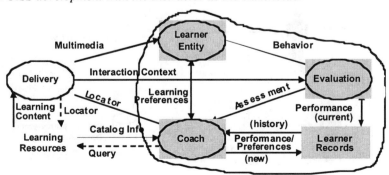

management system, '*Central Point*', to provide functionality for both staff and students. This includes bulletin and notice boards, Web-based assignment submission, provision of student marks via secure Web based lookup and provision of Web based subject configu- ration for subject coordinators. This system is well- documented in (Darbyshire and Wenn, 1998; Darbyshire and Wenn, 1999). The current research project is using agent technology to change the dominant interaction metaphor to one of *indirect-manipulation*. We hope to slowly delegate to the agents we write many of the tasks now directly initiated by human *direct-manipulation*.

As Central Point is basically a computer implementation of our existing manual efforts, it is definitely in a first stage of evolutionary development. Some of the benefits from implementation of this FES include:
- More timely dissemination of important notices for students and staff
- Flexibility in assignment submission for students
- Flexibility is access to submitted assignment for staff
- Reduction of paper handling and transfer (eg assignments, assignment sheets etc.)
- Flexibility in dissemination of results to students

With our CISS now in place, we are now in a position to pursue benefit acceleration implied by SES development.

Currently, the Central Point System (Darbyshire and Wenn, 1997), consists of a number of Microsoft Access databases which contain information submitted by both staff and students (Darbyshire and Wenn, 1999). A number of HTML and Cold Fusion scripts are provided for access to the system. The student gains access by one set of scripts and a second, secure, password protected set of scripts is provided for staff. This second set of scripts facilitates the subject management functions. An abstract representation of the structure of Central Point is shown in Figure 9.

The current research project is using autonomous agents to implement functionality described by three of the possible SES enhancements identified in the previous section. That is, Monitoring of assignment submission patterns by individual students; Notifying the subject lecturer of late assignment submission; Generating reminders of assignment due dates based on past late submission patterns. Three autonomous agents will implement this functionality. Three agents are not much, but this is a pilot research project to study the effectiveness of the approach and to guide future agent development. The implementation is anything but trivial.

The agents are implemented in Java and will reside on the server which also hosts the Central Point CISS. The architecture of the system of agents is based on the Ki architecture

Figure 9. Structure of Central Point system

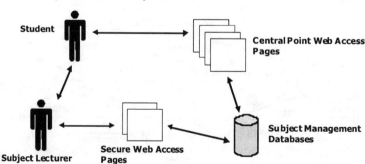

developed by Sundsted (Sundsted, 1998). There are many Java Classes involved in the agent system, but for conciseness a UML diagram showing an abstraction of the major Classes and their relationship is shown in Figure 10.

Figure 10. Abstraction of agent system architecture

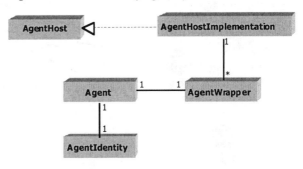

All of the agents in the system reside on a *'Host'* machine. The AgentHost class defines the basic functionality that all agent hosts must provide. In this research pilot, all agents will reside on the one Host, but this Class, and the AgentHostImplementation Class provides functionality that facilitates agent mobility. It was decided to retain this functionality from the original Ki architecture in case further research required agent mobility. The AgentHostImplementation Class provides further functionality of the Host environment, keeps track of every agent executing in the Host, allows for resurrection and saving facilities, and implements messaging capability between agents.

The Agent class defines the agent itself. There is an instance of this class for each agent executing on the host. The AgentWrapper class defines the agent interface to the Host. An instance of this class envelopes each agent and provides access to it via a well-defined interface. This class also interfaces with the AgentHostImplementation Class to facilitate communication between agents. It is only through this Class that agents have any contact with other agents on the Host. The AgentIdentity Class uniquely defines each agent's identity. There is an instance of this Class for each agent on the Host, and agents use this Class to identify other agents executing on the Host.

The collection of agents is referred collectively as EVE (an acronym for Evolutionary VEhicle). The three initial agents, which are all instances of the Class Agent in Figure 10, are named EVE-1, EVE-2, and EVE-3 respectively. The tasks of these agents are as follows:

EVE-1: monitors assignment submissions and as the due date approaches, will warn the students that have not submitted assignments of the impending deadline. Once the deadline passes for each assignment, it will close the assignment box and notify the subject coordinator of this, and any students that have not submitted work, that it is now outstanding and must be submitted in person. This agent also remembers submission patterns and prompts previously late students as deadlines approach.

EVE-2: will have access to both assignment submissions and grade information. This agent will monitor the grades received by students as they are entered and notify the poorer performing students early for each assignment, to start early and seek help at the beginning.

EVE-3: this agent communicates directly with both the students and the subject lecturers. This agent is an *interface* agent that is responsible for human-agent communication.

The tasks for these agents seem fairly simple, yet their implementation is complex. For instance, EVE-3, the interface agent communicates with both the student and instructor. Currently this communication is one-way only in the form of messages. EVE-3 communicates by sending e-mail messages to students and instructors via the university e-mail

Figure 11. EVE interaction with CISS

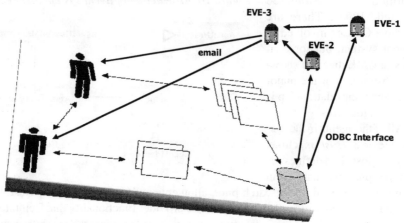

system, relayed from EVE-1 and EVE-2. The CISS databases holds the e-mail addresses needed by this agent. Communication between EVE-1, EVE-2 and EVE-3 is facilitated by the AgentHostClasses and uses a mail box technique. EVE-1 and EVE-2 both need to access the CISS databases, and this is achieved by using the Java ODBC interface. This is shown in Figure 11.

The individual agents also need to store their own accumulated knowledge upon which their behavior is based. If we recall, the definition of an autonomous agent is one that senses that environment and acts on it, over time, in pursuit of its own agenda and so as to effect what it senses in the future. In order to achieve this, EVE-1 and EVE-2 incorporate JESS (Friedman-Hill, 1999). JESS stands for Java Expert System Shell and is an expert system shell made available for researchers by Sandia National Laboratories CA, USA.

By using an expert system shell, the agents can collect *facts* by browsing the CISS database and apply *rules* (conditional actions) to these facts. The rules are continually applied to the accumulated knowledge base (facts), which expands over time as the agent accumulates knowledge. Additional knowledge is collected by the expert system shell making assertions into the knowledge base as:

(assert (assignment-submission (subject oops) (IDnum 3115678) (status Late) (days 2)))
 (assert (assignment-submission (subject opsys) (IDnum 3271189) (status OnTime))).

Both of the above assertions, add knowledge (facts) to the database, the first that Student # 3115678 submitted an assignment two days late for the oops subject, and the second, that Student # 3271189 submitted on time for opsys. The agents can then apply predetermined rules to the facts and take specific actions. For example, EVE-1, which monitors assignment submissions, will collect facts as above, and apply rules such as:

    (defrule late-rule-1
    (assignment-submission (subject ?W) (IDnum ?X) (status late) (days ?Y))
    (subject-coordinator (subject ?W) (name ?Z))
    =>
    (send-late-notice ?X ?W ?Y)
    (notify-coordinator ?W ?Z))
which states that
    if a late assignment submission exists for student X doing subject W

and
   the subject coordinator is Z
then
      send a late notice to student X that the submission is Y days late
      notify the subject coordinator Z that a late submission has been received

By allowing the agents to monitor the CISS database for a semester, collect facts and continually apply its rules, then over an entire semester the agents will be able to build a valuable profile of student submission patterns. These agents can perform automatically many mundane tasks that would take us, as academics, valuable time. If these tasks are not already performed, then this becomes a value added service to the CISS. The more we can get the agents to do, then that time savings will accumulate, perhaps to a point where it would be impractical to realize this functionality in the underlying IS domain (manually). According to our definitions, we would then have evolved our CISS. To add more functionality to existing agents, all we need do is add more rules to the agents knowledge base.

The agents just described have also been chosen for another reason. Because of what they do, their implementation will have no impact on the existing CISS in terms of code modification. In Figure 11 it can be observed that the three agents have no connections with the scripts and process of the CISS. They operate solely by continually mining the CISS database for new facts to store. Thus, as in Figure 11, they can be viewed as something almost apart from the CISS itself, akin to adding a new dimension to the system. This will not necessarily be true for all agents added to the CISS in future, as many may have to work closely with existing processes. However if the 'data-mining' type approach proves successful, it may direct future research.

The pilot research project is to run these agents for a semester with the CISS in daily use by the students, and this live run is targeted for semester 2, 2000. Over this period, the agents will perform many tasks, and we can then examine the overall work performed by the agents to determine the '*value added*' time they have given to the CISS.

RESULTS

As yet, there are no results, only some preliminary testing of the agents themselves, without using live data. The agents will log all performed tasks to a log-file that will accumulate for a semester. The entries in the log file are of the form:

EVE-1: 13/5/2000: subject bco3345: Notified student 3241112 by e-mail that assignment 2 was 3 days late
EVE-1: 13/5/2000: subject bco3345: Notified coordinator of late submission
EVE-2: 23/5/2000: subject bco3357: Alerted student 3115643 of due date for assignment
EVE-1: 10/5/2000: subject bco3345: Closed assignment box for assignment 3
EVE-1: 10/5/2000: subject bco3345: Notified student 1002377 assignment box closed
EVE-1: 10/5/2000: subject bco3345: Notified student 3111566 assignment box closed

This is only a sample of data to be collected at the end of the trial semester. Each of the different types of tasks that EVE will perform over the semester will be allocated a Human Equivalent Time (HET). The log-file will then be scanned, substituting the HET for each task to determine the total overall value added time to the system.

EVE is configurable so that not all subjects registered with Central Point will be monitored by EVE. Initially during the trial semester, only three small subjects will be trialed; however, the results can be scaled to give approximate estimations for larger subjects.

CONCLUSIONS

While there has been much written on the evolution of Information Systems, most (if not all) of this has concentrated on generational improvements based on some life cycle model. We need to identify meta-level stages of evolution in order to direct the overall evolution of an Information System. In this paper we have provided definitions of a first and second stage of evolution for an Information System. With the technology we currently have available, developers of many CISS's could use existing functionality to feedback into their design models and initiate further development based on this functionality, in effect evolving the underlying model from a first evolutionary stage to a second. Agent technology is one tool that would help facilitate this evolutionary step.

There is a current proliferation of research on agent technology, and many experts agree that agents will change the way we work with computers, but that this change will be a slower evolution, rather than a revolution. It is important that we understand the basic concepts of agents, and exactly what agents are. There is also much attention at the moment on the use of Web based agents (internet agents), and this is as much a result of the need to manage the information explosion, as it is the excellent environment that the Web provides for agent development.

With the development of Web based courseware, the development of autonomous agents to aid in managing the educational process could lead to significant improvements, and possible evolutionary progression. We have discussed in detail a research project that is using agent technology, and in particular, autonomous agents to aid in the Web based subject management software described in previous papers. The agents used in the project are constructed in Java and use a corresponding expert system shell to provide '*intelligence*' in their tasks. It is anticipated that some measurable benefit will be observed, thereby paving the way for more complex agent development as part of second evolutionary stage development for the courseware system described.

While the actual agent functions themselves are small, their successful implementation should result in some measurable improvement. Even if it is only something else the subject coordinator does not have to do, it indicates a step in a forward direction. The successful implementation will also result in expertise gained in order to implement further, more complex and rewarding second stage tasks via the use of autonomous agents.

FUTURE WORK

The project outlined in the paper seems to have only opened up more avenues for investigation. Initially, it is expected that the trial run in semester 2, 2000 will confirm future directions and possible further agent development. The ultimate goal is to evolve the CISS outlined into a tool which predominately implements the indirect-manipulation interaction metaphor.

One of the major areas for future work already flagged is enhancement of the agent-human communication. In the current system the agent EVE-3 is responsible for this, with only one way communication taking place in the form of e-mail. The e-mail interaction seems reasonable, but we would like to investigate the possibility of two-way communication with EVE-3. This will probably involve a number of agents taking the place of EVE-3 in future. With two-way communication, students could possibly email EVE with specific requests that they might otherwise be making with EVE's human counterpart, the instructor.

Such communication would need to be highly structured, but might take the form of an e-mail with a specific header requesting another copy of last week's assignment, or the lecture notes for a lecture they couldn't attend, or for their last assignment marks. Instructors could also e-mail EVE with specific requests, such as a request for submitted assignments to be e-mailed to themselves, or a list of students who have requested certain documents.

Another area for future work is that of long-term student patterns. For example, it is anticipated that EVE will at the moment operate on a semester by semester basis only. However, the student assignment submission patterns, for example, might be accumulated over a period of years during the students' entire stay. Such information may possibly be useful in aiding all subject coordinators in trying to motivate all students appropriately. The long-term storage of such information will need to be investigated as will its appropriate transfer from semester to semester.

REFERENCES

Anonymous. (1999). *Agent Technology - An Overview*. Paper presented at the Proceedings of Tenth Australian Conference on Information Systems, ACIS'99, Wellington, New Zealand.

Belady, L. A., & Lehman, M. M. (1971). *Programming System Dynamics or the Metadynamics of Systems in Maintenance and Growth* (RC 3546). T J Watson research center, NY: IBM research report.

Boehm, B. W. (1976). Software Engineering. *IEEE Transactions on Computers, C-25*(12), 1226-1241.

Brooks, F. P. (1974). The Mythical Man-Month. *Datamation, 20*(12, Dec 1974), 35-42.

Case, R., Cheikes, B., Goodman, B., Linton, F., Pioch, N., & Soller, A. . *PROPA*. Available: http://www.mitre.org/resources/centers/it/g068/propa.html2/7/2000].

Cheikes, B. A. (1995). *GIA: An Agent-Based Architecture for Intelligent Tutoring Systems*. Paper presented at the Proceedings of the CIKM'95 Workshop on Intelligent Information Agents.

Cheikes, B. A., Major, N., Murray, T., & Bloom, C. (1995). *Should ITS Designers Be Looking For A Few Good Agents?* Paper presented at the AI-ED'95 Workshop on Authoring Shells for Intelligent Tutoring Systems.

Darbyshire, P. (1999). *Distributed Web-Based Assignment Submission and Access*. Paper presented at the International Resource Management Association, IRMA '99, Hershey, PA.

Darbyshire, P., & Wenn, A. (1996). *Experiences With Using the WWW as a Multi-campus Instructional Aid*. Paper presented at the Teaching Matters Symposium, Victoria University of Technology, Melbourne, Australia.

Darbyshire, P., & Wenn, A. (1997). *Central Point: cyber classroom*. Available: http://www.business.vu.edu.au/cpoint/index.html.

Darbyshire, P., & Wenn, A. (1998). *Cross Campus Subject Management Using the Internet*. Paper presented at the International Resource Management Association, IRMA '98, Boston, MA.

Darbyshire, P., & Wenn, A. (1999). A Matter of Necessity: Implementing Web-based

Subject Administration, *Managing Web Enabled Technologies in Organizations* : Idea Group Publishing.

Franklin, S., & Graesser, A. (1996). *Is it an Agent, or just a Program?: A Taxonomy for Autonomous Agents.* Paper presented at the Proceedings of the Third International Workshop on Agent Theories and Architectures.

Friedman-Hill, E. J. (1999). *Jess, The Java Expert System Shell,* [Web page]. Distributed Computing Systems. Available: http://herzberg.ca.sandia.gov/jess [1999, 25/8/99].

Gilbert, D., & al., e. (1995). *The Role of Intelligent Agents in the Information Infrastructure* USA: IBM.

IEEE. (2000). *LTSA Specification Version 5* (base document), [Web accessable document]. Learning Technology Standards Committee, Architecture and Reference Model Working Group (IEEE 1484.1). Available: http://edutool.com/ltsa [2000, 25/6/2000].

IFIP. (1998). *A Framework of Information System Concepts (The FRISCO Report)* (Final Report), [Web Accessable Document]. IFIP WG 8.1 TAsk Group FRISCO. Available: ftp://ftp.leidenuniv.nl/pub/rul/fri-full.zip [1999, 8/11/99].

Landon, B. (1988). *On-line Educational Delivery Applications: A Web Tool for Comparative Analysis,* [Web Page]. Center for Curriculum, Transfer and Technology, Canada. Available: http://www.ctt.bc.ca/landonline/ [1998, 10/10/98].

Lehman, M. M. (1981, September 1981). *Programming Productivity - A Life Cycle Concept.* Paper presented at the Proceedings CompCon'81.

Lehman, M. M. (1982). *Program Evolution.* Paper presented at the Symposium on Empirical Foundations of Computer and Information Sciences, Japan Information Center of Science and Technology.

Lehman, M. M., & Belady, L. A. (1985). *Program Evolution: Process of Software Change*: Academic Press.

Maes, P. (1994). Agents that Reduce Work and Information Overload. *Communications of the ACM, 37*(7, July 1994).

Maes, P. (1995). Intelligent Software. *Scientific American, 273, Sept. 95*(3), 84-86.

Mills, H. D. (1980). The Management of Software Engineering, Part I: Principles of Software Engineering. *IBM Systems Journal, 19*(4).

Nwana, H. (1996). Software Agents: An Overview. *Knowledge Engineering Review, 11*(3).

Oman, P. W., & Lewis, T. G. (1990). *Milestones in Software Evolution*: IEEE Computer Society Press.

Ostwald, J. (1996). *Knowledge Construction in Software Development: The Evolving Artifact Approach.* Unpublished Doctoral Dissertation, Colorado University.

Ottmann, T., & Tomek, I. (Eds.). (1998). *ED—Media/ED—Telecom '98.* Charlottesville, VA.

Parker, M. M., & Benson, R. J. (1988). *Information Economics: Linking Business Performance to Information Technology*: Prentice-Hall.

Ritter, S., & Koedinger, K. R. (1995). *Towards lightweight tutoring agents.* Paper presented at the AI-ED 95—World Conference on Artificial Intelligence in Education, Washington, D.C.

Schneiderman, B. (1983). Direct Manipulation: A Step Beyond Programming Languages. *IEEE Computer, 16*(8), 57-69.

Sommerville, I. (1989). *Software Engineering.* (3rd ed.): Addison-Wesley.

Stanford, J. D., & Cook, H. P. (1987). *Computer Managed Learning - Its application to increase student achievement using formative self-assessment.* Paper presented at the CALITE 87, University of New South Wales, Sydney.

Sundsted, T. (1998, 6/98). An introduction to agents. *JavaWorld, June 1998.*

Weinberg, G. M. (1970). Natural Selection as Applied to Computers and Programs. *General Systems, 15.*

Weiss, M. (1999). *A gentle introduction to agents and their applications* : Mitel Corp.

Wooldridge, M., & Jennings, N. (1995). Intelligent Agents: Theory and Practice. *Knowledge Engineering Review, 10*(2, June 1995).

Zachman, J. A. (1987). A Framework for Information Systems Architecture. *IBM Systems Journal, 26*(3), 276-292.

ENDNOTE

1 According to our thinking, this is not an agent, yet.

Chapter VII

Intelligent Software Agents in Electronic Commerce: A Socio-Technical Perspective

Mahesh S. Raisinghani, University of Dallas, USA
Christopher Klassen, The Software Construction Company, USA
Lawrence L. Schkade, University of Texas, USA

"The future business culture will be one in which innovation is necessary, learning is constant, organizations need to act collaboratively and work is its own reward…It will not be business. It will not be government. It is the social sector that may yet save the society." ——Peter F. Drucker

INTRODUCTION

Although there is no firm consensus on what constitutes an intelligent agent (or software agent), an intelligent agent, when a new task is delegated by the user, should determine precisely what its goal is, evaluate how the goal can be reached in an effective manner, and perform the necessary actions by learning from past experience and responding to unforeseen situations with its adaptive, self-starting, and temporal continuous reasoning strategies. It needs to be not only cooperative and mobile in order to perform its tasks by interacting with other agents but also reactive and autonomous to sense the status quo and act independently to make progress towards its goal (Baek et al., 1999; Wang, 1999). Software agents are goal-directed and possess abilities such as autonomy, collaborative behavior, and inferential capability. Intelligent agents can take different forms, but an intelligent agent can initiate and make decisions without human intervention and have the capability to infer appropriate high-level goals from user actions and requests and take actions to achieve these goals (Huang, 1999; Nardi et al., 1998; Wang, 1999). The intelligent software agent is a computational entity that can adapt to the environment, making it capable of interacting with other agents and transporting itself across different systems in a network. "…The state of the running program is saved, transported to the new host, and restored, allowing the program to continue where it left off" (Kotz and Gray, 1999).

THE CURRENT STATE OF RESEARCH ON SOFTWARE AGENTS

Software agents were first used several years ago to automate repetitive behavior in simple tasks such as filtering and sorting information or making basic price comparisons (Maes et al., 1999; Kirsner, 1999). This first phase of software agents has been superceded by sophisticated software agents that keep a detailed profile of demographics and psychographics. They can track interests and preferences in order to offer customized services in business-to-business, business-to-consumer, and consumer-to-consumer e-commerce based on some embedded mobility metadata (Maes, 1999; Wong et al., 1999). In automated negotiation in retail, e-commerce, electricity markets, manufacturing planning and scheduling, distributed vehicle routing among independent dispatch centers, and electronic trading of financial instruments, computational agents find and prepare contracts on behalf of the real world parties they represent (Sandholm, 1999). Gloshko et al. (1999) believe that over time, most merchant web sites will provide agent-searchable catalogs that supply product descriptions and information about price and availability. The stage is set for applications that can benefit from the mobile agent paradigm, such as personal assistance by monitoring and notifying/information dissemination, secure brokering, distributed information retrieval, telecommunication networks services, and workflow applications, and parallel processing (Lange and Oshima, 1999; Hauk and Chen, 1999).

Much research and many articles have been devoted to this topic, and software products billed as having intelligent agent functionality are being introduced on the market every day. The articles and research, however, do not whole-heartedly endorse this trend. A growing number of computer information professionals recognize that there are certain problems and issues surrounding intelligent agent terminology and technology that must be resolved if agent technology is to continue to develop and mature.

The current research into intelligent agent software technology can be divided into two main areas: technological and social. The latter area is particularly important since, in the excitement of new and emergent technology, people often forget to examine what impact the new technology will have on people's lives. In fact, the social dimension of all technology is the driving force and most important consideration of technology itself. Technology is not created and produced for its own sake, but to improve people's lives. Technology and computers and software are not created simply to see what the human mind can achieve, they are created for the sake of human beings.

TECHNOLOGICAL ISSUES

The first and most fundamental technological aspect that must be considered is what constitutes an intelligent software agent: What is the definition of an intelligent software agent? It is here that the first major problem for intelligent agent technology emerges. "In order for this term [intelligent agent] to have any effectiveness, there must first be a universal definition that can be agreed upon and used consistently" (Vinaja and Sircar, 1999, p. 478). Unfortunately, though, there is in fact no commonly agreed upon definition of an intelligent agent or even an (software) agent. Many proposals for a formal definition of "intelligent agent" have been made, but none has been widely accepted (Franklin and Graesser, 1996, p. 3). The following are a few of the more promising definitions:

"An agent is anything that can be viewed as perceiving its environment
through sensors and acting upon that environment through effectors" (Russell
and Norvig, 1995, p. 33).

"Let us define an agent as a persistent software entity dedicated to a specific purpose. 'Persistent' distinguishes agents from subroutines; agents have their own ideas about how to accomplish tasks, their own agendas. 'Special purpose' distinguishes them from other entire multifunction applications; agents are typically much smaller" (Smith, Cypher, and Spohrer. 1994, p. 58).

"Intelligent agents are software entities that carry out some set of operations on behalf of a user or another program with some degree of independence or autonomy, and in so doing, employ some knowledge or representation of the user's goals or desires" (The IBM Agent).

"An **autonomous agent** is a system situated within and a part of an environment that senses that environment and acts on it, over time, in pursuit of its own agenda and so as to effect what it senses in the future" (Franklin and Graesser, 1996, p. 3).

Some of the key terms found in the preceding definitions are: sensing, environment, persistent, 'own agendas', autonomy, goals, and knowledge. Ma (1999) defines intelligent/ mobile/multi-system/profiling agents as working through actions and characterizes agents as "atomic, software entities that operate through autonomous actions on behalf of the user-machines and humans-without human intervention." Each of these terms seems to appropriately describe characteristics of what an intelligent agent is, yet none of them has gained wide recognition as *the* definition of a software (intelligent) agent. Woolridge and Jennings (1996), give a compelling reason why a definition consensus has not yet been reached. They point out that agent technology is so popular partly because the idea of an agent is extremely intuitive. The intuitive aspect of the term "intelligent agent" leads to many different people having different ideas of what an agent is. As Franklin and Graesser (1996), point out, most of the definitions proposed thus far seem to have originated from particular examples that the people who have proposed the definitions already had in mind. It is important to note here that the same intuitive aspect of the term "intelligent agent", while making it difficult to establish a broadly accepted formal definition, actually makes marketing a product billed as incorporating intelligent agent software technology much easier.

Another reason that a consensus has not been reached is that much of the agent research is proprietary. Companies that sponsor the research do not want to give away their work for free since they have made significant monetary contributions to this research. This makes standardization of the new technology difficult. Intelligent agent technology will continue to suffer from this difficulty either until the companies and individuals with the proprietary information recognize that sharing it will benefit everyone, including themselves, or until the companies and individuals with the proprietary information recoup enough of their expenditures to feel justified in making available their research.

A third reason for the difficulty in reaching a generally approved definition of what comprises an intelligent software agent is that so-called intelligent agent software does not seem to be qualitatively different from any other software. "Is it an agent, or just a program?" In their article of the same title as the previous question, Franklin and Graesser note, correctly, that all software agents are programs. They go on to state that not all programs are agents, the implication being that some programs, then, are in fact agents.

This third reason for the difficulty in reaching a generally approved definition of "intelligent agent software" revolves around a key term, "quality". The term "intelligent agent" does not simply mean a more complicated program. If it did, not much controversy would ever have been generated about what actually is an intelligent software agent. If "intelligent agent" only signified a more complicated program, the term "intelligent agent" would mean that a so-called intelligent agent software program was simply more complex and possibly more useful that other typical computer programs. This sense of "intelligent agent" is a *quantitative* sense.

However, those who are doing research into so-called intelligent agent software technology do not mean that an intelligent agent is only more complicated than other computer programs. A true intelligent agent would have to be *qualitatively* different from a mere computer program. An agent is, broadly speaking, someone or something that acts. However, in order to act, the thing that acts must have a purpose or a goal. This is included in the third and fourth proposed definitions set forth earlier. Do any computer programs have their own goals or purposes? Not really. All a computer program does is perform a set of instructions that were programmed into it. An intelligent software agent is no different from any other computer program in this respect. It simply has more possibilities than less complicated computer programs.

Even if we do grant that a computer program may act, it certainly does not act autonomously as the fourth definition asserts. For something to act autonomously it must have independence and freedom. Philosophically, for something to be autonomous, it must have knowledge of what it is doing and it must *will* to do what it is doing. Computer programs do not *will* to do anything. Again, we reiterate that the program may be quite complex and be able to react to many different events, but the key is that the computer simply reacts, it does not act on its own.

The word, "react", further clarifies the inherent limitations of computer programs, and why they cannot truly be called intelligent or autonomous agents. An agent, in the true sense of the word, initiates action. True agents are proactive as well as reactive. They have beliefs, intentions, and desires. It is absurd to speak of computer programs of any sort as having desires. This, then, sums up the problems with calling computer programs "intelligent agents".

This leaves us with a question. What are we to make of the all of the software currently on the market or in production that is billed as having intelligent agent functionality? Certainly we do not wish to demean all of the research that has gone into these products. Products such as e-mail filters, help engines (such as the Microsoft Office Assistant), data warehousing tools, news filters, etc. all have the potential to be highly useful to human beings. But look at how they work. They are all based on the detection of patterns in conjunction with explicit user commands and preferences. At their core, all of these computer programs are based on mathematics and logic. The help engines and data warehousing tools, for example, search for built-in patterns, but the programs do not generate the patterns on their own. They have the patterns pre-built into them.

The news and searching tools (often marketed as intelligent agents), while having great potential given the explosion of information accessible on the Internet, pose an interesting problem. The problem is this: if many users have news searching "intelligent agent" tools constantly searching for information, isn't it likely that the Internet may be clogged up? It is likely that each person would have quite a number of these programs running in order to get a wide variety of information. To further complicate this picture, there is also the possibility that these "intelligent agents" will be programmed with the capability to spawn other agents. Imagine if one of these "intelligent agents" had an error (bug) built in which caused the program to continuously spawn agents. What if each one of these spawned agents also spawned other agents?

Furthermore, it is conceivable that a certain number of the "intelligent agents" searching the Internet for information would get lost, that is, they would not return with the requested information to the entity which spawned them. Thus, one can begin see the technical dangers in having such "intelligent agents". They might create severe bottlenecks on the already crowded Internet.

TRANSITIONING TO THE KNOWLEDGE SOCIETY

The transition from the industrial age to the information age to the knowledge age is a continuum that is evolutionary. A final destination will never be reached since new knowledge and experiences are continually added and refined and outside forces can create a change in corporate strategy. Although there have been several definitions of knowledge management published, the one, which conveys the concept best in the context of this chapter is by Malhotra (1999):

"Knowledge Management caters to the critical issues of organizational adoption, survival, and competence in the face of increasingly discontinuous environmental change. Essentially, it embodies organizational process that seeks synergistic combination of data and information processing capacity of information technologies and the creative and innovative capacity of human beings".

This definition not only recognizes the discontinuous environment, but also the importance of both techno-centric and socio-centric approaches. The traditional view of knowledge management mostly relies on the prepackaged or taken for granted interpretation of the knowledge. Such knowledge is generally static and does not encourage the generation of multiple and contradictory viewpoints in a highly dynamic and ever-changing environment. The concept of "best practices" and "efficiency optimization" cannot provide the competitive advantage that companies may be striving for. This is where the concept of intelligent agents acting as catalysts of knowledge management is not only effective but also essential for the organization's survival.

According to Churchman (1971), "To conceive of knowledge as a collection of information seems to rob the concept of all its life...Knowledge resides in the user and not in the collection. It is how the user reacts to a collection of information that matters." Intelligent agents can facilitate the process of filtering and reacting to information. Since they are heterogeneous, robust, fault-tolerant and able to encapsulate protocols, adapt dynamically and execute asynchronously and autonomously, they can reduce the network load and overcome network latency (Lange and Oshima, 1999). Kotz and Gray (1999), state that the rise in the use of mobile agent technology on the Internet will be due to several factors such as availability of increased bandwidth, need of technology to ease information overload, increasing need for individual customization to meet user expectations, increasing use of mobile devices, dependence of Internet technology by mobile users, and proxy sites which will provide for the specific needs of individual users.

Knowledge Discovery Using Intelligent Agents: A Proposed Framework

The transformation of data into knowledge can be accomplished in several ways. In general, it is a process that starts with data collection from various sources. These data are stored in a database. Then the data can be preprocessed and stored in a data warehouse. To discover knowledge, the processed data may go through a transformation that makes it ready for analysis. The analysis is done with data mining tools which look for patterns and intelligent systems, which support data interpretation. The result of all these activities is generated knowledge. Both the data, at various times during the process, and the knowledge, derived at the end of the process, may need to be presented to users. Such a presentation can be accomplished by using presentation tools, and the created knowledge may be stored in a knowledge base (Turban, Mclean and Wetherbe (1999).

Having understood the need for a change in organization theory and managerial style, it is essential to develop a system architecture for implementation of knowledge management systems. Brook Manville, Director of Knowledge Management at the consulting firm McKinsey & Co. in Boston, proposes three architectures needed for implementing a shift from traditional emphasis on transaction processing, integrated logistics, and work flows to systems that support competencies for communication building:

- A new information architecture that includes new languages, categories, and metaphors for identifying and accounting for skills and competencies.
- A new technical architecture that is more social, transparent, open, flexible, and respectful of the individual user.
- A new application architecture oriented towards problem solving and representation, rather than output and transactions.

The application of this framework will facilitate business model innovation necessary for sustainable competitive advantage in the new business environment characterized by dynamic, discontinuous and radical pace of change. This proposed architecture helps integrate the key ideas of this chapter, i.e., a socio-technical perspective of intelligent agents facilitating the transition to the knowledge society. The social and ethical implications are discussed in the next section.

SOCIAL AND ETHICAL IMPLICATIONS

The social implications, as might be expected with a relatively new and partially developed technology, include both positive and negative issues. The authors recognize that the current discussion and research into intelligent agent software technology deals quite sparingly on the topic of the social and ethical implications of this new technology. This lack of serious consideration of the impact intelligent agent software technology on people's lives is a problem that this chapter hopes to begin to address.

The first area that must be addressed is the philosophical nature of technology itself. Technology is created by human beings for human beings. Technology has always been pursued by humankind in order to improve the quality of life. Sometimes men/women engage in technological projects to help themselves only, but more often they pursue technological improvements for the good of humankind in general. However, the view that technology is developed for the benefit of humankind is only one of several possible views on the interplay between technology and society. For instance, the field of Social Construction of Technology (SCOT) or the socio-technical school of systems development have additional perspectives on technology and society than those presented in this chapter. The social aspects on agent technology are the focus of this chapter.

All new technology must be tested in order to see if it meets the requirements of the person(s) who have invented them, and one of the tests must be: does the new technology provide significantly more benefit to humankind or a portion of humankind, than it causes harm? This is the most general test of any new technology, and it is also the most important test since if the new technology fails this test, it should not be implemented at all. So let us apply this test to the new intelligent agent software technology. A caveat is that there is an underlying assumption in this discussion that consequences of technology in social use can be anticipated, which may not always be true.

To begin with, let us consider the positive aspects of intelligent agents. One of the biggest benefits to intelligent agents is that they have the potential to free humans from the tedious work of searching for information on the Internet and in databases. The amount of information and data both on the Internet and in corporate databases is already enormous, and it is continuing to grow exponentially. For any given search by a human being, however, much of the information available on the Internet and in databases is of little value. The intelligent agent is supposed to aid in the searching by filtering out the information and data which is of little or no value with little human intervention. If the intelligent agents are successful in this task they certainly can provide a significant benefit to human beings.

Unfortunately, intelligent agents also have the potential to harm human beings. First, if human beings rely too much on intelligent agents, they (human beings) may possibly lose too much freedom. This is a problem with technology and computers in general. A very good article by Jason Lanier describes in detail the potentially harmful effects of technology on humans (http://www.well.com/user/jaron/agentalien.html). Lanier objects to the use of the words "intelligent agent" to describe any type of computer program. His argument centers around the concept that computers contribute substantially to the dulling of the human mind and human creativity. Confining oneself to an artificial world created by some human programmer(s) does limit human potential. This argument, though, lends itself more to the development of children's minds rather than human beings in general.

Another objection Lanier raises is that human beings end up degrading and lowering themselves when they accept computer programs as "intelligent agents". This argument is more applicable than the first to human beings in general. While information technology professionals and those more aware of what intelligent agents actually are and how they function realize the limitations and scope of so-called intelligent agents, the general public who are the intended audience and users of intelligent agents are less aware of the inner-workings and limitations of intelligent agents. These are the people who Lanier suggests will be psychologically harmed by "intelligent agent" terminology. When individuals begin to think of computers as actually possessing intelligence and autonomy, they will begin to treat the computers like people rather than the (helpful) tools which they are intended to be. The result of treating computers like people will actually be that people begin to view themselves and others around them as computers. "As a consequence of unavoidable psychological algebra, the person starts to think of himself as being like the computer." This is a serious problem that must be avoided at all costs.

Another more technical problem that Lanier raises is this:

"If info-consumers see the world through agent's eyes, then advertising will transform into the art of controlling agents, through bribing, hacking, whatever. You can imagine an "arms race" between armor-plated agents and hacker-laden ad agencies."

The point here is that if intelligent agents are used to find useful information what will end up happening is that the agents themselves will be manipulated by producers of goods and services. Imagine an agent searching for information on airline flights being manipulated by the various advertising agents sent out by the cleverer airline companies. This problem is not insurmountable for those creating "intelligent agents", but it is a significant problem that needs to be addressed.

CONCLUSION

In conclusion, while intelligent agent technology has the potential to be useful to humankind, many fundamental problems remain to be solved. These problems are both technical and social or ethical in origin and require careful thought and consideration by those who are developing intelligent agent technology. This chapter has been critical of the current state of intelligent agent software technology in the hope of making these developers aware of problems they do not seem to have taken into account. The issues such as lack of standardization in mobile agents may cause lack of ability of tracing identity due to multiple transfers among networks. Security concerns relate to machine protection without artificially limiting agent access rights. Finally, there are issues surrounding performance and scalability such as the performance effects that high levels of security would have on networks, as well as the effects of having multiple mobile agents in the same system. These issues are fundamental to the well-being of those for whom intelligent agent technology is ultimately intended and need to be carefully considered.

Intelligent agent software technology has made some progress but has much, much further to go before it can and should be accepted as a tool to improve the quality of people's lives. The emergence of intelligent mobile/software agents not only will change the way that we communicate across networks, but also have a profound impact on the way that we accomplish many tasks.

REFERENCES

Baek, S., Liebowitz, J., Prasad, S., and Granger, M. (1999) "Intelligent Agents for Knowledge Management—Toward Intelligent Web-Based Collaboration within Virtual Teams, in *Knowledge Management Handbook*, Jay Liebowitz (ed), CRC Press LLC, 11-1: 11-23.

Franklin, S., and Graesser, A. (1996) "Is It an Agent, or Just a Program?: A Taxonomy for Autonomous Agents," *Proceedings of the Third International Workshop on Agent Theories, Architectures, and Languages*, Springer-Verlag.

Hauk, R. V. and Chen, H. (1999), Coplink: A Case of Intelligent Analysis and Knowledge Management, *Proceedings of the Twentieth Annual International Conference on Information Systems*, Charlotte, North Carolina.

Huang, M., (1999), "Intelligent Diagnosing and Learning Agents for Intelligent Tutoring Systems," *Journal of Computer Information Systems*, Fall, 45-50.

Lange, D. B. & Oshima, M. (1999), "Dispatch your Agents, Shut off your Machine," *Communications of the ACM*, 42(3), 88-89.

Lanier, J., "Agents of Alienation," http://www.well.com/user/jaron/agentalien.html.

Kirsner, S. (1999), "The bots are back," *CIO*, 12:14. Section 2, 26-28.

Kotz, D., Gray, R. (1999), "Mobile Agents and the Future of the Internet," ACM Operating Systems Review, August, ftp://ftp.cs.dartmouth.edu/pub/kotz/papers/ chapters/ kotz:future2.ps.Z.

Ma, M. (1999), "Agents in E-Commerce,"*Communications of the ACM*, 42(3), 78-80.

Maes, P.(1999), "Smart Commerce: The Future of Intelligent Agents in Cyberspace, *Journal of Interactive Marketing*, 13:3, 66-76.

Maes, P., Guttman, R. H. and Moukas, A. G. (1999), "Agents that Buy and Sell," *Communications of the ACM*, 42:3, 81-87.

Malhotra, Y. "Deciphering the Knowledge Management Hype", Available at www.brint.com.

Nardi, B.A., Miller, J.R., and Wright, D. J. (1998), 'Programmable Intelligent Agents," *Communications of the ACM*, 41:3, 96-104.

Russell, S. J. and Norvig, P. (1995), *Artificial Intelligence: A Modern Approach*, Englewood Cliffs, NJ: Prentice Hall.

Sandholm, T. (1999), "Automated Negotiation," *Communications of the ACM*, 42:3, 84-85.

Smith, D. C., Cypher A., and Spohrer, J. (1994), "KidSim: Programming Agents Without a Programming Language," *Communications of the ACM*, 37, 7, 55-67.

Turban, Mclean and Wetherbe (1999), *Information Technology for Management, Making Connections for Strategic Advantages*, John Wiley & Sons, Inc. Second edition.

"The IBM Agent", http://activist.gpl.ibm.com:81/WhiteChapter/ptc2.htm.

Vinaja, R. and Sircar S. (1999), "Agents Delivering Business Intelligence," in *Handbook of IS Management*, Auerbach Publications, 477-490.

Wang, S. (1999), "Analyzing Agents for Electronic Commerce," *Information Systems Management*, Winter, 40-46.

Wong, D., Paciorek, N., and Moore, D. (1999), Java-based Mobile Agents, *Communications of the ACM*, 42:3, 92-95.

Woolridge, M. and Jennings N. R., (1996), "Pitfalls of Agent-Oriented Development," in *Intelligent Agents*, Section 4.2,, Springer-Verlag, Berlin.

QUESTIONS FOR DISCUSSION

1) What should a developer of agent technology think about in more specific terms with respect to issues and challenges in human-computer interaction? How should he/she go about it?

2) How can users of agent technology, particularly the less technically savvy users, be supported in understanding their rights and putting the right kind of pressure on the industry?

Chapter VIII

Knowledge Engineering in Adaptive Interface and User Modeling

Qiyang Chen, Montclair State University, USA
A. F. Norcio, University of Maryland, Baltimore County, USA

ABSTRACT

This chapter presents the issues of user modeling and its role in adaptive human-computer interface (HCI). Particularly, it focuses on knowledge acquisition and representation in user modeling. Several related problems in the traditional user modeling systems are also identified and discussed.

ADAPTIVE INTERFACE AND USER MODELING

The concept of an adaptive human-computer interface (HCI) has been recognized as a very promising and challenging area for both research and applications (Norcio and Stanley, 1989). The objective of an adaptive interface is to adapt system responses to the user effectively in a complex computer-based task. In the context of human computer interaction, the relationship between a human and a computer involves many factors such as the computing environment, the nature of the tasks to be performed, as well as various characteristics of the users. The effectiveness of a human-computer interface system is influenced greatly by its ability to adapt to these factors.

As the functionality of computer systems becomes more complex and users' tasks vary, users must adjust their behavior and problem solving strategies to the systems. This situation is often made worse because users lack the knowledge and experience to be effective. A well-designed interface can provide much more helpful information in a more appropriate manner during the interaction, especially for those users who have limited experiences. Therefore, an adaptive interface is not only beneficial for users but also for system resources management since the tasks and the related resources are better allocated between user and the computer.

Generally, an adaptive interface should be able to offer an effective interaction and allocate tasks dynamically between the user and the computer system. It is not unusual that users are frequently confronted with an overwhelming amount of information in interacting with computers. Users must decide what information to request and use. In these situations, it has been found that users do not usually perform optimally (Card, Moran and Newell, 1983). In addition, users may not have the necessary information or expertise to adjust their behavior. The adaptability of an interface is helpful for the users with different backgrounds, because the interface system can individualize its responses. An adaptive interface can increase user proficiency with a new system and allow novices and experts to use the system with equal ease.

To adapt to a user effectively and correctly, an interface system must be able to characterize and distinguish individual users. User modeling, a process of establishing a collection of the system's beliefs about various users' characteristics, has become an important component in adaptive interface systems. An interface equipped with user modeling component is able to tailor its responses to individual users. Generally, an adaptive interface has the following advantages:

- Economy of the interaction: The dialogue may be short, more precise, better focused and understandable. Since system responses can rely on default knowledge already stored in the user model, the system *knows* what the next optimal response should be to help the user perform the task.
- User acceptability: The dialog is individually tailored. Thus, it becomes more acceptable to the user. In addition to providing a clearer dialogue, a user model can provide the basis of explanations of the solution to users. It can also detect the user's misconceptions in the task performance; and therefore, it can provide justifications for the adaptation.
- Effectiveness and efficiency of use: The access to the target system and its use may become more effective and efficient, in terms of both quality and cost of the performance.

Research in the field of user modeling dates to the early seventies (Self, 1974; Bruce, 1975; Allen and Perrault, 1978; Cohen, 1978; Rich, 1979). It is widely recognized that computer systems should adapt to users in an intelligent and cooperative manner. It is also evident that computer systems can acquire these capabilities on a large scale only if they have the knowledge about users and the tasks that the users are performing. Constructing, maintaining, and utilizing user models has become an active research area. Since the mid-eighties, user modeling research has focused on four different but interrelated domains: human-computer interface (Murray, 1987; Dede, 1986; Botman *et al.*, 1987), natural language dialog systems (Wahlster and Kobsa, 1989), intelligent tutoring systems (Self, 1974; Kass, 1989, Selker, 1994), and information retrieval (Daniel, 1986; Allen, 1990; Kramer *et al*, 2000). From the viewpoint of system functionality, user modeling can be considered as a component of the interface for optimizing human-computer interactions.

Some studies of user interface management systems (UIMS) partially address adaptation of information displays based on features of the system's operation (Eberts and Eberts, 1989). With the UIMS approach, the interface becomes an important and separate system component to which software engineering techniques are applied. The UIMS approach facilitates interface design by providing a set of tools. A UIMS provides a definition language for representing the dialogue required and a generator that automatically produces the necessary code from a source definition in this language. A UIMS typically includes screen generation tools, a graphics package, and editors for help messages, error messages, prompts, forms, icons, and so on. The typical runtime functions are management of multiple windows and conversion of task output to user representation. However, the characteristics of users and tasks to which the system needs to adapt are not emphasized. The UIMS approach provides a flexible and reliable interface design strategy, but fails to make the interface adapt dynamically because the underlying cognitive models and other relative characteristics of users are not considered (Norcio and Stanley, 1989). It is acknowledged that in many applications such as tutorial systems, information retrieval systems, or security control systems, personalized interfaces are crucial to the success of the system (Kramer *et al*, 2000).

In an adaptive interface, user modeling is a primary mechanism that allows the system to tailor its responses to individual users during the interaction. A wide variety of user models have been proposed. In order to adapt to users, a user modeling system must address the following issues:

- The existence of information or knowledge about the user, the task, and the context of interaction;
- The approaches of eliciting the above information or knowledge;
- The strategies of utilizing this information or knowledge.

Figure 1 shows the framework of an interface system equipped with a user modeling component. The user modeling subsystem monitors the interaction and dynamically produces profiles for both the user and the tasks. According to these profiles, the system tailors personalized information from various system resources to provide to the user.

Without considering the application domain, the possible roles of user models in interactive systems can be illustrated as follows:

- User models can be used to analyze input and generate output. User models are helpful for determining what and how to prompt a user and interpreting a user's response without ambiguity. In a natural language system, it is often necessary to determine what a user really means. Uncertainties involved in a user's language need to be minimized. In addition, the system needs to determine a user's intended meaning, even though it is not explicitly stated. User models may provide prerequisite information that may not be directly stated in a user input, construct referring expressions, and make lexical choice so that the system is able to decide what and how to respond to a user input.
- User models assist in recognizing a user's goals and plans so that the system can better understand the user's information-seeking behavior. A user's goals and plans are related. A user's goal is what the user wants to achieve after interacting with a computer system, while the plan is considered as a sequence of actions that results in the realization of a goal. Furthermore, each action in a plan may have its own subgoals. One approach to recognize a user's goal is to observe and analyze the user's actions.
- User models help to evaluate when to provide information, as well as recognize and

Figure 1. A Framework of Adaptive Interface System

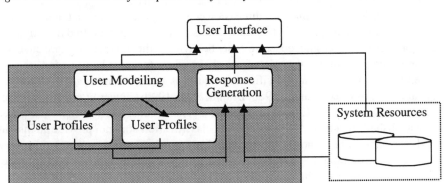

correct misconceptions, so that the system can provide more meaningful help and advice. Knowing what the user believes to be true is especially useful for many kinds of systems. Knowledge of the concepts that a user understands or misunderstands allows the system to produce appropriate responses. This feature is particularly necessary in instructional or tutorial systems.

DESIGN USER MODEL

The term "user model" is used in many different contexts to describe task-oriented information or knowledge that is used to support human-computer interaction. There are a variety of views of user model, and none is universally accepted. Thus, the best way for understanding user modeling mechanisms is to explore their features in terms of their organization and utilization.

Knowledge Sources of a User Model

The contents of a user model can directly affect the user-computer interaction. Given a task, different user models usually cause different system responses. Some or all of the following aspects might be incorporated into a user model:
- User's knowledge about the system and proficiency regarding the system operations.
- User's goals that underlie the tasks being performed; the plans that a user follows to achieve the goal; and the beliefs held by a user regarding a particular domain.
- User's preferences and cognitive characteristics.
- Characteristics about the tasks.

The contents of the user model vary greatly from application to application. For example, a tutorial system may need to capture all concepts known (or unknown) to a student (Paris, 1989; Nwana, 1991). A database query system may need to model data items with which a user is concerned (Chen and Norcio, 1997; Heger *et al.,* 1991). An expert system may need to model a user's domain goals (Chin, 1989). Rich (1979, 1983) classifies the information incorporated in a user model through three domain-independent dimensions:
- *The long-term/short-term dimension:* Long-term models describe relatively static characteristics of users, while short-term models describe specific topics and goals in the current discourse. The dimension characterizes the persistence of a user model established during an interaction.
- *Canonical / individual dimension:* A canonical model only describes the character- istics of a "typical" system without considering the individual differences among users, while an individual model concerns those characteristics that are highly salient and relevant to the task being performed by a specific user.
- *Explicit/implicit dimension:* This dimension concerns how to elicit and represent the information from the previous two dimensions. The model is specified directly by a user or established through observing user behavior in the interaction. A mechanism for inferring the individual models from observed events must be provided.

Given this context, similar classifications, such as given vs. inferred, or static vs. dynamic, are also proposed (Daniel, 1986; Brajnik *et al.,* 1990; Clowes *et al.,* 1985; Allen, 1990). The idea of this classification is to provide a generic consideration on how the user model is established and utilized. Obviously, this classification does not provide an insight into the dynamics of a user model, which includes a user's progressive or evolutionary capability, a user's cognitive style, as well as a user's mental workload in task performance. Allen (1990) also suggests that this classification is not clear about relationships or transitions between these dimensions.

These dimensional settings are consistent with each other. Some also imply others. Essentially, they attempt to characterize knowledge about a user in four aspects (Chen and Norcio, 1997):

- Information persistency or temporal extent
- Methods of knowledge elicitation and representation
- Degree of specification
- Relationships between these three aspects

The knowledge for constructing a user model may encompass three areas:

1) *User's domain knowledge and task related characteristics*. The user model should be able to characterize and to distinguish between individuals. The information about a user's domain knowledge, capacities, and cognitive preferences should be obtained for each user in order to adapt to the task being performed. Also, the predicted user's beliefs, goals and plans are the components of a user model.

2) *Task information*. While the term "user model" emphasizes the information about the person's long term and short-term characteristics, it is obvious that a great deal of task information may be encoded in the model. It is suggested that dynamic information about a user's current state in task performance is more important than the user's long-term characteristics for generating an appropriate system response. The GOMS model is one of the common approaches for predicting the task performance (Card *et al.*, 1983).

3) *Knowledge of the interaction*. A user model should be able to keep track of the current human computer dialogue. It requires knowledge about how the interaction is constructed and what information may be implied from it. A transition diagram of a dialogue can be considered as a representation of such knowledge in a user model.

In order to incorporate knowledge about users and their tasks in a structured way, some domain independent features must be implemented into a user modeling system. Finin (1989) suggests several important features that can be synthesized:

- *Separate Knowledge Base*: Information about a user is organized in a separate module rather then distributed throughout the system. This knowledge base distinguishes the system's knowledge about its user from the other target resources such as application databases, programs, etc.
- *Explicit and Declarative Representation*: Knowledge in a user model is encoded in a declarative rather than procedural manner. A user's profile is represented explicitly.
- *Support for Abstraction*: The modeling system provides a function of generalization so that it can address a class of users as well as individuals.
- *Multiple Use*: Since the user model is represented as a separate module, it can be utilized in several ways such as classifying a user, monitoring a user's performance, and tailoring the system response.

Knowledge Acquisition and Representation in User Model

Norcio and Stanley (1989) summarize three common approaches for establishing a user model. They are:

- Classify users from novices to experts according to their operational proficiency and domain expertise,
- Compare a user's knowledge against an expert's knowledge, and
- Characterize users by a set of stereotypical traits.

The ways of constructing a user model can be classified as explicit elicitation and implicit elicitation:

1) *Explicit information elicitation*. The information needed for a user model is learned directly from the user's input. The system may prompt the user for characteristics regarding a certain task. The user's response to these questions can be formed as an initial profile. An example is the Grundy system that is used to model a user's social status such as sex, age, and occupation (Rich, 1979; Hoeppner *et al.*, 1986).

2) *Implicit information elicitation*. Through monitoring the human-computer interaction, information about a user can be obtained indirectly. The system deducts the user model contents according to observations on various factors. These factors are usually domain dependent. However, they could be domain-independently classified as *behavior data* and *conceptual objects*.

Behavior data are statistics that focus on the user's performance during interactive sessions, such as the types of commands used, the error rate, the time span of a dialogue, the number of help requests, the usage of optimal command sequence, etc. Also, these data can be considered as explicitly obtained since they are primarily based on objective observation. However, the explanation of the implication from these data is crucial in user modeling. The most common usage of such statistics is to classify the user's operational proficiency toward the target system.

A user model functions only as the system's knowledge base about the user. Its establishment should not become the user's obligation and workload. Therefore, the balance between explicit elicitation and implicit elicitation is important for effectiveness of the interface system. The modeling process should be *transparent* to the user. Actually, explicit elicitation may not guarantee the validity of obtained information. For instance, a user's claimed programming skill as "excellent" may not fit the system's criteria. However, this transparency may raise some social or psychological issues. For example, a user may be reluctant to be modeled and may make his/her behavior abnormal for various reasons (Murray, 1987).

In the user modeling process consistency is a major concern in this process. The acquired knowledge should be incorporated into the existing user model without causing any contradiction. Usually default reasoning and evidential reasoning are utilized.

Default reasoning allows the modeling process to maintain hypothetical knowledge about a user in the absence of evidence to the contrary. In order to make a large number of inferences with a small number of observations, extensive default assumptions must be established, even though they may not be true during the interaction. Therefore, techniques for handling incomplete and inconsistent information must be involved in the modeling process.

If the model construction is driven by evidential reasoning, the numerical values of the beliefs about the facts and rules must be carefully defined. Further, modification of such belief values is necessary until adequate modeling performance is obtained. However, even if the system can identify the correlation between the observations and their implications, it is still difficult to make a probabilistic assignment especially for some intermediate concepts or conclusions that support inferences and explanations. Even with a well-understood situation, it is difficult to maintain probabilistic formalisms (*e.g.*, independence of probabilities) over the whole production system (Zadah, 1989). Many sources of uncertainties can lead reasoning systems to draw inconsistent conclusions (Bonissone *et al.*, 1985). In addition, off-line tuning of belief values is both time- consuming and inexact. It is often based on inadequate tests and a subjective judgment of how the interaction is progressing, and local improvement obtained by tuning one capability of the modeling process might be detrimental to other capabilities (Bonissone *et al.,* 1985).

ASSUMPTIONS AND STEREOTYPES

It is a common practice to use a set of predefined assumptions to initialize the system's beliefs about its users and the tasks they are performing. It is called the stereotype approach (Rich, 1979; Kobsa, 1990). Stereotypical knowledge is organized into a generalization hierarchy in which the stereotypes inherit knowledge from their ancestors. A stereotypes hierarchy is shown in Figure 2, in which each node in the hierarchy represents a stereotype regarding a certain task. Each node can also be associated with a set of attributes or assumptions that are used to justify or describe the corresponding stereotype. One stereo-type subsumes another if it can be considered to be more general. For example, a hierarchical user model S_h is a substructure of the generalization hierarchy S that can be represented as follows:

$$S_h \_ S = \{ \ S_i, \ S_i \text{ is a stereotype in the hierarchy} \}$$
$$S_i = \{ \ a_j^{(i)}, a_j^{(i)} \text{ is an assumption in } S_i \}$$

Usually, the modeling process proceeds from the root of the hierarchy. If one or more assumptions are verified by certain facts or observations during an interaction, the stereo-type that contains these assumptions is activated and then added into the current user model. As the interaction progresses, more and more stereotypes are activated and the user model becomes more informative. For example, in Figure 2 if *S1* is defined as a computer user, then *S2* can be defined as microcomputer user and *S3* as mainframe user. Furthermore, *S4* may be specified as an IBM PC user and *S5* as Macintosh user respectively. If a user is modeled as a PC user, then the user's profile consists of all assumptions contained in *S1, S2* and *S4.*

Initial knowledge about a user comes from the system assumptions. To infer a user's characteristics, user modeling system must establish extensive assumptions. Each assumption is predefined with conditions that need to be satisfied before that assumption can be applied to the user. If a user fulfills the conditions, the assumption can be ascribed to the user. This ascription is normally contingent on an absence of conflict with other information previously known to the system.

Applications of Stereotypes

The earliest application of the stereotype approach is Rich's GRUNDY system that is used to recommend books for users (Rich, 1979). Stereotypes are used to model a user's social status such as occupation, reading preferences, sex, age, etc. At the beginning of each session, a user is

Figure 2. Hierarchical Stereotypes

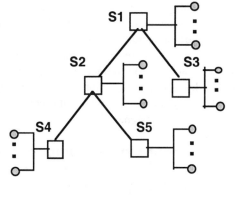

○ assumption

☐ stereotype

asked for a self-description regarding these social traits. Stereotypes are activated by the user's input in terms of matching the user's responses with the assumptions attributed to these stereotypes. This approach may work well for modeling a user's long term, static characteristics, but it does not fit the situation in which a user does not know how to describe the task-related characteristics. For example, in a tutorial system, the user (*i.e.*, a student) may not be able to respond correctly to the request about the domain knowledge level (Wenger, 1987). Even if the user does respond, the user's judgment may not fit the system's criteria. In addition, the traditional stereotype system does not provide any insight about the task being performed (Clowes *et al.,* 1985).

KNOME, a user modeling system developed by Chin (1989) for tutoring UNIX, avoids eliciting information from a user directly. Instead, it infers the user's knowledge levels by examining the evidence that the user knows or does not know some key concepts. It classifies four groups of users with different levels of expertise and associates each group with stereotypical expectations about the user's familiarity with UNIX commands of a certain difficulty level. However, such stereotypical knowledge does change as the user's proficiency progresses. This limits the adaptability of a user model (Totterdell *et al.,* 1990).

Stereotyping is also used in some user modeling shells that provide tool kits for constructing user models for various applications. Finin's GUMS system addresses the problems of revising stereotypical knowledge about the user's beliefs (Finin, 1989). It does not derive the assumptions itself, but provides a set of services for maintenance. It accepts and stores new facts about the user. The knowledge about the user is organized in a stereotype tree where each node represents a class of users.

The user model is revised when the application system observes new facts that conflict with the active stereotypes. It deduces the negated fact from the current assumptions, informs the application system about recognized inconsistencies and answers queries concerning its current assumptions about the user's level of expertise. The revision is done by replacing the active stereotype with its closest ancestor that does not conflict with the observed facts. The stereotypes in a parallel path are considered as possible replacements. As some authors pointed out (Huang, 1991; Kobsa, 1990), since the hierarchy is constrained to a tree, and only a single stereotype may apply to a user at a time, this revision approach is inappropriate because it only decreases the stereotypical knowledge. If the initial stereotype is chosen inappropriately, additional information about the user increases the likelihood that fewer stereotypes can be attributed to the user. Therefore, better fitting stereotypes can never be found. In addition, the GUMS exploits the closed world assumption as the basis of inference; whereby, any hypothesis that is unknown is assumed to be false. This might oversimplify the real world situation.

Kobsa (1990) presents a more comprehensive shell system, BGP-MS, to support the definition of the stereotype architecture in a user model for a particular application domain. A stereotype management utility is presented to monitor the current assumptions about the user and to automatically activate and retract stereotypes according to certain conditions specified by the user model designer. It attempts to maintain a sufficient number of activated and consistent stereotypes in run time. However, it seems to leave too much obligation to the shell users (i.e., user model designers).

Forming Assumptions

In a stereotype hierarchy, all assumptions are directly or indirectly activated by the user's input. There are various techniques for transforming a user's input into. Wahlster and

Kobsa (1989) summarized two types of approaches for forming assumptions:

1) *Forming the assumptions based on the user's input.* Sometimes a user's input can be directly incorporated into a user model as long as this input directly states the information about what is required and what the user believes. For example, the system can pose questions to the users that have been devised to elicit responses that are most relevant to the preconditions of the assumptions. If the assumption cannot be made directly from a user's input, a content-dependent inference must be conducted. For example, if a user's input is a question, it usually implies several alternative assumptions. The syntactic and linguistic analysis on how this question is prompted can also underlie a set of assumptions.

2) *Forming the assumptions based on the dialogue.* The interaction between the user and the computer system also contributes new entries to a user model. All traits involved in a dialogue, such as system's navigation plan, system response, user's utterances, and feedback actions can be these entries. For example, an answered question is assumed to be understood by a user. Therefore, the user should not ask the same question in a later dialogue.

In the context of modeling a user's domain knowledge or conceptual knowledge, some "common sense" rules can be used to form assumptions directly from the user's direct input.

- *Transitive rule.* If a user knows that the concept C implies B, and that B implies A, then the user knows that C implies A.
- *Inheritance rule.* If a user knows that concept A has attribute description X, and B is a subtype of A, then B also has attribute description X.
- *Compass rule.* If a user knows that concept A has attribute descriptions $X_1,..., X_n$, and B has $Y_1,..., Y_m$, and that each of the X_i is a special case of some Y_j, then the user knows B implies A.

The following rules can also be useful for indirectly adding the information into the user model.

- If a user mentions a concept in a dialogue, then the user either knows the concept or does not know the concept, depending on whether or not the user requests an explanation for this concept.
- If a user mentions an attribute description of a concept, then the user believes that the concept has such an attribute.
- If a user uses new terminology and the user does not ask for clarification, then the user understands the terminology.

Very often more than one stereotype can be ascribed to a user, and a given stereotype may be a subtype of more than one other stereotype (i.e., a node has more than one parent node in the hierarchy). This feature complicates the inheritance of information. The inherited information might conflict with each other. This is shown in Figure 3, where each stereotype has some inherited information (i.e., assumptions or attributes applied to a stereotype), except S_1. The S_2 and S_3 are the subtypes of S_1. S_4 is the subtype of both S_2 and S_3. The problem in this case is that, according to the feature of generalization, S_4 may inherit conflicting assumptions (i.e., a_1 and ÿa_1), which is not allowed in user modeling.

Figure 3 Inheritance conflict

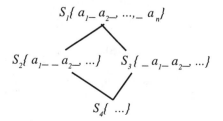

Conflict Resolution

Conflicts between the conclusions/predictions based on different stereotypes are difficult to solve. Rich (1979) presents several domain-dependent and domain independent resolution strategies. Domain-independent strategies suggest the selection of the following predictions instead of the conflicting stereotype predictions:

- The average value, if the predictions in a conflict are numerically valued.
- The least upper bound, namely the closest shared ancestor of two stereotypes in the generalization hierarchy.
- The prediction based on the stereotype that has been active longer since it should be better established.
- The prediction based on the more recently activated stereotype since it is more current.
- The prediction that has never been involved in any conflict.

In addition, as Ballim and Wilks (1991) suggest, an extension to inheritance hierarchy is necessary to allow for exceptions. However, the introduction of exceptions brings further problems and complexities to the inheritance reasoning. One such problem is that of ambiguity. Also, the solutions are often computationally expensive because of the time-consuming search that is required.

Ability of Learning

The learning mechanism in a user modeling system allows the user model to adapt dynamically to the user's current performance or status. This mechanism is crucial for the usability of a user modeling system. Usually the learning mechanism is enforced by revising the contents of an individual user model dynamically.

The requirement for learning stems from two realistic situations: first, it is difficult to predefine an accurate knowledge set about the system's user community; and secondly, the characteristics (*e.g.,* familiarity with the system, beliefs, goals, and preferences, etc.) about an individual user or a class of users may change over time. As the interaction progresses, the system's belief values or rules must be added, deleted or modified to reflect real time changes. These revisions may in turn cause further data generalization and specification. However, this kind of adaptation is passive because it lacks the ability of deductive inference and prediction.

Some user modeling systems utilize techniques for handling uncertainties as a learning mechanism in which the model is refined by modifying the belief values until adequate modeling performance is obtained (Rich, 1979; Brajnik *et al.,* 1990; Hoeppner *et al.*, 1986; Howard *et al.,* 1987; Simon, 1988). Off-line tuning is both time-consuming and inexact. It is often based on inadequate tests and a subjective judgment of how the interaction is progressing. The local improvement obtained by tuning one capability of the modeling process might be detrimental to other capabilities. In addition, if such a revision is not based on a view of the behavior pattern, the modeling process may face the dilemma of frequent conflict-resolution (Huang, *et al.*, 1991). In addition, when a conflict is detected, it is necessary to determine a minimal set of assumptions that is associated with this conflict. This is usually an NP-complete process (Barr and Feigenbaum, 1982).

Default Reasoning and Truth Maintenance

A user modeling system can draw a number of plausible conclusions about a user from a small base of definite knowledge. Thus, default reasoning becomes a major process in most user modeling systems. The stereotyping approach is one form of default reasoning. In a default reasoning system if the underlying knowledge never changes, or if a reasoning system never reexams any conclusion, it is called a monotonic system. A non-monotonic reasoning system differs from the monotonic reasoning in that it is often necessary, when a conclusion is deleted from the current knowledge base, to review other conclusions whose proofs depend on the deleted one.

In a default reasoning system, assumptions may need to be either eliminated or to have new proofs that are valid based upon the current knowledge base. Deleting a single assumption may have a significant effect on an entire knowledge base because all assumptions must be deleted to maintain the consistency. In turn, these deletions can cause further deletions in the knowledge base. Thus, a change is propagated throughout the knowledge base. It is very important that a non-monotonic reasoning process not spend all its time propagating changes. Otherwise, it is not a stable system, and the credibility of any conclusion it draws is doubtful.

Default reasoning and non-monotonic logic have been originally studied by McCarthy, McDermott and Doyle, as well as Reiter. McDemott and McCarthy introduced a formal discussion about non-monotonic logic (McDermott, 1980; McCarthy, 1980). Reiter presented a survey of the areas of AI in which such reasoning is involved (Reiter, 1980), and introduced a mathematical treatment of this subject (Reiter, 1980). Reiter (1980) presents the following reasons for the necessity of a non-monotonic reasoning system:

- The presence of incomplete knowledge requires default reasoning.
- A changing external environment must be adapted by the knowledge base.
- Generating a complete solution to a problem may require temporary assumptions about potential solutions.

To able to propagate changes in the knowledge base and to check the validity of the proofs, the default reasoning needs to keep track of all results in the process. Thus, a non-monotonic system requires more storage space and processing time compared to the monotonic system.

The Truth Maintenance System (TMS) by Doyle is an implemented system that supports non-monotonic reasoning (Doyle, 1979). It serves as a truth maintenance subsystem affiliated with a reasoning system. It does not generate new inferences, but maintains consistency among the conclusions generated by the reasoning system. When an inconsistency is detected, it evokes its own reasoning mechanism, called dependency backtracking, to resolve the inconsistency or conflict by updating a minimal set of beliefs. It has the following three essential functions (Boy, 1991):

- It stores all the inferences made by the problem solver. As a result, inferences that have already been made do not need to be repeated and the contradictions, once discovered, will be avoided in the future.
- It enables the problem solver to make non-monotonic inferences. The presence of non-monotonic justification forces the TMS to use a procedure that satisfies constraints in order to determine which facts should be believed.
- It ensures that the knowledge base does not contain contradictions. Contradictions are removed by identifying the missing justifications and adding corresponding justifications. The procedure of identifying and adding justifications is called dependency-directed backtracking.

SOME LIMITATIONS OF CONVENTIONAL
STEREOTYPE APPROACHES

Although the stereotype approach provides a simple way to initialize the modeling process and is successful in some applications, this approach limits the representational power of a user model in the following three aspects:

1) Reasoning under Uncertainties. Since reasoning is conducted with extensive default assumptions that may conflict with the new evidence obtained as the interaction progresses, the revision of stereotypical knowledge is necessary to handle the inconsistencies. This in turn can cause dependency-directed backtracking that is a non-monotonic process (de Kleer, 1986). This process is called truth maintenance and has been a fertile field for AI research. Since the conventional truth maintenance approach examines one piece of evidence at a time, it is often ineffective or even impossible to detect noisy or inconsistent inputs that should be ignored. This phenomenon, for instance, may be observed in a tutoring system where the student's input often carries some inconsistencies (*e.g.*, typing mistake, grammar mistake, or the way the student raises the question) that may have nothing to do with understanding the tutorial concepts and, therefore, should be ignored in the modeling process.

In addition, the stereotyping approach must be able to examine the continuity and overall user behavior pattern in task performance. Otherwise, the modeling process may not reflect the real world situation, and it is possible that current efforts of maintaining consistency may bring further conflicts in the subsequent interaction. Thus, model construction may fall into a dilemma where a non-monotonic process of conflict-resolution is frequently involved, and eventually no modeling decisions can be made after a period of interaction (Chen and Norcio, 1997).

2) Individualization. A generalization hierarchy also provides a simple way to classify a user into certain stereotypes. The user model must capture the individual differences in order to tailor the system response to fit a particular user. Therefore, very often this classification must be as subtle as possible. But the predefined hierarchical structure is sometimes too inexact to characterize a particular user. This limits the degree of individualization in the sense that all assumptions or attributes are confined within a stereotype. They must apply to a certain stereotype at all times. However, it is very possible that a user fits one stereotype, but may not fit some attributes defined in that stereotype. The generalization hierarchy lacks the ability to justify such a situation. In addition, it is obvious that the representation power depends on the number of stereotypes rather than the number of assumptions.

3) Feature identification. Since the stereotype hierarchy is logically organized, it may not be appropriate for dynamically extracting a user's short-term characteristics that change over time and temporally exhibit great varieties regarding the current task. For instance, it is very realistic that a user might demonstrate both expert and novice traits for the same task. In that case, the hierarchical classification of characteristics via few dimensions might not be able to provide consistent information for the system to adapt the current interaction. It may fail to recognize the *irrational* data about a user's behavior. Whether such data need to be taken into account should depend on the examination of overall behavior patterns.

Since the predefined attributes or assumptions are confined within each stereotype and can be only inherited by the descendant stereotypes, there is no effective way to update those attributes that are no longer significant in the context of task performance. In addition, most stereotyping approaches solve conflicts by simply replacing the active stereotypes with their ancestors in the hierarchy (Rich, 1979; Huang *et al.,* 1991). Thus, some assumptions that are still consistent to the current situation are lost. It is possible that a user may fail to fit any set of stereotypes, so that the hierarchical modeling process fails to associate any system decision to that user. In such a situation, some assumptions distributed among the stereotypes might be still useful for characterizing that particular user. Hierarchical approaches lack the ability to identify and reorganize the useful assumptions distributed among the stereotypes.

ARTIFICIAL NEURAL NETWORKS IN ADAPTIVE HUMAN-COMPUTER INTERFACE

It has been recognized that the ability of an Artificial Neural Network (ANN) to learn and recognize patterns in data can be utilized in the area of human-computer interaction (HCI). Unlike classical AI techniques, neural networks have the ability to adapt and to generalize. Many different types of HCI activities can benefit from these characteristics of neural nets (Maren, 1990; Stacey *et al.,* 1992; Chen and Norcio, 1997). The primary concern for utilizing ANN techniques can be summarized as follows:

1) Learning techniques. ANN models provide a family of numerical learning techniques. They are particularly useful in the applications of data-intensive pattern recognition. They can extract the rules from the examples. The feature of self-organization allows dynamic modeling of the run-time environment. ANN models have also shown the potential for the development of knowledge-based system in which the knowledge acquisition is often a bottleneck (Hayes-Roth, 1991). In human computer interaction, dynamic learning is particularly important for modeling user performance. The historical log of interaction can provide training samples for the classification of a user's behavior (Stacey *et al.* 1992).

2) Pattern completion and noise tolerance. The ANN technique is also useful for processing incomplete information. Successful matches between the input and output pattern can be accomplished with incomplete or imperfect patterns, even when there is noisy or ambiguous input. The performance is said to degrade gracefully. Similarly, when presented with unfamiliar data that are within the range of its exemplars, the network will generally produce an output that is a reasonable interpolation between the exemplar outputs. This feature also facilitates uncertainty management in the sense that it examines the current knowledge base in pattern-formatted view so that incomplete and imprecise information can be matched to the closest output pattern (Pao, 1989).

3) Efficient *system development and maintenance.* For some applications, ANN techniques provide an efficient development alternative. Building and adjusting an ANN model are relatively easier than building a large number of production rules (Fu, 1990). In the applications of data-intensive pattern recognition and classification, it is especially difficult to define a set of rules that covers all evidence-conclusion situations in pattern recognition. In addition, the parallel processing model makes the computation cost-effective. It avoids the overhead of required maintenance in conventional rule-based systems (Carpenter, 1989; Pao, 1989).

ANN and Rule-Based Systems: Comparison and Integration

The ANN approaches and rule-based systems are different in several aspects. The knowledge of ANN is implemented by its connections and associated weights; whereas, the

Table 1. A comparison between the ANN-based system and the rule-based system

	ANN-based system	**rule-based system**
knowledge representation	Connections and weights	production rules
computing unit	Numbers	symbols, belief values
information level	Signal level	knowledge level
adaptation	Good	poor
development cost	Low	high
explanation	None	good
pattern recognition ability	Good	poor
processing mode	Parallel	sequential
inference mode	Summation and thresholding propagation of activation	propagation of belief values, unification and resolution

knowledge of rule-based system lies in rules. The ANN processes information by numerically propagating and combining activations through the networks, but a rule-based system processes information through symbol matching and generation. Table 1 shows the primary differences between the two methods.

Since the interface systems must provide the dialogue in the symbolic form, any result from neural nets must be transformed, which needs the rule based processing. On other side, the ANN can facilitate the conventional rule-based systems in the aspects of adaptation, pattern recognition, and classification. It has been suggested that combining these two systems can enhance both of them (Caudill, 1990). Figure 4 illustrates an interface framework that integrates the two systems.

The neural network module functions as a component that analyzes the user's input and provides the intermediate results for generating system response and explanation. Both the pre-processing module and the post-processing module are the rule-based subsystems. The pre-processing component is used to transform the user's input into numerical stimuli for further neural-net processing. The output from the neural network activates system operations and needs to be symbolically interpreted. This is achieved by another rule-based module, the post-processing component. The system's knowledge base is a working memory that contains all supporting information, such as rules of transformation, meta-knowledge, and user or task profiles, usually in symbolic form. For example, if this

Figure 4. An integration of neural networks and rule-based system

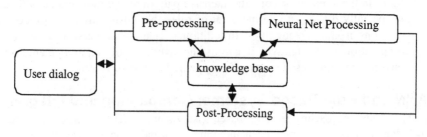

framework is implemented in an information retrieval environment, then the preprocessing component translates a user's query (e.g., subjects) into network input, and the network will propagate the activation. The output is a vector that corresponds to some subjects or documents. The post-processing component then searches the database according to the analysis on this vector. It also generates explanations if the system response to a user's query needs to be justified.

There are several strategies for combining neural networks with expert systems or other systems. The strategies for the integration vary from stand-alone systems to a fully integrated neural net and expert system (Caudill, 1990; Bailey and Thompson, 1990; Hillman, 1990; Bailey and Medsker, 1991; Boy, 1991). Bailey and Medsker (1991) classify these strategies in terms of structural topology: stand alone structure; transformation structure where two systems are linked one after the other, and the successor uses the output of the predecessor; loose coupling structure where the systems have dependencies such as feedback from one system to the other or both systems feed into a third; tight coupling structure; and full integration structure.

Applications of ANN in HCI

Artificial Neural Network (ANN) techniques that specialize in human computer interaction have been proposed and developed by a number of investigators. The earlier application of ANN in HCI is NETtalk, a system developed by Sejnowski and Rosenberg (1987), which uses three-layer back-propagation ANN to learn to "read aloud." The goal was to have an ANN convert English text to speech by learning through exposure to examples as opposed to entering phonological rules and handling exceptions with a look-up table. A back-propagation net was trained to transform an input vector that encodes a sequence of letters into an output vector that encodes the phonemic features of the sequence and which can be used to drive a speech synthesizer.

Maren (1990) summarizes three areas where ANN can be utilized to improve a system's ability to adapt in HCI: information control, diagnosis, and dialog monitoring. She suggests that neural networks can enhance the learning capability of adaptive interfaces in terms of sensing the extensive data about the interaction through various channels.

ANN in user modeling is also proposed for identifying user's domain knowledge (Chen and Norcio, 1997). The data about a user's behavior can be formed as stimuli for classification conducted by neural networks. The clues from the task performance can also be matched to a complete task path for system's navigation. Stacey *et al.* (1992) present an ANN paradigm for pattern analysis of the trace data generated by human-computer interaction. It is suggested that since a user interacting with a system follows patterns within a certain context, ANN techniques can be used to observe and predict the behavior pattern. Eberts (1991) proposed to use a back-propagation network to elicit knowledge about a user's proficiency of the UNIX command system for the design of help subsystems. Finley and Beale (1992) suggest modeling individual differences and habits of users as a means of providing support for common activities. They use a minimalist approach to the problem, and view user modeling as the composition of a number of stereotypical classifications. They propose the use of example-based classifiers as user modeling components.

ANN can provide an alternative intelligent interface for an information retrieval system. Heger and Koen (1991) developed an associative memory for database retrieval in which the causal relationships among key terms in a database are established and weighted. Given a user's initial query, the interface can activate all related key terms and induce the new queries. McGrew (1992) proposes the use of a neural network in the rapid validation and prototyping of task analysis in interface design. By mapping the task analysis onto a network, one can simulate the result of the analysis and quickly identify any errors. This is particularly useful for usability studies. Eichmann and Srinivas (1992) propose the use of an unsupervised network based on Adaptive Resonance Theory (ART) to perform retrieval software modules from a repository. It is done by partial matching and exploiting the generalization properties of the network. Habibi and Eberts (1992) also use neural networks to develop a filter to select relevant articles based on keywords of interests. Oakes and Taylor (1992) present a useful comparison of a number of retrieval techniques, ranging from string matching through the neural network methods. Their application is to classify terms in a medical thesaurus in which the terms may be related literally or conceptually.

There are also many studies of using neural network technology to design video/audio equipment for HCI. For instance, Bryn and Eichmann (1997) present a design and experiment of neural network approach to tracking eye position. The results show that accurate tracking of a human's eye position is possible by neural network based image processing built in the goggle-mounted miniature charge-coupled device.

All these studies demonstrate benefits of various useful properties of neural networks, which open up new research and applications in the field of HCI.

An Alternative Approach to User Modeling

Chen and Norcio (1997) proposed and tested an alternative to conventional stereotyping approaches. A set of associative networks is utilized as the knowledge base for modeling users' domain knowledge. In contrast to the conventional rule-based user modeling approaches, this study uses artificial neural network (ANN) techniques to store, maintain, and infer various task-related attributes about users. The proposed approach is referred to as associative user modeling. It is suggested that this approach provides an effective and simple way of user modeling in terms of the inherent features of ANN techniques.

In associative user modeling, all characteristics or assumptions about a user are referred to as concepts. These concepts are represented by the network nodes. There are two perspectives for defining the connections among the nodes (*i.e.*, concepts):
- The connections are viewed as the causal relationships among the concepts, which are conditionally weighted.
- The connections are obtained by supervised or unsupervised network training.

In associative user modeling, there is no need to group assumptions *a priori* for pre-defined user profiles. User modeling is a process that extracts the concepts and their weighted connections from associative networks to form a unique profile that fits a particular user or task. This process is conducted by propagating the activation level throughout the network. Since the propagation process allows any number of concepts to be activated, more combinations of concepts can be utilized to characterize individual users. This underlies a more flexible way of constructing of a user model.

Associative user modeling provides a pattern-formatted view of a user's characteristics. It examines the information about users through pattern recognition. The default reasoning is viewed as a process of pattern completion. The produced user models can be applied to predicting users' performance and evaluating users' domain expertise. The system equipped with such models can optimize its performance by making the dialogue strategy adapt to users' skills and tasks.

1) The ability of default reasoning. ANN's abilities of pattern completion and noise tolerance allow production of default assumptions based on incomplete, imprecise and inconsistent input. This means that based on a small number of inputs the system can produce a large number of outputs. Also, the inconsistent information about the user can be reconciled through pattern recognition. This approach avoids the complexity of truth maintenance in default reasoning that is required in conventional stereotype approaches.

2) *The ability of learning.* ANN models can learn from the exemplars (*i.e.*, training data). Using supervised or unsupervised training procedures, the ANN models can generalize the hypothetical information about user's characteristics such as the beliefs about user's domain knowledge and user classifications. The learning ability of ANN models can enhance the adaptability of user modeling that requires dynamic revision of its knowledge base.

3) *The system implementation and maintenance.* It is widely recognized that the implementation and maintenance of neural network models are much simpler than that of rule-based systems. Conventional rule-based systems require extensive work on knowledge elicitation to set up the appropriate rule bases, which tends to be a time-consuming and error-prone process. In contrast, the learning ability of a neural network eases the knowledge elicitation process. The consistency can be easily maintained in neural network systems due to their ability to handle inconsistent or incomplete information. In addition, the useful features of conventional stereotyping approaches, such as inheritance and fast classification, can be easily implemented by ANN-based pattern association process.

SUMMARY

This chapter presents the importance of user modeling techniques for improving the adaptability of human-computer interfaces. User models have become important components of adaptive human-computer interfaces. A system will be able to exhibit flexible user-oriented behavior if it has access to a model that consists of assumptions about the user's characteristics in performing certain tasks. These characteristics are usually task-related, such as the user's plans, goals, background knowledge, and cognitive preferences. There are different taxonomies about these characteristics depending on the time period while they hold, the way by which they are elicited and represented, as well as the degree to which they are specified.

It has been a common practice to use a set of stereotypes to initialize a system's beliefs about its users and the tasks being performed. The predefined stereotypical knowledge is organized into a generalization hierarchy. The modeling process proceeds with a stereotype assignment using default reasoning. This chapter discussed the issues of knowledge elicitation and representations involved in the modeling process. The limitations of the stereotyping approach in generalization, individualization, and default reasoning were presented. The uncertainties involved in the user modeling were identified. These uncertainties primarily originate from the incomplete and inconsistent information about users. Most user modeling systems use the *ad hoc* approach to handle the uncertain information, which may fail to generalize, and weakens the theoretical foundation of uncertainty management considerably.

In addtion, the study of user cognitive characteristics (*e.g.*, performance models or mental models) is also very important to user modeling. The performance models emphasize the decomposition of tasks in a generic way, and mental models are concerned about individual differences. These models may supplement each other to facilitate the understanding of human-computer interactions.

The ANN techniques have been used in the field of human computer interface design. The ANN techniques demonstrate strong ability of learning, pattern completion, and handling inconsistent information, which is required in the design of adaptive interface systems. They can also be used in user modeling. In addition, the ANN-based modeling systems are easier to develop and maintain compared with the traditional rule based systems, especially for data-intensive pattern recognition and classification.

REFERENCES

Allen, J. F. and Perrault, C. R., "Participating in Dialogue Understanding via Plan Deduction," *Proceedings of the Second National Conference of the Canadian Society for Computational Studies of Intelligence,* 1978.

Allen, R. B." User Models: Theory, Methods, and Practice," *International Journal of Man-Machine Studies,* Vol.32, 1990, 511-543.

Bailey, D. L. and Medsker, L. R., "Integrating Expert Systems and Neural Networks: Tutorial mp3." in *the Ninth National Conference on Artificial Intelligence* (AAAI-91), July 1991.

Bailey, D. L. and Thompson, D. M. "Developing Neural-Network Application," *AI Expert,* November 1990.

Ballim, A. and Wilks, Y. "Beliefs, Stereotypes and Dynamic Agent Modeling," *User Modeling and User-Adapted Interaction,* Vol. 1, No.1, 1991, 33-56.

Barr, A. and Feigenbaum, E. A., *The Handbook of Artificial Intelligence 2.* Los Altos, Kaufmann, 1982.

Bonissone, P. and Tong, R. M. "Editorial: Reasoning with Uncertainty in Expert Systems," *International Journal of Man-Machine Studies,* 1985, Vol. 30, 69-111.

Boy, G. A. *Intelligent Assistant Systems*, Academic Press, 1991.

Brajnik, G., Guida, G., and Tasso, C. "User Modeling in Expert Man-Machine Interfaces: A Case Study in Intelligent Information Retrieval," *IEEE Transactions on Systems, Man, and Cybernetics*, 1990, Vol. 20, No. 1, 166-185.

Bruce, B. C., Belief System and Language Understanding, *Report No. 2973*, Bolt, Beranek Newman (Ed.) Cambridge, MA, 1975.

Bryn, W. and D. Eichmann, "A Neural Network Approach to Tracking Eye Position," *International Journal of Human-Computer Interaction*, 1997, Vol. 9, No. 1, 59-79.

Buchanan, B. and Smith, R. G., Fundamentals of Expert Systems, *Ann. Rev., Computer Science*, 1988, Vol. 3, 23-58.

Card, S. K., Moran, T. P. and Newell, A., *The Psychology of Human-Computer Interaction,* Lawrence Erlbaum Associates, 1983.

Carpenter, G. A. and Grossberg, S., "A Massively Parallel Architecture for Self-Organizing Neural Pattern Recognition Machine," Computer *Vision, Graphics and Image Processing*, Vol. 37,1987, 54-115.

Carpenter, G. A. " Neural Network Models for Pattern Recognition and Associative Memory," Neural Networks, Vol. 2, 1989, 243-257.

Caudill, M. "Using Neural Nets: Fuzzy Cognitive Maps," *AI Expert*, 1990, 49-53.

Chen, Q. and A. F. Norcio, "Modeling a User's Domain Knowledge with Neural Networks", *International Journal of Human-Computer Interaction*, Vol. 9, 1997, No. 1, 25-40.

Chin, D. N., "Knome: Modeling What the User Knows in UC," *User Models in Dialogue Systems,* A. Kobsa and W. Wahlster (Ed), Springer-Verlag, Berlin, 1989.

Clowes, I., Cole, I., Arshad, F., Hopkins, C., and Hockley, A., "User Modeling Techniques for Interactive Systems," People *and Computers: Designing the Interface*, Ed. by Johnson P. and Cook, S., Cambridge University Press, 1985, 35-45.

Cohen, P. R. "On Knowing What to Say: Planning Speech Acts," Ph. D. Thesis, Computer Science Department, University of Toronto, 1978.

Daniel, P. J. "Cognitive Models in Information Retrieval - An Evaluative Review," *Journal of Documentation,* Vol. 42, No. 4, 1986, 272-304.

DARPA *Neural Network Study*, AFCEA International Press, 1988.

Dede, C. "A Review and Synthesis of Recent Research in Intelligent Computer-Assisted Instruction," International *Journal of Man-Machine Studie*s, Vol. 24, 1986, 329-353.

de Kleer, J. "An Assumption-Based TMS," *Artificial Intelligence*, Vol. 28 No. 2, 1989, 127-162.

Doyle, J. "A Truth Maintenance System," *AI,* Vol. 12, 1979, 231-272.

Eberts R. "Knowledge Acquisition Using Neural Networks for Intelligent Interface Design," *Proceedings of 1991 IEEE International Conference on Systems, Man, and Cybernetics*, 1331-1335.

Eberts, R. E. and Eberts, C. G. "Four Approaches to Human-Computer Interaction," Intelligent Interfaces: Theory, Research and Design, P. A. Hancock and M. H. Chignell (ed.), Elsevier Science, NY, 1989.

Eichmann, D. and Srinivas, K. "Neural Network-Based Retrieval from Software Reuse Repositories," *Neural Networks and Pattern Recognition in Human-Computer Interaction*, Beale, R. and Finlay, J. (Ed.), Ellis Horwood Publisher, 1992, 216-228.

Finin, T. W., "GUMS: A general user modeling shell," in *User Models in Dialogue Systems*, A. Kobsa and W. Wahlster (Ed.), Springer-Verlag, Berlin, 1989.

Finlay, J. and Beale, R. "Pattern Recognition and Classification in Dynamic and Static User Modeling," *Neural Networks and Pattern Recognition in Human-Computer Interaction.* R. Beal and J. Finlay (Eds.), Ellis Horwood Pub. 1992, 65-89.

Fu, L., "Integration of neural heuristics into knowledge-based inference," *Connection Science*, 1990, Vol. 1, No. 3.

Habibi, S. and Eberts, R. "Using Neural Networks to Route Messages," *Neural Networks and Pattern Recognition in Human-Computer Interaction*, Beale, R. and Finlay, J. (Ed.), Ellis Horwood Pub., 1992, 229-239.

Hayes-Roth, F, "Making Intelligent Systems Adaptive," in *Architecture for Intelligence*, K. Vanlehn (ed.), Lawrence Erbaum Associates, Hillsdale, NJ, pp. 301-321, 1991.

Heger, A. S. and Koen, B. V. "KNOWBOT: An Adaptive Data Base Interface," *Nuclear Science and Engineering*, Vol. 107, pp. 142-157, 1991.

Hillman, D. V., "Integrating Neural Networks and Expert Systems," *AI Expert*, June 1990, 54-59.

Huang, X., Mccalla, G. I., Greer, J. E. and Neufeld, E., "Revising deductive knowledge and stereotype knowledge in a student model," *User Modeling and User-Adapted Interaction,* 1991, Vol. 1, No. 1.

Hoeppner, W., Morik, K. and Marburgber, H., "Talking It Over: The Natural Language Dialog System HAM_ANS," *Cooperative Interfaces to Information Systems*, L. Bolc and M. Jarke (Ed.), Berlin, Springer-Verlag, 1986, 189-258.

Howard. S. and Murray, D., "A Taxonomy of Evaluation Techniques for HCI," *Proceedings of Human Computer Interaction (INTERACT'87)*, 1987, 453-459.

Kass, R. "Student Modeling in Intelligent Tutoring Systems: Implications for User Modeling," in *User Models in Dialogue Systems,* A. Kobsa and W. Wahlster, (Ed.), Springer-

Verlag, Berlin, 1989.

Kobsa, A. "Modeling the User's Conceptual Knowledge in BGP-MS, A User Modeling Shell System," *Computational Intelligence,* Vol. 6, No. 4, 1990.

Kramer, J., Noronha, S. and Vergo, J. "A User-Centered Design Approach to Personalization," *Communications of ACM,* Vol 43, No. 8, 2000.

Maren, A. J., "Neural Network for Enhanced Human-Computer Interaction," *IEEE Control Systems,* August, 1991

McCarthy, J., "Circumscription - A Form of Non-Monotonic Reasoning," *AI,* Vol. 13, 1980, pp. 27-39.

McDermott, D. and Doyle, J., "Non-monotonic Logic," *AI* Vol. 13, 1980, 41-72.

MaGrew, J., "Task Analysis, Neural Nets, and Very Rapid Prototyping," *Neural Networks and Pattern Recognition in Human-Computer Interaction,* Beale, R. and Finlay, J. (Ed.), Ellis Horwood Pub., 1992.

Minskey, M. L, "A Framework of Representing Knowledge," *The Psychology of Computer Vision,* P. H. Winston (ed.) NY: McGraw-Hill, 1975.

Murray, D., "A Survey of User Cognitive Modeling," *Report DITC 92/87,* National Physics Laboratory, Teddington, England, 1987.

Norcio, A. F. and Stanley, J., "Adaptive Human-computer Interfaces, A Literature Survey and Perspective," *IEEE Transactions on System, Man and Cybernetics,* Vol. 19, No. 2, 1989, 399-408.

Nwana, H. S., "User Modeling and User Adapted Interaction in an Intelligent Tutoring System," *User Modeling and User-Adapted Interaction,* Vol. 1, No. 1, 1991, 1-32.

Oakes, M.P. and Taylor, M. J. "Clustering of Thesaurus Terms Using Adaptive Resonance Theory, Fuzzy Cognitive Maps and Approximate String-Matching Techniques," *Neural Networks and Pattern Recognition in Human-Computer Interaction,* Beale, R. and Finlay, J. (Ed.), Ellis Horwood Pub.1992, 243-263.

Pao, Y., *Adaptive Pattern Recognition and Neural Networks,* Addision-Wesley Publishing Co., 1989.

Paris, C. L. "The Use of Explicit User Models in a Generation System for Tailoring Answers to the User's Level of Expertise," in *User Models in Dialogue Systems,* A. Kobsa and W. Wahlster, (Ed.), Springer-Verlag, Berlin, 1989, 200-232.

Reiter, R. "A Logic for Default Reasoning," *Artificial Intelligence,* Vol. 13, 1980, 81-132.

Rich, E., "User Modeling via Stereotypes," *Cognitive Sciences,* Vol. 3, 1979, 329-354.

Schank, R. *Scripts, Plans, Goals and Understanding.* Hillsdale, NJ: Lawrence Erlbaum, 1977.

Sejnowski, T. J. and Rosenberg, C. R. "Parallel Networks that Learn to Pronounce English Text," *Complex Systems,* Vol. 1, 1987, 145-168.

Self, J. A., "Student Models in Computer-Aided Instruction," *International Journal of Man-Machine Studies,* Vol. 6, 1974, 261-276.

Selker, T. "Coach: A Teaching Agent that Learns," *Communication of ACM,* Vol. 37, No.7, 1994, 92- 99.

Simon, T. "Analyzing the Scope of Cognitive Models in Human-Computer Interaction: A Trade-Off Approaches," *People and Computer IV,* D. M. Jones and R. Winder Ed., Cambridge Univ. Press 1988, 79-93.

Stacey, D. Calvert, D. and Carey T., "Artificial Neural Networks for Analyzing User Interactions," *Neural Networks and Pattern Recognition in Human-Computer Interaction,* Beale, R. and Finlay, J. (Ed.), Ellis Horwood Pub., 1992.

Wahlster, W. and Kobsa, A. "User Models in Dialogue Systems," in *User Models in Dialogue Systems,* A. Kobsa and W. Wahlster, (Ed.) , Springer-Verlag, Berlin, 1989.

Wenger, E. *Artificial Intelligence and Tutoring Systems*, Morgan Kaufmann Publishers, Los Altos, CA. 1987.

Zadeh, L. A. "Knowledge Representation in Fuzzy Logic," *IEEE Transactions on Knowledge and Data Engineering,* Vol. 1, No. 1, 1989, 89-100.

Chapter IX

Application of a Cognitive Model of Collaboration to a User Interface

John Sillince, Royal Holloway, University of London, UK
Duska Rosenberg, University of Zagreb, Croatia

INTRODUCTION

The problem considered in this chapter is how does an individual keep in touch with what everybody else is doing, in order to proactively participate, while ensuring they do not spend too much time on passively watching and listening? The chapter aims to consider several means of supporting the grounding process in computer mediated communication. These are the enabling factors of the user to browse the transcript of the interaction so far, evaluation of the interaction's effectiveness, keeping track of the state of the conversation, and tracking and summarizing the way that the shared artifact has been acted upon during the interaction.

BACKGROUND

It is not possible for all team members to know everything about what everyone is doing. Although current collaborative learning systems attempt to maximize shared information, this may not be the most appropriate way of achieving "meaningful learning" (Wan and Johnson, 1994). Therefore, keeping in touch requires knowledge of a basic stock of common information, or common ground. Common ground, involving folk wisdom, common assumptions, and mutual cultural beliefs and values is an important element in coordinating interaction between individuals.

One potential coordination problem is the user's inability to observe a synchronous electronic interaction in a way which enables the user to decide when and whether to join in. This involves a need for a means of gradual engagement and disengagement from the interaction, a set of alternative entry and exit points from the interaction and a means of enabling the user to "browse" the content of the interaction so far. Computer-mediated communication differs from face to face conversation because while for some individuals interaction may be continuous and synchronous, for others involvement is spasmodic and asynchronous and largely consists of deliberating over recorded interactions of the group. Much CSCW design, however, is based on an assumption of continuous involvement which may be largely misplaced.

In electronic interactions the coordination task is accomplished by means of periodic monitoring rather than by continuous discourse (Rosenberg and Hutchinson, 1994). Coworkers communicate across the gulf between these two modalities of periodic and continuous information (Devlin and Rosenberg, 1993; Hutchinson and Rosenberg, 1993). At present, no electronic schema can adequately evaluate the effectiveness of this communication activity in a way which picks up the gaps and quiet patches and considers the overall coherence of the developing interaction (Devlin and Rosenberg, 1996). However, it is possible to evaluate communication in terms of its coherence from an argumentation viewpoint (Sillince, 1999; 1995). Current CSCW models of collaboration tend to assume that coordination is effected by means of continuous interaction; whereas, often remote coworkers go quietly or attend to other foci (Rosenberg and Hutchinson, 1993).

COORDINATION IN COMPUTER-MEDIATED COLLABORATION

When coordination fails, and a listener misunderstands what the speaker is saying, then repair activity is necessary. However, common ground has been argued to be a concept of wider application than merely conversation, and that it is fundamental to all coordination activities (Clark and Brennan, 1991) and to collaboration (Flor, 1998). An addressee must deliver appropriate and timely feedback if restarts and conversational breakdowns are to be avoided. Indeed, Clark and Brennan (1991) have argued that, instead of the principle of individual least effort (Grice, 1975) conversation should be studied in terms of the principle of the least collaborative effort because so much of conversation is aimed at achieving shared understanding. These concepts are important for designers of collaborative tools because if common ground is fundamental to collaboration, it is necessary to discover what are the representations which should be used in designing better support technologies.

There are various representations for interaction which have been viewed as necessary to successful coordination within the collaborative technology literature. Two of these are as follows:

1. *Representations for situated cognition.* A large amount of an individual's cognition is occupied with current, contextualized aspects of their work such as current tasks and current objects (Clancey, 1997). Indeed, some have argued that there is no cognitive core which exists independent of content and context (Resnick, 1991). Situated cognition depends upon knowledge of organizational identity and norms and on heuristics (what works in particular situations), which depends upon physical and social awareness. Awareness of what coworkers are doing and seeing has been argued to be useful in order to prevent misunderstandings. Awareness and a sense of co-presence are affected by the types of media used such as large and good quality video pictures.

2. *Representations for generalization and reflection.* Such representations include meta-knowledge (Wan and Johnson, 1994), or conceptual frameworks which enable sensemaking of sets of ideas and the analysis of relationships between them and therefore, which lead to reflection on experience (Schon, 1983) and the construction of new meanings (Ausubel, 1963; Ausubel *et al.*, 1978). It has been suggested that they offer a potential answer to problems of 'information overload' and 'lost-in-hyperspace' which afflict collaborative systems such as virtual classrooms (Hiltz, 1988) and hypermedia (Yankelovish et al., 1988; Halasz *et al.,* 1987).

THE SETTING

The setting in which data was collected was a construction project studied during the 'Collaborative Integrated Communications for Construction' (CICC), (ACTS No. 017) project on the development and use of interactive technology in the workplace. The research is user-driven and interdisciplinary. It is motivated by the needs of people working in construction and manufacturing industries, where poor communication causes serious problems in day to day activities and requires cooperation and coordination. Interactive multimedia technology is hoped to improve communications and to offer a richer information environment for the repair of breakdowns and misunderstandings. Such a facility is particularly useful in project teams where a stable organizational form is absent. For example, in construction, the tendering process is competitive, yet is followed by a period during which cooperation is vital. Problems of lack of shared culture have to be addressed and this is usually done with a series of induction meetings and seminars at the start of the project. This is a vital yet time-consuming team building stage of the project and is undermined by teams joining projects at later stages with consequent integration problems (Rosenberg *et al.*, 1997).

The project sought to observe and record computer-mediated interactions between the professionals who were playing different roles in the construction process. Project teams for architectural and engineering design for construction are characterized by working under high levels of uncertainty to tight time pressures deploying a wide variety of high grade professional skills (Winch *et al.*, 1997).

COGNITIVE MODEL OF COLLABORATION

We distinguish two areas of activity, process and content (Clark and Brennan, 1991; Grosz and Sidner, 1986; Clark and Schaefer, 1989). The process or task activity is the process by which a team working is carried out between the team's members, by means of communication. The content, centered around the design or media object, is the topic of the interactions and the focus of the work. Process comprises actions on tasks (e.g. finding new tasks, justifying them and checking they have been done), responsibilities, abilities, and

Figure 1. Transcript 1.

Transcript	Actions on tasks	Actions on design objects
\<break in conversation as people continue about their business in the room\> KC: 'Hullo?' AC: 'Hi KC..'	Suspect inattention to task	
\<break for 20 seconds\> KC: 'Hullo?' AC: 'Hi KC..' KC:'...can you hear me?' AC: 'Yes I can'.	Misunderstanding due to ambiguity of what silence means Suspect poor reception Reassurance of good reception	

negotiated authority. Content comprises actions on design or media objects (e.g. showing a file or drawing), the design or media objects themselves, and organizational authority. Examples of the transcripts and the identification of actions on tasks and actions on objects are shown in Figures 1 to 8.

Figure 2. Transcript 2.

Transcript	Actions on tasks	Actions on design objects
\<at this point KF leaps out of her chair and shoots across the room, whilst KC is engaged in a quite detailed discussion. KC continues – not realizing what she's done. Then DS goes too. KC realises that he's not getting any verbal feed back\>		
KC: 'do you have any drawings for building B, alt. 1? \<waits but no answer\> ..any.. \<he murmurs quietly\>	Task suggestion Suspect inattention to task	Request other to show object
AC: \<pause, leans towards speakerphone\> 'Kate is looking for them right now'.	Reassurance of good reception	Promise other to show object
KC: 'OK'	Check task done	Acknowledge other's promise to show object

Figure 3. Transcript 3.

Transcript	Actions on tasks	Actions on design objects
\<problem is discussed. KC goes silent – to think about this – the team present – AC, KF and DS then talk amongst themselves. At one point, they check whether KC is still (virtually) present\>		
KF: Is KC still with us? \<KF is standing near the computer or microphone\>	Suspected inattention to task	Use object
AC: \<appears to interpret this as a request – because KC may not be able to hear this\> 'are you still there KC?'	Assume suspicion not communicated	
KC: 'I'm trying to figure out what I did'.	Justify inattention	Use object

Figure 4. Transcript 4.

Transcript	Actions on tasks	Actions on design objects
KF: 'There's a PowerPoint file on our group directory called..' \<breaks off and	Justify task suggestion	Inform other about object
looks at the computer> '..can you type it in the chat' \<i.e. the 'chat' window> '.. the name of the file, KC?'	Task suggestion	Request other to show object
KC: \<reads filename out>	Misunderstand task	Show object
DS: \<shouts across the room> 'Yeah, can you type it in...in chat...can you ask him to type it in?'		Request other to show object
KF: \<looks at screen> 'Dave wants you to type it in.. can you have,...' \<murmur from KC> '..chat yeah!'	Task suggestion	Request other to show object
\<name of file appears in chat window> \<pause> \<KF stands up> 'This is crazy'	Task acceptance (proxy)	Acknowledge other's showing of object

PROCESS

1) *Tasks*. Examples of tasks include discussing Building B (Transcript 2), typing a filename into the chat window (Transcript 3), or opening an e-mail (Transcript 4).

2) *Actions on tasks*. Actions on tasks include the *core process of the task* (in the Transcripts these actions are requesting or finding a new task, justifying a task, suggesting a task, accepting a task, and checking the task has been done) as well as *peripheral tasks* (examples in the Transcripts of these actions are solving problems, clarifying misunderstandings, and shifting focus). Being able to shift from core (tight coordination) to peripheral (loose coordination) tasks is an indicator of smoothness of coordination from one task context to another (Ishii *et al.*, 1994; Ishii and Kobayashi, 1992; Ishii *et al.*, 1992). Actions on tasks are associated with particular speech acts (see Figure 9).

3) *Individuals*. Individuals have three key characteristics:

   a) *Responsibilities*. Examples of responsibilities are sharing a drawing in Transcript 2, sharing a filename in Transcript 4 and reporting on work done in Transcript 5). Because a large part of conversations is taken up by pairwise interactions (pairs of interactants taking the floor and their exchange lasting several turns – Parker, 1988), an important aspect of responsibilities is the actions of giving and taking ("push" and "pull" in Flor, 1998). Responsibilities are situation-specific – they indicate when in the interaction particular coworkers need to be alerted that must participate, and when they need to be provided with summarization and tracking information.

   b) *Abilities*. Abilities comprise both knowledge such as Kate finding the drawings in Transcript 2 and awareness such as AC able to hear KC in Transcript 1.

Figure 5. Transcript 5.

Transcript	Actions on tasks	Actions on design objects
KC: 'I sent you an e-mail just now Kate' KF: 'OK'	Justify task suggestion	Inform other about object
KC: 'If you can open my email..'	Task suggestion	Request other to use object
RF: \<turns to Kate> 'you open it then'		Request other to use object
KF: \<to KC> 'Yeah, let me open your e-mail' [cut]	Task acceptance	Promise other to use object
\<KF goes over to a Sun machine to open an elm/e-mail session>		Use object
RF: 'So do you want to show me KC, er, what you've been working on, this week?'	Task suggestion	Request other to show object
KC: 'Actually, it's not on our Web page yet' [cut]	Problem suggestion	Inform other about object
\<they then need to find out the location of this file on the UNIX based group space>	Problem acceptance	Use object
AC: 'So what is the name of your file, KC?' [cut]	Transform problem into subtask	Request other to inform about object
KC: 'Look in the email directory' \<Kate tries to find the e-mail in the elm session she is now running>	Subtask definition	Request other to use object
KF: 'I'm looking..\<she finds the e-mail with the filename in it>..Oh, yes! \<quietly> ' It's a very long name' \<then louder, to KC> 'OK'	Subtask acceptance	Promise other to use object Use object Inform other about object
[cut]	Check subtask done	Inform other of use of object
KF: \<reads out the filename to AC who types it in to the NetMeeting – networked PC, which they try to use to share the file with KC>	Task acceptance	Show object Show object

Figure 6. Transcript 6.

Transcript	Actions on tasks	Actions on design objects
KF: 'OK, what else do we want to talk about? What was on our agenda? Didn't I have some things I wanted to talk about?'	Request/find new task	Use object
AC: 'Yeah, shall I go look on my e-mail?'	Task suggestion	Offer to use object
KF: 'Why don't you do that...'	Task acceptance	Accept other's offer to use object
<AC goes over to another computer to look at KF's e-mail to him with the agenda on it. Over the course of the meeting, AC then keeps track of the questions that KF wanted to ask, looking at what they've already discussed and making sure that they covered all topics that they needed to>		Use object
	Check task done	

Figure 7. Transcript 7.

Transcript	Actions on tasks	Actions on design objects
<KF discusses RF's design requirements; as she does so, AC flicks through his project file. Looking for things to aid her with>	Request/find new task	Use object
KF: 'Do you have this list?' <the question is directed to AC>	Task suggestion	Request other to show object
AC: 'Yeah, here' <he takes a piece of paper and passes it to KF>	Task acceptance	Show object
KF: 'All right' <she takes the paper, passes it to GL, pointing to a sentence on it, and murmurs quietly to him. GL examines the paper. KF then shows him information on the Web space relating to the requirements on the sheet of paper, using the mouse to point out features, then at times, using her hands, pointing to the screen>	Check task done Request/find new task Task suggestion	Acknowledge other's showing of object Show object Use object Show object

Figure 8. Transcript 8.

Transcript	Actions on tasks	Actions on design objects
KC: 'Um, the filename is very long, so I suggest that you open my email? I sent my filename in my e-mail' Inform other about object	Justify task suggestion Task suggestion	Inform other about object Request other to use object Justify task suggestion
RF: 'Yes, Kate is looking at it now. <Kate has returned to the second computer, and has an elm/emacs window open on the Sun machine> <pause for 20 seconds>	Task acceptance	Inform other about using object Use object
KF: 'Um, KC do you send your Request other to inform e-mails to, er, AEC98?' <the team's group email account>		Check task done
KC: 'Our team number?'		Request other to inform about object
KF: 'Uh huh. Do you send your e-mails to the, er, hypermail archive? <mail only archived on hypermail if it is sent to AEC98>		Request other to inform about object
KC: 'I just sent my familiar email, so I didn't <unclear>		Inform other about object
KF: 'Oh, you just replied? Okay, um..'	Task not done	Request other to inform about object
KC: 'Look in your e-mail object directory'.	Task suggestion	Request other to use object Inform other about using
KF: 'I'm looking..oh, yes! , quietly to AC and RF> 'there it is' <then louder, to KC> 'It's very, a long name. OK'.	Task acceptance Check task done (proxy)	object Inform other about object Inform other about object
KC: 'Long name'.	Check task done	Inform other about object
KF: 'Yeah, uh huh'.		
RF: 'And, is it in your web's work space?'	Check task done	Request other to inform about object
KF: 'It's in our group space'.		Inform other about object

c) *Negotiated authority.* Negotiated authority is the weight given to each coworker at a particular point in the dialogue and determines who can at any moment direct the conversation. It varies quickly and is negotiated during talk, depending on who takes the initiative and who has relevant knowledge. The coworker who has initiated a sequence of actions (such as KC requesting a drawing in Transcript 2) has negotiated authority, no matter how lowly his/her position in the organization. The coworker who misunderstands something shows the lack important knowl-

Figure 9. Actions on tasks and speech acts.

Action on task	Speech act
Task suggestion	Directives: request ('do you have any..'), suggestion ('I suggest that you..'), command ('Look in..')
Suspect inattention to task	No answer or directives: question ('Is KC still with us?')
Suspect poor reception	Directives: question ('..can you hear me?')
Reassurance of good reception	Representatives: assertion ('Yes, I can')
Check task done	Declaratives: ('OK', 'All right', 'Oh, yes!')
Justify inattention	Representatives: assertion ('I'm trying to..')
Justify task suggestion	Representatives: assertion ('There's a PowerPoint file..', 'I sent my filename')
Task acceptance	Representatives: positive assertion ('Yeah, here', ' Yes, Kate is looking..')
Problem suggestion	Representatives: negative assertion ('it's not on our website')
Transform problem to subtask	Directives: request name ('what is the name?')
Define subtask	Directives: command ('Look in..')
Request/find new task	Directives: question ('What do we want..?')

edge and, therefore, cedes negotiated authority to the coworker who assumes the responsibility for repairing the misunderstanding, (as DS does when KS misunderstands in Transcript 4).

CONTENT

1. Design or media objects. Objects are design objects (written or graphical representations of what the team are building) or media objects (means through which such objects are communicated). Although objects and media can be distinguished in some cases (a list is an object and video is a medium), they are sometimes overlapping (e-mails are both objects as well as media). Other examples taken from the transcripts include: Chatroom, elm/e-mail, phone, video, Unix groupspace, Web page, hypermail archive, Web workspace, list, file, e-mail message, design requirements, piece of paper, drawing, and agenda.
2. Actions on design or media objects. Examples include requesting a file, showing a drawing, pointing to a list or using the phone.
3. Organizational authority. For example, in Transcript 4 RF's request to KC ("show me what you've been working on this week") is justified by RF's high organizational position.

Although the sequence of actions on tasks revealed by the Transcripts is not completely predictable, there are some sequences of actions on tasks which occur frequently (for example, they occur frequently in Transcripts 1 to 8). They, therefore, form a grammar (see Figure 11). The grammar gives a central role to representations for attention, understanding and agreement (Daly-Jones *et al.,* 1998: 25): *attention* (suspecting inattention, justifying inattention), *understanding* (misunderstanding the task, misunderstanding due to ambiguity or delay, recognising the misunderstanding) and *agreement* (accepting the task, accepting

Figure 11. Grammar of actions on tasks. Thin lines identify actions requiring sharing with at least one other coworker. Thick lines identify actions requiring sharing with all coworkers.

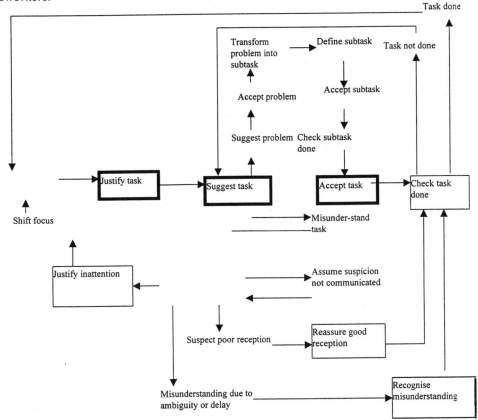

the problem, accepting the subtask).

Similarly, actions on design and media objects form a grammar (see Figure 12).

The primary purpose of these grammars is to enable coworkers to share these workflow and conversational flow expectancies, in order to provide *shared feedback* (Dourish and Bellotti, 1992), but also to make this conditional on the declared need for it. This has two implications.

1. *Reciprocity.* Firstly, the coworker to whom an adjacency pair opener (e.g. promise, request, question) has been uttered should be the coworker with whom any response (thanks, acceptance, answer) must be shared. For example, if one coworker currently suspects poor reception (Figure 11), then it is important that that coworker should be reassured. And if one coworker promises another that they are going to use an object (Figure 12), then the knowledge that they are now currently using that object should be shared with them. An example is in Transcript 5 where KF says "It's a very long name" to RF and AC to explain why KC wanted to look in the email directory.

2. *Need to share.* Some actions require confirmation or even discussion, whereas others do not. Indeed, the degree to which actions must be shared can vary from no need to share (e.g. "suggest problem" in Figure 11, "use object" in Figure 12), to a need for feedback from at least one other coworker (e.g. "misunderstand task" in Figure 11,

Figure 12. Grammar of actions on objects. Thin lines identify actions requiring sharing with at least one other coworker. Thick lines identify actions requiring sharing with all coworkers.

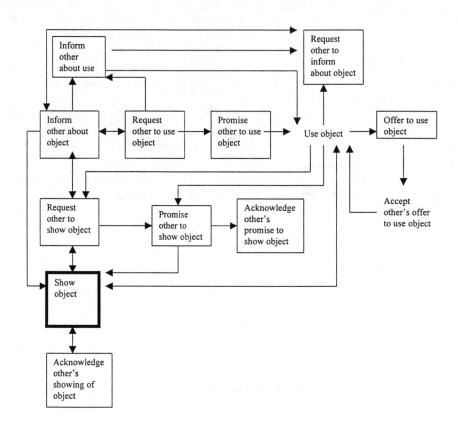

"promise other to show object" in Figure 12), to a need for all coworkers to share the action (e.g. "request or find new task" in Figure 11, "show object" in Figure 12). An example of information that everybody needed at that moment is in Transcript 5 where KC says "Actually, it's not on our Web page yet".

APPLICATION OF COGNITIVE MODEL TO USER INTERFACE

The cognitive model can be applied to a user interface as a means of enabling the recording and representation of the interactional activities of the user. This information would be collected when the user chose particular options within the interface. For example, if the collaborative tool user chooses the "Request new task" screen in which to type a message, the next screen becomes "Justify task" unless the user chooses (more effortfully) otherwise. The user's pattern of choices (sequential, frequency) is recorded and available for later evaluation. Some uses of this representation are outlined on the following pages.

GRADUAL ENGAGEMENT AND DISENGAGEMENT FROM THE INTERACTION

In order to minimize the amount of time spent in synchronous electronic interactions between colleagues working closely together (such as R&D teams, design teams, and project teams), mechanisms are needed which provide points of entry for members who wish to float in and out without disrupting the proceedings by demanding summarisation or by bringing in inappropriately new topics. The action grammars in Figures 11 and 12 distinguish between core and peripheral actions, and therefore enable the signaling of high (core) and low (peripheral) priority for joining.

Managers spend a large proportion of their working day in meetings, the majority of these unscheduled (Mintzberg, 1973, 1975; Kotter, 1982). These unscheduled meetings enable rapid exchange of views and information which is targeted to narrowly defined and topical decisions the manager needs to make. Face to face engagement and disengagement is very sensitive to judging how necessary is the interruption, and there is a wide variety of politeness behaviors which people use for disengagement. Electronic interactions, however, do not provide the same facilities for engagement and disengagement. In order to engage someone in a conversation one needs to know how important their current activity or list of activities is. So, if someone has been passively listening to an interaction, or if they have been 'inattentive', or if an individual has been interrupted frequently without taking avoiding action, these patterns could be signaled to someone who wishes to interrupt his work.

Figure 13. Relationships between process (tasks) and content (objects)

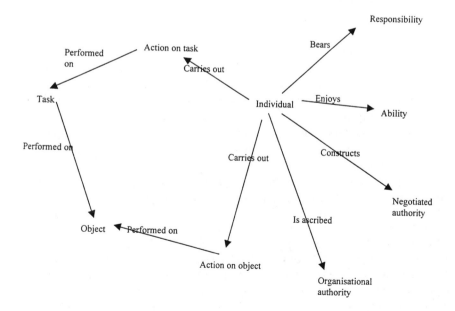

Process and content are relevant to disengagement in the sense of providing warrants justifying an individual's preoccupation elsewhere: for example, an individual with responsibility for action on a current and urgent task could be provided by the interface with protective mechanisms for disengagement. These mechanisms need to be made explicit (Flor, 1998: 220). This and other such excuses are suggested by Figure 13.

A MEANS OF ENABLING THE USER TO "BROWSE" THE INTERACTION SO FAR

Many individuals may wish to be passive interactants. However, overhearers do not understand as much of a conversation as do the conversants (Schober and Clark, 1989). Passivity, overhearing, and browsing all require accessible summarization. We have suggested that the principal means of summarizing the interaction could be provided by the two grammars of Figures 11 and 12. In Figure 11, the core tasks are requesting or finding a new task, justifying, suggesting, accepting a task and checking it has been done. These can provide the top level information about the state of the conversation so far as regards process. With regard to the content part of the conversation, Figure 12 suggests that core actions are showing, using and informing about design and media objects.

EVALUATION OF THE EFFECTIVENESS OF ELECTRONIC INTERACTIONS

Evaluation is difficult even in traditional face to face settings, largely because it is difficult to set up and construct believable performance metrics for naturalistic groups, which have histories and realistic tasks. The conventional approach to evaluation of interactions is measurement of outcomes (Mott, 1972) or decisions (Vroom and Jago, 1988). This ignores the process of decision making, which may or may not be important in the quality of the final result (Watts *et al.*, 1996; Daly-Jones *et al.*, 1998).

An alternative is to evaluate communication process rather than task outcome. Several ways of evaluating communicative process are possible, each with its own implications for the cognitive model introduced above.

1. It has been argued that in highly volatile business environments the key to high performance is breaking down hierarchical and functional constraints on interaction (Lawler, 1992). This suggests the *equality of interaction* as a useful indicator of interactional effectiveness so that all participants feel involved and in control (Silver *et al.*, 1994; Carletta *et al.*, 1998). The cognitive model we have suggested provides a finer grain for assessing this – for example, coworkers may vary on equality of participation between process and content ('managers' might tend to concentrate on process, delegating content to subordinates).

2. Also, reflexivity, or the amount that a group spends talking about its goals and the processes by which it reaches a decision, is thought to be linked to team effectiveness (West, 1996). Reflexivity (a) provides an opportunity for groups to coordinate their goals, and (b) directs groups to revisit opportunities for missed contributions. This suggests a measure of the *opportunity for reflection* by enabling easy switching between synchronous and asynchronous or between new and old ideas (Ausubel, 1963; Ausubel et al., 1978; Baker and Lund, 1997). The objective of the cognitive model introduced above is to facilitate this switching behavior.

3. Alternatively, Daly-Jones *et al.,* (1998) used *conversational fluency* and *interper-*

sonal awareness. These are not addressed by our cognitive model. Rather, they are aspects of face to face communication that may be less appropriate when considering computer-mediated communication. For example, some have argued that metaphors from face to face environments should not be the only ones used for designing computer-mediated communication (Terveen, 1993).

4. Another possible measure is the degree of coordination achieved – for example by *counting misunderstandings* and *time taken on repairs* (Garrod and Anderson, 1987), or the *existence of linguistic conventions* (Garrod and Doherty, 1994). However, there is little evidence of any association between linguistic coordination and team effectiveness (Smith *et al.,* 1994).

5. Another measure (on which computer-mediated communication compares favorably with face to face meetings) is the degree to which discussion is *task-focussed* rather than having social significance (Sillince, 1996). The action grammar in Figure 11 provides a very fine grained measure of task focus.

6. Managing coherence and argumentative orientation at the same time is something which causes many people difficulty (Andriessen *et al.*, 1996). This suggests that another measure is the overall *coherence* of the discourse (Grimes, 1984; Halliday, and Hasan, 1976; Mann and Thompson, 1988; Penman, 1987; Sanders *et al.*, 1992; Tyler, 1994) in terms of a set of *connected propositions* and one central macro-proposition (van Dijk 1997; Sillince, 1999) or a set of non-propositional concepts or images (van Dijk, 1997). An alternative approach to coherence within computer-mediated interaction would be to consider the proportion of interactions conforming to the grammars in Figures 11 and 12.

7. Another approach is analysis of collaborative interaction in terms of separable constructs – dialectical (rational criticism), rhetorical (cognitive effect on partici-pants), epistemological (the nature of the knowledge involved), conceptual (the form of the cognitive representations) and interactive (the mutual refinement of meaning and knowledge) (Baker, 1998). Although all of these are relevant, we shall merely consider the dialectical level here. The dialectical level suggests the need for information about how much of the interaction is bound up with negotiating. The grammar enables analysis of such negotiations. For example, requesting the other to use an object will lead to a promise by the coworker to use an object, unless this is contested, in which case an informing action is done - see Figure 12.

8. Argumentation coding of transcripts (e.g. Canary *et al.,* 1987) provides a series of elements and sequences which may indicate that something is wrong. For example, studies of the Challenger and Watergate disasters which used such coding schemes have shown that committee members failed to *question or challenge unwarranted assumptions* and *poor conclusions* (Gouran *et al.*, 1986), did not base decisions upon *factual evidence* (Hirokawa and Pace, 1983) and *overlooked facts for opinions* (Hirokawa, 1984). This suggests the need for information about how much of interactions is contested (see the point above). But it also suggests the need to distinguish between misunderstanding and contesting. Both of these lead to regress within the grammar flow diagrams of Figures 11 and 12, but they are very different from an evaluative point of view.

The actions on tasks introduced above reveal useful information here. The following are some examples of useful data from the grammar of actions on tasks: frequency of 'misunderstandings' (poor communication), mean time to repair 'misunderstandings' (effect on slowing down interactions), ratio of 'suggested' to 'accepted' tasks, frequency of 'problems' (effect of slowing down task completion), a high proportion of actions predicted by the grammar (an indicator of high task analysability), frequency of 'new tasks' (innovativeness), and frequency of 'focus shifts' (Sillince, 1995) (above a certain level this may be a possible indicator of ineffectiveness of electronic interactions). Evaluation could be more finely tuned to seek correlations between particular significant events and media choice. Such as: suspect poor reception' and audio only, or 'misunderstand task' and interface design issues or 'misunderstand task' and the user's recorded sequence of media choices (Whittaker, 1995). Or, evaluation could use correlations between particular signifi-cant events and media-oriented actions such as time spent looking towards the video monitor (Watts and Monk, 1996). The following are some examples of useful data from the grammar of actions on tasks: proportion of promises honored (relevant to commitment and trust), proportion of offers accepted (an indicator of whether coworkers understand each other), and the ratio of 'showing' to 'using' (a low ratio indicates low interactivity).

KEEPING TRACK OF THE STATE OF THE CONVERSATION

The representation enables the provision of information about:

1. The current state of the interaction, such as where one is in the core task chain (find new task, justify, suggest, accept, check task).
2. The current state of design objects, in terms of which objects are shared or not shared, and which objects have been used.
3. What design objects are currently being shown to whom, by whose organisational authority.
4. What was last done to objects, for what task, and whether the task is done or still waiting to be done.
5. What kinds of tasks currently require what kinds of negotiated and organizational authority – i.e. what is the power pattern surrounding the current task focus of the group.

However, these items unfortunately produce a list of uninterpreted data instead of an informative summary of the latest position. What would be more useful would be the enduring rather than the temporary outcomes of past interactions. For example, in Transcript 5 the whole of the interaction yields one important outcome – the name of a file (sent in an e-mail to KC).

DEIXIS – THE WAY THAT THE SHARED ARTIFACT HAS BEEN ACTED UPON DURING THE INTERACTION

Of course, the sequences described in the grammar of actions on objects Figure 12 do not apply uniformly to the same object, but to a collection of objects or object parts. The way that the shared artifact has been 1) talked about, made references to, pointed to, and 2) transformed by the talk, must somehow be distinguished.

1) *Pointing*. This is most directly possible by means of visual association of state (the grammar) with the visual image on screen (the representation of the artifact). So for example, "promise other to show object" might be associated with the in-valve, whereas "show object" might be associated with the out-valve, so that immediate identification of misunderstanding becomes possible. For example, in Transcript 6 the e-mail containing the agenda was used to check the task was done – AC pointed to each agenda item.

2) *Transforming*. Transformation of images requires different representation. For example, a collaborative support tool such as CLARE (Wan and Johnson, 1994) would be able to associate artifact parts with different node primitives such as Question or Suggestion. The Question of "Why are the two artifacts different – in and out valve?" is transformed into a Suggestion "Suspect inattention to task".

CONCLUSION

Users of computer-mediated communication systems have the problem of not wanting to participate fully in ongoing interaction, but needing to be up-to-date on team decisions and aware of current thinking. In particular, the latest position on team thinking is of the highest importance – one possible reason why formal reports are accorded less value by managers than corridor discussions.

The cognitive model suggested here provides a number of practical advantages for handling this tradeoff. In terms of points of entry to and exit from the group's interaction, the grammar in Figures 11 and 12 provides a method of prioritising when to join or leave the interaction. The current action history signals interruptibility (for engagement), and authority signals authorization to disengage. Each of the measures of evaluation of interaction effectiveness can be approached and enriched using the cognitive model. The cognitive model also provides a structure for keeping track of actions which both points to artifacts and which transform them. The grammars also provide a summary of interactions and hence make the group's discussion more accessible for browsing.

REFERENCES

Andriessen, J.E.B., de Smedt K., and Zock M. 1996. 'Discourse planning, experimental and modelling approaches', 247-278 in Dijkstra A., and de Smedt (eds) *Computational psycholinguistics: symbolic and network models of language processing,* Taylor and Francis, London.

Ausubel, D. P. 1963. *The psychology of meaningful verbal learning*, Grune & Stratton, New York.

Ausubel, D.P. Novak J., and Hansesian H. 1978. *Educational psychology: a cognitive view*, Rhinehart & Winston, New York.

Baker, M., and Lund K. 1997. 'Promoting reflective interactions in a CSCL environment', *Journal of Computer Assisted Learning*, 13, 175-193.

Baker, M. 1998. 'Argumentation and constructive interaction', in Andriessen J. & Coirer P., (eds), *Foundations of argumentative text processing*, University of Amsterdam Press, Amsterdam.

Canary, D.J., Brossman B.G., and Seibold D.R. 1987. 'Argument structures in decision-making groups', *Southern Speech Communication Journal*, 53, 18-37.

Carletta, J., Garrod S., and Fraser-Krauss H. 1998. 'Communication and placement of authority in workplace settings – the consequences for innovation', *Small Group Research,* 29, 531-559.

Clancey, W.J. 1997. *Situated cognition: on human knowledge and computer representations,* Cambridge University Press, Cambridge.

Clark, H., and Brennan S. 1991. 'Grounding in communication', 127-149 in Resnick L.B., Levine J.M., and Teasley S.D., (eds) *Perspectives on socially shared cognition*, American Psychological Association.

Clark, H., and Schaefer E. 1989. 'Contributing to discourse', *Cognitive Science,* 13, 259-292.

Daly-Jones, O., Monk A., and Watts L. 1998. 'Some advantages of video conferencing over high-quality audio conferencing: fluency and awareness of attentional focus', *International Journal of Human-Computer Studies*, 49, 21-58.

Devlin, K & Rosenberg, D. (1993), Situation theory and Cooperative Action, in Aczel P, Israel D, Katagiri Y & Peters S (eds) *Situation theory and Its Applications* vol 3, CSLI Lecture Notes, Stanford University, 215-266.

Devlin, K & Rosenberg, D. (1996), *Language at work: analyzing communication breakdown in the workplace to inform systems design.* CSLI Lecture Notes, 66. CSLI Publications.

Dourish P., and Bellotti V. 1992. 'Awareness and coordination in shared workspaces', *Proceedings of CSCW'92,* ACM, New York.

Dijk, T.A. van, 1977. *Text and context: explorations in the semantics and paragmatics of discourse,* Longman, London.

Garrod, S.C., and Anderson, A. 1987. 'Saying what you mean in dialogue: a study in conceptual and semantic co-ordination', *Cognition,* 27, 181-218.

Garrod S.C., and Doherty, G.M. 1994. 'Conversation, co-ordination and convention: an empirical investigation of how groups establish linguistic conventions', *Cognition,* 53, 181-215.

Gouran, D.S., Hirokawa, R.Y., & Martz, A.E. 1986. 'A critical analysis of factors related to decisional processes involved in the Challenger disaster', *Central States Speech Journal,* 37 (1), 119-135.

Grice, H.P. 1975. Logic and conversation, 225-242 in Cole P., and Morgan J.L., (eds) *Syntax and semantics Vol 3,* Seminar Press, New York.

Grimes, J.E. 1984. *The thread of discourse,* Mouton, Berlin.

Grosz B., and Sidner C., 1986, 'Attentions, intentions and the structure of discourse', *Computational Linguistics,* 12, 175-204.

Halasz, F.G., Moran, T.P., and Trigg, R.H. 1987. 'Notecards in a nutshell', 45-52 in *Proceedings of the ACM CHI + GI'87 Conference on Human Factors in Computing Systems and Graphics Interface.*

Halliday, M.A.K., and Hasan, R. 1976. *Cohesion in English,* Longman, London.

Hiltz, S. 1988. 'Collaborative learning in a virtual classroom: highlights of findings', 282-290 in *Proceedings of ACM 1988 Conference on Computer Supported Cooperative Work.*

Hirakawa, R.Y., & Pace R.C. 1983. 'A descriptive investigation of the possible communication-based reasons for effective and ineffective group decision-making', *Communication Monographs,* 50, 363-379.

Hirakawa, R.Y. 1984. *Why 'informed' groups fail to make high-quality decisions: an investigation of possible interaction-based explanations,* Paper presented at the meeting of the Speech Communication Association, Chicago.

Hutchinson, C. & Rosenberg, D. (1993) 'Cooperation and Conflict in Knowledge-Intensive Computer Supported Cooperative Work', in Easterbrook S (ed.) *CSCW: Cooperation or Conflict?* Springer-Verlag CSCW series.

Hutchinson, C. & Rosenberg, D. (1994) 'The Organizations: Issues for Next Generation Office IT', *Journal of Information Technology* 9.

Ishii, H., Kobayashi, M., and Arita, K. 1994. 'Iterative design of seamless collaboration media', *Communications of the ACM,* 37, 83-97.

Ishii, H., and Kobayashi, M. 1992. 'Clearboard: a seamless medium for shared drawing and conversation with eye contact', *Proceedings of CHI'92,* ACM, New York.

Ishii, H., Kobayashi, M., and Grudin, J. 1992. 'Integration of inter-personal space and shared workspace, clearboard and experiments', *Proceedings of CSCW'92*, ACM, New York.

Kotter, J. 1982. 'What do really effective managers really do?', *Harvard Business Review*, November-December, 156-167.

Lawler, E.E. 1992. *The ultimate advantage: creating the high-involvement organization*, Jossey-Bass, San Francisco.

Mann, W.C., and Thompson, S.A. 1988. 'Rhetorical structure theory - toward a functional theory of text organization', *Text,* 8, 243-281.

Mintzberg, H. 1973. *The nature of managerial work*, Harper & Row, New York.

Mintzberg, H. 1975. 'The manager's job: folklore and fact', *Harvard Business Review,* July-August, 49-61.

Mott, P.E. 1972. *The characteristics of effective organizations*, Harper & Row, New York.

Parker, K.C.H. 1988. 'Speaking turns in small group interaction: a context-sensitive event sequence model', *Journal of Personality and Social Psychology*, 54, 965-971.

Penman, R. 1987. 'Discourse in courts: cooperation, coercion and coherence', *Discourse Processes,* 10, 201-218.

Resnick, L.B. 1991. 'Shared cognition: thinking as social practice', 1-20 in Resnick L.B., Levine J.M., and Teasley S.D., (eds) *Perspectives on socially shared cognition*, American Psychological Association.

Rosenberg, D. & Hutchinson, C. (eds.) (1994) *Design Issues in CSCW,* Springer-Verlag CSCW Series.

Rosenberg, D. (1996) 'Sociolinguistic inquiry + situation theory = contribution to CSCW'. In Connolly & Pemberton (Eds) *Linguistic concepts and methdods in CSCW.* London: Springer-Verlag.

Rosenberg, D., Perry, M., Leevers, D., Farrow N. 1997. 'People and Information Finder: informational perspectives', in Williams R. (ed) *The Social Shaping of Multimedia: Proceedings of International Conference COST-4,* European Commission DGXIII, Luxembourg.

Sanders, T.J.M., Spooren, W.P.M., and Noordman, L.G.M. 1992. 'Toward a taxonomy of coherence relations', *Discourse Processes*, 15, 1-35.

Schober, M.F., and Clark, H.H. 1989. 'Understanding by addressees and overhearers', *Cognitive Psychology*, 21, 211-232.

Schon, D.A. 1983. *The reflective practitioner*, Harper Collins, New York.

Sillince, J.A.A. 1994. 'Multi-agent conflict resolution: a computational framework for an intelligent argumentation system', *Knowledge-Based Systems*, 7, 2, 1994, 75-90.

Sillince, J.A.A. 1995. 'Argumentation dynamics: justifying shifts in focus and scope', *Journal of Pragmatics*, 24, 413-431.

Sillince, J.A.A. 1996. 'A model of social, emotional and symbolic aspects of computer-mediated communication within organizations', *Computer-Supported Cooperative Work*, 4 (2) 1-31.

Sillince, J.A.A.,1999. 'The role of political language forms and language coherence in the organizational change process', *Organization Studies*, 20 (3), 485-518.

Sillince, J.A.A., and Saeedi, M.H. 1999a. 'Incorporating rhetorical and plausible reasoning in an electronic conferencing system.' *Knowledge Based Systems* , 12, 113-127.

Sillince, J.A.A., and Saeedi, M.H. 1999b. 'A formal model of organisational argumentation: applications of informal logic to a committee meeting', *Cybernetics and Systems: An International Journal,* 30, 365-409.

Silver, S.D., Cohen, B.P., and Crutchfield, J.H. 1994. 'Status differentiation and information exchange in face to face and computer-mediated idea generation', *Social Psychology Quarterly*, 57, 108-123.

Smith, K.G., Smith, K.A., Olian, J.D., Sims, H.P., O'Brannon, D.O., and Scully, J.A. 1994. 'Top management team demography and process: the role of social integration and communication', *Administrative Science Quarterly*, 30.

Terveen, L. Panel discussion comment, in Terveen L. (ed.) *Proceedings of the Workshop on Collaborative Problem Solving: Theoretical Frameworks and Innovative Systems, August 1993 World Conference on AI and Education,* 1993, Edinburgh .

Tyler, A. 1994. 'The role of repetition in perceptions of discourse coherence', *Journal of Pragmatics,* 21, 671-688.

Vroom, V.H., and Jago, A.G. 1972. *The new leadership*, Prentice-Hall, Englewood Cliffs, NJ.

Walker, M. 1992. 'Redundancy in collaborative dialogue', 345-351 in *Proceedings of the International Conference on Computational Linguistics.*

Wan, D., and Johnson, P.M. 1994. 'Experiences with CLARE: a computer-supported collaborative learning environment', *International Journal of Human-Computer Studies,* 41, 851-879.

Watts, L., Monk, A. and Daly-Jones, O. 1996. 'Inter-personal awareness and synchronization: assessing the value of communication technologies', *International Journal of Human-Computer Studies,* 44, 849-873.

West, M.A. 1996. 'Reflexivity and work group effectiveness: a conceptual integration', in West M.A., (ed) *The handbook of work group psychology,* Wiley.

Whittaker, S. 1995. 'Rethinking video as a technology for interpersonal communications: theory and design implications', *International Journal of Human-Computer Studies,* 42, 501-529.

Winch G.M., Usmani A., and Edkins A., 1997, 'Towards total project quality: a gap analysis approach', *Construction, Management and Economics*, 14.

Yankelovich N., Haan B.J., Meyrowitz N.K.Y., and Drucker S.M., 1988, 'Intermedia: the concept and the construction of a seamless information environment', *Computer,* 21, 81-96.

Chapter X

Structure- and Content-Based Retrieval for XML Documents

Jae-Woo Chang, Seoul National University of Korea
Du-Seok Jin, Chonbuk National University of Korea

ABSTRACT

As the number of XML documents is dramatically increasing, it is necessary to develop an XML document retrieval system that can support both structure-based retrieval and content-based retrieval. In order to support the structure-based retrieval, we design four efficient index structures, i.e., keyword, structure, element and attribute index, by indexing XML documents based on a basic element unit. In order to support the content-based retrieval, we design a high-dimensional index structure based on the X-tree so as to store and retrieve both color and shape feature vectors efficiently. Finally, we do the performance evaluation of our XML document retrieval system in terms of system efficiency, such as retrieval time, insertion time, and storage overhead, as well as system effectiveness, such as recall and precision measures.

INTRODUCTION

The XML (eXtensible Markup Language) was proposed as a standard markup language to make Web documents in 1996[W3C, 2000]. It has as good expressive power as SGML and is also easy to use like HTML. Recently, it has been common for users to acquire through the Web a variety of multimedia documents written by XML. Meanwhile, because the number of XML documents is dramatically increasing, it is difficult to reach a specific XML document required by users. Moreover, an XML document not only has a logical and hierarchical structure commonly, but also contains its multimedia data, such as image and video. Thus, it is necessary to develop an XML document retrieval system that can support both the retrieval based on document structure and the retrieval based on image content.

In general, since the conventional XML document retrieval systems support only structure-based retrieval, it is impossible to deal with a user query which requires both structure- and content-based retrieval for XML document. In this chapter, we design and implement an XML document retrieval system that can efficiently retrieve XML documents based on both document structure and image content. In order to support the structure-based retrieval, we design four efficient index structures, i.e., keyword, structure, element and attribute index, by indexing XML documents based on a basic element unit and implement them by using the o2store storage system. For supporting the content-based retrieval, we design a high-dimensional index structure based on the X-tree so as to store and retrieve both color and shape feature vectors efficiently.

This chapter is organized as follows. We introduce related works in the area of structure-based and content-based document retrieval systems. We design an XML document retrieval system supporting structure-based and content-based retrieval. We show the interface of our XML document retrieval system. In Section 5, we present the performance analysis of our system. Finally, we draw conclusions and provide some issues for future research.

RELATED WORK

Structure-Based Retrieval

Because an element is a basic unit that constitutes a structured document (i.e., SGML or XML document), it is essential to support not only retrieval based on element units but also retrieval based on logical inclusion relationships among elements. Since there are a lot of studies on SGML documents, we, in this section, describe some related work on the representation of SGML document structures. First, RMIT in Australia proposed five query types for structure-based retrieval that should be supported in SGML information retrieval (Sacks-Davis, Arnold-Moore and Zobel, 1994). Most of the types consist of retrieval on upper-level elements (e.g., parent element), or on lower-level elements (e.g., child elements) from a given element. For supporting the five types of queries, RMIT proposed a *subtree model* which indexes all the elements in a SGML document and stores all the terms which are appeared in the elements (Lowe, Zobel and Sacks-Davis, 1995). Although the model supports efficient retrieval on a specific query, it has disadvantages of long indexing time and high storage overhead because index information should be repeatedly stored according to a tree depth. Secondly, RMIT proposed a *SCL structure* that extends the *GCL structure*(Dao and Sacks-Davis, 1996). After assigning numbers to both terms and markups in SGML documents, they use the *SCL structure* to store term interval, markups and inclusion relationships among elements. The *SCL structure* has an advantage that it can handle graph-structured documents, but it has two disadvantages that it requires a deletion operation and it cannot represent the depth of the elements effectively. Finally, SERI in South Korea proposed a *K-ary Complete Tree Structure* which represents a document as a K-ary complete tree (Han, Son, Chang and Zhoo, 1999). In this method, each element corresponds to a node in a K-ary tree. Therefore, a relationship between two elements can be acquired by calculation. This method has an advantage that it is fast to find an element including a given logical relation by calculation. But, as the depth of a K-ary tree is deeper, the number of nodes is increasing exponentially with a large number of unused nodes. In the cases of partial insert and deletion, almost all of nodes should be changed in their assigned number.

Content-Based Retrieval

There have been many researches on content-based retrieval techniques in multimedia DBMSs. The key issues of the studies include keyword extraction for text-based retrieval, image-processing techniques used for feature extraction of images, and multi-dimensional indexing techniques for fast retrieval, and content-based image retrieval based on color histogram, texture, and shape. First, *QBIC (Query By Image Content) project* (Niblack,

1993) (Flickner, 1995) of IBM Almaden research center studied content-based image retrieval on a large on-line multimedia database. The study supports various query types based on the visual image features such as color, texture, and shape. Secondly, the *Chabot project* (Ogle and Stonebraker, 1995) of UCB made use of a spatial indexing method on the relational database management system, POSTGRES, so as to perform simple attribute-based retrieval, text-based retrieval, and content-based image retrieval using color histo-gram. Thirdly, VisualSEEk (Smith and Chang, 1996) of the Colombia University of USA is a developed database system as a tool for content-based retrieval and browsing. It processes user queries that combine a spatial location of image object and color. Its purpose is an implementation of CBVQ(Content-Based Visual Query) which supports efficient retrieval functionality for content-based database system. Fourthly, the *CORE (Content-base Retrieval Engine)* (Wu, 1995) of the National University of Singapore studied novel indexing techniques based on image features so that the engine provides content-based retrieval on multimedia objects. The engine provides the functionality of query feedback to support query refinement. The engine also uses the image features such as keyword, color, shape, texture so as to support visual browsing, similarity retrieval, fuzzy retrieval, and thesaurus-based text retrieval. Finally, NoD (Jin, Jung and Chang, 2000) of the Chonbuk National University of Korea designed a low-level storage manager for efficient storage and retrieval of multimedia data. The low-level storage manager not only efficiently stores video stream data of news video itself, but also handles its index information. It provides an inverted file method for efficient text-based retrieval and an X-tree index structure for high-dimensional feature vectors. In addition, the low-level storage manager was implemented based on SHORE(Scalable Heterogeneous Object REpository) storage system.

A STRUCTURE-AND CONTENT-BASED XML DOCUMENT RETRIEVAL SYSTEM

A structure-and content-based XML document retrieval system mainly consists of five parts, such as a preprocessing part for parsing XML docu-ments and doing image seg-mentation, an indexing part for generating index keys of the documents used in storing and querying, a storage manager part for storing index informa-tion into a specific database, an unified retrieval part for re-sults and finding integrating them into an unified one, and a user interface part for answer-ing user queries by using Web browser. Figure 1 shows the whole system architecture of our XML document retrieval system supporting structure-and content-based retrieval.

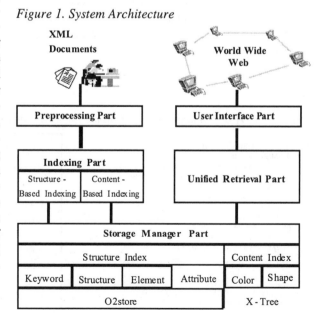

Figure 1. System Architecture

When an XML document is given, we first parse it and do image segmentation from it through the preprocessing part. The parsed document information is transported into the structure-based indexer in order to index its document structure consisting of element units. And the parsed image information is transported into the content-based indexer in order to get the index information of its color and its shape. The structure-based and content-based index information are separately stored into index structures for structure-based retrieval and one for content-based retrieval, respectively. Using the stored index information extracted from a set of XML documents, some documents are retrieved by the retrieval part in order to obtain an unified result to answer user queries. Finally, the unified document result is given to users through a convenient user interface such as Web browser.

Document structure-based indexing

Because an element is a basic unit for retrieving an XML document, it is required to support not only the retrieval based on document unit that is used in the traditional document retrieval system, but also the retrieval based on element unit in a given depth. In addition, it is necessary to support a query on a logical inclusion between elements and on the characteristic value of elements. For this, we design a document retrieval system that efficiently supports element-based queries by constructing an index on a document structure after analyzing XML documents based on DTD. For instance, suppose XML documents include Korean porcelain information with images. Figure 2 depicts a DTD grammar for representing XML documents and one of XML document instances. The XML document instance contains document structure between elements and attribute information. For example, the *porcelain* element has the *name* element as a child and the *decoration* element has the *detail* element as a sibling. In addition, the attribute name of the *porcelain* element is 'TYPE' and its value is 'CHONG_JA'.

To make a document structure tree for XML documents, we first parse the XML documents by using sp-1.3 parser (James, 1999). Next, we construct the document structure tree from the parsed result. Then the constructed tree is delivered into a low-level storage manager. Finally, the storage manager extracts document structure information and image content information from the tree and stores them into a database. Figure 3 shows a procedure to make a document structure tree, and Figure 4 describes the constructed document structure tree.

Figure 2. A DTD grammar and an instance for XML documents

```
<! ELEMENT relic (porcelain)*>
<!ELEMENT porcelain
  (name,year,possession,classification,description,image)>
  <!ATTLIST porcelain TYPE CDATA #REQUIRED>
  <!ELEMENT name (#PCDATA)>
  <!ELEMENT year (#PCDATA)>
  <! ELEMENT possession
  (museum|university|personal)>
  <! ELEMENT museum   (#PCDATA)>
  <!ELEMENT university (#PCDATA)>
  <!ELEMENT personal  (#PCDATA)>
         :

<! ELEMENT image (align)*>
  <!ATTLIST image SRC CDATA #REQUIRED>
  <!ELEMENT align (#PCDATA)>
```

```
<relic>
  <porcelain TYPE="Chung-Ja">
    <name>
      Chung-ja kettle
    </name>
    <decoration>
      lotus flower
    </decoration>
         :
    <detail>
      It is Chung-ja kettle in little gourd shape ...
         :
    <detail>
    </description>
    <image SRC="hc_1">
    </image>
  </porcelain>
</relic>
```

Image content-based indexing

For image content-based retrieval, we analyze image objects of XML documents and extract image feature vectors by separating object regions from the background of images. To extract the object regions, we use the fuzzy c-mean (FCM) algorithm which is a generally famous clustering one to divide object regions from color images (Bezdek and Triedi, 1986). When we divide an image into two clusters, the FCM calculates the distances of a pixel from the center point of each cluster and assigns it to a cluster with shorter distance. It has an advantage that the separation of image objects from its background can be performed well when an image has little noise, as shown in our porcelain images.

In order to obtain an image feature vector for shape, we use the image object produced by the preprocessing and generate a 24-dimensional feature vector based on distances between the center point and a set of edge points. An algorithm for generating a shape feature is as follows.

1. After sorting each pixel of object in a column and a row respectively, calculate the central point of object using its maximum and minimum values.
2. By increasing 15 degrees at the central point, starting from the X-axis, select 24 pixel points met at the edge.
3. Compute the distance between the central point and the 24 pixel points on the edge.
4. Normalize the 24 distances by dividing them by the maximum distance.
5. Generate a 24-dimensional feature vector.

Figure 5 describes a procedure to generate a 24-dimensional feature vector. Also, our algorithm for shape feature vectors can be directly applied to such applications as cyber museums, where an image has only a couple of salient objects.

Since the proximity among colors in the RGB color space doesn't mean their similarity among colors, we use HSV (Hue, Saturation, Value) color space model. This model provides a uniform distribution of colors and makes color transformation easy. In this model, H means a shade of color, ranging from 0 to 360 degree. S means the chrome of color, and V means the brightness of color. Here, we propose an algorithm to generate a 22-dimensional color feature vector as follows.

1. Transform all color pixels of an image object in the RGB color space into those in the HSV color space.

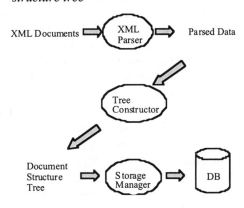

Figure 3. A procedure to construct document structure tree

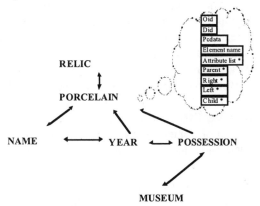

Figure 4. Document structure tree and its element information

2. Generate a color histogram by using color histogram generation algorithm.
3. Normalize the color histogram by dividing it by the number of all the pixel.
4. Generate a 22-dimensional feature vector.

Figure 5 shows an example in which a 22-dimensional feature vector is extracted from its real image. Also, our algorithm for color feature vectors can be directly applied to content-based multimedia information retrieval applications when we transform the RGB color space of an image into its HSV color space.

Low-level storage manager

For structured- and content-based retrieval for XML documents, its low-level storage manager consists of two parts. The index structures for structure-based retrieval are constructed by indexing XML documents based on an element unit, i.e., the basic unit of XML documents, and consist of keyword, structure, element, and attribute index structures. The index structure for content-based retrieval is a high-dimensional index structure based on the X-tree so as to store and retrieve both color and shape feature vectors efficiently.

(1) Keyword index

The keyword index consists of three files, i.e., keyword index file being composed of keywords extracted from data token element (e.g., PCDATA, CDATA) of XML documents, posting file including the IDs of document and element where keywords appear, and location file containing the location of keyword appearance in elements. Figure 6 describes the keyword index structure and shows an extendible form of an index structure used for the conventional information retrieval system by adding an element information of a document.

DF (document frequency) represents the number of documents containing a given keyword. DID is the identifier of the document stored. Because a keyword can be appeared in a set of elements constituting a document, the index includes the different value of EF (element frequency) per each document where EF means the number of elements having a

Figure 5. Feature vector extraction of color and shape

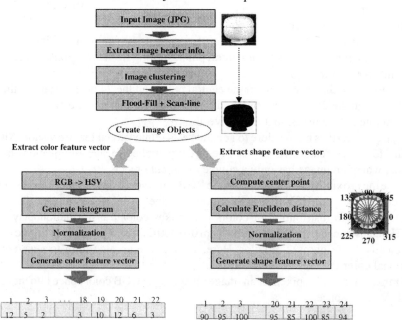

Figure 6. Keyword index structure

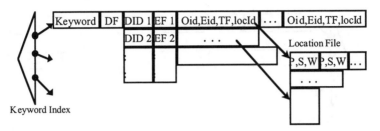

given keyword in each document. Oid is the identifier of the element stored. Eid is an identifier for an element name. Here we use Eid (element name ID) rather than the actual element name because the element name being variable in size is appeared repeatedly. TF (term frequency) represents the number of keyword occurrences in an element. locId is the identifier of location information, i.e. paragraph (P), sentence(S), and word(W), in the location file. Since the location information is only used to answer a keyword adjacency query, we can access only the posting file except the location file to answer a general query, leading to fast response time.

(2) Structure index

The structure index is used for searching an inclusion relationship among elements. So, it should represent the logical structure of a document and should guarantee good performance on both retrieval time and storage overhead. In this chapter, we propose an element unit parse tree structure to represent the hierarchical structure of a document. In the structure, we easily find an inclusion relationship among elements because an element contains the location of its parent, its left sibling, its right sibling, and its first left child. Figure 7 shows the element unit parse tree structure of a given parse tree.

Figure 8 shows the structure index structure based on the element unit parse tree where an element is identified by Oid and Eid. For fast searching of inclusion relationship among elements, we makes use of the identifier of a parent element (ParentOid), that of a left sibling element (LeftOid), that of a right sibling element (RightOid), and that of the first left child element (FchildOid). In addition, NW(node weight) represents relevance degrees between a parent node and one of its child nodes. It is computed as the similarity between a parent term vector and its child term vector.

(3) Element index

For structure-based retrieval, the element index is used for locating a start element. It also plays an important role in mapping into an actual element name the Eid of the element obtained from the keyword index or the attribute index. Figure 9 describes the element index where the meaning of each field is the same as that in Figure 6.

Figure 7. Element unit parse tree structure

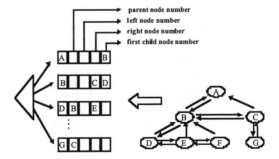

Figure 8. Structure index structure

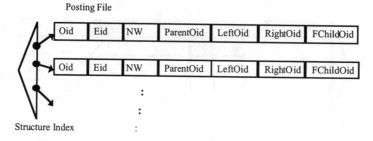

(4) Attribute Index

The attribute index is used for retrieval based on an attribute name and an attribute value assigned to an element. The domain of attribute values exists in several types. But we store an attribute value as character value due to its simplicity. Figure 10 describes the attribute index where VLen means the length of an attribute value, and Value means an attribute value. In order to fast access to the posting information of the next document, we store a length of document posting information into PS (post size). The number of element names and attribute names, depending on the corresponding XML, DTD is fewer than that of keywords. Therefore, we can reside the element index and the attribute index into memory for fast searching

(5) High-dimensional index structure based on the X-tree

A main focus on managing a large number of documents is retrieval performance. As the number of dimensions of feature vectors is increasing, the retrieval time of the traditional index structures is exponentially increasing. To cope with this problem, the X-tree (Berchtold, Keim and Kriegel, 1996) was proposed as an efficient high-dimensional index structure to achieve good retrieval performance even though the dimension of feature vectors is high. The X-tree makes use of special super nodes being extended in size so as to minimize the size of overlapped region due to node splitting. This is, when the overlapped regions become large due to the partitioning of a node, the X-tree converts the node into a super node being double in size, rather than partitioning the node. The X-tree uses a hierarchical directory structure in a low dimension, while it uses a linear directory structure that can save a memory space and can lead to fast accesses to nodes with high-dimensional feature vectors. Thus, we in this chapter construct a high-dimensional index structure based on the X-tree for efficiently retrieving high-dimensional feature vectors of both color and shape. Because our index structure is made based on the X-tree, it can support various types of queries, like point, range, and k-nearest neighbor search. Figure 11 shows color and shape indexes which are constructed using our high-dimensional index structure.

Figure 9. Element index structure

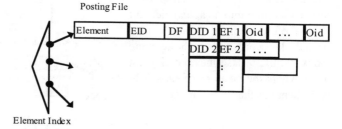

Figure 10. Attribute index structure

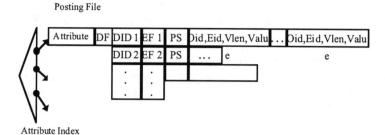

Unified Retrieval

Even though there have been various retrieval models in the traditional text-based information retrieval, there is little research on retrieval models for structured- and content-based multimedia information retrieval. To answer a document structure query, a similarity (S_w) between an element q and an element t is computed as the similarity between the term vector of node q and that of node t (Salton and McGrill, 1983), as shown in the following equation.

$$S_w = COSINE(NODE_q, NODE_t) = \frac{\sum_{k=1}^{m}(TERM_{qk} \cdot TERM_{tk})}{\sqrt{\sum_{k=1}^{m}(TERM_{qk})^2 \cdot \sum_{k=1}^{m}(TERM_{tk})^2}}$$

Figure 11. Color and shape indexes

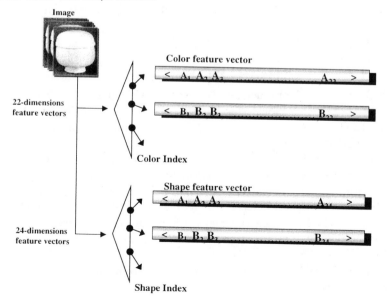

When a result to answer user query is a set of documents, the documents can be represented as $D = \{ E_0, E_1, ..., E_{n-1} \}$ where E_i means an element i in a document D. Also, a similarity (D_w) between an element q and a document D is computed as follows.

$$D_w = \text{MAX} \{ COSINE(NODE_q, NODE_{E_i}), 0 \leq i \leq n\text{-}1\}$$

To answer an image content query, we first extract color or shape feature vectors from a given query image. Then we compute Euclidean distances between a query color (or shape) feature vector and the stored image color (or shape) feature vectors by searching the color (or shape) index. Finally, we compute a similarity between the query feature vector and the image feature vector as 1 – (Euclidean distance / maximum distance), and retrieve relevant documents with high similarity in the decreasing order of the similarity. In case we require content-based retrieval based on both color and shape feature vectors, we compute one unified similarity by the multiplication of both the color and the shape similarities. A similarity, $C_w(q, t)$, between a query image q and a target image t in the database is calculated as the following equation. Here Distc(q, t) and Dists(q, t) mean a color vectors distance and a shape vector distance between a query image q and a target image t, respectively. Nc and Ns mean the maximum color and the maximum shape distances for normalization, respectively.

$$C_w = \begin{cases} 1 - \dfrac{Distc(q,t)}{Nc}, & \text{if a query contains only a color feature.} \\[2mm] 1 - \dfrac{Dists(q,t)}{Ns}, & \text{if a query contains only a shape feature.} \\[2mm] (1 - \dfrac{Distc(q,t)}{Nc}) \times (1 - \dfrac{Dists(q,t)}{Ns}), & \text{if a query contains both color and shape feature.} \end{cases}$$

Finally, when a is the relative weight of the structured-based retrieval compared with the content-based retrieval, a similarity (T_w) for both structured- and content-based composite query is calculated as the following equation. If the weight of the structured-based retrieval is equal to that of the content-based retrieval, a is 0.5.

$$T_w = \begin{cases} C_w \times \alpha + D_w \times (1-\alpha), & \text{if results are document for user query} \\[2mm] C_w \times \alpha + S_w \times (1-\alpha), & \text{if results are element for user query} \end{cases}$$

USER INTERFACE

XML documents are constructed with a proper XML DTD format from a porcelain book published in Korean National Museum. In order to design an efficient structure- and content-based document retrieval system, we classify XML queries into two types, which are simple and composite query types. The simple query can be divided into keyword, structure, attribute, and image query. The examples of the simple query are as follows:

- Keyword query : find documents which contain 'Buddist image' term.
- Structure query : find all children elements of [Porcelain] element.
- Attribute query : find documents or images whose attribute type is 'chong-ja'
- Image query : find documents or images which has a specific color and shape.

The composite query is the composition of simple queries. The examples of the composite query are as follows:

- Structure + Keyword query : find documents which contain 'buddist image' term in [detail] element.

Figure 12. User query interface

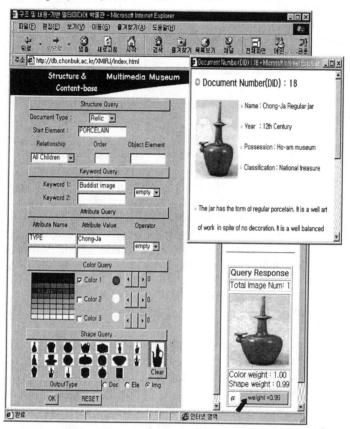

- Structure + Attribute query : find documents whose attribute type is 'chong-ja' and which contain [museum] element in children of [possession] element.
- Image + Keyword query : find documents or images which contain 'buddist image' term among those documents containing a 'blue' color image.
- Image + Structure query : find children element of [Porcelain] element among documents containing images with the shape of 'cup'.

The following Figure 12 shows a user query interface. It consist of five parts for making a user query, that is, structure query, keyword query, attribute query, color query and shape query. For example, a user wants to retrieve documents that have 'buddist image' keyword in all children element of [porcelain] element whose attribute type is 'chong-ja' and that include an image whose color is 'green' and whose shape is like 'kettle'. The figure shows result for the query and its similarity for the combination of structure and image content query. When a user wants more detailed information, another window can browse the detail of the result.

PERFORMANCE ANALYSIS

We implement our structure- and content-based XML document retrieval system under SUN SPARCstation 20 by using GNU CCv2.7 compiler. For this, we make use of O2-Store v4.6 (Deux, 1991) as a storage system and Sp-1.3 as an XML parser. To evaluate our system efficiency, we measure retrieval time, insertion time, storage overhead. Table 1 shows a test data set used for the performance analysis.

Table 1. A test data set

The number of Documents	10000 XML documents
Document average size	1.29K + 40.7K(image)
The number of elements	165800

For insertion time, it takes about 0.02 second to insert the feature vectors of image into color and shape index. Meanwhile, it takes about 1.6 seconds to insert the document structure of a XML document into keyword, attribute, structure, and element index structures. Figure 13 shows retrieval times for queries base on keyword, attribute, structure, color, and shape. It takes less than one second to retrieve a color, a shape and an attribute query. It takes about three seconds to retrieve a keyword query. It takes about six seconds to retrieve a structure query. Consequently, it is shown that retrieval time for answering the structure query is the longest. Figure 14 shows retrieval times for complex queries, such as structure + keyword, structure + attribute, keyword + color, and structure + shape queries. It takes eight seconds to answer the combination of structure and attribute queries or the combination of structure and shape queries. It takes about 4 seconds to answer the combination of color and keyword queries. Consequently, it is shown that a complex query including the structure type takes more time than other composite queries to answer it.

To evaluate retrieval effectiveness, we measure recall and precision (Salton and McGrill, 1983) with a test group consisting of ten graduate students in our Computer Engineering Department. Table 2 shows the recall and precision measures of our XML document retrieval system when we find the most similar K porcelains. As K is increasing, the precision is decreasing while the recall is increasing. In case of K=10, the recall is 0.6 and the precision is about 0.4 for the color query, while the recall is about 0.6 and the precision is about 0.3 for the shape query.

Table 3 shows an average retrieval time of our system and its competitors. Because it is difficult to find other systems to support both structure and content-based retrieval, we compare our system with the StIR system for structure-based query and compare our system

Figure 13. Retrieval time for simple queries

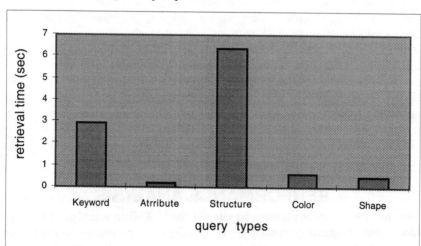

Figure 14. Retrieval time for complex queries

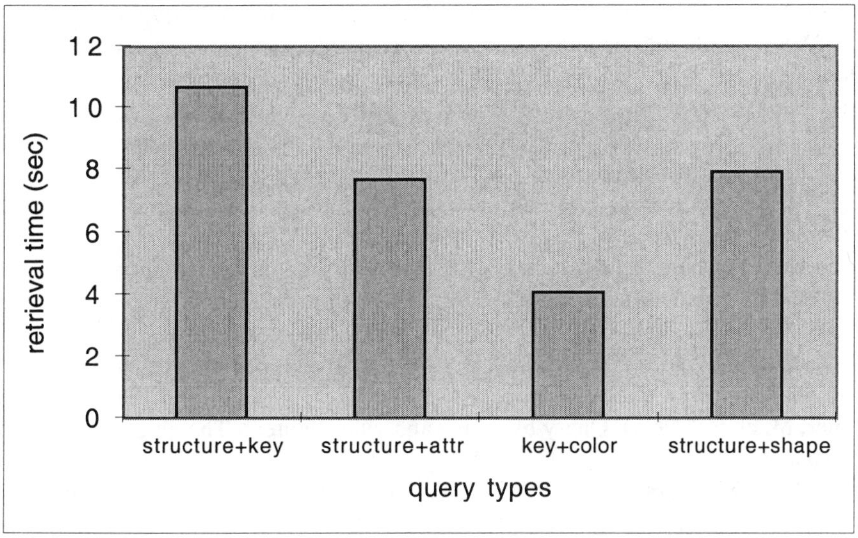

with the NoD system for content-based query. In the structure-based query, both our system and the StIR take about six seconds, showing the similar retrieval time. In the content-based query, our system takes less than one second while the NoD system takes about three seconds.

Table 2. Precision and recall measures

	Color		Shape	
	Precision	Recall	Precision	Recall
K = 7	0.64	0.33	0.57	0.23
K = 10	0.60	0.37	0.55	0.32

Table 3. Average retrieval time

	Our System	StIR[Han,1999]	NoD[Jin,2000]
Structure query	6.5 sec	6.3 sec	N/A
Content query	0.6 sec	N/A	3.5 sec

CONCLUSIONS

In this chapter, we designed and implemented an XML document retrieval system that can efficiently retrieve XML documents based on both document structure and image content. In order to support efficient structure-based retrieval, we designed our keyword, structure, element, and attribute index by indexing XML documents based on the basic element unit and implemented them by using the o2store storage system. For efficient image content-based retrieval, we designed a high-dimensional index structure based on the X-tree for both color and shape feature vectors. In our XML document retrieval system, the retrieval time for the structure query is about six seconds while that for the image content query is below one second. Also, the retrieval time for the combination of structure and keyword queries is shown to be the longest, i.e. about ten seconds. Our XML document retrieval system spends about 1.6 seconds for inserting a document. As further research, in order to make our XML document retrieval system popular, we need to implement it by using a public storage system, like the Shore storage system developed by the University of Wisconsin.

REFERENCES

eXtensible Markup Language. (2000). Available: http:// www.w3.org/XML.

Sacks-Davis, R., Arnold-Moore, T., & Zobel, J. (1994). Database systems for structured documents. *In Proc. Informational Symposium on Advanced Database Technologies and Their Integration.*

Lowe, B., Zobel, J., & Sacks-Davis, R. (1995). A formal model for databases of structured text. *In Proc. Database Systems for Advanced Applications.*

Dao, T., & Sacks-Davis, R., (1996). Indexing structured text for queries on containment relationships. *In Proc. the 7th Australasian Database Conference.*

Han, S., Son, J., Chang, J., & Zhoo, Z. (1999). Design and implementation of a structured information retrieval system for SGML documents. *In Proc. Database Systems for Advanced Applications.*

Niblack, W. et. al. (1993). The QBIC project: Quering by image content using color, texture, and Shape. *In Proc. the SPIE Storage and Retrieval for Image and Video Databases.*

Flickner, M. et. al. (1995). Query by image and video content: The qbic system. *In IEEE computer.*

Ogle, V.E., & Stonebraker, M. (1995). Chatbot: Retrieval from a relational database of images. *IEEE computer* (Vol. 28, 40-48).

Smith, J. R., & Chang, S. F. (1996). VisualSEEk: a Fully automated content-based image query system. *ACM Multimedia Systems.*

Wu, J. K. et. al. (1995). Core: a content-based retrieval engine for multimedia information systems. *ACM Multimedia Systems* (Vol. 3, 25-41).

Jin, K., Jung, J., & Chang, J. (2000). Design and implementation of a low-level storage manager for efficient storage and retrieval of multimedia data in NoD Services. *Korea Information Processing Society* (Vol. 7).

Sp-parser. (1999). Available: http://www.jclark.com/sp. [1999, July 17].

Bezdek, J. C., & Triedi, M. M. (1986). Low level segmentation of aerial image with fuzzy clustering. *IEEE Trans. on SMC* (Vol. 16, 589-598).

Berchtold, S., Keim, D., & Kriegel. H. P. (1996). The x-tree: An index structure for high-dimensional data. *In Proc. the 22nd Conf. on Very Large Databases.*

G. Salton. & M. McGill. (1983). An introduction to modern information retrieval. McGraw-Hill.

O. Deux et al. (1991). The O_2 System. *IEEE Communication of the ACM* (Vol. 34).

Chapter XI

MESH: A Model-Based Approach to Hypermedia Design

Wilfried Lemahieu
Katholieke Universiteit Leuven, Belgium

INTRODUCTION

A Brief History of the Hypermedia Concept

The term *hypermedia* denotes an approach to computer data organization in a manner similar to the functioning of the human brain. In essence, human cognition is organized as a semantic network in which related concepts are linked together. New information we come across is integrated into our mind's semantic structures of existing knowledge. These structures allow for the stored information to be accessed *by association*.

A precursor of current hypermedia systems was mentioned as early as in 1945, i.e. long before the introduction of the modern computer, by (Bush, 1945). He described an imaginary device called *Memex* as "*a sort of mechanized private file and library ... in which an individual stores all his books, records, and communications, and which is mechanized so that it may be consulted with exceeding speed and flexibility. It is an enlarged intimate supplement to his memory*". One of the key concepts of *Memex* was said to be its ability to *link* items together such that they could be accessed by association, rather than through indexing.

In 1965, Nelson came up with the term *hypertext*, which he defined as "*a body of written or pictorial material interconnected in a complex way that it could not be conveniently represented on paper. It may contain summaries or maps of its contents and their interrelations; it may contain annotations, additions and footnotes from scholars who have examined it*" (Nelson, 1965).

Generally, the concept of *hypertext* can be seen as the structuring of standard text with the addition of *links* that allow for navigation through this text in a non-linear order; each portion of the text can *anchor* a link that leads to a related text fragment when the anchor is 'stimulated'. In parallel to the human brain, hypertext organizes data (i.e. text fragments) into a network structure, with semantic relationships being established through links. These links allow for navigating through and accessing data *by association*. Hence, the purpose of the links is not only to model data *interrelations*; they also represent a *navigational path* throughout the resulting network structure. Therefore, hypertext differs from other data organization techniques in that directives about how to navigate through the information space are included within the data themselves.

Most so-called *first generation* hypertext systems were implemented on mainframes and were strictly text-only (Halasz, 1988). Generally, the anchors were represented by underlining the relevant text portion, with the stimulus being provided by 'clicking' the anchor. As PC's inundated the computer market in the eighties, the term *hypermedia* became a synonym for hypertext, emphasizing the said data organization methodology being enhanced with *multimedia* capabilities. In such *second generation* hypermedia systems, the chunks of data not only consisted of text, but also pictures, animations, video and audio fragments or even virtual reality objects. As a consequence, links anchoring and the stimuli to provoke link access have become more diverse, befitting the corresponding media type. The principle, however, remains the same, according to a more up-to-date definition by (Smith and Weiss, 1988): "*an approach to information management in which data is stored in a network of nodes connected by links. Nodes can contain text, graphics, audio, video as well as source code or other forms of data*".

The components of current hypermedia systems comprise a *user interface*, an *authoring environment* to create and manage both node *content* and *structure* and a hypermedia *engine* with an associated *storage system* for the possibly heterogeneous multimedia data.

The appeal of hypermedia is based upon its ability to store complex, cross-referenced bodies of information, which can be browsed according to the user's personal preferences. The latter, along with the resemblance to human cognition, makes hypermedia highly suitable as a tool for end user exploring and learning. Or, as put in (Bieber, 1993): "*Hypertext systems provide a non-sequential and entirely new method of accessing information unlike traditional information systems which are primarily sequential in nature. They provide flexible access to information by incorporating the notions of navigation, annotation, and tailored presentation*".

Many hypermedia systems have been conceived, some of which did not even outgrow the stadium of obscure experimental systems in research labs. Some were special-purpose built to be applied in a clear-cut field; others were general-purpose 'shells' to accommodate various areas of data. Among the most publicly known (commercial) implementations are certainly *Hypercard*, which comes free with every Macintosh computer sold since 1987 and the *Microsoft Windows Help System*. However, the environment that really brought hypermedia to the public eye is undoubtedly *the World Wide Web* (Berners-Lee and Cailliau, 1994), promoting the hypertext paradigm as the primary access mode to all Internet-connected networks across the globe. Unfortunately, the latter *WWW* presents a genuine enlargement to many shortcomings that exist to some degree in *all* current hypermedia implementations.

Where Current Hypermedia Applications Fall Short

Indeed, along with increasing popularity and worldwide adoption of hypermedia, limitations and downright deficiencies became painfully apparent. The concepts inherent to hypermedia led to inconveniences that prohibited satisfactory information retrieval by the *end user* as well as adequate hyperbase *maintenance*. Whereas non-linear navigation resulted in disoriented end users, the disorderly network of links involved an unacceptable amount of 'manual' work to keep the hypermedia structure up-to-date (Ramaiah, 1992).

-User disorientation

Users *navigating* in a hypermedia environment are confronted with questions such as "Where am I?", "Where do I go?" and "How do I get there?" (Rivlin et al, 1994). The problems surrounding hypermedia navigation have been thoroughly discussed in literature, e.g. (Nelson, 1987); (Nielsen, 1990b); (Bernstein, 1991). The explorative, non-linear nature of hypermedia navigation imposes a heavy processing load upon the end user. This phenomenon is known as *cognitive overhead* (Ramaiah, 1992). If the freedom and flexibility become "too much" to the end user, the latter is distracted from their initial focus of attention (Hammond, 1993). This process of cognitive overhead effecting into user disorientation and losing one's chain of thought is referred to as the 'lost in hyperspace' phenomenon (Nielsen, 1990a).

-Limited maintainability

A problem often obscured by the one described above, but nonetheless at least as stringent, is the *maintenance* problem. The latter was certainly less than a sinecure in the pioneering hypermedia implementations.

A heavy burden upon hyperbase maintainability is the fact that, due to the absence of workable abstractions, many hypermedia systems implement links as direct references to the target node's *physical location* (e.g. the *URL* in a *WWW* environment). To make things worse, these references are embedded within the *content* of a link's source node (Davis, 1995). As a result, moving a single node demands heavy maintenance efforts to restore hyperbase integrity; *all* nodes' bodies have to be searched for a reference to the now-obsolete location and all found references have to be adapted. Hyperbase maintenance has become a synonym for manually editing the nodes' *contents*.

Whereas manually created links already reduce maintainability to a great extent, they also have a disastrous impact upon *consistency* and *completeness* (Ashman et al., 1997). The inability to enforce integrity constraints and submit the network structure to consistency and completeness checks, results in a hyperbase with plenty of *dangling links*. Needless to say that the consequences of inferior maintenance will also frustrate the end user and effect into additional orientation problems.

Objectives of this Chapter

The *MESH* hypermedia framework as deployed in (Lemahieu, 1999) proposes a structured approach to both data modeling and navigation, so as to overcome said maintainability and user disorientation problems. *MESH* is an acronym for *Maintainable, End user friendly, Structured Hypermedia*. Its fundaments are a solid underlying *data model* and a *context-based navigation paradigm*.

The data model is based on concepts and experiences in the related field of database modeling, taking into account the particularities inherent to the hypermedia approach to data storage and retrieval. Established entity-relationship (Chen, 1976) and object-oriented (Rumbaugh et al., 1991); (Jacobson et al., 1992); (Meyer, 1997); (Snoeck et al., 1999) modeling abstractions are coupled to proprietary concepts to provide for a *formal hypermedia data model*. While uniform layout and link typing specifications are attributed and inherited in a *static* node typing hierarchy, both nodes and links can be submitted *dynamically* to multiple complementary classifications. The *MESH* data model provides for a firm hyperbase structure and an abundance of meta-information that facilitates implementation of an enhanced navigation paradigm.

This *context-based navigation paradigm* builds upon the data model to reconcile navigational freedom with nested, dynamically created *guided tours*. Indeed, the intended navigation mechanism is that of an "intelligent book", which is to provide a disoriented end user with a *sequential path* as a guidance. Such *guided tour* is not static, but is adapted dynamically to the *navigation context*. In addition, a node is able to tune its *visualization* to the context in which it is accessed, hence providing the user with the most relevant subset of its embedded multimedia objects.

These blueprints are translated into a high-level implementation framework, specified in an abstract and platform independent manner. The body of this chapter is dedicated to the *MESH* data model. Thereafter, the *context-based navigation paradigm* and the *implementation framework* are briefly discussed. The last section makes comparisons to related work and formulates conclusions.

A MODEL-BASED APPROACH TO HYPERMEDIA APPLICATION DEVELOPMENT

Orientation and Comprehension in Hypermedia

In (Thüring et al., 1995), a distinction is made between hypermedia systems that are destined for being *wandered* through, picking up information here and there, and the ones that are specifically aimed at deep understanding. It is argued how especially the second kind benefits from a structured approach. In this way, two factors are denoted as being crucial in hypertext readability and comprehensibility: *coherence* as a positive influence and *cognitive overhead* as a negative one.

Coherence

Coherence was already described in an earlier effort by the same authors (Thüring et al., 1991). A coherent hypermedia document would enable the reader to construct a mental model that represents the objects and relations described in its content. Coherence should exist both on the level of a single node and of the whole hypermedia structure. At the latter level, it can be increased by explicitly representing semantic relationships between nodes, to indicate what these nodes have to do with each other. A second measure can be to provide information about the *context* in which a node is displayed. This conveys a sense of continuity across separate nodes and reduces the impression of information *fragmentation*. Other remedies include aggregation and providing *overviews* of the information space.

Cognitive overhead

Cognitive overhead according to (Conklin, 1987) is *"the additional effort and concentration necessary to maintain several tasks or trails at one time"*. (Thüring et al., 1995) claim that *"Every effort additional to reading reduces the mental resources available for comprehension. With respect to hyperdocuments, such efforts primarily concern orientation, navigation and user-interface adjustment."*

As a solution, they suggest how the hypermedia environment should offer the reader maximal support to identify his/her current position within the hypermedia structure and to reconstruct the way that led to this position. Moreover, it should make the selection of the next step as easy as possible.

Improved orientation through increased comprehensibility

Moreover, it is claimed how "*memory for content and memory for spatial information are different aspects of the same mental representation, i.e. the reader's mental model*". This is said to explain the close correlation between comprehension and memory for location: both *orientation* difficulties and difficulties in *understanding* the hypertext are symptoms of the same disease. As such, every feature that facilitates the construction of such a model by reducing mental effort or increases a model's quality by improving completeness and consistency affects both comprehension and orientation.

The authors suggest how readability of hyperdocuments, hence also orientation, can be improved by supporting the construction of a mental model in terms of a dual approach based on both *increased document coherence* and *reduced cognitive overhead*. Therefore, they suggest eight design principles, which will also feature prominently in the *MESH* framework:

- *Typed link labels* that allow for understanding semantic relations between information units and reduce fragmentation
- The indication of *equivalencies between information units* also reduces the impression of fragmentation
- The preservation of the *context in which information units are displayed* further reduces fragmentation
- *Higher-order information units* should be available, e.g. composite nodes, to induce a stronger sense of structure
- *Visual information about the hypertext structure* should be available as overviews, maps, etc.
- The user should be provided with cues about his/her *current position and available navigational options*
- Navigation facilities should cover aspects of *direction and distance*
- A *stable screen layout* diminishes cognitive overhead

Advantages of a Formal Hypermedia Data Model

Whereas the design principles above already hint at the need for hypertexts to be *structured* according to a conceptual model, similar to the ones applied in database modeling, other authors support this vision with partially similar and partially complementary arguments.

Consistency

In (Garzotto et al., 1995), consistency is regarded as one of the most important evaluation criteria of hypertext systems: "*treat conceptually similar elements in a similar fashion and conceptually different elements differently*".

(Nanard and Nanard, 1995) insist that tools must enable the designer to work both at the abstract model level and at the level of instances. Therefore, they advocate the use of a conceptual model. Abstract semantic types should offer a means for handling an actual structure both at a global and a local level. This would enforce consistency of the hypertext structure, increase modularity and allow users to recognize similarities. Both node and link types would model similar semantic properties across different entities and enforce the regularity of structure. Moreover, even a few node instances would allow for evaluating the global design and implementation.

Abstractions

(Rivlin et al., 1994) describe the importance of hierarchies and aggregations to navigation. A well-defined hypermedia structure greatly facilitates end-user orientation. It has been proven that insight into the underlying abstractions is a key condition to orientation in a hypermedia environment (Halasz, 1988).

(Botafogo et al., 1991) explicitly refer to the object-oriented paradigm as a means for structuring hypertext and providing meaningful abstractions so as to reduce the complexity of large numbers of nodes and links. Therefore, nodes and links are to be collected into more abstract structures, both through aggregation and generalization. This allows for dealing with a set of nodes and links as a single (higher-level) object, which reduces cognitive overhead.

(Garg, 1988) also describes the usefulness of abstractions in hypermedia. They yield richer information structures and more natural specifications of domain knowledge. Also, the expressive power of queries is increased. Moreover, they allow for a whole collection of information units to be denoted by a single reference. Finally, support for collaboration and versioning is facilitated.

In (Mayes, 1994), a distinction is made between *hyperspace* and *conceptual space*. The former refers to the hypermedia structure itself, whereas the latter involves the actual concepts and interrelations represented in the hypermedia system. A *close correlation between hyperspace and conceptual space* is claimed to significantly advance comprehension and orientation. Therefore, the objects in the hypermedia structure are to reflect the concepts from the domain model as accurately as possible.

Typed links

Arguably the most significant abstraction of all, at least in the context of hypermedia, is the *link type*. The importance of a conceptual data model with typed links to support navigation was already emphasized by (Halasz, 1988). Whereas (Thüring et al., 1991) stress the influence of typed *links* upon the coherence of hyperdocuments, (Knopik and Bapat, 1994) advocate the use of both typed *nodes* and *links*. They should provide the user with hints at what awaits him/her in the next node, such that they can make a well-founded decision about their next move. Therefore, they plead for those types not to be "technical" as is the case in many implementations, e.g. implicit versus explicit or internal versus external. Rather, they should reflect the semantic relationship between source and destination node, i.e. as specified in the application domain. Moreover, link typing should not be limited to attaching labels, but should also influence browsing behavior, allow for displaying properties in different contexts and enforce semantic constraints.

Authoring advantages

The advantages to the *author* of a formal design model are described in (Garzotto et al., 1993): first, it improves the *communication* between analyst, end user and system designer and allows for complex constructs to be discussed on an application domain independent level. Moreover, *design methodologies* can be tested, analyzed and compared at a high level of abstraction, independently of individual nodes. This permits certain constructs and components to be *reused* in different applications as well. Furthermore, a formal data model allows for powerful *design tools* to support authoring in a systematic, structured way. Another very important factor is that it enables these tools to enforce *consistency and completeness constraints* and *predictable representation structures*, which in turn will be of benefit to the end user and reduce disorientation.

E.R. and O.O.-Based Hypermedia Models

The first conceptual hypermedia modeling approaches such as *HDM* (Garzotto et al., 1993) and *RMM* (Isakowitz et al., 1995); (Isakowitz et al., 1998) were based on the entity-relationship paradigm. Object-oriented techniques were mainly applied in *hypermedia engines*, to model functional behavior of an application's *components*, e.g. *Intermedia* (Meyrowitz, 1986); (Haan et al., 1991), *Microcosm* (Davis et al., 1992); (Hall et al., 1992); (Beitner et al., 1995), *Hyperform* (Wiil & Leggett, 1992); (Wiil & Leggett, 1997) and *Hyperstorm* (Bapat et al., 1996). Along with *EORM* (Lange, 1994) and *OOHDM* (Schwabe et al., 1996); (Schwabe & Rossi, 1998a); (Schwabe & Rossi, 1998b), *MESH* is the first approach where modeling of the *application domain* is fully accomplished through the object-oriented paradigm. The following section presents *MESH*'s data model in detail.

MESH'S OBJECT-ORIENTED HYPERMEDIA DATA MODEL

The Basic Concepts: Node and Link Types

On a conceptual level, a *node* is considered a black box, which communicates with the outside world by means of its *links*. External references are always made to the node *as a whole*. True to the O.O. *information-hiding* concept, no direct calls can be made to its multimedia content. However, internally, a node may encode the intelligence to adapt its visualization to the *navigation context*, as discussed in section 5.

Nodes are assorted in an inheritance hierarchy of *node types*. Each child node type should be compliant with its parent's definition, but may fine-tune inherited features and add new ones. These features comprise both node layout and node interrelations, abstracted in *layout templates* and *link types,* respectively.

A *layout template* is associated with each level in the node typing hierarchy, every template being a refinement of its predecessor. Its exact specifications depend upon the implementation environment, e.g. as to the Web it may be HTML or XML-based. Node typing as a basis for layout design allows for uniform behavior, onscreen appearance and link anchors for nodes representing similar real world objects.

A *link* represents a one-to-one association between two nodes, with both a semantic and a navigational connotation. A directed link offers an access path from its *source* to its *destination node*. Links representing similar semantic relationships are assembled into *types*. Link types are attributed to node types and can be inherited and refined throughout the hierarchy. Link type *properties* allow for enforcing constraints upon their instances and can be overridden to provide for stronger restrictions upon inheritance. This mechanism is discussed in full in an upcoming section..

For example, whereas an **artist** node can be linked to any **artwork** through a *has-made* link type, an instance of the child node type **painter** can only be linked to a **painting**, by means of the more specific child link type *has-painted*.

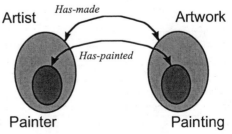

The Use of Aspects to Overcome Limitations
of a Rigid Node Typing Structure

Definition of aspect descriptor and aspect type

The above model is based on a node typing strategy where node classification is total, disjoint and constant. The aspect construct allows for defining *additional* classification criteria, which are not necessarily subject to these restrictions. Apart from a single "most specific node type", they allow a node to take part in other secondary classifications that are allowed to change over time. Although we deliberately opted for a single inheritance structure, aspects can provide an elegant solution in many situations that would otherwise call for multiple inheritance.

An *aspect descriptor* is defined as an attribute whose (discrete) values classify nodes of a given type into respective additional subclasses. In contrast to a node's "main" subtyping criterion, such aspect descriptor should not necessarily be *single-valued* or *constant over time*. Aspect descriptor properties denote whether the classification is *optional/mandatory*, *overlapping/disjoint* and *temporary/ permanent*.

Each *aspect type* is associated with a single value of an aspect descriptor. An aspect type defines the properties that are attributed to the class of nodes that carry the corresponding aspect descriptor value. An aspect type's instances, *aspects*, implement these type-level specifications. Each aspect is inextricably associated with a single node, adding characteristics that describe a specific "aspect" of that node.

A node instance may carry multiple aspects and can be described by as many aspect descriptors as there are additional classifications for its node type. If multiple classifications exist, each aspect descriptor has as many values as there are subclasses to the corresponding specialization. Its cardinalities determine whether the classification is total and/or disjoint. As opposed to node types, aspects are allowed to be volatile. Hence, dynamic classification can be accomplished by manipulating aspect descriptor values, thus adding or removing aspects at run-time. Aspect types attribute the same properties as nodes: *link types* and *layout*. However, their instances differ from nodes in that they are not directly referable. An aspect represents the *same real-world object* as its associated node and can only be visualized as a subordinate of the latter.

For example, to model an **artist** who can be skilled in multiple disciplines, a non-disjoint aspect descriptor *discipline* defines the **painter** and **sculptor** aspect types. Discipline-specific node properties are modeled in these aspect types, such that e.g. the **Michelangelo** node features the combined properties of its **Michelangelo.asPainter** and **Michelangelo.asSculptor** aspects.

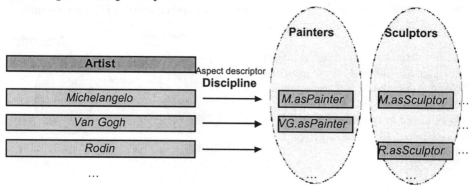

Delegation of node properties to aspect descriptors

Node type properties (i.e. layout and link types) can be *delegated* to aspect descriptors, such that they can be inherited and overridden in each aspect type that is associated with one of the descriptor's values.

An aspect type's *layout* template refines layout properties that are delegated to the corresponding aspect descriptor. Link types delegated to an aspect descriptor can be inherited and overridden as well. In addition, each aspect type can define its own supplementary link types. The inheritance/overriding mechanism is similar to the mechanism for supertypes/subtypes, but because an aspect descriptor can be multi-valued, particular care was taken so as to preclude any inconsistencies. Further details will be provided.

Inheritance of aspect types throughout the classification hierarchy

Aspect types themselves are node type properties that can be inherited and overridden across the node type hierarchy. The *aspect descriptor* is used as a vehicle for the inheritance of aspect types. This ability yields the opportunity to use aspects as real building blocks for nodes. Link types and layout definitions pertaining to a single "role" a node may have to play, can now be captured into one aspect type. If the corresponding aspect descriptor is attributed at a generic level in the node hierarchy, the aspect type can be inherited where necessary by more specific node types. This allows for the modeling of a similar 'aspect' in otherwise completely unrelated node types. The aspect type *art-collector* could be defined at root level and inherited by both *museum* and *private-collector*, modeling the fact that both node types can behave as owners of artwork. Node types can be 'assembled' by inheriting the proper aspect types, complemented by their own particular features. In this way, different aspects associated with the same node instance can have different editing privileges, such that updating multimedia *content* can be delegated to different parties.

Link Typing and Subtyping

Introduction

In common data modeling literature, subtyping is invariably applied to *objects*, never to *object interrelations*. If additional classification of a relationship type is called for, it is *instantiated* to become an object type, which can of course be the subject of specialization. However, as for a hypermedia environment, node types and link types are two separate components of the data model with very different purposes. It would not be useful to instantiate a link type into a node type since such nodes would have *no content* to go along with them, and thus, each instance would become an 'empty' stop during navigation.

This section demonstrates how specialization semantics can be enforced not only upon node types, but also upon the *link types*. A sub link type will model a type whose set of instances constitutes a subset of its parent's, and which models a relation that is more specific than the one modeled by the parent.

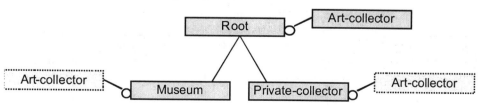

Definition and domain of a sub link type

A link instance is defined as a source node - destination node tuple (n_s, n_d). Tuples for which this association represents a similar semantic meaning are grouped into link types. A link type defines instances that comply with the properties of the type and is constrained by its *domain*, its *cardinalities* and its *inverse link type*.

The *domain* of the link type is the data type to which the link type is attributed. This can be either a node type or an aspect type. The domain casts a restriction upon which nodes are valid as *source* nodes of the tuples represented by the link type:

$$(n_s, n_d) \in L \Rightarrow n_s \in Dom(L)$$

If L_c is a sub link type resulting from a specialization over L_p, the set of (n_s, n_d) tuples defined by L_c is a subset of the one defined by L_p. As a consequence, L_c's domain should be the same as or define a subset of (i.e. a sub node type or an aspect type) of L_p's domain:

$$L_c \subset L_p \quad \Rightarrow ((n_s, n_d) \in L_c \text{ fi } (n_s, n_d) \in L_p)$$
$$\Rightarrow Dom(L_c) \subseteq Dom(L_p)$$

If the domains are the same, we speak of a sub link type resulting from a *horizontal* specialization. If the sub link type is inherited in a sub node type or aspect type, we speak of a *vertical* specialization.

A *vertical link specialization* is the consequence of a parallel classification over the links' *source nodes*, in either node subtypes or aspect types. The term denotes that each sub link type is attributed at a 'lower', more specific level in the node typing hierarchy than its parent; since L_c's domain is a subset of L_p's domain and they both model similar semantics,

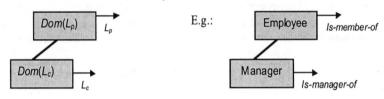

$$L_c \{ L_p, Dom(L_c) \{ Dom(L_p) \}$$

If L_c and L_p share the same domain, L_c can still define a subtype of L_p in the case where L_c models a more restricted, more specific kind of relationship than L_p, independently of any node specialization. Both parent and child link type are attributed at the same level in the node type hierarchy, hence the term *horizontal* specialization.

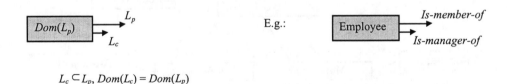

$$L_c \subset L_p, Dom(L_c) = Dom(L_p)$$

Cardinalities of a sub link type

A link type's *cardinalities* determine the minimum and maximum number of link instances allowed for a given source node. If the domain is an aspect type, the cardinalities pertain to a node's corresponding aspect.

$$MinCard(L) = 1 \Leftrightarrow \forall\, n_s \in Dom(L): \exists\, (n_s, n_d) \in L$$
$$MaxCard(L) = 1 \Leftrightarrow [\forall\, n_s \in Dom(L): (n_s, n_{d1}) \in L \,\&\, (n_s, n_{d2}) \in L \Rightarrow n_{d1} = n_{d2}]$$

Upon overriding link type cardinalities, care should be taken so as not to violate the parent's constraints, particularly in case of a non-disjoint classification. The following tables present feasible combinations, respectively in function of a *horizontal* and a *vertical* specialization over a given parent link type. Note that a '-' sign stands for "not inherited". Moreover, the mechanism for link type inheritance in a "real" node subtype is similar to delegation to a (1,1) aspect descriptor, as represented in the rightmost column of the vertical link specialization table.

Parent link type cardinality	
(0,n)	(0,n) (0,1)
(1,n)	(0,n) (0,1) (1,n) (1,1)
(0,1)	(0,1)
(1,1)	(0,1)

Horizontal link specialization

Parent link type cardinality	Aspect descriptor cardinality			
	(0,n)	(1,n)	(0,1)	(1,1)
(0,n)	- (0,n) (1,n) (0,1) (1,1)	- (0,n) (1,n) (0,1) (1,1)	- (0,n) (1,n) (0,1) (1,1)	- (0,n) (1,n) (0,1) (1,1)
(1,n)		(1,n) (1,1)		(1,n) (1,1)
(0,1)	- (0,1) (1,1)	- (0,1) (1,1)	- (0,1) (1,1)	- (0,1) (1,1)
(1,1)		(1,1)		(1,1)

Vertical link specialization

Inverse of a sub link type

The *inverse link type* is the *most specific* link type that encompasses all of the original link type's tuples, with reversed source and destination. There are two possibilities. If the 'inverse-of' relationship is mutual, we speak of a *particular* inverse, notation: $L \,\acute{}\, Inv(L)$. If this is not the case, we speak of a *general* inverse, notation: $L \, \cancel{E} \, Inv(L)$.

A *particular inverse* models a situation where two link types are *each other's* inverse. Not counting source and destination's sequence, the two link types represent the same set of tuples. The term *particular inverse* is used because no two link types can share the same particular inverse.

$$L \leftrightarrow Inv(L) \Leftrightarrow [(n_s, n_d) \in L \Leftrightarrow (n_d, n_s) \in Inv(L)]$$
$$\Leftrightarrow L = Inv(Inv(L))$$

E.g. **employee.*is-member-of* ↔ department.*members***

A child link type can override its parent's inverse with its own particular inverse, which is to be a subtype of the parent's inverse.

E.g. **employee.***is-manager-of* ↔ **department.***manager*

However, if no suitable particular inverse exists for a given child link type, it has to inherit its parent's inverse as a *general inverse*, without overriding. Hence a *general* inverse can be shared by multiple link types with a common ancestor.

As to a *general inverse*, the set of tuples represented by L is a *subset* of the one represented by $Inv(L)$. This is equal to stating that $L \subset Inv(Inv(L))$.

$$L \to Inv(L) \Leftrightarrow [((n_s, n_d) \in L \text{ fi } (n_d, n_s) \in Inv(L)), \exists\, (n_d, n_s) \in Inv(L): (n_s, n_d) \notin L]$$
$$\Leftrightarrow L \subset Inv(Inv(L))$$

The *general* inverse of a child link type must be the *particular* inverse of one of this child's ancestors.

E.g. **employee.***is-manager-of* → **department.***members*

Summarizing, a child link type either inherits its parent's inverse as a *general* inverse, or the inverse property is overridden with a subtype of the parent's inverse becoming the *particular* inverse of the child link type:

$$L_c \subset L_p \Rightarrow [(\exists\, K_c: L_c \leftrightarrow K_c, K_c \subset Inv(L_p)) \text{ or } (L_c \to Inv(L_p))]$$

Link type specialization properties

Properties for *node type specialization* determined whether the latter was total and/or disjoint. On the other hand, no such properties are attributed to a *link type classification* itself. Without a concession to generality, we can force each specialization to be *total* by defining an additional child link type L_{cRest} where necessary, to collect instances of the parent that could not be classified into any of the other children. Each (n_s, n_d) tuple that belongs to the parent link type L_p, also belongs to *at least* one of its subtypes L_{ci}.

$$L_p := L_{c1} \cup L_{c2} \cup L_{c3} \cup L_{c4} \cup \dots \cup L_{cRest}$$
$$\Leftrightarrow [(\forall\, L_{ci}: L_{ci} \subset L_p) \,\&\, (\forall\, (n_s, n_d) \in L_p: \exists\, L_{ci}: (n_s, n_d) \in L_{ci})]$$

Whether *overlapping* subtypes are allowed is not enforced at the *specialization* level, but as a property of each subtype separately, leaving space for a finer granularity. This is accomplished by a child link type's *singularity* property, which denotes whether its instances are allowed to also belong to sibling child types. We can force L_{cRest} to be disjoint to any other child link type by denoting it as a *singular* link type.

Just like node types can have multiple aspect descriptors, multiple classifications can be defined over a link type. Since each classification should be total, the union of all sub link types described by one such specialization returns the full parent link type. Conversely, each instance of the parent link type should also belong to at least one subtype for each specialization defined.

Department.*members* can be subclassed according to either a person's *function* (worker, clerk or manager), or his/her *mode of employment* (full-time or part-time). Two sets of sub link types result, any instance of **department.***members* will have to be classified according to both criteria:

department.*members*
:= **department.*workers*** ∪ **department.*clerks*** ∪ **department.*manager***
  := **department.*full-time-members*** ∪ **department.*part-time-members***

Whereas, the data model could stand on its own to support the analysis and design of hypermedia applications, its full potential only becomes apparent in the light of its role as a foundation to the *context-based navigation paradigm*, briefly discussed in the next section.

MESH'S CONTEXT-BASED NAVIGATION PARADIGM

The navigation paradigm as presented in *MESH* combines set-based navigation principles with the advantages of typed links and a structured data model. The typed links allow for a generalization of the *guided tour* construct. The latter is defined as a linear structure that eases the burden placed on the reader, hence reducing disorientation.

As opposed to conventional static guided tour implementations, *MESH* allows for complex structures of nested tours among related nodes to be generated *at run-time*, depending upon the *context* of a user's navigation. Such context is derived from *abstract navigational actions*, defined as link type selections. Indeed, apart from selecting a single *link instance*, similarly to the practice in conventional hypermedia, a navigational action may also consist of selecting *an entire link type*. Selection of a link type L from a given source node n_s results in a *guided tour along a set of nodes* being generated. This tour includes all nodes that are linked to the given node by the selected link type:

$$n_s.L := \{n_d \mid (n_s, n_d) \in L\}.$$

For example, the action **Van Gogh.*has-painted*** yields a guided tour along all paintings painted by Van Gogh:

Van Gogh.*has-painted* := {Irises, Potato eaters, Starry night, Sunflowers, Wheatfield,
…}

Navigation is defined in two orthogonal dimensions: on the one hand, navigation *within the current tour* yields linear access to complex webs of nodes related to the user's current focus of interest. On the other hand, navigation *orthogonal to a current guided tour*, changing the context of the user's information requirements, offers the navigational freedom that is the trademark of hypertext systems. In addition, the abstract navigational actions and tour definitions sustain the generation of very compact overviews and maps of complete navigation sessions. This information can also be *bookmarked*, i.e. bookmarks not just refer to a single node, but to a complete navigational situation, which can be resumed at a later date.

A GENERIC APPLICATION FRAMEWORK

The *information content* and *navigation structure* of the nodes are separated and stored independently. The resulting system consists of three types of components: the *nodes*, the *linkbase/repository* and the *hyperbase engine*. Although a platform-independent implementation framework is provided, all actual prototyping is explicitly targeted at a *Web* environment.

A node can be defined as a static page or a dynamic object, using e.g. HTML or XML. Its internal content is shielded from the outside world by the indirection of link types playing the role of a node's interface. Optionally, it can be endowed with the intelligence to tune its reaction to the *context* in which it is accessed. Indeed, by integrating a node type's set of attributed link types as a parameter in its layout template's presentation routines, the multimedia objects that are most relevant to this particular link type can be made current upon node access, hence the so-called *context-sensitive visualization* principle.

Since a node is not specified as a necessarily searchable object, linkage information cannot be embedded within a node's body. Links, as well as meta data about node types, link types, aspect descriptors and aspects are captured within a searchable *linkbase/repository* to provide the necessary information pertaining to the underlying hypermedia model, both at design time and at run-time. This repository is implemented in a relational database environment. Only here, references to physical node addresses are stored, these are never to be embedded in a node's body. All external references are to be made through location independent *node ID*'s.

The *hyperbase engine* is conceived as a server-side application that accepts link (type) selections from the current node, retrieves the correct destination node, keeps track of session information and provides facilities for generating maps and overviews. Since all relevant linkage and meta information is stored in the relational DBMS, the hyperbase engine can access this information by means of simple, predefined and parameterized *database queries*, i.e. without the need for searching through *node content*.

CONCLUSIONS

Advantages of the *MESH* Framework with Respect to Orientation

MESH's primary ambition was to reduce the orientation problems perceived by the end users of a hypermedia environment. As explained earlier, this can be accomplished by striving towards increased coherence and reduced cognitive overhead.

Evidently, *consistency* is improved by *MESH*'s structured data modeling approach, with *typed links* explicitly representing *relationship semantics*, i.e. *why* the source and destination nodes are related, and the practice of node and aspect typing offering maximal facilities for indicating *equivalencies between information units*. Moreover, end- user comprehension of how the hyperbase is conceived and what kind of relationships exist between the distinct nodes, already facilitates orientation to a great extent.

The use of *higher-order* information units such as object classes, but also the representation of collections of nodes as (node, link type) combinations, induces a stronger sense of structure and decreases *cognitive overhead*. The latter is even further reduced thanks to the *uniform user interface* that is supported by inheriting and refining layout templates in the node typing hierarchy and through the practice of capturing layout properties into aspect types as well. Consistent interface properties not only facilitate interaction with the system, but providing a similar layout to similar nodes also increases the user's ability to grasp the underlying data structure.

Visualizing the hypertext structure is also beneficial to reducing cognitive overhead. The latter is facilitated by two factors; first, the hyperbase structure being stored within a *searchable* relational database, such that (partial) maps and overviews can be generated at run-time, without the need to search through the node's *contents*. Second, the abundance of meta-information as node, aspect and link types allows for incorporating these abstractions into the overview, so as to be able to present concepts of varying granularity. This is applied e.g. in *fish eye views*, where more distant items can be shown with less detail, i.e. in aggregated form.

Although *MESH*'s data model could be efficacious on its own merits, it was contrived with specific navigation semantics in mind. The principle of context-based navigation offers a dynamic linear path throughout the information space, diminishing the risk of disorientation; whereas, the task of exhaustively exploring a certain topic becomes much easier. The navigation paradigm is easily understandable and supports a certain notion of *direction and position*.

Whereas, context-based navigation mainly affects cognitive overhead; it also has a positive influence on coherence by indicating the *context in which information units are displayed*, as a representation of what these units have in common. Obviously, this positive effect is even enlarged through the principle of *context sensitive node visualization*, which causes a node to present that subset of its embedded information that is most relevant to the current context.

Advantages of the *MESH* Framework with Respect to Application Development and Maintenance

Whereas the development advantages of object-oriented analysis and design are too numerous to mention them all, a few topics can be named that particularly apply to the *MESH* approach. Obviously, the notion of *abstraction* is strikingly present in *all* components of the framework. Both *layout templates* and *link types* can be designed on a high level of generality and refined and enriched on more concrete levels through inheritance and overriding. This not only facilitates authoring, but also benefits consistency, hence the overall quality of the application.

The practice of attributing link types to node types, rather than just attributing links to individual nodes, along with the ability of enforcing *constraints* such as cardinalities and inverse, allows for checking on consistency and referential integrity. Such constraint preservation should not necessarily be "repressive", but may well be "preventive", by suggesting mandatory links and feasible destination nodes to the author. Such would be a great asset, especially in larger hypermedia systems.

Other hypermedia approaches such as *EORM*, *RMM*, *HDM* and *OOHDM* are also based on conceptual modeling abstractions, either through E.R. or O.O. techniques. Among these, *OOHDM* is the only other methodology to explicitly incorporate a subtyping and inheritance/overriding mechanism. However, subtyping modalities are not explicitly stipulated. Rather, they are borrowed from *OMT* (Rumbaugh et al., 1991), a general-purpose object-oriented design methodology. *MESH* deploys a proprietary approach, specifically tailored to hypermedia modeling, where *structure* and *relationships* prevail over *behavior* as important modeling factors. Its full O.O. based data modeling paradigm should allow for hypermedia maintenance capabilities equaling their database counterpart; with unique object identifiers, monitoring of integrity, consistency and completeness checking, efficient querying and a clean separation between authoring *content* and *physical hyperbase maintenance*. *MESH* is the only approach to formulate specific rules for inheriting and overriding layout and link type properties, taking into account the added complexity of plural (possibly overlapping and/or temporal) node classifications. Links are treated as first-class objects, with link types being able to be subject to multiple specializations themselves, not necessarily in parallel with node subtyping. It is also clear that a model-based approach in general facilitates information sharing, reuse, development in parallel, etc.

Separation of node content from link structure and meta information allows for the latter two to be stored in a *relational database*; whereas, node content can be maintained in whatever facility is most suitable. Consequently, *link maintenance* is uncoupled from *content maintenance*. The former can be carried out almost entirely through queries upon the *linkbase*, without having to alter the internals of the nodes involved. Links become independent of physical node location and can be created or adjusted without accessing the nodes themselves, resulting in minimal repercussions of updates.

The very loose definition of the node concept allows for an open system where documents of almost any type can be used as nodes and be seamlessly integrated into the system, while retaining full navigational flexibility. Furthermore, nodes can be designed to be sensitive to different types of links, without knowledge of all nodes they are linked to. Only the various link *types* have to be taken into consideration, not every separate instance. The latter approach can be considered as more natural in that a node does not react to *from which node* it is accessed, but to the *reason why*.

Another benefit of abstraction lies in *MESH*'s *navigation paradigm*, where navigational actions are specified on an abstract level as much as possible, resulting in link *type* selection taking the place of link *instance* selection. This not only facilitates the *design*, with such actions being specified on node/aspect *type* level, but also yields node implementations with anchors that are *independent of the actual link instance*. As a consequence, links can be reallocated without any modification to the source node. Moreover, the context-based navigation paradigm supports a completely *automated generation of guided tours, maps* and *indices*, in contrast to e.g. *RMM, HDM* and *OOHDM*, where these are conceived as *explicit design components*, requiring extensive authoring efforts. In *MESH*, the author is not even engaged in their realization. Finally, it goes without saying that a well-maintained hyperbase will in its turn mean an invaluable asset to the end user.

REFERENCES

Ashman, H., Garrido A., and H. Oinas-Kukkonen, H.(1997). Hand-made and Computed Links, Precomputed and Dynamic Links, *Proceedings of Hypertext - Information Retrieval - Multimedia (HIM '97)*, Dortmund.

Bapat, A., Wäsch, J., Aberer, K., and Haake, J.(1996). An Extensible Object-Oriented Hypermedia Engine, *Proceedings of the seventh ACM Conference on Hypertext (Hypertext '96)*, Washington D.C. .

Beitner, N., Goble, C., and Hall, W. (1995). Putting the Media into Hypermedia, *Proceedings of the SPIE Multimedia Computing and Networking 1995 Conference*, San Jose.

Berners-Lee, T., and Cailliau, R.(1994). The World-Wide Web, *Commun. ACM, 37(8)*.

Bernstein, M. (1991). The Navigation Problem Reconsidered, *Hypertext/Hypermedia Handbook*, E. Berk and J. Devlin Eds., *McGraw-Hill*, New York.

Bieber, M. (1993). Providing Information Systems with Full Hypermedia Functionality, *Proceedings of the twenty-sixth Hawaii International Conference on System Sciences (HICSS-26)*, Hawaii.

Botafogo, A., and Shneiderman, B. (1991). Identifying Aggregates in Hypertext Structure, *Proceedings of the third ACM Conference on Hypertext (Hypertext '91)*, San Antonio.

Bush, V. (1945). As We May Think, *The Atlantic Monthly* (Jul.).

Chen, P. (1976).The entity-relationship approach: Toward a unified view of data, *ACM*

Trans. Database Systems, 1(1).

Conklin, J. (1987). Hypertext: An Introduction and Survey, *IEEE Computer, 20(9).*

Davis, H., Hall, W., Heath, I., Hill G., and Wilkins, R. (1992). MICROCOSM: An Open Hypermedia Environment for Information Integration, *Computer Science Technical Report CSTR 92-15.*

Davis, H. (1995). To Embed or Not to Embed, *Commun. ACM, 38*(8).

Duval, E., Olivié, H., Hanlon, P., and Jameson, D. (1995). HOME: An Environment for Hypermedia Objects, *Journal of Universal Computer Science, 1(5).*

Garg, P. (1988). Abstraction mechanisms in hypertext, *Commun. ACM, 31*(7).

Garzotto, F., Paolini P., and Schwabe, D. (1993). HDM - A Model-Based Approach to Hypertext Application Design, *ACM Trans. Inf. Syst., 11*(1).

Garzotto, F., Mainetti L., and Paolini, P. (1995). Hypermedia Design, Analysis, and Evaluation Issues, *Commun. ACM, 38*(8).

Ginige, A., Lowe D., and Robertson, J. (1995). Hypermedia Authoring, *IEEE Multimedia 2(4).*

Haan, B., Kahn, P., Riley, V., Coombs, J., and Meyrowitz, N.(1991). IRIS hypermedia services, *Commun. ACM, 35*(1).

Halasz, F. (1988). Reflections on NoteCards: Seven Issues for Next Generation Hypermedia Systems, *Commun. ACM, 31*(7).

Hall, W., Heath, I., Hill, G., Davis, H., and Wilkins, R.(1992). The Design and Implementation of an Open Hypermedia System, *Computer Science Technical Report CSTR 92-19*, University of Southampton.

Hammond, N. (1993). Learning with Hypertext: Problems, principles and Prospects, *HYPERTEXT a psychological perspective*, C. McKnight, A. Dillon and J. Richardson Eds., *Ellis Horwood*, New York.

Isakowitz, T., Stohr, E., and Balasubramanian, P. (1995). RMM, A methodology for structured hypermedia design, *Commun. ACM, 38*(8).

Isakowitz, T., Kamis, A., and Koufaris, M.(1998). The Extended RMM Methodology for Web Publishing, *Working Paper IS-98-18, Center for Research on Information Systems*, 1998 (Currently under review at ACM Trans. Inf. Syst.).

Jacobson, I., Christerson, M., Jonsson, P., and Övergaard, G. (1992). Object-Oriented Software Engineering, *Addison-Wesley*, New York.

Knopik, T., and Bapat, A. (1994). The Role of Node and Link Types in Open Hypermedia Systems, *Proceedings of the sixth ACM European Conference on Hypermedia Technology (ECHT '94)*, Edinburgh.

Lange, D. (1994). An Object-Oriented design method for hypermedia information systems, *Proceedings of the twenty-seventh Hawaii International Conference on System Sciences (HICSS-27)*, Hawaii.

Lemahieu, W. (1999). Improved Navigation and Maintenance through an Object-Oriented Approach to Hypermedia Modeling, *Doctoral dissertation (unpublished)*, Leuven.

Mayes, M. (1994). A method for evaluating the efficiency of presenting information in a hypermedia environment, *Computer in Education, 18*(1).

Meyer, B. (1997). Object-Oriented Software Construction, Second Edition, *Prentice Hall Professional Technical Reference*, Santa Barbara.

Meyrowitz, N. (1986). Intermedia: The Architecture and Construction of an Object-Oriented Hypermedia System and Applications Framework, *Proceedings of the Conference on Object-oriented Programming Systems, Languages and Applications (OOPSLA '86)*, Portland.

Nanard, J., and Nanard, M. (1995). Hypertext Design Environments and the Hypertext Design Process, *Communications. ACM , 38*(8).

Nelson, T. A (1965). File Structure for the Complex, The Changing and The Indeterminate, *ACM Twentieth National Conference.*

Nelson, T. (1987). Literary Machines. Vers. 87.1, *the Distributors*, South Bend.

Nielsen, J. (1990a). The Art of Navigating Through Hypertext, *Communications. ACM, 33*(3).

Nielsen, J. (1990b). Navigating through Large Information Spaces, Hypertext and Hypermedia, *Academic Press*, Boston.

Ramaiah, C. (1992). An Overview of Hypertext and Hypermedia, *International Information, Communication & Education, 11*(1).

Rivlin, E., Botafogo, R., and Shneiderman, B. (1994). Navigating in hyperspace: designing a structure-based toolbox, *Communications. ACM, 37*(2).

Rumbaugh, J., Blaha, M., Premerlani, W., Eddy, F., and Lorensen, W. (1991). Object Oriented Modeling and Design, *Prentice Hall*, Englewood Cliffs.

Schwabe, D., Rossi, G., and Barbosa, S. (1996). Systematic Hypermedia Application Design with OOHDM, *Proceedings of the seventh ACM conference on hypertext (Hypertext '96)*, Washington DC.

Schwabe D., and Rossi, G. (1998a). Developing Hypermedia Applications using OOHDM, *Proceedings of the Ninth ACM Conference on Hypertext (Hypertext '98)*, Pittsburgh.

Schwabe, D. and Rossi, G. (1998b). An O.O. approach to web-based application design, *Draft*.

Smith, J., and Weiss, S. (1988). An Overview of Hypertext, *Communications. ACM, 31*(7).

Snoeck, M., Dedene, G., Verhelst, M., and Depuydt, A. (1999). Object-Oriented Enterprise modeling with MERODE, *Universitaire Pers Leuven*, Leuven.

Thüring, M., Haake, J., and Hannemann, J. (1991). What's ELIZA doing in the Chinese Room - Incoherent Hyperdocuments and how to Avoid them, *Proceedings of the third ACM Conference on Hypertext (Hypertext '91)*, San Antonio (Nov. 1991).

Thüring, M., Hannemann J., and Haake J. (1995). Hypermedia and Cognition: Designing for comprehension, *Communications. ACM, 38*(8).

Wiil, U., and Leggett, J. (1992). Hyperform: Using Extensibility to Develop Dynamic, Open and Distributed Hypertext Systems, *Proceedings of the fourth ACM European Conference on Hypermedia Technology (ECHT '92)*, Milan.

Wiil, U., and Leggett, J. (1997). Hyperform: a hypermedia system development environment, *ACM Trans. Inf. Syst. , 15*(1).

Chapter XII

User Considerations in Electronic Commerce Transactions

Jonathan Lazar, Towson University, USA
A.F. Norcio, University of Maryland Baltimore County, USA

ABSTRACT

This chapter will provide a discussion of user considerations in electronic commerce transactions. A consumer in an electronic commerce transaction is essentially a user. There are a number of user considerations that must be addressed for an electronic commerce transaction task to be successful. This chapter will address the functionality and usability needs of a user in an electronic commerce transaction. Results of a study of over 150 users and the factors that influence their decision to purchase textbooks will be presented, analyzed, and discussed.

INTRODUCTION

The most important element of a business-to-consumer transaction in electronic commerce is the consumer. Businesses can place whatever site they choose on the Internet, but it is the consumer who chooses whether to purchase something and therefore, the consumer decides whether to make a transaction occur. For the consumer to make an electronic commerce transaction, the user must interact with the computer. Therefore, a consumer is just another name for a user, and the focus should be on designing an electronic commerce transaction around the needs of the user (Miles, Howes and Davies, 2000).

In a traditional information system in an organization or company, the user may need to access the system as part of their job. In fact, the user may be required to use the system. In electronic commerce, the opposite scenario is true. The user will only perform an electronic commerce transaction if they want to. No one is forcing the user to perform an electronic commerce transaction. In addition, there are many alternatives to using a specific electronic commerce site. Users can choose to purchase their products from traditional brick-and-mortar stores, as well as mail-order catalogs. There are many other e-commerce sites that sell similar products, and there are virtually no costs involved for a user to switch from one site to another (Nielsen and Norman, 2000). Therefore, the user interaction experience in electronic commerce must be a good one for an electronic commerce site to be successful, and for the transaction to actually take place.

Electronic commerce creates a number of new concerns. Electronic retailers must deal with issues of electronic payment, security, supply chain management and delivery. In dealing with all of these new concerns, frequently, the human interaction factors in the transaction are forgotten. The customer in an electronic commerce transaction is, in reality, a user. To purchase products from an electronic retailer, the customer/user must perform a set of computer tasks. The electronic commerce transaction cannot successfully be completed without the user. In this chapter, we will focus on the user factors in an electronic commerce transaction. Our discussion will address the human-computer interaction literature as it relates to the electronic commerce transaction. The electronic commerce transaction will be approached from the traditional human-computer interaction viewpoints of functionality and usability.

FUNCTIONALITY

One of the first considerations in an electronic commerce transaction is whether an e-commerce site has something interesting and valuable for the user. No one is going to go to an e-commerce site to purchase a case of cola for fifteen dollars when any food store in the country sells the same case of cola for four dollars. There are a number of reasons why a user might want to purchase something through an e-commerce site:

- The e-commerce site might offer a better selection of products than the brick-and-mortar store. It is possible that the e-commerce site might offer items of a higher quality than that the brick-and-mortar store, or offer products that the brick-and-mortar store simply does not offer (Turban, Lee, King and Chung, 2000).
- The e-commerce site might offer better pricing than a brick-and-mortar store. (Turban et al., 2000).
- The e-commerce site might offer better customer service than a brick-and-mortar store (Mossberg, 1999; Turban et al., 2000). For instance, the e-commerce store can be open 24 hours a day, which most brick-and-mortar stores are not.

Another functionality consideration is simply whether an e-commerce site can respond to a request from a consumer/user. Assuming that a user wants to purchase from a specific e-commerce site, and assuming that the e-commerce site is easy to use so that there are no usability problems, the transaction will take place, right? Not necessarily. There might be a number of technical problems that could keep the transaction from taking place. For instance, in a study done by Anderson Consulting during the 1999 Holiday season, over 25% of transactions could not take place due to server error (Reuters, 1999). Another study done by the Boston Consulting Group estimated that 28% of attempted transactions failed (Bonisteel, 2000). For some reason, the e-commerce server could not respond to the user request. It is quite possible that this was due to overwhelming transaction demand. A number of e-commerce sites simply could not keep up with the demand for transactions.

An interesting concern from the user point of view is what took place when the server could not respond to the user request. Did users receive an error message? If so, what type of error message did the users receive? In user interactions, novice users tend to blame themselves for errors, even if the errors were not due to the actions of the user (Lazar and Norcio, 1999; Lazar and Norcio, 2000b). In addition, error messages often are unclear and do not provide guidance to the user (Lazar and Norcio, 2000a). These error messages often increase the frustration level for the user. When the user attempted to complete an electronic commerce transaction, but the server was not able to respond, did the error messages clearly let the users know that e-commerce site was having technical problems, and that none of this was the fault of the user? Did the error message encourage the user to attempt their transaction again later the same day? Error messages need to be positive, and need to let the user know what actions to take.

USABILITY

There are a number of factors that affect the usability of a web site. All of these web usability rules apply to e-commerce. Usability is an extremely important consideration in electronic commerc since the user is not being forced to use the system, but rather, the e-commerce web site is competing with a number of brick-and-mortar stores and mail-order catalogs. In an ideal world, e-commerce sites would be created with user-centered design techniques, where the user is the main focus of the design process (Lazar, 2001; Norman, 1986). In user-centered design, there are a number of different techniques for evaluating the usability of an interface. For instance, usability testing involves users in determining whether an interface is easy to use and what problems exist (Nielsen, 1994). Expert reviews consist of usability experts critiquing an interface for usability problems (Nielsen and Mack, 1994). Unfortunately, many e-commerce sites are not built with user-centered design techniques, but instead are built quickly to meet short deadlines. The next sections discuss some of the important concepts of web usability as they relate to e-commerce.

Navigation

As Jakob Nielson says, "…if the customer can't find a product, then he or she will not buy it." (Nielsen, 2000a, p. 9). The user needs to be able to find what they are looking for on a web site. If the user cannot find what they are looking for, then the e-commerce transaction will not take place. Navigation needs to be provided to allow users to find what they are looking for among the many web pages on a web site. Traditionally, navigation on each page should be provided so that the users can easily access all of the main topical sections of the web site (Nielsen, 2000a). In addition, a search engine might be helpful (Lynch and Horton, 1999).

On the web page, the navigation should be provided on either the top of the web page, or the left side of the web page (Lynch and Horton, 1999). Navigation should not be placed on the bottom or the right side of the web page. The user may never scroll to the bottom of the web page, and therefore would not see the navigation. If navigation was placed on the right side of the web page, it is possible that the user might not have the browser window open to the full screen size, or that the screen size would be smaller than the intended web page size. In either of these situations, the user would not be able to see the navigation. Navigation should be text-based and should be simple. If navigation is provided graphically, users who have graphics turned off may not be able to effectively use the web site. Also, those who have JavaScript or Java applet functionality turned off will not be able to use the site if those technologies are required for navigation (Nielsen, 2000a).

Navigation on an e-commerce site should be easy. Users should not have to struggle to find the products that they want, nor should they have to struggle to get from one part of the e-commerce site to the other (Tilson et al., 1999). The user should not be required to click a lot of times to get to the item that they are interested in (Tilson et al., 1999). Tilson, Dong, Martin, and Kieke suggest limiting the use of drop-down menus in navigation, as they obscure the choices from view, and they require extra clicks just to see a complete list of items (Tilson et al., 1999). The easier it is for a user to find the item that they are looking for, the more likely it is that the user will purchase the item.

Browser Compatibility

The issue of browser compatibility is one of the most serious issues facing designers of web sites. The same web page can appear very differently in the two main web browsers, Internet Explorer and Netscape Navigator (Niederst, 1999). Both browsers (as well as the many versions of each browser) respond differently to HTML code, JavaScript, and stylesheets. Designers of e-commerce sites must make sure that their site displays properly in both browsers. Proper testing can assist in meeting this goal.

Download Time

Web pages that take a long time to download can frustrate the user (Nielsen, 2000a). In fact, the perceived quality of a web page can be affected by the download speed (Ramsay, Barbesi and Preece, 1998). The longer the page takes to download, the lower the perceived quality of the content. Therefore, the longer the page takes to download, the less likely the user is to complete the e-commerce transaction. Web pages should include a minimal amount of graphics, to help limit download time. If a page must have a large number of graphics, and therefore, will take a long time to download, users should be notified and be prepared to expect a slow download (Nielsen, 2000a). Users do not want to wait long to view a web page.

When the user sends a request for information or to complete a transaction, server response time can be both a functionality and usability problem. If a server is slow to respond to user requests, this is a usability concern. However, as server response time increases, it can become more than frustrating. The user may perceive that there is a functionality problem; that the server isn't just taking too long to respond, but rather, the user may perceive that the server cannot provide the services that the user needs.

Page Layout

Meaningful design and organization of the information on the screen is important for creating an interaction environment that enables effective user performance (Wickens & Andre, 1990). It is well established that the chunking process forms the basis of human cognitive processing, and that we have limits on how much information we can take in at one time (Miller, 1956). Consequently, page layout needs to conform to the chunking principle in order to be sure that the user can comprehend and correctly process the information on the page. For instance, it will be overwhelming to the user if they are provided with a list of fifty items (such as men's shirts) from which to choose. It will be easy for the user if these fifty items are chunked into ten categories of five items each. Effective information organization allows the user to search a page in a manner that conforms to the user's style (Hornof and Kieras, 1997). The number of colors on the page also needs to be minimal so as not to overwhelm the user (Lynch and Horton, 1999).

Metaphors

Metaphors provide useful conceptual models for designing interfaces (Carroll and Thomas, 1982). Metaphors are used to compare objects in an interface to items in the user's real-world setting. Metaphors are especially valuable as design models in e-commerce systems because the majority of e-commerce users are typically casual computer users. The more obvious the interface is to the users, the more satisfying the interaction becomes for the user (Igbaria and Nachman, 1990). This results in customers who are highly likely to return to the e-commerce site for additional transactions.

Some useful metaphors for novice users are the shopping cart metaphor and the desktop metaphor. In the desktop metaphor, which is used in the MacOS and MS-Windows interfaces, objects in the interface are compared to objects in the user's real world setting, such as trash cans, recycling bins, folders and printers. In most e-commerce sites, the shopping cart metaphor is used. Users "load" items into their shopping cart, which is a metaphor that relates to the real world shopping experience for most users. Users then go to the "check-out," at which point the transaction becomes final. Again, this relates to the real world shopping experience for most users. These metaphors are easy to understand because they are representative of the commonplace real world experience of the typical user (Nielsen, 2000a). The shopping cart metaphor has become a standard in e-commerce, and when a company deviates from that standard, sales may go down (Nielsen, 2000b).

SURVEY METHODOLOGY

To learn more about the functionality and usability factors that contribute to a successful electronic commerce transaction, a survey was created. After a pilot study to refine our survey instrument, we distributed our survey to a targeted population of users. The purpose of the study was to learn more about the factors that influence a user decision to purchase textbooks from an electronic commerce site.

Two of the reasons why users might not purchase items on-line are that 1) they are not comfortable using computers and the Internet, and 2) they do not have access to computers and the Internet. Our study specifically focused on users who are students majoring in computer science or computer information systems or information systems. By definition, these users are all comfortable with using computers; they have chosen to spend a large amount of their time taking computer courses, with the goal of working in the information technology field. Also, Internet access is not an issue; these students all have access to a number of computer labs. Not only do students have access to the open campus labs, but they also have access to computer labs that are reserved for only CS/CIS/IS majors. Therefore, Internet access would not be an issue for these students. By taking these two major factors out of the equation, we were able to isolate other factors that influence the decision to purchase textbooks from an electronic commerce site.

Pilot Study

In September, 1999, thirty students took part in a pre-testing of the survey instrument. Their responses were not counted, rather, their feedback was used to help improve the survey instrument. The post-pilot survey that was developed as a result of their feedback can be seen in Appendix A.

RESULTS

Surveys were collected during the Fall 1999 and Spring 2000 semesters. A total of 159 surveys were collected. Of the respondents 46 out of 159 (28.9%) were female, while 113/159 (71.1%) of respondents were male. The average age of respondents was 23.47 years, with the range being 19 years old to 46 years old. Figure 1 displays the estimated graduation dates of respondents.

Out of 159 respondents, 13/159 (8.1%) were computer science majors, 143/159 (89.9%) were computer information systems majors, and 3/159 (1.9%) of respondents were

Figure 1. Estimated graduation dates

Estimated Graduation Date	Respondents	Percentage
1999	22/159	13.8%
2000	79/159	49.7%
2001	47/159	29.6%
2002	9/159	5.7%
No answer	2/159	1.3%

other majors. Based on the age, gender and graduation year, it is possible to determine that we had a diverse sample that is representative of college students who major in the computing and information sciences.

Reasons for not purchasing textbooks on-line

Out of the 159 surveys, 24/159 (15.1%) of respondents indicated that they had purchased textbooks on-line during the current semester, while 39/159 (24.5%) of respondents indicated that they had purchased textbooks on-line sometime in the past. Figure 2 displays the reasons given by respondents for not purchasing textbooks on-line.

Other reasons cited for not purchasing textbooks on-line include respondents being worried that the bookstore wouldn't "buy back" books at the end of the semester if they were purchased from e-commerce sites, instructors frequently changing the textbooks during the first week of the semester or the name of required textbooks not being available until the first week of classes, university scholarships only allowing them to purchase textbooks from the bookstore, and students trying not to purchase books until after the first class, since they frequently add and/or drop classes.

Reasons for purchasing textbooks online

Figure 2. Reasons for not purchasing textbooks on-line

The traditional campus bookstore has all of the textbooks that I need	88/120	73.3%
I am concerned about giving out my credit card number over the Internet	35/120	29.2%
I find the Internet-based textbook sites hard to use	1/120	00.8%
I did not see the need to use an Internet-based textbook seller	52/120	43.3%
I was not sure whether I would receive the books in time	45/120	37.5%
I did not want to pay for shipping and handling costs	46/120	38.3%
The Internet-based textbook seller did not accept my credit cards	0/120	0%
I browsed to learn more about the books, but I did not purchase	20/120	16.7%
I attempted to purchase textbooks on-line, but the site was confusing to use	4/120	3.3%
I attempted to purchase textbooks on-line, but the site was having technical problems	1/120	00.8%

Figure 3. Reasons for purchasing textbooks on-line

Reason for purchasing books on-line		
I did not want to wait on a long line at the campus bookstore	10/39	25.6%
The Internet-based bookstore offered better prices	25/39	64.1%
The Internet-based bookstore offered books that the campus bookstore was out of	4/39	10.3%
The traditional campus bookstore was closed when I wanted to purchase books	1/39	2.6%
I enjoy purchasing items on-line	8/39	20.5%

For those who had purchased textbooks on-line, 3/39 (7.6%) had purchased all of their books on-line during the current semester, while 24/39 (61.5%) had purchased some of their books on-line during the current semester. Some of the e-commerce sites that respondents had purchased textbooks from include amazon.com (14), varsitybooks.com (9), ecampus.com (4), barnesandnoble.com (3), borders.com (2), bigwords.com (2), textbooks.com (2), and bestbooksbuys.com (1). Figure 3 displays the reasons why respondents chose to purchase textbooks on-line.

Satisfaction

The average response on the scale of satisfaction for survey respondents who had purchased textbooks on-line was 4.09, where 1 is "very satisfied" and 9 is "very unsatisfied." Final comments from respondents include being frustrated about books being out of stock at the e-commerce bookstore, concern over shipping and handling costs, concern about long delivery times, and concern about purchasing used books on-line without being able to see the condition of the textbooks.

Analysis

Why did people choose to not purchase textbooks on-line, or if they did purchase textbooks on-line, why did they do so? It is interesting to note that the two most cited reasons for not purchasing textbooks on-line were 1) *the traditional campus bookstore has all of the textbooks that I need* (73.3%) and 2) *I did not see the need to use an Internet-based textbook seller* (43.3%). Respondents did not cite problems with the e-commerce textbook sites themselves, but rather, did not see any convincing need to use the e-commerce sites. This is an important finding because e-commerce companies may need to refocus their advertising to convince people to use their web sites.

A large percentage of respondents indicated that 1) *I did not want to pay for shipping and handling costs* (38.3%) and 2) *I wasn't sure whether I would receive the books in time* (37.5%). This may point to the need for e-commerce textbook companies to improve their distribution networks, allaying consumer fears about delivery costs and delivery time. In addition, 29.2% of respondents indicated that *I am concerned about giving out my credit card number over the Internet*. This finding reinforces the findings of Tilson et. al. (1999), who found that consumers fearing the theft of their credit card numbers was one of the biggest hindrances to an e-commerce transaction (Tilson et al., 1999). This finding may also point out the need for alternative payment methods for e-commerce transactions, such as "digital cash" (Turban et al., 2000).

For survey respondents who had purchased textbooks on-line, the most popular reason for purchasing textbooks on-line was that *The Internet-based bookstore offered better prices* (64.1%). The second-most cited reason for purchasing textbooks on-line was that *I did not want to wait on a long line at the campus bookstore* (25.6%). These statistics point to two of the reasons that people like shopping on-line: better prices and better customer service. When attempting to market their web sites, e-commerce companies might want to focus on the main reasons that users come to web sites: better prices and better service.

It is interesting to note that the interface design, and the usability of the web sites, did not seem to play a major part in users deciding to perform or not to perform an e-commerce transaction in the textbook market. This may be due to a number of factors. For instance, e-commerce textbook sites may, as a group, be well designed. The target population of this study (university students who are majoring in the computing and information sciences) may all have fast connections to the Internet, so download time might not have been a problem. It is interesting, however, to note that the satisfaction score reported by those who had purchased a textbook on-line was 4.09, on a scale of 1 to 9 where 1 is very satisfied and 9 is very unsatisfied. Users who responded to this study are not overwhelmingly satisfied with their on-line shopping experience. In addition, a large majority of those who responded to this study had never purchased textbooks on-line, even though they are comfortable using the Internet and have access to the Internet. For most of the respondents, they just didn't feel that the e-commerce textbooks sites offered anything more valuable than the campus bookstore. The users who responded did not see any reason to purchase on-line.

Usability is a very important consideration in designing web sites, to ensure a successful user experience and increase on-line sales (Tedeschi, 1999). However, once usability is taken into consideration, and the connection speeds and experience levels of the users are taken into account, the major advantages and disadvantages of e-commerce are still the same: users go to e-commerce sites because they want better prices and better customer service, and users are frightened about giving out their credit card numbers on the Internet. These are important findings, which can be used to create a more successful experience for the user in an e-commerce transaction.

SUMMARY

This chapter focused on user considerations in an e-commerce transaction. The e-commerce site must offer functionality that the user is interested in, and the e-commerce site must also be easy to use. In this study, the usability of e-commerce textbook sites did not appear to be a problem. For those who did not purchase textbooks on-line, the most frequently cited reasons were that there was no need to use the e-commerce site, concerns about shipping and delivery time, and concerns about credit card security. For those who did purchase textbooks on-line, the most frequently cited reasons were improved prices and customer service. All of these findings point to what users want, both those who have not purchased on-line, and those who have purchased on-line. Users want: 1) Good prices and customer service, 2) Quick and inexpensive delivery of products, and 3) Secure methods of payment. By focusing on these areas, e-commerce sites can provide a more positive experience for the user and possibly increase sales for the e-commerce company.

APPENDIX A. CUSTOMER SATISFACTION SURVEY

The purpose of the following survey is to learn more about factors that contribute to the success of Internet-based textbook sellers. This study includes both sites that focus on textbooks, such as efollett.com , varsitybooks.com, and ecampus.com, as well as mainline booksellers, such as amazon.com, borders.com, and barnesandnoble.com

1. Age _____
2. Gender___
3. Expected year of Graduation _____

4. Major   Computer Science ___   Computer Information Systems ___
   Other _____ (please indicate)

5. Have you used an Internet-based textbook seller to purchase your textbooks this semester?
   Yes _____   Which seller(s?)_____
   No _____

6. Have you ever used an Internet-based textbook seller?
   Yes _____   Which seller(s?) _____
   No _____

If you have NEVER purchased textbooks from an Internet-based textbook seller, please complete question number 7, and then turn in your survey. If you HAVE purchased textbooks from an Internet-based textbook seller, please complete the questions (starting with number 8) on the other side of this survey

7. If you HAVE NOT purchased textbooks from an Internet-based textbook seller, why not?
   (Check as many as you wish)
   _____   The traditional campus bookstore has all of the textbooks that I need.
   _____   I am concerned about giving out my credit card number over the Internet.
   _____   I find the Internet-based textbook sites hard to use.
   _____   I did not see the need to use an Internet-based textbook seller.
   _____   I was not sure whether I would receive the books in time.
   _____   I did not want to pay for shipping and handling costs.
   _____   The Internet-based textbook seller did not accept my credit cards.
   _____   I browsed to learn more about the books, but I did not purchase.
   _____   I attempted to purchase textbooks on-line, but the site was confusing to use.
   _____   I attempted to purchase textbooks on-line, but the site was having technical   problems.
   _____   Other (please elaborate_____
              _____
              _____)

8. If you HAVE used an Internet-based textbook seller this semester, please complete the rest of the survey.

(Check only one)

_____   I purchased all of my books this semester through an Internet-based textbook seller.

_____   I purchased some of my books this semester through an Internet site, and some of my books through a campus bookstore or traditional bookstore.

9. Why did you choose to use an Internet-based textbook seller?
(Check as many as you wish)

_____   I did not want to wait on a long line at the campus bookstore.

_____   The Internet-based bookstore offered better prices.

_____   The Internet-based bookstore offered books that the campus bookstore was out of.

_____   The traditional campus bookstore was closed when I wanted to purchase. books.

_____   I enjoy purchasing items on-line

_____   Other _____

10. How satisfied were you with your experience purchasing textbooks on the Internet?

Very Satisfied   Very Unsatisfied
1   2   3   4   5   6   7   8   9

11. Any other comments?

_____

REFERENCES

Bonisteel, S. (2000). More on-line shopping; more unhappy shoppers - study. *Andover News Network (www.andovernews.com)*, March 7, 2000.

Carroll, J., & Thomas, J. (1982). Metaphor and the cognitive representation of computing systems. *IEEE Transactions on Systems, Man, and Cybernetics, 12*(2), 107-116.

Hornof, A., & Kieras, D. (1997). *Cognitive modeling reveals menu search is both random and systematic.* Proceedings of the CHI: Human Factors in Computing Conference,107-114.

Igbaria, M., & Nachman, S. (1990). Correlates of user satisfaction with end-user computer: An exploratory study. *Information and Management, 19*, 73-82.

Lazar, J., & Norcio, A. (1999). *To Err Or Not To Err, That Is The Question: Novice User Perception of Errors While Surfing The Web.* Proceedings of the Information Resource Management Association 1999 International Conference, 321-325.

Lazar, J., & Norcio, A. (2000a). *Intelligent Error Message Design for the Internet.* Proceedings of the World Multiconference on Systemics, Cybernetics, and Informatics, 532-535.

Lazar, J., & Norcio, A. (2000b). System and Training Design for End-User Error. In S. Clarke & B. Lehaney (Eds.), *Human-Centered Methods in Information Systems: Current*

Research and Practice . Hershey, PA: Idea Group Publishing, 76-90.

Lazar, J. (2001, in press). *User-Centered Web Development*. Sudbury, MA: Jones and Bartlett Publishers.

Lynch, P., & Horton, S. (1999). *Web style guide: Basic design principles for creating web sites*. New Haven: Yale University Press.

Miles, G., Howes, A., & Davies, A. (2000). A framework for understanding human factors in web-based electronic commerce. *International Journal of Human-Computer Studies, 52*, 131-163.

Miller, G. (1956). The magical number seven, plus or minus two: Some limits on our capacity for processing information. *Psychological Review, 63*(2), 81-96.

Mossberg, W. (1999). On-line drugstores offer some remedies and a few headaches. *Wall Street Journal*, April 29, 1999.

Niederst, J. (1999). *Web Design in a Nutshell*. Sebastopol, CA: O'Reilly and Associates.

Nielsen, J. (1994). *Usability Engineering*. Boston: Academic Press.

Nielsen, J, and Mack, R. (eds.) (1994). *Usability Inspection Methods*. New York: John Wiley & Sons.

Nielsen, J. (2000a). *Designing web usability: The practice of simplicity*. Indianapolis: New Riders Publishing.

Nielsen, J. (2000b). Jakob Nielsen's Alertbox: the Sales Paradox. Available at: http://www.useit.com/alertbox/20000806.html.

Nielsen, J., & Norman, D. (2000). Usability on the web isn't a luxury. *Informationweek*, February 14, 2000.

Norman, D. (1986). *User-centered system design: new perspectives on human-computer interaction*. Hillsdale, NJ: Lawrence Erlbaum Associates.

Ramsay, J., Barbesi, A., & Preece, J. (1998). A psychological investigation of long retrieval times on the World Wide Web. *Interacting with Computers, 10*, 77-86.

Reuters. (1999). One in four on-line purchases thwarted. *Reuters News*, December 20, 1999.

Tedeschi, B. (1999). Good Web Site Design Can Lead to Healthy Sales. *The New York Times*, August 30, 1999.

Tilson, R., Dong, J., Martin, S., & Kieke, E. (1998). *Factors and principles affecting the usability of four e-commerce sites*. Proceedings of the 1998 Conference on Human Factors and the Web.

Turban, E., Lee, J., King, D., & Chung, H. (2000). *Electronic commerce: A managerial perspective*. Upper Saddle River, NJ: Prentice Hall.

Wickens, C., & Andre, A. (1990). Proximity compatibility and information display: Effects of color, space, and objectness on information integration. *Human Factors, 32*(1), 61-77.

Chapter XIII

Computer-Supported Social Networking Based on E-mail Exchange

H Ogata and Y. Yano, Tokushima University, Japan
N. Furugori, INES Corporation, Japan

ABSTRACT

The exploration of social networks is essential to find capable cooperators who can help problem-solving and to augment cooperation between workers in an organization. This chapter describes PeCo-Mediator-II to seek for capable cooperators with the chain of personal connections (PeCo) in a networked organization. Moreover, this system helps gathering, exploring and visualizing social networks in an organization. The experimental results show that the system facilitates users encounter cooperators and develop a new helpful relationship with the cooperators.

INTRODUCTION

Recently, opportunities for communication and collaboration via computer networks have immensely been increased in networked organizations (Sproull and Kiesler, 1991). A fundamental problem is how to encounter people who can help problem-solving. We are focusing on the problem of discovering such people through social networks. Social networks are at least as important as the official organizational structures for tasks ranging from immediate, local problem-solving (e.g., fixing a piece of equipment), to primary work functions, such as creating collaborative groups (Kautz et al., 1997a).

In CSCW, researchers are interested in the role of social networks between organizational members. Clement stated that users developed informal collaborative networks to know how to use a new software (Clement, 1990). Then, private networks are important for workers to solve problems by providing helpful information. A number of studies have shown that one of the most effective channels for gathering information and expertise within an organization is its informal networks of collaborators, colleagues and friends. The networks of helping relationships are called Help Network (Eveland et al., 1994). However, the networks are not collected and generally follow work group alignments rather than technical specialization. Therefore, it is significant to use members' interpersonal connections effectively in their activities.

Our research focuses on "Personal Connection" (PeCo) which is a starting point for finding a capable cooperator. We propose PeCo-Mediator-II (Ogata et al., 1996a, Ogata et al., 1997) for gathering, seeking, and visualizing social networks in a networked organization. PeCo-Mediator-II is a distributed system with a personal database (PeCo-Collector) and a software agent (PeCo-Agent). Every user has the two softwares on the respective site. PeCo-Collector incrementally gathers information on its user's acquaintances and the relationships through watching the exchanges of e-mail. PeCo-Agent moves to colleagues' sites and negotiates with other agents and users to find cooperators. Although the users of both NetNews and mail lists are often passive to find answers, our system can actively discover cooperators with the chain of personal connection from the user and the cooperators.

OVERVIEW OF PECO-MEDIATOR-II

When a computer network connects people or organizations, it is an on-line social network. Just as a computer network is a set of machines connected by a set of cables, a social network is a set of people connected by a set of social relationships, such as friendship, co-working, or information exchange (Garton et al., 1997). Computer-Mediated Communication (CMC) systems also reduce the transaction costs of initiating and maintaining interpersonal ties (Pickering and King, 1992). Weak ties created by CMC expand the channels of information sources for the individual and have potential for strong ties.

Social network analysis is focused on uncovering the patterning of people's interaction (Scott, 1992, Wasserman and Faust, 1994, Wellman and Berkowitz, 1997, Hiramatsu, 1990, Yasuda, 1997). Network analysis is based on the intuitive notion that these patterns are important features of the lives of the individuals who display them. Network analysts believe that how an individual lives depends in large part on how that individual is tied into the larger web of social connections. Many believe, moreover, that the success or failure of societies and organizations often depends on the patterning of their internal structure. Typically social networks are obtained in two ways: socio-centric and ego-centric approach. First, socio-centric approach considers a whole network based on some specific criterion of population boundaries such as a formal organization. A whole network describes the ties that all members of a population maintain with all others in that group. Although this method is available for handling incomplete data sets, this requirement places limits on the size of networks that cat be examined. Second, the ego-centric approach considers the relations reported by a local individual. This approach is particularly useful when the population is large.

Our initial system called PeCo-Mediator (Ogata et al., 1995) was based on socio-centric approach. PeCo-Mediator is a groupware system that allows sharing of PeCo in a group and to search for connections between the user and targets. The users need to share PeCo with the common database of PeCo-Mediator. Although the system was very available in some small groups, it was reluctant in terms of users offering their private information like PeCo into the common database.

In this chapter, our target is a large-scale organization. Therefore, PeCo-Mediator-II gathers PeCo based on ego-centric approach. PeCo-Mediator-II consists of the two systems, PeCo-Collector and PeCo-Agent (see Figure 1). Every organizational member has the two software on the respective site. PeCo-Collector gathers information on its user's acquaintances and the relationships through watching the exchanges of e-mail.

Figure 1: Overview of PeCo-Mediator-II.

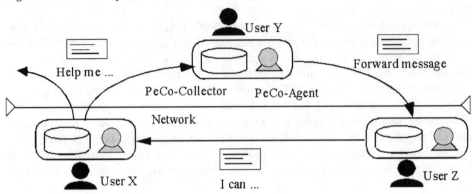

PeCo-Agent moves between members' sites to find a partner in the community. The user's PeCo is a starting point for the exploration. The user's acquaintance acts as a liaison between the user and the partner in this situation. In this figure, user X requests user Y to help the problem solving, and user Y introduces user Z. After that, user Z can help user X by request. Particularly in Japan, the mediation of mutual acquaintances is very effective for success in negotiation of cooperation, because social relationships have an influence on decision making (Matsushita, 1993).

The characteristics of this system are:

1. Accumulation of on-line and off-line social networks: Mainly, our system deals with PeCo based on the exchange of e-mails, PeCo-Mediator-II automatically stores relationships based on e-mail tags. In addition, the user can provide on-line relationships; e.g., based on the exchange of name-cards.

2. Measurement of PeCo strength: The strength of PeCo is estimated with the frequency of e-mail exchange. This degree is very useful for deciding the receivers of the request.

3. Privacy protection: PeCo-Mediator-II manages individual ties with a distributed personal database in the user's own site. Personal data is safer in a personal database than in a common database. Therefore, it is easy for this system to protect user's privacy and to be accepted in a large scale organization.

4. Compatibility: The architecture of PeCo-Mediator-II is compatible with existing e-mail mechanisms. Compatibility reduces user overhead in taking advantage of the e-mail tools.

5. Scalability: Even if the number of users increase, this system can work robustly because of an agent-based distributed system architecture.

6. Parallel exploration assisted by agents: PeCo-Agent supports the user to search for a cooperator through social networks while negotiating with other users and PeCo-Agents. Moreover, the user can visually understand the current status of the exploration and easily control that process.

7. Mitigation of cooperators' overload: The questions are possibly concentrated on a part of users (experts). This system provides a common database of answers and navigates the questions with strategies on educating the secondary cooperators and on spreading the answers.

SOCIAL NETWORKS BASED
ON E-MAIL EXCHANGE

This section presents how to gather individual ties through the exchange of e-mail and how to estimate the strength of PeCo.

Collection of Social Networks

We can divide PeCo into explicit and implicit according to an e-mail header. The former is a human relation between a sender and a receiver who has directly exchanged an e-mail each other. On the other hand, the latter connection is between persons who have never exchanged an email directly, and it is derived from the header of e-mail. Implicit ties are available for collecting friends linked with some relationship. Table 1 shows ties of user A when he/she has sent or received e-mail. A connection has a direction from a sender to a receiver. A sender is written in "From" field, and a receiver is in "To" and "Cc" fields. If user A sends e-mail to user X, Y and Z, then the system stores the explicit connections from user A to user X, Y, and Z. Also, if user A receives e-mail from user B, the relationship from user B to user A is collected explicitly. Moreover, if user S and T also receive the e-mail, the system stores the connection from user A to user S and T. Since the system automatically gathers the user's connections, it greatly lightens the user's burden of the data entry.

Table 1: Relationship derived from e-mail header.

The user A		Sender	Receiver
Header of email		From: A To: X Cc: Y, Z	From: B To: A, S Cc: T
PeCo	Direct	A ⇒ X A ⇒ Y A ⇒ Z	B ⇒ A
	Indirect		A ⇒ S A ⇒ T

Strength of Social Networks

PeCo (ties) have been classified in social networking theory as either strong or weak (Granovetter, 1973). To evaluate the relationship, the strength of it is very useful. We propose the scale derived by the e-mail exchanging. The connection is strong if the following conditions are satisfied:

1. Exchanging e-mail frequently;
2. Exchanging e-mail recently; and
3. Exchanging e-mail reciprocally.

Based on this consideration, we propose the following equation for representing the closeness between the two person *(Pi)* and *(Pj)*:

$$M_{i,j} = \frac{1}{2}\left\{ \sum_{k=1}^{P} w_k \times \frac{n(s_k)}{N(s_k)} + \sum_{k=1}^{P} w_k \times \frac{n(r_k)}{N(r_k)} \right\}$$

where,

$$W_k = \frac{200(P - k + 1)}{P(P + 1)}$$

$$\sum_{k=1}^{P} W_k = 100.$$

The first and second expression of this equation respectively shows how frequently the user has sent and received messages during a certain defined period of time k, P . n(sk) and n(rk) shows the number of delivery and accept messages between the user and one of his/her acquaintances during the sub-term of the user-defined period. The total number of the messages during the term denotes N(sk) and N(rk) separately. The weight to the sub-term, Wk is given by the user and the sum of all weight is 100. The weights mean the level of importance at the period. For instance, if the user has a very close relationship with the friends who exchanged e-mail at a recent time, the user might give high weight to the term. The maximum of this scale is 100 and the minimum is 0. The closeness is used as search criteria in exploring social networks. This system searches for the relationships over the criteria given by user.

EXPLORATION OF SOCIAL NETWORK

This section proposes a data diagram of PeCo exploration that is based on speech-act-theory (Winograd and Flores, 1987, Suchman, 1994). Speech Acts are utterances that contain information needed to assert and perform actions, or, according to Austin "things that people do with words" (Austin, 1962). Speech Act Verbs are verbs used in speech acts utterances, to perform actions. We describe user's actions in the exploration of social networks and how to support the exploration of social networks using the diagram.

PeCo Exploration Diagram

Figure 2 shows the data diagram of exploring social networks. User A is a sender of e-mail and user B is its receiver. Each node denotes the state during the exploration, and it moves to the next state if the user acts on the activity of the arc. The starting point is the state one and the ending point is the state five and six. The state 2 shows the exploration is continued from the state 2 after changing the receiver. The sender has three options: request, cancel and remind. The receiver has five options: read, not-read, accept, forward, and reject. For example, if user A sends a request to user B, the receiver either reads it or does not read it. If user B does not read it, user A may remind user B to read it. If user B reads it, he/she either accepts the request, rejects it, or forwards it to his/her friends. Until someone accepts the request or user A cancels it, the exploration of social networks is continued.

Figure 2: Data diagram of exploring social networks with e-mail.

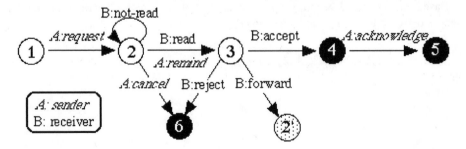

Awareness in Social-Networks Exploration

It is very meaningful for the system to provide awareness about the exploration process of social networks. According to the exploration diagram of social networks, the system tells users up-to-minute activities of receivers. From this awareness the user can know where the request is transmitted from, who introduces whom, etc. The awareness are classified according to:

1. Awareness of receiver's actions: This informs the receiver did not read the user's request, or the receiver rejected it, etc.
2. Awareness of social relationships: This shows the connections between the user and the receiver.

The first awareness gives the user the opportunities to communicate with the receiver. The second awareness facilitates the communication between the user and the receiver through the chain of the connections.

Control of Exploring Social Networks

It is necessary to give some restrictions to the exploration of social networks, not to continue to explore concurrently for a long time. Therefore, we propose the following ways to control the seeking:

1. Control by initial settings: Before the user starts the searching, the user sets a deadline, the minimum strength of relationships, and the maximum depth from the user to a receiver. If the exploration exceeds the settings, and the request is automatically deleted the branch of the exploration is over.
2. Control by remote commands: The user can control the request remotely according to awareness of receiver's reactions. The system allows the user to cancel or remind the request based on the diagram. Canceling the request enables the user to prune off the exploration tree. This command reduces the information overload of the receivers and prevents the request chaining. On the other hand, remind command encourages the user to make a response if the user wants a fast reply. If there is a loop message, the system automatically cancels the weaker message of the two.

History of PeCo Exploration

To support the exploration of social networks, PeCo-Mediator stores the history of PeCo exploration when the user has sent or received messages. We represent the history with the following attributes:

1. Who: Who did the user send the request to, or receive it from?
2. When: When did the user do it?
3. What: What did the user send or receive the request about?
4. Which: Which action did the user do?
5. How: How strong was the relationship between the user and the requester?
6. Path: Which path was the message sent through?

Based on PeCo exploration diagrams, the attribute "Which" includes the following user's actions: request, accept, reject, forward, receive request, receive-forward, receive-accept, receive-reject. The topic of the request is represented with keywords that are derived from e-mail.

Table 2: Taxonomy of users with the exploration history.

User type	Condition
Cooperator	*accept?* †*f ¿* and *accept* > *reject* and *accept* > *forward*
Semi-cooperator	*receive_accept?* †*accept?* †*f Å*
Mediator	*forward?* †*f Å* and *forward* > *reject*
Non-cooperator	*reject?* †*f Å* and *accept* = 0

Taxonomy of Users

Based on the above history, we divide users into the five types (see Table 2):

1. Cooperator: The cooperator is a user who usually accepts the request during this system use. The cooperator is often an expert about the request.
2. Semi-cooperator: The semi-cooperator is a user who potentially has the capability for cooperation about the request. We assume that a semi-cooperator receives the answer from others rather than accepting requests.
3. Mediator: The Mediator is the user who usually forwards the request to his/her friends.
4. Non-cooperator: The non-cooperator is a user who almost rejects the request.
5. Unknown user: If a user has never received or sent a request, the user is unknown for the system.

PeCo-Agent understands the users' capability through watching the exchanges of questions and answers. We represent the capability of the user and his/her acquaintances with the keywords in the e-mail. For example, a friend is a cooperator about C programming language although the friend is a non-cooperator about Tcl/Tk.

Supporting PeCo Exploration with History

PeCo-Agent helps a user in the following situation:

1. Request support: When the user decides a receiver of the request, this system shows the user the following information about the receiver:
   a) User's type (a cooperator, semi-cooperator, mediator, non-cooperator, or unknown user): If the receiver is a cooperator, the user may find the answer easily.
   b) Strength of relationship: If the connection between the user and the receiver is strong, it is easy to ask for cooperation.
   c) The number of requests left unattended: If the receiver has many requests, his/her answer may be late.
   d) System usage: If the receiver uses this system at that time, the user can obtain the response as soon as possible.
2. Acceptance support: If the user accepts a request, the system provides the reply of the request to the user. The user edits the past results to answer it.
3. Forward support: PeCo-Agent shows the user the possible acquaintances who can help the user with the results of the past exploration. If the user has a friend who is a cooperator, semi-cooperator or mediator, PeCo-Agent recommends them as the receiver.
4. Reject support: PeCo-Agent automatically rejects the request if the relationship strength between the user and the request sender is lower than the given value by the user.

Reducing the Overload of Cooperators

Cooperators are often burdened with the requests from others. To mitigate that, we propose the following support in this system.

1. Educating semi-cooperators: If semi-cooperators are educated and reach a level of cooperators, the number of cooperators increases. Therefore, PeCo-Agent recommends a cooperator to send the request to semi-cooperators. The cooperator sends the answer to the requester after checking and correcting the answer from the semi-cooperators reduce the overload of cooperators. Next time, PeCo-Agent recommends that the requester sends the request directly to the semi-cooperator. After that, the semi-cooperator becomes a new cooperator and the requester becomes a new semi-cooperator. Moreover, the free-rider issue (Salomon, 1992), which is a user who obtains information without giving any, might be settled also.

2. Sharing answers with a database: Organizational memory has been proposed as a concept for sharing organizational members' knowledge (Conklin, 1992). We also adopt that concept into our situation. If both a cooperator and a requester permit sharing of an answer, it is entered into a shared database. The decision about this depends on the relationship and the answer. Because the requesters can refer to the answers in the database before sending the requests, cooperators need not write down the same answer repeatedly.

3. Spreading answers: When a cooperator permits propagation of the answer, the system sends the answer to the mediators between the cooperator and the requester as well as the requester. By this facility, mediators can also know the answer.

IMPLEMENTATION

This section describes the development of PeCo-Mediator-II.

Data of PeCo

The data of PeCo consists of the three classes; person, e-mail and relationship.

1. Person object: PeCo-Collector automatically creates a new person object and enters his/her e-mail address through referring "From", "To", "cc" of an e-mail header. After this, the user inputs some data such as an office address and interest during this system use. User has to enter, and update personal data of her/his acquaintances by himself/herself, e.g., place of employment or URL. However, the exchange log of e-mail is automatically updated until the limited time. The user gives the deadline of the exchange log, e.g., one year.

2. E-mail object: PeCo-Collector manages e-mails, and they are hypertextual linked with keywords. The signatures are convenient to access people by WWW or e-mail. The e-mail object is automatically linked with the senders and receivers objects.

3. Relationship object: PeCo-Collector also generates a new relationships object at the delivery and accept time of e-mail. A relationship object has attributes of the social relationships such as classmates. Moreover, the relationship object is automatically connected to the sender and receivers objects.

System Configuration

We developed a prototype system on a workstation with Tcl/Tk (Ousterhoult, 1994). The system consists of PeCo-Collector and PeCo-Agent. Every group user has the two systems on the respective site.

Figure 3: System configuration of PeCo-Mediator-II.

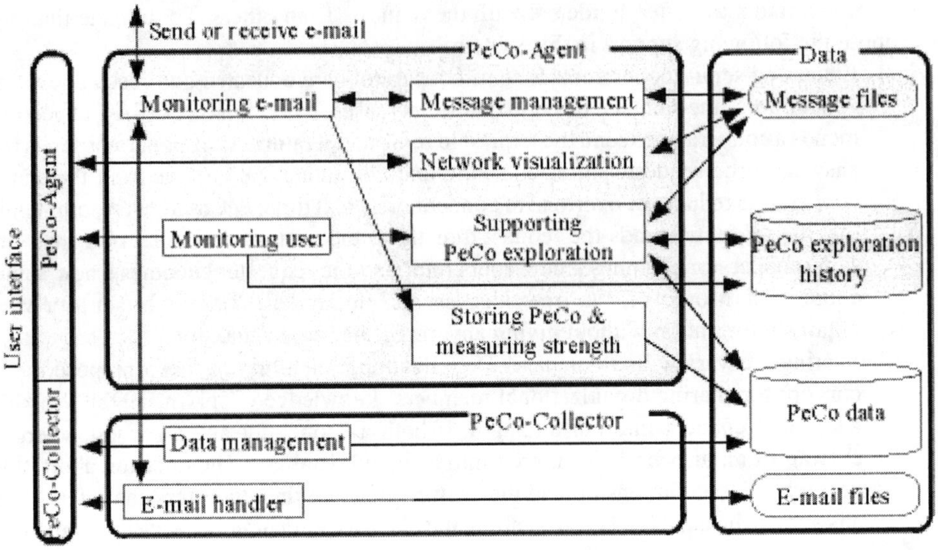

(1) PeCo-Collector

This system has two components: data management and e-mail handler. All the data is managed by TRIAS (Yamamoto et al., 1989) and the e-mail tool is tkMH based on MH (Mail Handler) (Peek, 1994). PeCo-Collector links an e-mail object and its sender's or receiver's object automatically and the user can make hypertextual links among e-mails.

(2) PeCo-Agent

The characteristics of PeCo-Agent are:
1. It represents capability of users with keywords about e-mails.
2. It obtains the capability of users from the user and other agent.
3. It can move around the Internet and communicate with other users and agents.
4. It finds the candidates of cooperators concurrently.

In PeCo-Mediator-II, a user communicates and negotiates with others through e-mail. In the same way, PeCo-Agent communicates with other agents with structured e-mail (Malone, 1986). User sends / receives the modified e-mail messages based on the data diagram, in the exploration of social networks. For example, when a user sends a request, PeCo-Mediator-II adds a special tag (X-action: request) into the e-mail header. By processing the special tags in e-mail, the system classifies the messages.

Free keywords given by user are used for seeking similar questions and answers. Only noun keywords are extracted from messages with Chasen (Matsumoto, 1997) that is a Japanese morphological analysis tool. PeCo-Agent calculates the similarity between the given keywords and the stored questions by matching keywords elicited from Chasen filter. In the Q&A matching process, we use a statistical similarity score. A Q&A pair is represented by a keyword vector that associates a significance value with each keyword in Q&A. We use TF/ITF (Salton and McGill, 1983) for weighting keywords. The TF (term frequency) component of this weight depends on the within-document frequency of the term, and the IDF (inverse document frequency) component varies inversely with the frequency of the term in the Q&A corpus.

PeCo-Agent consists of the following components:

1. Monitoring e-mail: PeCo-Agent watches the e-mail exchange of users and it distinguishes between normal e-mail and PeCo e-mail. If an e-mail is normal, it gathers the user's ties into PeCo-Collector. Otherwise, PeCo-Agent interprets tag fields of the messages and sends the results to the message management module.
2. Managing messages: This module stores PeCo e-mail into a message files database and it manages system's messages based on PeCo exploration diagram in Figure 2.
3. Monitoring user: PeCo-agent monitors user's actions in the exploration process and stores them into his/her PeCo exploration history database.
4. Network visualization: This component graphically shows the exploration process of social network at real time.
5. Supporting PeCo exploration: Using the local databases, PeCo-Agent helps the user to find suitable cooperators and connections.
6. Storing PeCo & measuring strength: This module stores the user's PeCo and the frequency of the e-mail exchange into his/her PeCo database.

Interface

PeCo-Collector

Figure 4 shows a screen of PeCo-Collector of user "aiso". The user manages e-mail in the window (A), e.g., moving a message into folders. The window (B) shows the class hierarchy of the database. The user can search for the data of a person, relationship or e-mail from this window. For example, personal data of user "Gouji" is shown in the window (C).

Figure 4: Screen shot of PeCo-Collector.

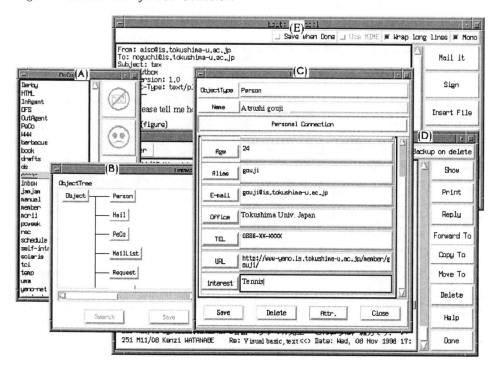

The user can easily update these data and add attributes. The window (D) is a list of e-mails of a folder. When the user sends the e-mail in the window (E), PeCo-Collector stores PeCo data.

Exploration of social network

Figure 5 shows the interaction after user "aiso" requests his/her PeCo-Agent. In the window (A) "aiso" writes the request message. In the window (B), the user sets time out for seeking social networks, the minimum strength of PeCo and the maximum steps between "aiso" and the receiver. PeCo-Agent finishes the exploration according to this setting. In the window (C), PeCo-Agent assists "aiso" to decide who is the better receiver of his/her acquaintances, and the user agent provides information about the candidates of the receivers. The window (D) displays the list of the requests that the user has sent.

The window (E) shows the flow of the exploration from the user graphically. This tree is the result of traveling with the connections of "aiso". The icons except "aiso" denote the candidates of cooperators. The shorter the distance between two icons, the stronger the relationship they have. While the dotted line denotes the receiver has not read the message yet, the solid line shows the receiver has already read it. The black icon means the user has rejected the request. The node icon shows the user has forwarded the message to his/her friends. The leaf and white icon means the user has accepted the cooperation. In this figure, "mendori" refused aiso's request, and "ogata", "abe", and "kawasaki" agreed to his/her request. "Akagi" has not read the message yet. If the user reminds the reply to the request from this window, PeCo-Agent of "akagi" tells him/her to read the message. From this result, "aiso" is the most familiar to "goji" and can easily access the cooperator "ogata" through the mediation of "goji".

Figure 5: Screen shot of PeCo exploration with PeCo-Mediator-II.

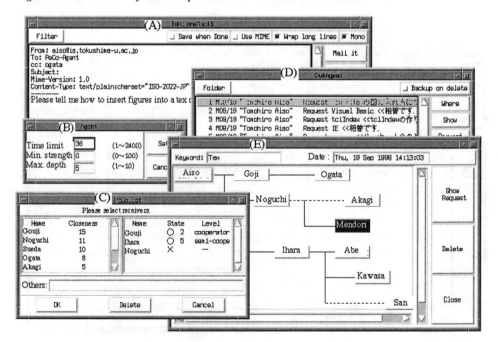

EXPERIMENTAL USE

Because it is necessary to consider both a point of technology and a point of sociology, it is very difficult to validate the effectiveness of PeCo-Mediator-II in general. In this research, we experimentally tested and evaluated it in a special small community.

Users and Tasks

In this experiment, we arranged thirteen master course students (group A) and 94 undergraduate students (group B) who had no relationship with the members of group A at the first stage of the experiment. Only one person, user VI, knows all the members of group A and B. They used the prototype system during nine weeks of a class in programming language C. Group B was given some homework every week. We divided nine weeks into four terms. Because this experiment was short, α, β, γ and δ were set to one in table 2.

- Term 1: In the first three weeks, each group member communicated among the internal group members without the contact of the other group. The system gathered their usual ties in this term.
- Term 2: We allowed group A and B to communicate and collaborate with each other to solve problems. The users solved the given problems through this system without supporting PeCo exploration with history.
- Term 3: In this period, we evaluated the function for supporting PeCo exploration with the history that was stored in the term 2.

Experimental Results

Social network analysis

Figure 6 shows the social networks between the users after six weeks from the beginning of this experiment. While the user of group A is indicated by a circle, the user of group B is shown by a square. The thick arrows denote the requested messages from the sender to the receiver. The thin arrows represent the forwarded messages over one time. This figure shows only the message flow across each group. The intra-group flow is not depicted in the figures. Of course, usual questions and answers occurred within each group. The weight of the arrow shows how many times e-mail was exchanged from the sender to the receiver. The user VI was a central person and acted as a liaison between group A and B. As shown in this figure, group A and B learned to communicate with each other through the introduction of user VI, although they did not have connections beyond the group. Moreover, most of the requests from group B concentrated on user VI and III, and the cooperators were almost fixed at six persons of group A. In this case, there was no cooperator in group B.

In the previous experiment (Ogata et al., 1998), we compared this system with e-mail, mailing lists and NetNews during four weeks. This experiment was executed in the same class. Both mailing list and NetNews were not often used for getting an answer because the student hesitated to ask a question. On the other hand, both this system and e-mail were frequently used. In this case, social networks were stable because direct and explicit relationships were used to get collaborative help. Likewise, (Yamakami, 1995) describes the interaction patterns of e-mail and bulletin board are stable from the long-term usage observation.

Figure 7 depicts the message flow in the term 3. Some members of group B became cooperators because our system lead the users to reduce the incipient cooperators' load. For

Figure 6: Network forming in the term 2.

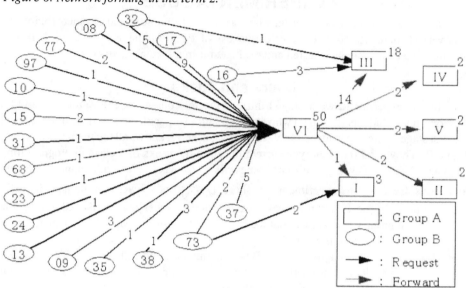

example, the system recommended user VI to forward the request from user 32 to user 17 who was a semi-cooperator. After that, user 32 directly requested user 17 to cooperate with problem-solving.

Figure 8 shows the comparison of the cooperators in the term 2 and 3. In term 2, the user VI and II accounted for 78% of all cooperators, and here was no cooperator in group B. In term 3, the cooperation rate of the user VI and III decreased 69 % and some of group B became cooperators. This experimental result seems to show that the facility of this system is available to prevent the cooperators from being fixed and to facilitate mutual cooperation.

Questionnaire

We evaluated the facilities of PeCo-Mediator-II with a questionnaire. Users had to answer giving a number between one and five to each one of thirteen questions. The obtained average was 4.2. Table 3 summarizes the results of the questionnaire.

Questions (1) and (2) were for evaluating the ways to store PeCo and to measure their strength. According to question (1), most of the users were satisfied with the PeCo data gathered by this system although the experimentation term was very short. It was especially effective in storing implicit connections. Question (2) indicated the strength of relationships given by PeCo-Mediator-II was nearly the same as that of real ones. Therefore, our method to measure PeCo strength was adequate. However, some users commented that it was quite a job to entry and update the personal data of their own friends one by one, e.g., their interests or telephone number, though the social closeness is automatically measured using the e-mail exchange log. In future work, we will investigate an effective way to extract automatically personal data from the signature of an e-mail message.

Questions (3) and (4) are provided for testing the support of PeCo exploration. As shown in the result of question (3), the visualization of PeCo was very effective for the senders to understand the current exploration process and the receivers' actions. Moreover, most of the users commented that the remote control facility of exploration was very

Figure 7: Network forming in the term 3.

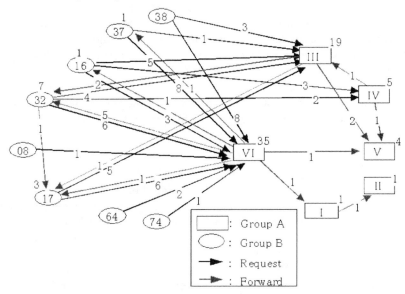

Figure 8: Rate of cooperators in the term 3.

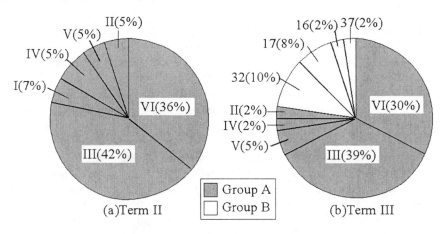

Table 3: Results of questionnaire.

Question	Ave.
(1) Could this system collect most of your firends?	4.1
(2) Could this system give correct priority to your friends?	4.0
(3) Was it effective to make the process of exploring networks visible?	4.1
(4) Was it available to control exploration of social networks?	4.4
(5) Did this system facilitate to find experts or partners?	4.5

convenient in that it did not disturb the receivers. Finally, the result of question (5) showed the users could easily find cooperative and capable persons near themselves through PeCo-Mediator-II. As for privacy, the user in PeCo-Mediator-II manages the personal database in his/her site, and the other users can not access his/her database without his/her permission. Then, most of the users did not protest against both collecting individual ties and using them reciprocally.

On the contrary, they were pleased to use this system for maintaining ties and developing a new connection with a collaborator. We evaluated this system in very special and small social environment. In future work, we will continue to use, estimate and improve this system.

RELATED WORKS

There are many possible sources for determining direct relationships. The initial version of our system imposed the entry of relationship lists upon organizational members (Ogata et al., 1995). The provision of individual ties makes the burden heavy for the users. Schwartz and Wood (Schwartz and Wood, 1993) proposed a way to obtain relationships by analyzing e-mail logs. However, the use of such information raises concerns of privacy and security that are hard to allay. ReferralWeb (Kautz et al., 1997a, Kautz et al., 1997b) an IKNOW(Inquiring Knowledge Networks On the Web) (Contractor et al, 1998) system uses the cooccurrence of names in close proximity in any documents publicly available on the Web as evidence of a direct relationship. Although these systems called communityware are readily available to discover public relationships, it may be difficult to find real private networks. Our system focuses on current and personal ties based on the exchange of e-mail.

A concept of organizational memory is proposed as organizational knowledge with persistence (Conklin, 1992). Answer Garden (Ackerman, 1994, Ackerman and McDonald, 1996), FAQFinder (Burke et al., 1997) FISH (eki et al., 1994) and COMES (Ogata et al., 1996b) have been proposed to record and use organizational memory. In an organization, however, information seeking is not straight-forward information transfer. Colleagues chose not to go to the channel of the highest quality for information, but rather to go to the channel of heights accessibility (Allen, 1977). Accessibility is concerned with psychological cost that is in the potential lack of reciprocity between giving and obtaining information and so on. PeCo makes it easy to agree to the cooperation and to access information.

To increase communication opportunities, awareness is one of the most interesting topics. Awareness is an understanding of the activities of others, which provides a context for personal activity (Dourish and Bellotti, 1992). For example, CRUISER (Root, 1988) VideoWindow (Fish et al., 1990), Portholes (Dourish and Bly, 1992) and VENUS (Matsuura et al., 1995) were developed to support informal communication. However, through only such awareness, it is hard to realize collaboration on the specific task with other users or accomplish tasks and common goals. Therefore, social aspects are very important to get other's cooperation and valuable information.

Foner (Foner, 1995) proposes Yenta that is a matchmaker agent to bring people together. In this approach, a broker agent automatically introduces other agents and people. On the other hand, our work pays much attention to human-centered approach for enhancing cooperation between organizational members. Therefore, the agency of PeCo-Agent is weak.

CONCLUSION

This chapter proposed PeCo-Mediator-II as a support to find capable cooperators with the chain of personal connections (PeCo) in a networked organization. This system helps gathering, seeking, and visualizing social networks of organizational members.

PeCo-Mediator-II is a distributed system to deal with e-mail-based PeCo. This system consists of PeCo-Collector as a personal database and PeCo-Agent as a user's assistant. We proposed the ways to gather PeCo by watching the e-mail exchange, how to measure their strength, and how to support exploration of social networks. PeCo-Mediator-II was experimentally tested and evaluated in a C programming language course. The results showed the system could help the user to encounter a cooperator and developed the new relationship with the cooperator. In our experiment at a classroom, we did not have such serious social problems. But we might find a new problem in different social situations, e.g., in a company. In future work, our system will be used and evaluated in several different societies.

CSCW literature includes an expanding body of sociological studies on work and collaboration. However, the technological support from social aspects has received little attention in the CSCW research studies. As shown in this chapter, it is very important to look at sociologyl and technology together for activating cooperation between workers.

ACKNOWLEDGMENT

This research has been supported in part by the Grant-in-Aid for Encouragement of Young Scientists (A) No.09780291 and the Grant-in-Aid for Scientific Research on Priority Areas No.09230214 from the Ministry of Education, Science, Sports and Culture in Japan.

REFERENCES

Ackerman, M. S. (1994). Augmenting the Organizational Memory: A Field Study of Answer Garden, Proceedings of CSCW 94, ACM Press, 243-252.

Ackerman, M. S. and McDonald, D. W. (1996). Merging Organizational Memory with Collaborative Help, Proceedings of CSCW 96, ACM Press, 97-105.

Allen, T. (1977). Managing the Flow of Technology, MIT Press.

Austin, J.L. (1962). How to do things with words, Harvard University Press.

Burke, R., Hammond, K., Kulyukin, V., Lytinen, S., Tomuro, N., and Schoenberg, S. (1997). Question Answering from Frequently Asked Question Files Experiences with the FAQ FINDER System, AI Magazine, Vol.18, no.2, 57-66.

Clement, A. (1990). Cooperative Support for Computer Work: A Social Perspective on the Empowering of End Users, Proceedings of CSCW 90, ACM Press, 223-236.

Capturing Organizational Memory, Groupware 92, 133-137.

Contractor N., Zink, D., and Chan, M. (1998). IKNOW: A tool to assist and study the creation, maintenance, and dissolution of knowledge networks, In Toru Ishida (Ed.), Community Computing and Support Systems, Lecture Notes in Computer Science 1519, Springer-Verlag, 201-217.

Dourish, P. and Bly, S. (1992). Portholes: Supporting awareness in a distributed work group, Proceedings of Computer Human Interaction 92, ACM Press, 541-548.

Dourish, P. and Bellotti, V. (1992). Awareness and Coordination in Shared Workspaces, Proceedings of CSCW 92, ACM Press, 107-114.

Eveland, D. J., Brown, W. and Mattocks, J. (1994). The Role of "Help Networks" in Facilitating Use of CSCW Tools, Proceedings of CSCW 94, ACM Press, 265-274.

Fish, R., Kraut, R. and Chalfonte, B. (1990). The video window system in informal communications, Proceedings of CSCW '90, ACM Press, 1-12.

Foner, N. L. (1995). Clustering and Information Sharing in an Ecology of Cooperating Agents, Proceedings of AAAI Spring Symposium on Information Gathering from Distributed, Heterogeneous Environments, AAAI Press.

Garton, L., Haythornthwaite, C., and Wellman, B. (1997). Studying On line Social Networks, Journal of Computer Mediated Communication, vol. 3, no. 1. (http://www.usc.edu/dept/ annenberg/vol3/ issue1/ garton.html)

Granovetter, M. (1973). The strength of weak ties, American Journal of Sociology, 78, 1360-1380.

Hiramatsu, H. (1990). Social Network Analysis, Fukushima Press. (in Japanese).

Kautz, H., Selman, B. and Shah, M. (1997a). Referral Web: Combining Social Networks and Collaborative Filtering, Communications of ACM, vol. 40, no. 3, 63-65.

Kautz, H., Selman, B. and Shah, M. (1997b). The Hidden Web, AI Magazine, vol. 18, no. 2, 27-36.

Malone, T. W. (1986). Semi-Structured Messages are Surprisingly Useful for Computer Supported Coordination, Proceedings of CSCW 86, ACM Press, 102-114.

Matsumoto, Y, Kitauchi, A., Yamashita, T., Hirano, Y., Imaichi, O. and Imamura, T. (1997). Japanese Morphological Analysis System ChaSen Manual, Nara Institute of Science and Technology Technical Report NAIST-IS-TR 97007. (in Japanese)

Matsushita, Y. (1993). A Social and Cultural Study on Groupware, Technical Report of the trans. of IPSJ, vol.93, no.34, 93-GW-1, 1-10. (in Japanese)

Matsuura, N., Hidaka, T., Okada, K. and Matsushita, Y. (1995). VENUS: An informal communication environment supporting interest awareness, Transactions on Information Processing Society of Japan, vol. 36, no. 6, 1332-1341 (in Japanese).

Ogata, H., Yano, Y., Furugori, N., and Jin, Q. (1995). PeCo-Mediator: Development and Modeling of a Supporting System for Sharing and Handling Personal Connections Transactions on Information Processing Society of Japan, vol. 36, no. 6, 1299-1309. (in Japanese)

Ogata, H., Goji, A., Jin, Q., Yano, Y. and Furugori, N. (1996a). Distributed PeCo-Mediator: Finding Partners via Personal Connections, Proceedings of 1996 IEEE Systems, Man and Cybernetics (SMC), vol. 1, Beijing, China, 802 - 807.

Ogata, H., Tsutsumi, K., Jin, Q., Yano, Y. and Furugori, N. (1996b). COMES: Collaborative Organizational Memory System, Proceedings of 1996 IEEE Systems, Man and Cybernetics (SMC), vol. 2, Beijing, China, 983-987.

Ogata, H., Furugori, N., Jin, Q. and Yano, Y. (1997). PeCo-Mediator-II: Supporting to Find Partner(s) through Personal Connections in a Networked Environment, Transactions of the Institute of Electronics, Information and Communication Engineers, D-I, vol.J80- D-I, no.7, 551-560. (in Japanese)

Ogata, H., Aiso, T., Furugori, N., Yano, Y. and Jin, Q. (1998). Computer Supported Social Networking in Virtual Communities, IEEE International Conference on Intelligent Processing Systems, 47-51.

Ousterhoult, J. (1994). Tcl and the Tk Toolkit, Addison-Wesley.

Pickering, M. J. and King, L. J. (1992). Hardwiring Weak Ties: Individual and Institutional Issues in Computer Mediated Communication, Proceedings of CSCW'92, ACM Press, 356-361.

Peek, D. J. (1994). MH and xmh: E-mail for users and programmers, O'Reilly and Associates, Inc.

Root, R. W. (1988). Design of a Multi-Media Vehicle for Social Browsing, Proceedings of CSCW 88, ACM Press, 25-38.

Salomon, G. (1992). What Does the Design of Effective CSCL Require and How Do We Study Its Effects?, ACM SIGCUE Outlook. (http:// www.cica.indiana.edu/ cscl95/ outlook/ 62_Salomon.html)

Salton, G., and McGill, M. (1983). Introduction to modern information retrieval, McGraw-Hill.

Schwartz, F. M. and Wood, M. C. (1993). Discovering Shared Interests Using Graph Analysis, Communications of ACM, no.36, vol.8, 78-89.

Scott, J. (1992). Social Network Analysis: A Handbook, Sage.

Seki, Y., Yamakami, T. and Shimizu, A. (1994). Flexible Information Sharing and Handing System -Towards Knowledge Propagation-, IEICE Transactions of Communications, vol. E77-B, no.3, 404-410.

Sproull, L. and Kiesler, S. (1991) Connections: New ways of working in the networked organization, MIT Press.

Suchman, L., Speech Acts and Voices: Response to Winograd et al., (1994). Computer Supported Cooperative Work,Vol.3, No.1, 85-95.

Yamakami, T. (1995). Information Flow Analysis: An approach to evaluate groupware adoption patterns, Transactions of Information Processing Society of Japan, vol.36, no.10, 2511-2519.

Yamamoto, Y., Kashihara, A., Kawagishi, K., and Tsukamoto, S. (1989). A tool for construction of personal database: TRIAS, Transactions of Information Processing Society of Japan, vol.30, no. 6, 733-742 (in Japanese).

Yasuda, Y. (1997). Network Analysis, Sin'yo-sha Press. (in Japanese)

Wasserman, S. and K. Faust (1994). Social Network Analysis, Cambridge University Press.

Wellman, Barry and S.D. Berkowitz (1997). Social Structures: A Network Approach (updated edition), JAI Press.

Winograd, T. and Flores, F. (1987). Understanding Computers and Cognition: A New Foundation for Design, Addison-Wesley.

Chapter XIV

The Cultural Aesthetic of Virtual Reality: Simulation or Transparency?

Ron Purser
San Francisco State University, USA

INTRODUCTION

The cultural significance of Virtual Reality (VR) extends far beyond the fact that it is an innovative technological device. Indeed, VR technology is embedded in, and a byproduct of, a much larger social, cultural, and scientific milieu. Changes in technological devices have paralleled the shifts in the way human cultures have ordered and represented their worlds. Historically, the emergence of new technologies often provides the base for profound changes in the structure of the self, as well as radical alterations in the collective field of perception. Donald Lowe, (1982) in his study, *The History of Bourgeois Perception*, argues that perception is shaped by a collective interplay of factors. Communication media, one of the main factors in Lowe's theory, acts to frame and filter the way we perceive the world. Basing much of his theory on the work of Walter Ong (1988), Lowe traces shifts in culture that correspond to changes in media: from orality to chirograpgy in the Middle Ages; from chirography to typography in the Renaissance; from typograpy to photography in bourgeois society; and from photography to cinema and television in the modern world.

We now stand at the brink of another profound cultural shift, moving from mass communication to interactive digital media—what Paul Levy (1998) refers to as a process of virtualization. The question that will be answered in the next few decades is whether VR will be actualized as an enabling technology for human betterment, or whether it will simply be another consumerist distraction, throwing culture deeper into a nihilistic void. This question, and the way that it will be answered, depends on the choice of cultural aesthetic, as well as the epistemological assumptions that end up informing the development, distribution and use of VR technology. This chapter explores and interrogates the potential destiny of VR technology in terms of its potential benefits to society, as well its possible abuses. I begin by first providing a brief overview on the mechanics of VR technology. I then situate VR technology within a larger cultural context of postmodern society by examining the sensibility of the hyperreal simulation, and how such notions that are operative in VR worlds differ markedly from conventional notions of the representation. The latter half of the chapter sets out to explore two possible future scenarios or trajectories of VR technology; what I refer to later as "VR1" versus "VR2". Finally, I conclude by offering some speculative suggestions on the potential role of VR technology as a new form of cultural expression and its implications for the transformation of human consciousness.

A BRIEF PRIMER ON VIRTUAL REALITY

Virtual reality is both a technology and an experience. Heim (1998, p.7) defines virtual reality technology as consisting of three interrelated components: immersion, interactivity, and information intensity. Immersion is the feeling or effect the user has of being situated in a qualitatively different space, which is achieved through devices that isolate the human senses. Interactivity is the feeling that responses made by the users are effected in real-time, providing the capability for "teleaction." Information intensity refers to the degree to which the VR experience provides a sense of telepresence and vividness. *Telepresence* occurs when there is a sufficient degree of feedback between the users' perceptions and the VR environment. Like other computer configurations, VR technology consists of hardware, software and peripheral/interface devices. Hardware usually requires very high speed computing capability along with large storage systems. Most of the innovative software that has been developed is purely experimental, much of it done in either collaboration with media artists or programmers specializing in VR programming and 3-D graphics. What are most unique to VR technology are the input-output interface devices, which serve to create the immersion effect. Users typically wear light-weight head-mounted displays, often referred to as the "falcon hood." Other installations—often referred to as the CAVE—use projection wall panels that display real-time 3-D graphics, with sophisticated tracking devices to monitor and detect the position of the user's movements. Both systems also utilize surround sound techniques that envelop the user. It is interesting to note that a key feature of VR systems is the visual tracking system. With the falcon hood device, the movement of the head is fed as input into the computer0 while the visual output appears on the small display monitors covering the eyes. In addition, some VR systems also include data gloves for tracking hand gestures. Others even include whole data suits that track the movements of the whole body.

The apparatus of VR technology as described above tracks the sensory and kinesthetic movements of the sensory-motor body into signals that are processed and instantaneously reproduced as visual and auditory displays. The virtuality that is reproduced is a consequence of the interface devices which, in the case of the falcon hood, completely blocks out the actual world. The user in effect wears a pair of "eyephones," so that his or her attention is completely captivated by the images appearing on the visual display. A user wearing a data-glove may reach out to pick a virtual flower; there is a constant and real-time feedback between the user's hand movements and changes in the 3-D graphics display. Sophisticated VR technology has the capability of transporting the user into a qualitatively different space and time, an artificial world of experience.

VIRTUALIZATION

The Virtual Reality experience is unique. According to Morse (1998, p.24), virtuality is "a dematerialized, and for that reason, ontologically uncertain mode of presence." Our cultural response to VR technology, I believe, is not predetermined or inevitable. Virtualization, in principle, has the potentiality of having either a culturally enriching or degrading effect. Paul Levy (1998, p.26) defines virtualization as a dynamic that leads to a

"...change in identity, a displacement of the center of ontological gravity of the object being considered". But Levy's definition, while helpful, is deceptively neutral in its tone. Because virtualization can alter identity, further analysis is needed to explore how VR technology could be received in culture and it potential impact on human consciousness. In this chapter, I will also examine how the dynamic of virtualization might unfold with the advent of VR technology, particularly as a new mode of aesthetic expression. While VR technology is still in a very embryonic stage of development, its potential can be discerned in how it is already beginning to be used commercially in rudimentary applications, but also, and perhaps more significantly, in how VR has been equated to being an emblematic symbol of postmodern culture.

Virtual Reality and the Hyperreal

Conquest of space would not have been possible without the products of linear perspectivisim—accurate maps and representations of the actual physical terrain—which allowed explorers to navigate the globe. There was a sensibility, however, that the map was an imperfect representation of the actual terrain—that the "map was not the territory." VR technology introduces a fundamentally different sensibility, where the image no longer needs to stand in for or represent the "real world" because in virtual reality the image is "a world." We can speak then of inhabiting virtual environments, or virtual worlds. Within a virtual world, *the map is the territory*, and, following Baudrillard's (1995) argument, even precedes or supersedes the actual world. The potential for vivid experience in virtual reality precedes the virtual world it purports to trace. In this respect, VR technology produces a new epistemic order, wherein it becomes increasingly difficult to differentiate the boundary between actual reality and virtual reality. Blurring the boundaries between actual and virtual worlds was vividly portrayed in William Gibson's sci-fi novel, *Neuromancer* (and a recent Hollywood movie, "Matrix," that was based on it).

We can consider Descartes abstract realm of geometry also as a type of virtual world— a mental space—which created a new epistemic order for representing objects in an imaginary, mathematical-coordinate space. Computer graphics using digital images are also mapped onto abstract mathematical spaces. Rather than accurately representing the actual world on canvass or a map, graphics programmers build models to simulate reality; the source of their art is not the actual world, but a code, a mathematically constructed image. Their aesthetic motivation is not representation, but *simulation* or hyperrealism.

Normally we might think of a simulation as merely a cheap imitation of the "real thing." In the actual world, we can usually intuit or sense that there is something essentially absent or missing in the imitation which the original possessed. We can easily spot a cheap Mona Lisa reprint from the Rembrandt original. But in virtual worlds, technology allows image creation to move into the pure realm of abstraction; the source of the simulation no longer needs to be derived from the actual world. In this case, how can we tell if something is missing or absent if there is no longer any original in which to compare? For if an original no longer exists, one can no longer speak of a "counterfeit." This raises the question of the ontological status of appearances in virtual reality. What appears in virtual reality is an image of a totally self-contained world that requires no grounding or reference in reality. Appearances have a "simulated presence." *Postmodern* and cultural theorists have referred to this state as a "crisis of representation," in which differences between the sign and referent have been obliterated. What is left is simply a play of signs or surfaces—"a precession of simulacra," to use Baudrillard's phrase— where nothing can be taken too seriously.

What is key to this development is that images, or simulacra, no longer need to be situated or grounded in a geographical or historical context. Such notions of origin or locale can simply be erased, and the social relations that lie behind the image can also be conveniently concealed from view. Such an ability to sanitize the image is the power that is derived from substituting information for direct knowledge and embodied experience. As a new medium, virtual reality has a great deal of affinity with postmodern culture where "image is everything, and everything appears as art." The obliteration of the distinctions between sign and referent goes hand in hand with obscuring the differences between absence and presence.

Alternate World Syndrome

Virilio (1997) argues that diffusion of VR into society could lead to new types of psychological disorders as people experience greater difficulty discerning image from reality. Rather than simply having to deal with the actual world, people will be confronted with the challenge of having to maintain a "split-perspective" between actual and virtual worlds, and to live in what Virilio (1997) calls "stereo-reality." VR theorists have already noted this trend, in what they now call *Alternate World Syndrome* (AWS) (Heim, 1993, 1998). This perceptual disorder seems to erode what Freud referred to as the "reality principle." Heim (1993, 1998) has reported that frequent immersion in VR can lead to a profound perceptual disorientation and a distorted sense of context. Early indications of this perceptual disorder were first observed in pilots in flight simulators. Due to the time lag of the pilots' actual physical movement and the perceived motion of the simulator, some pilots experience nausea and/or disorientation. With VR, some users become experience kinesthetic confusion; sensations arising from their "cyber-body" compete for attention with sensations in their "bio-body." Heim (1998, p.53) describes AWS as a technology sickness, "a lag between the natural and the artificial environments."

One possible social scenario, as VR technology becomes more sophisticated, is that users will become addicted or frequently immersed in virtual worlds. Preferring to be immersed in VR worlds, those suffering from AWS would have a difficult time coping with the demands of the actual world. After long and frequent periods of being immersed in VR worlds, transitioning back to "reality" produces stress, hypersensitivity and flashbacks (see Heim, pp.183-184). "Real presence" begin to seems "heavy" and burdensome in comparison to the "lighter fare of the hyperreal" (Borgman, 1992). This may not be far-fetched as it sounds. Consider how fast and pervasive usage of PCs occurred. With new advances in computing speed on the horizon, the cathode ray screen could quickly be supplanted by various types of VR interfaces. Consider the fact that simulator sickness is well-documented, and such use was limited to a very small percentage of the population. Moreover, simulators were designed strictly for flight-training. What will be the response to large segments of the population when VR systems offer a plethora of simulated worlds that go well beyond technical training? When people can change their body-image, identity, and engage in virtually any sort of act in VR worlds, what will be the personal and social consequences?

In virtual worlds, distance—whether spatial or temporal—can be technologically compressed, encoded, reified, and then reproduced as simulation. We need not enter the "real world" as embodied subjects, but are enticed to shed the weight of our embodied existence and disburden ourselves so we can enjoy the simulated presence of the hyperreal without resistance, without being encumbered by the gravity of the real. As VR technology produces images that are as vivid and real as the actual object or experience—we have achieved what Giddens calls a "reality inversion." Noting the displacement of actual reality, Mitchell (1992, p.57) states, "the connection of images to solid substance has become tenuous....images are no longer guaranteed as visual truth." For example, someone seeking to experience unspoiled nature may, in the future, enter a Virtual Reality room and "visit" Yellowstone National Park and its various wilderness areas. Why bother actually going to Yellowstone when nature can be "appreciated" in a Virtual Reality simulator?

Habitual immersion in, and addiction to, VR worlds—in which people lose interest in living in the actual world—would result not only in an appreciative loss of embodiment, but also massive social inertia. Tele-action reduces the need for movement and mobility. Commenting on this foreseeable trend, Virilio (1995) states:

> ...the overequipped able becomes the equivalent of the equipped disabled. There is a menace of infirmity and paralysis. But also a psychological menace, for the future generations of implemented interactivity who could see the world reduced to nothing. Generations may experience a feeling of "great internment," of an Earth too small for the speeds of transport and transmissions, a feeling of "incarceration." (p.101)

As this new cultural aesthetic becomes normalized over time, we may even question why we should bother caring about the "real" when it becomes harder to differentiate the realm of *physis*, *bios*, and *ecos* from the realm of *techne*? We may, in fact, cross a threshold where a sort of collective amnesia sets in, as traces of our history and origins are imperceptibly erased from our long-term cultural memory. This is also not actually that far-fetched given the fact that we are shifting from typographic to digital storage media. Despite the reliability and economy of digital storage, this media is actually quite fragile and subject to recurring cycles of technological obsolescence. As Stewart Brand (1999) points out, file formats quickly become obsolete, and even the physical media for data storage—such as disks and tapes—lose their integrity in five to ten years. The book may not be consigned to museum display cases, but may gradually fade out as the medium of choice as digital technologies take ascendancy.

The development of VR and its use could move toward a progressive withdrawal of our participation in the actual world. Morse (1998) captures the potential danger of telepresence of VR: "What concerns cyberculture is not the fact of telematic imagery per se but the telepresent danger of engagement with the image world at the cost—ethical and psychic—of disengagement or remoteness from the actual effects of one's actions. (p.23)" The dominance of the image in postmodern society has been enabled by developments in digital media. While the ontological shift to seeing the "world as a picture" can be philosophically traced back as far as Plato's notion of *eidos,* its technological genesis is in the Renaissance. *Being* (in the Heideggerian sense) in the perspectival world suddenly became something that appeared through our own unique point of view—our own picture. In the digital age, *Being* is now reduced—with the aid of digital media—to the ontology of the image. In postmodern culture, not only is the world a product of our point-of-view, but Being is now, exclusively, for us. As Levin (1988) points out, "Everything which presences, which is, must present itself for our representation. And only representation is regarded as real." Another way of understanding this shift is in terms of a shift from meaning to value (Simpson, 1995). That which is of any value in hyperreality must be that which can lend itself to control, consumption, or utility. Value is purely instrumental in nature.

The trend toward the *hyperreal* was intimated by Heiddeger's analysis of the modern age, which he characterized as the "age of the world picture." Heidegger (1977) noted that "the world picture, when understood essentially, does not mean a picture of the world, but the world conceived and grasped as picture." His analysis was concerned over the fact that what was considered real was now totally determined by humanity's collective representations, which are unconsciously imposed upon the world for gaining control and power. Heidegger explains:

> "...to represent means to bring what is present at hand [das Vorhandene] before [or in front of] of oneself as something standing over against oneself, ...and to force it to remain in this relationship..Therewith, man sets himself up as [the godlike arbitrator] of the setting in which whatever is must henceforth set itself forth, must present itself, i.e., be picture" (quoted in Levin, 1988, p.119).

VR, cyberspace and digital technologies have increased our capacities, to use Heidegger's phrase, to "enframe" the world. In hyperreality, our *Being* is digitized into a simulated presence, derived from images which are engineered, coded, and reproduced for mass consumption. It is interesting to note this movement toward digital enframing of the world corresponds with the intent to develop higher quality photographic resolution in virtual displays. As Morse (1998) points out:

> "this has as much to do with controlling physical objects as it does with aesthetics. An art if virtual spaces that simply aims toward realism of fit with appearance with a physical landscape may then risk merely serving instrumental or hegemonic purposes of military and business interests in an information society." (pp.184-185)

With the advent of digital media, the world as picture could literally become a reality (an image) by conceiving of the world as information. Consider the pervasive root metaphor for genetic engineering: DNA as an information code. The basic building blocks of all living organisms are now seen as fundamentally reducible to a binary like code. This is all part of the shift in the epistemic order of modern society that I alluded to earlier. It is a shift that entails becoming more dependent on mediated knowledge of the world. This increasingly dominant mode of perception, based on what I refer to as "distanced knowing," is possible because we have also collapsed the distinctions between such elementary notions as "data," "information," "knowledge," and "wisdom." Acquiring knowledge about the world is now simply equated to having "the facts," which can be conveniently accessed by logging on to the Internet. As knowing—mediated by technologies of image production—is reduced to simply "having information about things," the difference between absence and presence becomes harder to discern" (Borgman, 1992).

VIRTUALIZATION OF CONSCIOUSNESS OR CONSCIOUS VIRTUALIZATION?

In this section, I differentiate between two modes of virtualization, which are mirrored in the design and conception of different trajectories of Virtual Reality (VR) technology, what I will refer to as "VR1" and "VR2." The first mode, VR1, as we shall see, is a further amplification of the hyperreal trajectory which I have discussed in previous sections. The modality of VR1 accelerates the dynamic of virtualization, but in a direction that spirals downward, into a nihilistic void of pure simulacra. In fact, I argue that with VR1, culture is drawn into a closed world with a proliferation of commodified images, making human consciousness more fixated and one-sided. The very meaning of human intelligence descends to a functionary level, ruled by the logic of algorithmic reasoning. What emerges is an image of the human subject that is colonized by *cyborg* and artificial intelligence "anticonsciounsess" discourse, and metaphors of the brain as a cybernetic information process-ing device. Indeed, cyborg brain implants are no longer mere science fiction; they are already beginning to emerge.

The other alternative, VR2, is a trajectory that has the potential for bringing about a new collective aesthetic and liberating forms of cultural expression. In VR2, users have the opportunity of learning more about the workings of their perception and how it actively constructs the phenomena they come to know. Donning a data suit or stepping into a VR CAVE in VR2 would provide users experiences very different from those typical of VR1. VR2 worlds use the medium of virtual reality to produce evocative experiences aimed at de-automatizing our perceptual habits (this will be addressed in further depth in the next section). If VR2 develops momentum, it could potentially trigger a new renaissance movement, a cultural mutation, which stimulates a personal and collective inquiry into the nature of our existence. What follows below is a brief exposition of the features and characteristic differences between VR1 and VR2 worlds.

VR1: A Dystopian Scenario

The path of VR1 results in the virtualization of consciousness. VR1 worlds are aimed to simply satisfy the ephemeral and fanciful desires of the consumer-self. Such experiences will likely alter our sense of self, radically de-centering and fragmenting it into a solipsistic, disembodied subject, and compliant instruction follower. Driven mainly by commercial interests, VR1 systems could have far reaching consequences in terms of their impact on human consciousness. Mass consumption of programmed experiences would be equivalent to stepping inside a video game. While interactivity and information intensity would be greatly enhanced, the programmatic nature of the experience is essentially routine and mechanical. There may even be an array of immersion programs or different worlds that the user could choose from, but the aesthetic aim of VR1 is mainly to entertain by presenting 3-D versions of existing commercial media.

A number of the original developers and pioneers in VR systems such as Mark Pesce and Jaron Lanier, also express grave misgivings about this dystopian scenario. Pesce presented his concerns in a paper, "Final Amputation: Pathogenic Ontology in Cyberspace" at the Third International Conference in Cyberspace held at the University of Texas. In this paper, Pesce builds on McLuhan's insight—that every technological advance can be seen as a simultaneous gain and loss—what McLuhan referred to as a "metaphorical amputa-tion." So, for example, with the driving of an automobile, the driver no longer uses the legs for locomotion. The legs have undergone a metaphorical amputation. Since VR is totalizing in its ability to dominate the human sensory field, VR amputates everything—hence, his notion of the "Final Amputation." The automization of perception achieved in VR1 goes beyond the pathological symptoms as exhibited in simulator sickness. As Pesce notes, the physical pathology at work in the flight simulators is rather innocuous compared to the psychological pathologies brought about by the highly suggestive content of the images in VR1. Formation of strong ego identity is necessary for healthy adult development. Certainly, the intensity of stimulation combined with the perceptual disordering effects of VR1 will put children and young adults especially at risk.

What is at issue with VR1 is its potential to progressively automatize human intelligence. This phenomenon manifests itself as humans descend and subordinate their capacities to the level of the machine. Talbott (1995) addresses this issue at length in his book, *The Future Does Not Compute*. He questions whether it is the case computers are getting smarter, or whether human beings are simply becoming less intelligent by narrowing their ways of knowing to algorithmic reasoning. Let us imagine that Kurzweil's (1999) vision of the future fifty years out unfolds: that "spiritual machines" will attain the ontological status of super-humans. In this future scenario, VR systems will not only be as commonplace as PC computers, they will be ubiquitous. Human beings will delegate most, if not all of their major decisions to these spiritual machines. The natural and actual world will be a historical relic. In such a dystopian VR-dominated world, human beings will find solace in visual hallucinations-the world of simulacra.

What are to we make of the way human beings will think, their values, their ethics? In many respects, what may emerge is a mentality that operates and acts very much like the sort of "*bi-cameral mind*" that Julian Jaynes (1990) describes was operative in pre-civilized societies. According to Jaynes' bi-cameral mind theory, archaic humans did not possess consciousness, conscious minds, or subjectivity, and lacked the ability to introspect. Volition, planning and initiative can all occur, according to Jaynes, without consciousness. Instead, archaic humans were rather robotic in their behavior; they took their commands from the "gods" received through auditory hallucinations, which in reality was one hemisphere of the brain communicating via the corpus callosum to the other hemisphere. Bi-cameral civilizations in the Near East (circa 5000 B.C.) were notoriously rigid theocracies. Social order was invested in the formation of "idols…carefully tended centers of social control, with auditory hallucinations instead of pheromones." (Jaynes, 1990, p.144). In a culture which human consciousness has been effectively amputated by VR1, people will not hear the voices of the Gods telling them what to do, but the instructions will be issued ubiquitously by the computers that surrounds their lifeworld.

This pathway toward virtualization scatters human awareness across the surfaces of images. Knowledge proliferates in scope, but not in depth. Rather than serving to intensify awareness and active imagination, VR1 plunges culture into the manifold distractions and seductions of simulacra. VR1 breeds "con-fusion," an outcome of a fusion of mere fancy with the real. Fancy is not equivalent to imagination. The products of fancy are of many varieties, like the various fractal patterns generated in a kaleidoscope. But such images are only rearrangements of existing fragments, collages pasted together to excite and titillate. Imagination is subverted to mere fancy, constructing images that exploit the self's insecurity and narcissistic desire for recognition, along with its insatiable appetite for more stimulation. The worldview of modernism, with its image of a alienated, separate Cartesian self is reproduced, and even amplified by the VR1 aesthetic. In fact, VR1 inscribes a representation of the subject as a passive consumer of technologically constructed and packaged experiences. This mode of consciousness, which is exploited by VR1 type technologies, is intentionally directed toward generating not just images, but experiences as mass commodities. VR1 technologies are intentionally designed and marketed as a means of procuring the unlimited desires of an isolated consumer self.

The commercial promise of VR1 is to offer the consumer a self-contained realm of unencumbered and sanitary enjoyment. Surely, the whole meaning of "safe sex" will be taken to whole different order as VR1 technologies become more advanced with body suits, allowing its users to enjoy simulated sexual sensations and encounters. This is actually a hideous path of how our imaginative capacities could collectively devolve to the level of mere fancy. As Morse (1998) notes, this form of VR is a closed system, in which the user if enticed with fantasies of omnipotence and interaction with a "non-other." This type of closed world "in which the map can obliterate the real adds a kind of willful blindness to what is inherent in technology" (Morse, 1998, p.29). Over time, as VR1 proliferates, it eventually could lead to a progressive displacement of imagination in culture. The seductive attraction of VR1 as a sophisticated form of sensory escape, essentially privatizes human experience, and virtualizes what remains of our public spaces.

The technological marvel of VR1 is that it can literally substitute information for reality. What appears in VR1 has brilliance, vividness, and a "separate reality" that seems more real than reality itself. However, the "separate reality" experienced in VR1 does not have any likeness in quality to the altered state of consciousness that Carlos Casteneda describes. Rather, this "separate reality" is but a heightened manifestation of modern idolatry (Barfield, 1988). We might liken the VR1 world as being emblematic of what Nichol (2000) refers to as "radical idolatry." By radical idolatry, Nichol refers to Owen Barfield's (1988) notion that images, which are in effect our own creation, in the course of time, can soon be perceived as completely separate objects and things. As Barfield (1988) states, *idolatry* "...results when man begins to take his models—his representations—literally" (p.51).

VR2: A Socially Responsible Alternative

The consciousness-raising potential of VR2 could result in the rebirth of the collective imagination, where society at large, in different fields and domains, radically shifts to considering how human beings participate in the co-creation of their worlds. This shift in consciousness will legitimize and support a new form of discourse, fostering a collective inquiry into the processes by which we construct and call the world (and self) into being. As a new artform, VR2 could inspire an aesthetic in culture that provides evocative spaces for exploring proprioceptively the dynamics of perceptual experience. VR2 technologies would not simply entertain people with pre-packaged experiences—the realm of fantasy or fancy—but would rather tap into the primary imagination. I use the word imagination in the Barfieldian/Coleridgian sense, which "in its deepest sense signifies that very faculty of apprehending the outward form as the image or symbol of an inner meaning" (Barfield, 1977; p.19). Ultimately, the evolutionary path of VR2 presentiates conscious virtualization, whereby we gain more refined powers of apperception, that carry-over into the actual world.

When we first step into the artificial skin of a VR2 suit, we soon become aware our movements and actions are not quite natural. It takes some time to synchronize our actions with the events transpiring in the virtual world. In effect, we feel like a child that must learn how to walk, as we have to unlearn many movements or actions. Our proprioceptive sense suddenly becomes salient. VR2 worlds would be designed to amplify our *proprioceptive awareness* to include not just our muscular movements and kinesthetic sense, but also our very process of thinking. As the late quantum physicist David Bohm (1995) pointed out, we usually view the content and the process or movement of our thoughts as two separate and unrelated domains. Heightening our proprioceptive awareness in VR2 worlds would allow us to take this learning with us when we take off our technological skin and reenter back into our biological skin.

We can think of VR2 then as an enabling technology, which can provide civilization a new aesthetic expression that fundamentally alters our identity and calls into question the ontological status of reality. However, I want to stress that an enabling technology, in this case, VR2, does not automatically guarantee that such a new consciousness would arise. History demonstrates that new artforms often precede epochal changes in cultural consciousness (Gebser, 1985). A notable example is the convention of linear perspective art in the Renaissance. While geometric perspective in paintings was not the "cause" of the

Enlightenment consciousness, it certainly was a critical precursor to a new way of representing the world, which provided the cultural context for the emergence of the scientific worldview. Similarly, VR2 technology has the potential of stimulating a collective dialogue around in a new art form that in turn could lead to a fundamental change in the epistemic order of society. In other words, VR2 could be a critical cultural trigger on par in magnitude to that of the linear perspectival art.

One of the unique features of VR2 technology is that it would provide the capability for ordinary people to program their own software, allowing an individual, or even groups of people, to project their own imagination into a collective space (Lanier, 1994). Essentially, VR2 technology would empower the average individual to be an artist in virtual reality. According to Jaron Lanier (1998), a pioneer of Virtual Reality technology:

"The result will be a mass theatre of spontaneous shared imagination and dreaming. My fond hope is that it will take the form of networked VR with inspirational authoring tools that are capable of quick, improvisatory creation. But whatever the specific form, what we are building will encourage people to share interior vision and treat it as a tangible, worthy thing, even into adulthood.
"

As Lanier suggests, VR2 would be an empowering, interactive art form, allowing the average user to invent the contents of a virtual world. Not only this, VR2 would, according to Lanier, come with a shared virtual world interface, allowing users to share and co-mingle with their imaginative creations in a collective virtual space. Whereas VR1 is a con-fusion of fancy with the real, VR2 is a jazz-fusion of participation with imagination. It allows the user to consciously participate, and experience in real-time, what it means to invent and co-construct a reality with others. The architecture and software design assumptions of VR2 are epistemologically aligned with radical constructivism (Von Glasersfeld, 1995). The observer in VR2 can experience directly the simulated world as a product of their own interiority, an admixture of collective representations and a dynamic mosaic of their own mental constructs.

Certainly the most radical feature of VR2 is the capacity for users to directly share the contents of their imaginative experiences directly with others. Lanier predicts that this new media could give rise to a "post-symbolic order," transcending the limits associated with the narrative structure of language. In a VR2 world, images can be projected and experienced directly, without the mediation of words or language. In many respects, a VR2 environment is analogous to our dream world, where we encounter and experience events that are projected by our own imagination. As Lanier (1998) elaborates:

"It's really different than language. It's a new way to communicate, where people would directly create a shared world by programming it, by modeling it in real time, as opposed to merely using words, the intermediaries that we have to describe things. So it's like cutting out the middleman of words, and finding a new form of communication where you directly create shared reality—real-time, waking-state, improvised dreaming."

If VR2 technology evolves to the point that Lanier envisions, I believe it could provide the necessary aesthetic mutation for the *evolution of consciousness*. Just as linear perspectival art was a catalyst for the mutation into the rational-mental structure of consciousness, VR2 could do the same for what cultural historian Jean Gebser (1985) refers to as "the integral structure." Linear perspectival art in the Renaissance was also a symbolic order, which intensified consciousness to the point that it could break from the medieval mythical structure. Consciousness was able to mutate to a rational structure, whereby it could see itself as a separate and independent observer of the phenomena—a distant on-looker. So what does the next mutation lead to or break away from? The mutation is from being a detached bystander, an on-looker—to one of being a conscious participant, or co-creator. The characteristic differences between these two modes of virtualization and their techno-logical correlates (VR1 vs. VR2) are reflective of the cultural tensions similar to the transitional crisis periods during paradigmatic shifts in science that Thomas Kuhn has described. The movement toward and the emergence of a new era is usually uneven and full of contradictory developments. Clearly, the transition to a new era is far from smooth. VR1 is a technological extension of linear perspectivism, while VR2 offers the possibility of a discontinuous break from the mental-rational structure, leaping into an integral mode of consciousness.

A Step Toward VR2: OSMOSE

One attempt to move away from VR1 toward VR2 can be found in the recent work of virtual artist Char Davies. Her VR system, known as OSMOSE, radical departure from the controlling and manipulative epistemology inherent in VR1 technology. Char Davies created OSMOSE for expressed purpose of exploring the depth of consciousness and "de-automatizing" our habitual perception. OSMOSE is a fully interactive and immersive world that presents metaphors of nature, designed in accordance with a visual aesthetic based on semi—transparency and ambiguity of spatial relationships. The gallery description of OSMOSE states:

"OSMOSE is an immersive virtual space exploring the interrelation between exterior Nature and interior Self. The work explores the potential of immersive virtual space a medium for visual/aural expression and kinesthetic experience of philosophical ideas. In biology, osmosis is a process involving passage from one side of a membrane to another. Osmosis as a metaphor means the transcendence of difference through mutual absorption, the dissolution of boundaries between inner and outer, the inter-mingling of self and world, the longing for the Other. OSMOSE as an artwork seeks to heal the rational Cartesian mind/body subject/object split which has shaped so many of our cultural values, especially towards nature." (cited in Heim, 1998, p.162).

There are numerous immersive world-spaces within OSMOSE. Immersants first encounter a Cartesian Grid which serves as an orientation space. Next, immersants travel through various metaphorical worlds, such as the "Clearing," "Forest," "Tree," "Leaf," "Cloud," "Pond," Subterranean Earth," and "Abyss." In addition to these serene natural worlds, there are two additional world-spaces called the "Code" and the "Text." The Code actually contains visual representations of the software code used for OSMOSE. The Text includes quotations from artists and philosophers related to technology, space and the body.

What is quite unique about OSMOSE is the interface device for navigation. Rather than utilizing a data-glove or joystick, maneuvering through OSMOSE's immersive environment is controlled by the movement of breath and balance. The user wears a specially designed vest that is fitted with breathing and balance sensors. Vertical movement up-and-down is synchronized to the movement of the user's inhalation and exhalation. Horizontal movement is controlled through shifting the angle of the user's balance. Inspiration for this means of navigation and interface comes from Davies' experience of deep-sea diving, where the experience of floating is quite common. Davies explains her choice for using the breath as an interface:

"Whereas in conventional VR, the body is often reduced to little more than a probing hand and roving eye, immersion in OSMOSE depends on the body's most essential living act, that of breath—not only to navigate, but more importantly—to attain a particular state-of-being within the virtual world." (Davies, 2000).

Davies noticed that when users were first immersed in OSMOSE, they tended to rely on their habitual modes of awareness, attempting to travel around and see as much as possible, in what appeared to be a "goal-oriented, action-based behavior" (Davies, 2000). However, after about ten minutes of immersion, users facial expressions and bodies seemed to relax, and instead of rushing through the experience and trying to grasp images, they slowed down and entered what seemed to be a more contemplative state. During the last phase of their immersion experience, users directed their attention more to the unusual sensations of floating and the uncanny perceptual ability of being able to see objects as semi-transparent (Davies, 2000).

Since 1995, over 7,500 people have been immersed in OSMOSE and the experiences that they report are quite unusual. Through written responses and post-immersion interviews, a substantial number of participants have described their OSMOSE experience in highly emotional terms, reporting a profound sense of joy or euphoria, feelings of transcendence of time and space, ineffability, and a paradoxical sense of being both in and out of the body. Others reported losing track of time, a heightened awareness of their own Being, a deep sense of mind/body relaxation, and an overwhelming sense of loss, tears, when the experience was coming to a close. These unusual sensibilities are expressive of the evocative potential of a VR2 world. Char Davies attributes these responses of participants to the de-habituation of perception that tends to occur in OSMOSE. Moreover, the altered states of consciousness that immersants report having experienced can be understood as a "de-automatization" of perceptual sensibilities. According to Harvard psychologist Arthur Deikman (1990), those who practice meditation or other contemplative techniques experience enhanced feelings of clarity, concentration and attention. In many respects, the de-automatization of experience evoked by OSMOSE is similar to the de-automatization of experience that occurs in meditative absorption.

What accounts for the experience of de-automatization in OSMOSE? A key feature is the unique visual aesthetic that is based on the VR2 notion of transparency. Related to this is a profoundly different understanding and experience of space. Davies is fond of quoting from the philosopher Gaston Bachelard (1994), who in his book *The Poetics of Space*, wrote: "By changing space, by leaving the space of one's usual sensibilities, one enters into communication with a space that is psychically innovating...For we do not change place, we change our nature." Our normal conception of space is that of a vacant and empty container, set in contrast to solid objects or things with real or defining edges. Our habitual perception is based on fundamental dualities between subject/object, space/thing, figure/ground, inner/outer. However, in OSMOSE, rather than encountering a world of solid objects set over and against the one subject who perceives, these rigid dichotomies and distinctions break down. OSMOSE typifies a VR2 aesthetic; it uses transparent images, embellishing them with a shimmering luminosity or glow that dissolves habitual spatial distinctions. At a recent conference in San Francisco, I had the fortunate experience of hearing Char Davies present a videotaped simulation of OSMOSE. Even though I was more of spectator and not actually immersed in OSMOSE, I can attest to the fact that Davies' artistic vision as expressed in a VR world was truly remarkable. OSMOSE represents just the tip of the VR2 iceberg. The potential for creating evocative spaces that challenge the Western techno-scientific worldview and rampant consumerist mentality is unlimited.

"WORLD AS SPECTACLE" VERSUS "WORLD AS SHARED LUCID DREAM"

Whereas VR1 technology posits the world as a distant spectacle, VR2 technology presents the world as a shared dream. VR1 seeks to maximize the capacity for interactivity for the sake of interactivity. VR2 on the other hand utilizes interactivity as a means to achieve transcendence and insight. Virtual Reality technology (whether VR1 or VR2), relies on sophisticated sensors—typically head-goggles and hand-gloves—which are donned by the user to enter a virtual world. These sensors track the changes and movements in the user's sense organs, and then digitally represent these changes as visual and kinesthetic outputs that feedback to the user's senses. In effect, the user becomes part of the cybernetic circuit. From a hardware standpoint, VR1 and VR2 are not far apart. But when it comes to the software, and the design assumptions that determine the user interface, it is here that these two technological variants part company.

Within a VR1 world, the depths of user's imagination, the source of figuration, is not incorporated into the experience. Instead, the user of VR1 enters into a pre-programmed world, perhaps rich in the variety and range of interactive experiences that can be accessed, but it is by design, limited to experiencing artificial worlds packaged for mass consumption. In addition, since a VR1 user cannot actively participate in creating a shared virtual world with others, this limitation is compensated for by injecting content that is designed to shock the senses. VR1 presents imagery in such a way that it forces the user to stay within a dualistic posture, albeit in a so-called interactive mode. Participation within a VR1 world is primarily vicarious in nature. One feels the thrills and exhilaration of the simulation through immersion in a world designed to titillate and over-excite the senses. We already see indicators of this in the rise of shock TV, docu-dramas depicting "ER" victims with blood and guts, "COPS," and the fascination with the suffering of others—as spectacle. VR1 dazzles the user through both sensory overload and by presenting an array of images which can be explored interactively in succession. Clearly, the allure of VR1 will be the intensity of experience that it offers. However, like recreational drug addiction, as the threshold of excitation shifts after prolonged drug use, higher dosages are required to secure the desired effect or "high". We can expect VR1 will have a similar mass appeal, and hence the need for more novelty, more shocking experiences, and a continuous upstaging of previous narratives.

The emphasis on pure sensory stimulation suggests that VR1 harbors an empirical bias. Its design assumptions and architecture reflect a belief that our only form of contact with phenomena—is through our senses. The interiority and imagination of the user is simply not part of the VR1 equation. VR2, on the other hand, is used as a tool that can extend and display the user's imagination. The connection between the phenomena and the user goes deeper than simply what meets the eye (or other senses). The link between the user and the phenomena in a VR2 world has a non-material, imaginative connection, which goes beyond mere passive sensory stimulation.

VR1 confines the user to a structure of interactivity that is preordained by the software, with the purpose of defining the user as a consumer of commercialized VR experiences. In other words, in VR1 the user has the experience of being active, interacting with vivid images in real-time, but all the while maintaining a cognitively passive receptive stance-not unlike a highly engaged teenager engrossed in a video game. VR2, on the other hand, puts the user into an active mode of configuring the software so as to be able to project and share their imagination with others in a virtual world. To summarize: VR1 merely copies experiences and makes them available for mass consumption; VR2 is a tool for tapping one's own creative imagination and sharing it with others, providing a real-time experience of co-creating a virtual world.

We can liken VR2 to a new aesthetic that is akin to a state of lucid dreaming. In lucid dreams, the dreamer is conscious and aware of the fact that he or she is dreaming. Awake within the dream the lucid dreamer can alter the dream, and is not deceived by the illusory nature of dream images. Similarly, the heightening of perception in VR2 awakens the immersant to recognize that they are awake in a real-time dream. Simulating an ecstatic experience, VR2 opens our perspective from that of a detached bystander looking—a subject viewing objects—shifting our perception to a participatory mode of knowing. What appears then in a VR2 world appears as a magical display, as phenomena are seen and felt to co-arise in participation with the observer. In VR2, the visual field of objectivism is rendered transparent and opens into the whole. What we see, what we experience is an undivided movement of phenomena. Subjects and objects still appear, but they are seen and experienced in a new light. As transparent images, appearances appear without substance.

The integral potentialities of VR2 are apparent in several respects. The VR2 user, in constructing and interacting within a highly imaginative virtual world, draws upon long repressed magical and mythical dimensions of human consciousness. The richness and depth of the virtual world can inspire awe and appreciation for the myriad dimensions of consciousness that are co-present all at once. Virtual worlds in VR2 are evocative, requiring the user to consciously become aware of their participation in the figuration of appearances. Rather than repressing or disengaging the user's consciousness, VR2 turns the lights on, intensifying perception and active imagination. In other words, VR2 could open up human experience to a simulation of integral consciousness, providing a technologically mediated glimpse of a new vision, a new way of seeing the self in relation to the whole.

This is an exciting possibility since it could potentially provide the capacity for people to express and participate in the creation of "aperspectival" virtual worlds (Gebser, 1985). However, VR2 differs from VR1 in that it does not simply provide more surfaces to interact with, or a greater span of visuality. Rather, VR2 offers the possibility for entering into the interiority of space, of expanding inwardly into the depth of the image. In VR2, the user can, for example, see how a rainbow arises as an active construction or collective representation, involving both the user's perception, the image that is apparently distant, and the meaning-giving process that flows between percipient and the phenomena (Barfield, 1988). In other words, the user would have the opportunity to actually experience what a participatory consciousness feels like in a VR2 environment. Experience within VR2 would evoke a meta-awareness of participation-as-observer.

The capacity to share and exchange interior images in VR2 shifts the center of gravity away from a fixed vantage point. Indeed, the whole meaning of what it means to be an observer with a "point-of-view" is radically decentered and transparentized in VR2, but in a way that enhances human freedom. This technology actually would allow one to virtually get inside another person's shoes, to feel and experience the other's perspective. Not only could a user try on for size another person's psycho-physical embodiment, we can expect that more sophisticated versions of VR2 technology would provide multiple users shared interfaces that would allow any one user to see from any perspective. In what would amount to a collective, improvisational virtual world, it would quickly become difficult to know who was the subject and who was the object. Entering a virtual world of subject-object reversals would be somewhat dizzying and disorienting at first. But the intensity of subject/

object blurring experiences would generate a sort of ecstasy, a Sufi dervish-like whirl, and a sense that one was everywhere and nowhere at once.

The most radical implication of VR2 is, I believe, its evocative power to simulate a mode of consciousness in which appearances become virtualized. Appearances within a VR2 world would appear and be experienced as projections of light, as phantoms, including the appearance of the observer that is watching. That which appears to the observer in a VR2 world is recognized as not being the ultimate reality, but as having virtual substance, vivid but transparent, like an apparition, like a mirage, like an echo, like a dream object. Advanced VR2 worlds such as the ones I have described could offer the possibility of making the fundamental truths of quantum physics an embodied and lived experience. It is this transparentizing aesthetic that could potentially transform our vision into aperspectival knowing by open the viewing angle to the whole.

Instead of vision being refracted and distorted through the cone of linear perspectivism, instead of only perceiving with the light of reason, ratio opens up into the whole, into the zeroless dimension (Tulku, 1994). What arises is a sort of "a-dimensional" mode of awareness, whose origins are "ever present," prior to the establishment of a viewpoint, prior to the splitting of the perceptual field into duality, prior to the ratio, "before" measurement takes hold (Gebser, 1985). Vision opens perception into the depth of space, accommodating the observer and the observed simultaneously, in what Gebser terms "a synaresis," an arrangement of dynamic intensities. As transparentizing of awareness intensifies, expanding inwardly into greater depth, space becomes more accommodating of multiple modes of consciousness.

CONCLUSION

The hypertrophied rationality so characteristic of the current Information Age is the virus that no software program can cure. Ratio without grounding in a human matrix of the whole will continue to infect every corpuscle of society, its radiance so brilliant, so piercing, so inexorable that it blinds rather than enlightens. Without the proper antidote of a more balanced, integral consciousness, the ratio virus will proliferate, seeking to maximize and diffuse its power both outwardly in our material affairs, and inwardly, into the information matrix of the biosphere. In whatever domain, ratio, now fused with the powers of information technology, can rapidly spread, altering our sensibilities to a point that we may lose touch with our very sense of humanness. Computation now reigns supreme as the dominant metaphor for modeling our understanding of the world—whether of brain functioning and intelligence, economics, or biology. This hyperrational metaphor promises a world of total calculability and control, where the clarity of rationality supersedes the search for meaning. We have been led to believe that ratio, on its own, could solve all our problems. Computation delivers us to the Promised Land of Accuracy, but upon our arrival we discover that it is a rather cold and desolate place, devoid of human meaning.

The colonization of VR by commercial interests simply mirrors our progressive decrease in intrinsic awareness. The production of endless simulacra, images, and spectacles never get down to the key issue: to realize the true nature of reality. Instead, these media will keep us preoccupied and entranced, which, in reality, simply mimics our "real world" ignorance and state of deception in duality. I am sure that VR1 will no doubt appear at first glance as a technical marvel of the highest order, and why shouldn't it be an object of awe? This technology has the capacity to project a world that in reality has no substance. Yet, despite this technological feat, our consciousness in VR1 will still be habituated to grasping at experiences that we will predictably judge as either pleasurable or hideous. Our intoxication with consuming novel experiences will perpetuate a way of knowing that remains trapped within a perspectival world. We will continue to be mesmerized and taken in by the proliferation of images—real or virtual—all the while mistaking the image, the appearance, for the thing-in-itself. The modern spell of idolatry will not have been broken.

Whether we are inside or outside VR, we inevitably remain locked within our own self-made 3-dimensional universe, confined to the VR cave, unable to see through it. Lacking transparency, our knowing will remain dimly aware of the virtual nature of our everyday lived experiences. William Gibson, who coined the term "cyberspace," likened it to a "consensual hallucination." It's true, cyberspace, but especially VR1, will also appear as a dream, but with a key difference: infected with the ratio virus, the consciousness of the dreamer will continue to be divided against itself. Disjunctive thinking, dominated by a mode of consciousness still caught in subject-object duality, will be bound to a Cyber-Faustian dream—a delusionary state of hubris, where seductive techno-dreams eventually turn into nightmares with real consequences for sentient beings.

In this respect, VR1 stands as a cultural symbol for our hypertrophied rational structure of consciousness. The wizardry of VR1 is a "wizardry of wrong notions," an entrancement to a magical display which results in a proliferation of spatio-temporal displacements, time-space compression, and a dimming of Being (Rab-'Byam-Pa Klong-Chen, 1976). The texture of experience in VR1—excitation, nervousness, and acceleration—is very different in quality from that of VR2. VR2 can be thought of as ritual technology that not only inspires the collective imagination, but also deepens the intensity of awareness. In VR2, we are allowed to enter a world that has become more spacious, where time is a friend rather than an enemy. We are granted the ability to exercise our imagination and intelligence, to observe the observer, and to use VR technology to help us witness and pay attention to the subtle process of proprioception, witnessing our habitual bodily reactions and thought processes (Bohm, 1995). In this virtual world, the habitual reflexes of mind can slow down, allowing us to cultivate awareness, to deepen our capacity for intelligence, and to seed the ground for insight to grow.

Ultimately, though, even VR2 depends on the intentionality and consciousness of the user. VR2 is not some magical "techno-enlightenment" machine. This technology is not a substitute for active and disciplined inquiry. However, VR2 can serve as a new cultural symbol, functioning as a sort of souped-up bio-feedback device for the perceptual apparatus of mind. Having the power to transport the experiencer into a virtual world where imagination and speculation can alter all the rules and conventions of space and time holds great potential for the inception of a new cultural aesthetic. In this connection, VR2 could function as an intermediate and experimental space for the evolution of consciousness. The next great mutation, the leap into the integral mode of consciousness, will ultimately mean shifting from experiencing the world (and the self) as substance to experiencing the world as one virtual holomovement, as emanating from an ever present origination, an on-gong presencing of the whole, the pure wizardry of Being.

REFERENCES

Bachelard, G. (1994). *The Poetics of Space*. (trans. By Maria Jonas; Originally published in 1966). New York: Beacon Press.

Barfield, O. (1977). *Rediscovery of Meaning, and Other Essays*. Middletown, Conn.: Wesleyan University Press.

Barfield, O. (1988). *Saving the Appearances: A Study in Idolatry* (Wesleyan Revised Edition; Originally published in 1957). Hanover, New Hampshire: University Press of New England.

Baudrillard, J. (1995). *Simulacra and Simulations*. (trans. By Sheila Faria Glaser). Ann Arbor: University of Michigan Press.

Bohm, D. (1995). *Wholeness and the Implicate Order* (Originally published in 1980). London: Routledge.

Borgmann, A. (1992). *Crossing the Postmodern Divide*. Chicago: University of Chicago Press.

Borgmann, A. (1999). *Holding On to Reality:The Nature of Information at the Turn of the Millennium*. Chicago: University of Chicago Press.

Brand, S. (1999). *The Clock of the Long Now: Time and Responsibility*. New York: Basic Books.

Davies, C. (2000). OSMOSE www.immersence.com/osmose.htm

Deikman, A. (1990). De-automatization and mystical experience. In C. Tart (Ed.), *Altered States of Consciousness*. New York: Harper Collins.

Gebser, J. (1985). *The Ever-Present Origin*. (Noel Barstad and Algis Mickunas trans.Originally published in 1953). Athens, Ohio: Ohio University Press.

Giddens, A. (1990). *The Consequences of Modernity*. Cambridge: Polity Press.

Giddens, A. (1991). *Modernity and Self-Identity: Self and Society in the Late Modern Age*. Stanford, Calf.: Stanford University Press.

Heidegger, M. (1977). *The Question Concerning Technology and Other Essays* (trans. By William Lovitt). New York: Harper Torchbooks.

Heim, M. (1993). *The Metaphysics of Virtual Reality*. New York: Oxford University Press.

Heim, M. (1998). *Virtual Realism*. New York: Oxford University Press.

Jaynes, J. (1990). *The Origins of Consciousness and the Breakdown of the Bicameral Mind* (paperback edition). Boston: Houghton Mifflin.

Kurzweil, R. (1999). *The Age of Spiritual Machines*. New York: Penguin.

Lanier, J. (1998). "Without Interactions We Live in Absurdity: Virtual Reality as a Way of Sharing the New Worlds," MediaMente, March 8. http://www.mediamente.rai.it/english/bibliote/intervis/1/lanier.htm

Lanier, J. (1994). "Karma Vertigo: or Considering the Excessive Responsibilities Placed on Us by the Dawn of the Information Infrastructure." http://www.well.com/user/jaron/essay.html

Levin, D. M. (1988). *The Opening of Vision: Nihilism and the Postmodern Situation*. London: Routledge.

Levy, P. (1998). *Becoming Virtual: Reality in the Digital Age* (trans. By Robert Bononno). New York: Plenum Trade.

Lowe, D. (1982). *The History of Bourgeois Perception*. Chicago: University of Chicago Press.

Mitchell, W. (1992). *The Reconfigured Eye: Visual Truth in the Post-Photographic Era*. Cambridge: MIT Press.

Morse, M. (1998). *Virtualities: Television, Media Art, and Cyberculture*. Bloomington, IN: Indiana University Press.

Nichol, L. (2000). Personal conversation.

Ong, W. (1988). *Orality and Literacy: The Technologizing of the Word*. London: Routledge.

Rab-'Byams-Pa Klong-Chen. (1976). *Kindly Bent to Ease Us: Wonderment (Vol. 3)*. (trans. By Herbert Guenther). Berkeley, CA: Dharma Publishing.

Simpson, L. (1995). *Technology, Time and the Conversations of Moder*nity. New York: Routledge.

Talbott, S. L. (1995). *The Future Does Not Compute: Transcending the Machines in Our Midst*. Sebastopol, Calf.: O'Reilly & Associates.

Tulku, T. (1994). *Dynamics of Time and Space*. Berkeley, CA: Dharma Publishing.

Virilio, P. (1997). *Open Sky* (trans. Julie Rose). London: Verso.

Virilio, P. (1995). *The Art of the Motor*. Minneapolis, MN: University of Minnesota.

Von Glasersfeld, E. (1995). *Radical Constructivism*. New York: Palmer Press.

Chapter XV

HCI: The Next Step Towards Optimization of Computer-Assisted Surgical Planning, Intervention and Training (CASPIT)

Rudy J. Lapeer, Polydoros Chios, Alf D. Linney,
Ghassan Alusi and Anthony Wright

INTRODUCTION

The introduction of computerized systems in medicine started more than a decade ago. The first applications were mainly focused on archiving and the general database management of patient records with the aim of building fully- integrated Hospital Information Systems (HIS) and fast transfer of data and images (e.g. PACS - Picture Archiving and Communication Systems) between HIS. In parallel with this more general development, specialized computer systems were built to process and enhance image data from such systems as Magnetic Resonance Imaging (MRI) and Computed Tomography (CT) scanners. The use of enhanced CT and MRI images led to the birth of Image Guided Surgery (IGS). Other terminology for similar concepts has since been used, e.g. Computer- Assisted Surgery (CAS), Computer Integrated Surgery and Therapy (CIST) (Lavallée et al, 1997) and Computer-Assisted Medical Interventions (CAMI). In this chapter, we shall look mainly at Computer-Assisted Surgery (CAS) systems and related systems which are aimed at the training of surgeons and the simulation and planning of surgical interventions. The emphasis will be on the Human-Computer Interaction (HCI) aspect rather than the technological issues of such systems. The latter will be briefly discussed in the next section, to make the reader familiar with the terminology, the history and the current state of the art in CASPIT.

COMPUTER ASSISTED SURGICAL PLANNING, INTERVENTION AND TRAINING (CASPIT) - BACKGROUND

One of the early applications of computer-assisted surgery (CAS) was in the field of stereotactic neurosurgery where 3D visualization of anatomical structures on computer was used as a guidance to navigate the surgical tool to the target area. Today, CAS has become popular in a variety of surgical fields including cranio- and maxillo-facial surgery, ENT (ear, nose and throat) surgery, orthopaedic surgery, cardiac surgery, laparoscopy, interventional radiology and several other surgical disciplines (Lapeer et al, 2000a).

The term 'assisted' in CAS implies that the operator, i.e. the surgeon, is still responsible for the outcome and the overall control of the operation. The system is there as an aid; thus, the surgeon has to decide as to whether the information provided by the system is reliable or not.

Surgical simulation and planning was developed in parallel with CAS, possibly because of its solid base for testing new technologies which might prove too unreliable for direct use in a real clinical intervention. At the end of the 80's, simple 3D visualization of the anatomy of the patient, mainly obtained from Magnetic Resonance Imaging (MRI) and Computed Tomography (CT) images, was already a major step forwards in the planning and simulation of surgery. A few years later, **image guided surgery** (IGS) systems came in the development which allowed to display a virtual surgical tool into the 3D virtual scene, hence allowing more realistic planning and execution of such interventions like stereotactic and endoscopic surgery which previously provided the surgeon with only local visual information. Displaying the trajectory of the surgical tool in 2.5/3D was a useful aid to the surgeon even if the accuracy was not much better than a few millimetres. Nowadays, **computer-assisted surgery** (CAS) systems are still not accurate enough to be fully relied upon by the surgeon. However, they are a useful aid to provide the surgeon with spatial image formation which he/she previously had to reconstruct mentally, i.e. by observing a series of 2D images and then trying to mentally visualise the 3D anatomy.

The computer proves useful not only for major surgical interventions but also for smaller-scale and non-invasive interventions or examinations, e.g. interventional radiology, videostroboscopy, etc. Also, training of junior surgeons and nurses, be it in major or minor interventions, can be significantly improved using interactive and multimedia computer-based training (CBT) software.

The concept of **augmented reality** (AR) has become the new challenge in microsurgical disciplines such as ENT- and neurosurgery, which target the patient's head and involve the use of a surgical stereo microscope. The stereo images as obtained through the microscope are augmented with a virtual image from 3D rendered patient data, e.g. from MRI or CT images. This allows the surgeon to view structures which are not visible in the original image, thus providing him/her with more anatomical information. However, it is hardly necessary to mention that one crucial problem in CAS applications using AR is the accuracy of the overlay of the real image with the virtual image: poor registration of the two images may result in less reliable feedback than the original system would have provided.

Robotic surgery is one step further towards the minimization of human error during surgery. Currently, there are only a few surgical interventions, e.g. stereotactic neurosurgery, where the entire operation can be done by a robot. Even then, the robot is still supervised by a surgeon. Not only is the necessity for further technological developments a restriction for shifting the responsibility more and more towards the machine, but ethical issues also come into play!

HCI FOR CASPIT

From the previous section, it is obvious that a significant amount of research and technological advancement are necessary, especially for the more critical CAS systems to allow them to be used in full confidence by the surgeon. However, the success of such a system depends not only on purely technological concepts, but also on the interaction between the surgeon and his/her computerized aid. A clear interface to operate the CAS system is of major importance, not only because of the general inexpertise of a majority of surgeons to operate computerized systems, but also because they need their hands to do more important things than just twitching a knob to get some computerized image a tiny bit sharper! Basically, the CAS system functions as an aid, and its tuning should not distract surgeons from their more important tasks to be performed in the operating theatre.

For the less critical applications such as planning, simulation and minor or non-invasive interventions, better systems are available, but further optimization from the HCI point of view is still possible.

The next section discusses theoretical and practical concepts of HCI and how they fit in with the needs in CASPIT and related applications. In section 3.2, examples of some commercial and academic systems for different medico-surgical applications are given.

Theoretical considerations

A definition, as cited in (ACM SIGCHI, 1992) states that human-computer interaction (HCI) is a discipline concerned with the design, evaluation and implementation of interactive computing systems for human use and with the study of major phenomena surrounding them.

Visibility and affordance

Norman (Norman et al, 1992) identifies two main principles to ensure good HCI:

visibility Controls need to be visible which implies that there is a good mapping between the controls and their effects. For example, the controls on a driver's dashboard have good visibility whilst video-recorders have not (Preece et al, 1994).

affordance is a technical term that refers to the properties of objects, e.g. a door 'affords' to be opened. More important in HCI is perceived *affordance* which implies what a person thinks can be done with the object, e.g. does the door suggests it should be pushed or pulled?

Even though a surgeon should be made familiar and properly trained in the operation of the computer, the monitor, additional tools, etc., it is important that the controls have good visibility and affordance. This is because the surgeon should not be distracted from his/her main task by, for example, spending too much time to figure out which button will do which task, or by operating the wrong control because of poor affordance.

Usability

Another important concept of HCI is **usability**. Usability is concerned with making systems easy to learn and easy to use and, thus, requires good visibility and affordance.

Usability can be subdivided into four components (Bennett, 1984):

Learnability is the time and effort required to reach a specified level of user performance.

Throughput involves the tasks accomplished by experienced users, the speed of task execution and the errors made.

Flexibility is the extent to which the system can accommodate changes to the tasks and environments beyond those first specified.

Attitude or the 'positive' attitude engendered in users by the system.

The first issue, *learnability*, is probably more applicable in the fields of surgical simulation and planning. Many of the earlier systems were considered to be cumbersome to operate and did seldom reflect realistic situations. The current technology of graphical user interfaces (GUI's) has solved this problem to a considerable extent. Also the introduction of haptic feedback systems can make simulations more realistic and relieve the surgeon from learning tedious and unrealistic manipulations. The second issue, throughput, may not seem directly relevant; however, one should take into account that an efficiently designed CAS system may speed up the surgical procedure significantly. *Flexibility* is an important concept during the design phase of CASPIT applications. For instance, ergonomic issues may require a flexible design to adapt the system to different surgical environments. Attitude is obviously a crucial issue: medical doctors and surgeons tend to be skeptical when a new technology or advancement is introduced. Lack of a clear interface or an easy way of learning how to use the system tends to discourage surgeons; hence they revert back to their original and more familiar approaches.

Safety

The design of a HCI module often involves the consideration of **safety-critical components** to ensure human and/or environmental safety. In CAS systems, the safety of the patient depends on the system's reliability. If the latter is poor, fatal mistakes could be made by the surgeon who relies on its output. Poor reliability may not only result from technological shortcomings but also from a badly designed or cumbersome interface.

Ergonomic issues

The objective of ergonomics is to maximize an operator's safety, efficiency and reliability of performance, to make a task easier, and to increase the feelings of comfort and satisfaction (Preece et al, 1994). The concept of ergonomics is very important to the surgeon. A well-designed CAS system should not only preserve the state of ergonomics of the earlier non-computerized procedure, but also aim to improve it.

One of the important fields in ergonomics is the analysis of the human behavior in dynamic systems where people interact with machines. This implies observation of events such as tasks, postures, movements, gestures or episodes of communication or cooperation. The latter procedure is not straightforward since, for specific applications, some of the events run in parallel and/or show overlapping. In this case, the observer designs a **mental model** which he/she derives after being introduced to the environment of the HCI and the total number of events at the time of operation (Held, 1999). Mental models are either analogous representations or a combination of analogous and propositional representations. They are distinct from, but related to images. A mental model represents the relative position of a set of objects in an analogous manner that parallels the structure of the state of objects in the world (Johnson-Laird, 1988). An alternative definition by Donald Norman (Norman, 1988) explains a mental model as the model people have of themselves, others, the environment, and the things with which they interact. People form mental models through experience, training and instruction. Important human factors that are studied through the mental model are the prioritization of events and their sequence of occurrence. Knowledge

Figure 1: The spectrum of mixed reality according to Milgram (Milgram et al, 1994).

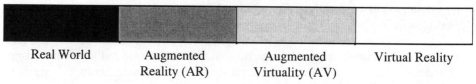

Mixed Reality

| Real World | Augmented Reality (AR) | Augmented Virtuality (AV) | Virtual Reality |

of these factors contributes to the better understanding of usability requirements, thus ensuring good HCI.

Virtual environments, virtual reality (VR) and augmented reality (AR)

VR systems/environments usually refer to interactive systems that provide the user with a sense of direct physical presence and direct experience. These systems may provide **visual, aural** and **haptic feedback** or some combination. They also allow natural interaction by manipulating computer-generated objects using gestures similar to those one would use to manipulate real objects (Preece et al, 1994).

Two types of virtual reality systems can be distinguished:

Immersion systems which include peripherals such as helmets and gloves.

Desktop systems use a single, usually large color display, a 3D pointing device or 3D mouse and a keyboard.

Between the extremes of real life and virtual reality (VR) lies the spectrum of mixed reality (see Figure 1). Mixed reality can be roughly divided into two categories, i.e. *augmented reality* (AR) and *augmented virtuality* (AV). Augmented reality lies near the real world end of the line with the predominate perception being the real world augmented by computer generated data (Milgram et al, 1994).

Augmented reality CAS systems have been tested by using a VR helmet, hence *immersing* the surgeon into an 'operating world'. Surgeons do not prefer this *immersion* since they feel isolated from the real operating scene. Moreover, the VR helmet causes increasing discomfort and is, thus, not suitable for relatively long interventions. Therefore, desktop systems are preferred. In section 4 we describe the CAESAR system (Computer-Assisted ENT Surgery using Augmented Reality) which uses a 3D autostereoscopic display.

Examples of HCI from commercial and academic CASPIT implementations

Computer-based training (CBT) software for general medical training and surgery is not a novelty. The current availability of commercial and academic products is widespread. A product developed at the Institute of Laryngology and Otology, University College London, is a computer-based training course in interactive rhinology. The software is implemented using HTML and Java and, thus, only requires an Internet browser to run. The user interface is windows based and has the structure of a webpage with buttons and images to click on, areas which show more information when the mouse cursor is placed in them, a general menu and on-line help which are accessible in every window and scrolling text messages in the lower part of the screen just in case the user is unsure what to do next (see Figure 2). The software also contains multi-media implementations, e.g. videos of surgical

Figure 2: The interaction panel from the 'Interactive Rhinology' CBT course as developed at the Institute of Laryngology and Otology (ILO), University College London (UCL) - with permission. The basic menu is on the left hand side and is constantly displayed. Note the scrolling message bar at the bottom of the window which prompts the user which operations can be done.

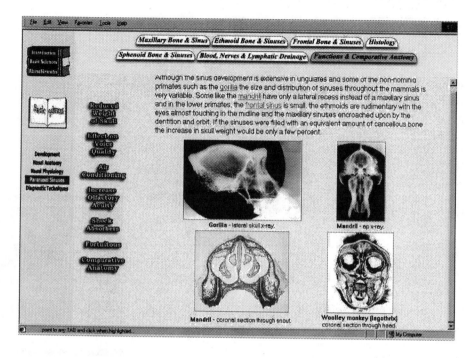

interventions and movies of 3D anatomical parts reconstructed from CT or MRI images (see Figure 3).

Smaller commercial systems, usually for diagnostic examinations or minor interventions, tend to have well-designed interfaces and have a compact and ergonomic overall design. Figure 4 shows a system for stroboscopy/endoscopy as developed by Kay Elemetrics Corp.

Software for *image-guided surgery* (IGS) and surgical navigation is fairly standard these days although its general lack of sub-millimetric accuracy makes it still not to be routinely used for most standard surgical procedures. Figure 5 shows the interface of IGS software as developed by MTT (Medical Technology Transfer). The position of the surgical tool is indicated by a white cross-hatch, on the three orthogonal views of CT/MRI images of the patient. The middle panel allows displaying of cryosections (colored images) of the same patient or 3D volume- or surface-rendered reconstructions from the MRI and/or CT data.

The introduction of *haptic feedback* is a significant improvement to create a more realistic feel of the simulation or planning of a surgical intervention. Figure 6 shows the DextroScope™, a medical and scientific tool for visualizing and interacting with 3D volumetric data. One of the applications, based on its virtual reality (VR) environment is a neurosurgical planning system. It has a *passive haptic feedback* allowing to control a virtual control panel. Another commercial system, as developed by ReachIn™, provides *active haptic feedback*, i.e. objects within the virtual scene are tangible. The interface is general,

Figure 3: The interaction panel from the 'Interactive Rhinology' CBT course as developed at the Institute of Laryngology and Otology (ILO), University College London (UCL) - with permission. The basic menu is on the left hand side and is constantly displayed. Multi-media can be activated as is shown in the bottom right hand side where a movie allows to study an anatomical part in 3D, from different orientations.

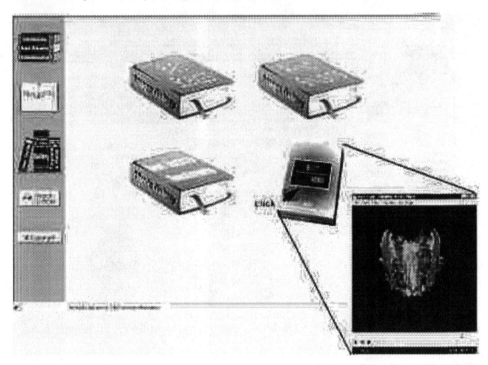

thus any application can be programmed and different material properties for the objects in the scene can be specified (see Figure 7).

CASE STUDY: ERGONOMIC ISSUES FOR COMPUTER ASSISTED ENT SURGERY AND AUGMENTED REALITY (CAESAR)

Introduction

The CAESAR (Computer-Assisted ENT Surgery using Augmented Reality) project is currently under development at the Institute of Laryngology and Otology, University College London. The project aims to improve surgical procedures by augmenting the real scene of the operated area as seen by the surgeon through a 3D surgical microscope, by superimposing a virtual scene which shows structures that are not visible in the real image (Lapeer et al, 2000a,b). The advantage of an augmented image from a surgical point of view was explained in section 2. The alternative of being presented with a 3D augmented image as compared to, for example, three orthogonal views (i.e. sagittal, transverse and coronal) which is commonly used in standard IGS software (see for example Figure 5) is also a significant improvement from a HCI point of view since it displays the object of interest

Figure 4: Kay's digital video stroboscopy/ endoscopy system (Kay Elemetrics Corp., with permission). The computer, monitor, printer, rhino-laryngeal stroboscope and other hardware components are stored in a single cabinet. The examiner can activate major functions using foot switches and a footpedal, thus keeping his hands free to operate the endoscope.

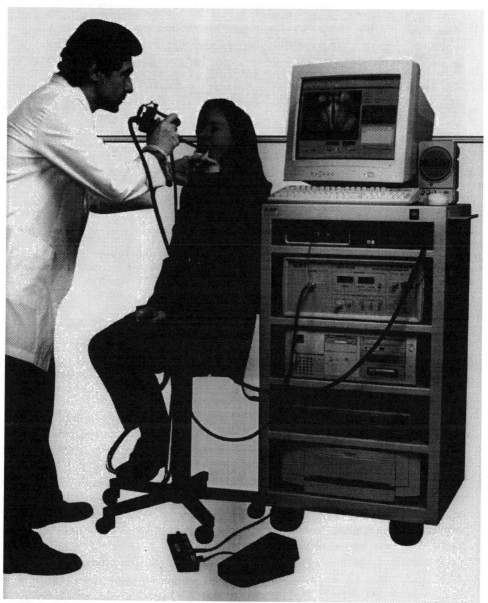

(OOI) in a more realistic fashion. The augmented image is composed of a stereo pair of two real images, captured by a surgical stereo microscope, and a stereo pair of virtual images obtained from a volume- or surface-rendered CT or MRI dataset. The depth cue for the virtual dataset is typically obtained using a computer-graphics based shading technique called ray-tracing. Figure 8 shows an augmented image.

Figure 5: An IGS interface as developed by MTT (Medical Technology Transfer, with permission). Three orthogonal views of MRI images, i.e. coronal, axial and sagittal, are shown on the left hand side. The position of the surgical tool is indicated by a white cross-hatch. The middle panel shows a cryo-section of the same patient.

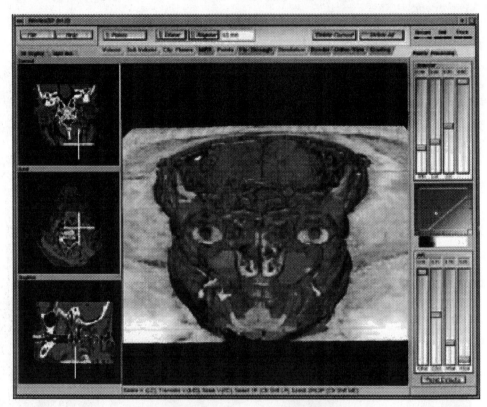

Equipment for microsurgery

In ENT surgery the binocular operating stereo microscope is the most important piece of equipment for the surgeon. The instrument offers the surgeon stereoscopic viewing, which is important for the perception of depth. Surgical microscopes use a single objective lens that allows the eyepieces to receive two different views of the region of interest (ROI), thus producing stereo vision effects. The field of view under the objective covers a sensing area of 20-30mm in diameter. Magnification and the physical properties of the lens derive the depth of field, which is the area above and below the focal plane in the ROI that is still perceived as a sharp image. Further magnification in the instrument's eyepiece enhances the relative depth between two or more points.

Scientific advancement in the field of stereo vision initiated the production of desktop systems (see section 3.1.5). Recent technological developments have led to the creation of 3D autostereoscopic displays for which the user does not require specialized headsets. The new devices offer a more realistic approach to 3D viewing, provide greater viewing freedom than the microscope's eyepieces and are also used for single or multi-view image presentations. Flat panel and Twin-LCD systems are considered of great prospect, as they are compact, lightweight and small in size, allowing easy implementation with other equipment found inside the operating theatre. Figure 9 shows two autostereoscopic displays.

Figure 6: The DextroScope™ (Copyright© 2000, Volume Interactions, with permission) is a medical and scientific tool for visualization and interaction with 3D volumetric data. Its virtual reality (VR) interface allows the user to manipulate two hand-held tools - a stylus for precision manipulation and a control handle for volume orientation. Unambiguous control of the application (push buttons, dragging sliders, controlling curves) is achieved by means of a virtual control panel, visualized within the 3D workspace and providing passive haptic feedback.

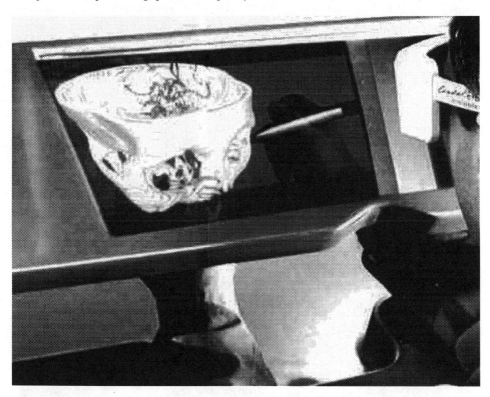

The arrangement of devices, tables and stools inside the operating theatre is fairly standard and follows strict health and safety regulations. The surgical microscope is usually attached to the end of a mechanical arm that stands at the other side of the operating table. The microscope itself is small and compact so that it can move freely to all directions. The introduction of new computer equipment, such as the autostereoscopic 3D display, inside the operating theatre forms a separate ergonomic study for which one has to consider hospital regulations, space availability, cabling, as well as the best possible conjunction of the new equipment with the existing apparatus (see Figure 10).

Ergonomic issues of the CAESAR project

The CAESAR project (Lapeer et al, 2000a,b) aims to create a tool that reduces the risk factor in ENT surgery by improving the way the surgeon perceives visual data. This will allow complex surgery to be performed with a greater degree of accuracy, reducing the risk of morbidity, including deafness to the patient. It will also allow routine surgery to be carried out faster and easier. The project introduces the use of a prototype 3D autostereoscopic display unit which complements the viewing end of the surgical microscope, thereby

Figure 7: The ReachIn display (ReachIn™, with permission) with active haptic feedback. The system combines a stereo-visual display, a haptic device and a six degree-of-freedom positioner. The user interacts with the virtual world using one hand for navigation and control and the other hand to touch and feel the virtual objects. The use of a semi-transparent mirror creates an interface where graphics and haptics are co-located - so the user can see and feel the object in the same place. The image shows an application for training a medical professional to draw blood from a bloodvessel in the hand using a syringe. The stylus provides the haptic interface by allowing the user to position his virtual tool (the syringe in this case) and also give haptic feedback whenever the virtual tool touches an object in the scene (the hand in this case). The user is wearing stereo goggles (shutter system) and thus perceives the objects in 3D.

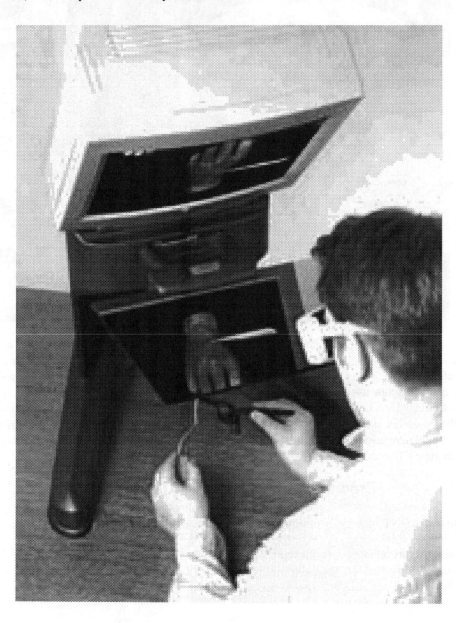

making surgery less stressful for the surgeon, thus less hazardous for the patient. The ergonomic study of the system at this stage included three aspects of research: analysis of the surgeon's actions during surgery, depth perception using a prototype autostereoscopic 3D display and structural implementation of the new system with existing equipment in the operating theatre.

Figure 8: Augmented image with superimposed virtual surgical tool.

Analysis of the surgeon's actions

Preliminary studies were conducted to analyze the surgeon's behavior during the surgical procedure. Seven independent actions, which occur during the critical stages of mastoid and skull base surgery, were identified and timed. These events and their weight of occurrence during surgery, as a result of time measurements, are listed in Table 1.

It was also found that events run in parallel. Seven possible combinations of such parallel events are:

1. Drilling or cutting, and viewing.
2. Communicating with consultant, and viewing.
3. Teaching or training, and viewing.
4. Observing the 2D monitor, and teaching.
5. Arranging the patient's position, and teaching.
6. Moving the microscope and arranging the patient's position.
7. Fixing the surgical tools, and teaching.

(a) NEC-GWT   *(b) SHARP*

Figure 9: Newly developed autostereoscopic 3D displays (with permission).

Figure 10: Typical arrangement of staff and equipment inside the operating theatre before the introduction of the 3D autostereoscopic display.

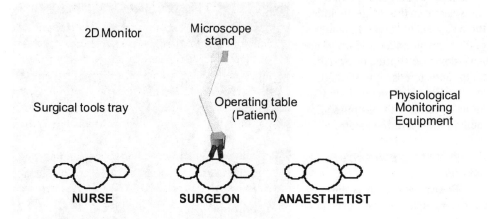

Depth perception using an autostereoscopic 3D display

One of the primary aims of the CAESAR project is to use an autostereoscopic 3D display for visual feedback instead of the microscope eyepieces. After adaptation of the 3D microscope, we investigated the potential use of the autostereoscopic display in microsurgery. In (Chios et al, 1999) it was shown that the display provided the same depth perception as by viewing through the eyepieces of the microscope.

A drawback of the autostereoscopic 3D display is its sensitivity to the position of the observer; thus, head motion is limited as it reduces the depth perception.

Equipment arrangement

The design of the 3D microscope-display system must be consistent with its usage criteria at the time of augmented reality microsurgery. The microscope, together with the remaining instruments used in the operating theatre, must be in a safe and ergonomically convenient position around the operating table. Since the surgeon operates whilst looking directly at the 3D autostereoscopic display, it is necessary that the latter be placed at the appropriate distance (usually between 30-50cm) from the viewer. With the existing arrangement of equipment (see Figure 10) around the table this proved difficult because the microscope is mounted at the lower end of a stand, thus affecting the surgeon's line of sight. To solve this problem, an inverted gamma-shaped arm was designed which lowered and

Table 1: Event recording at time of operation.

Event list	Weight
Performing surgery using the microscope	68%
Arranging the microscope's position	4%
Arranging the patient's position	3.5%
Observing the monitor or physiological monitoring equipment	4.5%
Communicating with other consultant or anaesthetist	4%
Teaching medical students	5%
Fixing surgical tools, communicating with nurse	11%

horizontally displaced the microscope.

DISCUSSION AND FURTHER DEVELOPMENT

It is clear from the outline in the previous sections that particular applications of CASPIT have well-thought-out and well-designed user interfaces whilst the more advanced applications still have a long way to go. Indeed, the applications targeted at training, planning and simulation are the least critical and have, therefore, been going through a sufficiently long development process. However, some GUI's of commercial systems still tend to suffer from shortcomings such as *color pollution* (Tufte, 1990) i.e. the excessive use colors. Also, excessive information is often stuffed into a single window which may cause confusion to the user.

Further improvement of the human-computer interface in surgical planning and simulation software, to reflect more realistic interaction, can be achieved using the *haptic feedback* system. Some commercial haptic feedback systems provide a general interface upon which any application, be it medical or non-medical, can be built (see Figure 7 for an example). For medical applications, the degree of 'realism' is, thus, dependent on the knowledge of material properties of the tissues involved in the simulated surgical intervention. This is the main problem at this stage since these properties are only known for a small percentage of human biological tissue.

A more advanced application of CAS involves the augmentation of surgical images as perceived through the operating microscope (the AR concept). Most of the current systems are still in their infancy, thus, little attention to HCI has been given at this stage. The main problem with surgical systems using augmented reality is the requirement of extra equipment, i.e. tracking devices with cables, a 3D autostereoscopic display and extra cameras on the microscope. This is mainly an ergonomic issue since the extra equipment should not obstruct the surgeon, the assistants and nurses in doing their job. The fact that the equipment also needs to be sterile when used in the operating theatre, requires consideration during the ergonomic design. As most standard (computer) equipment needs to be 'wrapped up' to allow sterilization, more space is required for each additional piece of equipment.

In a preliminary ergonomic analysis of the CAESAR project (Computer-Assisted ENT Surgery using Augmented Reality), it was shown that the surgeon's main activity is the use of the microscope. This frequent use of the microscope during surgery may result in discomfort such as sore eyes and strains of the upper back and neck muscles from a constant bent-over position. The choice to introduce the autostereoscopic 3D display as a complementary visualization tool, thus, relieves the surgeon from discomfort. It was also shown in (Chios et al, 1999) that the depth perception with the autostereoscopic 3D display was equivalent to the stereo operating microscope.

Improvements of HCI during surgery, for example to adjust the augmented image, could be done using for example *footpedals*, a *footmouse*, or a *speech recognition* system.

Some commercial systems have been built which provide an entire set-up for IGS or CAS, very often including imaging equipment based on ultrasound, fluoroscopy or low magnetic field MRI. The problem here is that the latter visualization techniques are not very accurate. Complete CAS or IGS systems including the far better CT or high magnetic field MRI scanners would be difficult to build in a standard commercial package. So despite these systems being well-designed from the HCI point of view and specifically in terms of ergonomics, their use for most surgical procedures is limited because of lack of accuracy.

CONCLUSION

In this chapter we discussed theoretical concepts of human-computer interaction (HCI) and put them in the context of computer-assisted surgical interventions, training and planning (CASPIT). Practical examples of HCI in commercial and academic applications in CASPIT were given. Furthermore, a case study on the ergonomic issues of computer-assisted ENT surgery using augmented reality (CAESAR), as implemented at the Institute of Laryngology and Otology (ILO), University College London (UCL), was presented.

It has been shown in this chapter that the consideration of HCI for CASPIT systems is not a novelty. Further development will eventually result in more accurate, flexible and ergonomically designed systems, which therefore will become standard, routinely used tools for CASPIT.

REFERENCES

Bennett, J. (1984). Managing to meet usability requirements. In J. Bennett, D. Case, J. Sandelin, and M. Smith, editors, *Visual Display Terminals: Usability issues and Health concerns.* Prentice-Hall Englewood Cliffs, NJ.

Chios, P., Tan, A. C., Linney, A., Alusi, G. H., Wright, A., Woodgate, G. J., and Ezra, D. (1999). The potential use of an autostereoscopic 3D display in microsurgery. In C. Taylor and A. Colchester, editors, *Medical Image Computing and Computer-Assisted Intervention - MICCAI' 99*, volume 1679 of *Lecture Notes in Computer Science.* Springer, 998-1009, September 1999.

Held, J. (1999). Fitting the mental model: A new technique for computerised event recording. In D. Harris, editor, *Engineering psychology and cognitive ergonomics.* London, Ashgate.

Johnson-Laird, P. N. (1988). *The Computer and the Mind.* Harvard University Press, Cambridge MA .

Lapeer, R. J., Chios, P., Alusi, G., Linney, A., Davey, M. K., and Tan, A. C. (2000a). Computer Assisted ENT Surgery using Augmented Reality: Preliminary results on the CAESAR project. In *MICCAI'2000 Conference Proceedings*, October 2000.

Lapeer, R. J., Chios, P., Alusi, G., Linney, A., Davey, M. K., and Tan, A. C. (2000b). Augmented reality for ENT surgery: an overview of the CAESAR project. In *ISA/ICC-2000 Conference Proceedings*, December 2000.

Lavallée, S., Cinquin, P., and Troccaz, J. (1997). *Computer integrated surgery and therapy: state of the art*, volume 30 of *Technology and Informatics*, chapter 10. IOS Press.

Milgram, P. et al. (1994). Augmented reality: A class of displays on the reality-virtuality continuum. In H. Das, editor, *SPIE Proceedings: Telemanipulator and Telepresence Technologies*, volume 2351, 282-292.

Norman, D. A. (1988). *The Psychology of Everyday Things.* Basic Books, NY.

Norman, D. A. et al. (1992). *Turn Signals are the Facial Expressions of Automobiles.* Addison-Wesley, Reading, MA.

Preece, J. et al. (1994). *Human-Computer Interaction.* Addison-Wesley.

ACM SIGCHI (1992). *Curricula for Human-Computer Interaction.* ACM Special Interest Group on Human-Computer Interaction.

Tufte, E. R. (1990). *Envisioning Information.* Graphics Press, Cheshire, CT.

About the Authors

Qiyang Chen is an Associate Professor of MIS at the School of Business, Montclair State University. He earned his PhD in information systems from the University of Maryland, Baltimore. His research interests are in the area of human-computer interaction, database development, soft computing and information resource management. His recent publications are in the *International Journal of Human-Computer Interactions*, *Human System Management*, *Journal of Neural Network Computing and Applications*, etc. Dr. Chen has consulted with those in industry on various issues in information systems. He regularly serves on program committees for national and international conferences and is included in 2001 edition of *International Who's Who of Information Technology*.

***

Ghassan Alusi is an ear nose and throat surgeon with an interest in image guidance for skull base surgery. He is a fellow of the Royal College of Surgeons in Edinburgh and London and is currently working as a Senior Registrar at the Royal Marsden Hospital. He is an Honorary Clinical Lecturer at the Institute of Laryngology and Otology and is about to complete his PhD dissertation in Surgery and Medical Physics.

Scott W. Ambler is President of Denver-based Ronin International. Scott is the author of *The Object Primer 2nd Edition* (1995, 2000), *Building Object Applications That Work* (1998), *Process Patterns* (1998) and *More Process Patterns* (1999), and co-author of *The Elements of Java Style* (2000) all published by Cambridge University Press. He is also co-editor with Larry Constantine of the Unified Process book series from CMP books, including *The Unified Process Inception Phase* (Fall 2000), *The Unified Process Elaboration Phase* (Spring 2000), and *The Unified Process Construction Phase* (Summer 2000) all of which focus on best practices to enhance the Unified Process. He has worked with OO technology since 1990 in various roles: Process Mentor, Business Architect, System Analyst, System Designer, Project Manager, Smalltalk Programmer, Java Programmer, and C++ Programmer. He has also been active in education and training as both a formal trainer and as an object mentor. Scott is a contributing editor with *Software Development* (www.sdmagazine.com) and writes columns for *Computing Canada* (www.plesman.com). He can be reached via e-mail at scott.ambler@ronin-intl.com.

Gerardo Ayala received a BE in Computer Engineering from the National Autonomous University of México (UNAM) in 1985, presenting a graduation thesis on the application of expert systems in education. He obtained an MS degree in Computer Science in 1990 from the Muroran Institute of Technology, Japan while working on Intelligent Tutoring Systems in the domain of rule-based programming. He received a PhD in March 1996 from the University of Tokushima, Japan while doing research on the modelling of 0intelligent agents for computer-supported collaborative learning environments. Currently, he is the

Director of the Research Center of Information and Automation Technologies (Centro de Investigación en Tecnologías de Información y Automatización, CENTIA) of the Universidad de las Américas-Puebla. His current research fields are computer-supported collaborative learning environments based on software agents in the context of knowledge management, the social construction of knowledge and lifelong learning. E-mail: ayalasan@mail.udlap.mx, http://gente.udlap.mx/~ayalasan.

Jae-Woo Chang received a BE degree in Computer Engineering from Seoul National University of Korea in 1984, and MS and PhD degrees in Computer Science from Korea Advanced Institute of Science and Technology (KAIST) in 1986 and 1991, respectively. In 1991, he joined the Department of Computer Engineering at Chonbuk National University, Chonju, Korea. He is currently an Associate Professor of the Faculty of Electronic, Information Engineering at Chonbuk National University. His research interests include multimedia databases, multimedia information retrieval, structured document retrieval, and database access methods.

Polydoros Chios obtained a BSc in AppliedPhysics and an MSc in Engineering and Physical Sciences in Medicine. He is currently completing a PhD at the Department of Medical Physics and Bio-engineering at University College London. His main interests are in computer assisted surgery, medical imaging, video microscopy, ergonomics and HCI.

Paul Darbyshire is a lecturer in the Department of Information Systems at Victoria University of Technology, Melbourne Australia. He lecturers in object oriented systems, C and Java programming and has research interests in the application of Java and Web technologies to the support of teaching. Paul's current research is into the use of the Web for university subject management and the use of AI techniques for the development of second generation Web-based teaching support software.

Antonio Drommi is an instructor of Computer Information Systems and the Instructional Technologist for the College of Business at the University of Detroit, Mercy. His area of focus and research is human computer interaction, interface design, advance programming, and database design. He is a frequent lecturer for Wayne State University and is the coordinator for the University of Detroit Mercy Quality Systems Center for the academic, Detroit manufacturing and business community.

Nobuko Furugori received a BA degree in mathematics from International Christian University (Tokyo, Japan) in 1973. She joined INES Corporation (Tokyo, Japan). At present, she is a manager of the Systems Research Center of INES Corporation (Yokohama, Japan). Ms. Furugori is a Certified Information Systems Auditor (CISA). She is interested in the research works on database and knowledge-based systems, human-computer interaction, and groupware. She is a member of Japan Society for Artificial Intelligence, JSiSE, the Operations Research Society of Japan, and Information Systems Audit and Control Association. E-mail: furugori@ines.co.jp.

Du-Seok Jin received a BE degree in Computer Engineering from Chonbuk National University of Korea in 1998. His research interests include multimedia databases, structure document retrieval, content-based retrieval, and data mining.

Christopher N. Klassen is a software consulting and design specialist for The Software Construction Company and a part-time MBA student at the University of Dallas, Graduate School of Management. He has a BA in Philosophy from the University of Dallas and is currently an Oracle Certified Professional DBA. His work has been presented at the Information Resources Management Association 2000 International Conference.

Rudy Lapeer obtained master's degrees in Mechanical Engineering and Computer Science and did a PhD in Biomedical Engineering at the University of Cambridge. He currently is a Senior Research Fellow at the Department of Medical Physics and Bio-engineering at University College London. His main research interests are in computer assisted surgery, medical imaging, video microscopy, ergonomics and HCI.

Jonathan K. Lazar is an Assistant Professor in the Department of Computer and Information Sciences in the College of Science and Mathematics at Towson University. Dr. Lazar earned his PhD in Information Systems at the University of Maryland. Dr. Lazar has a number of research publications focusing on human-computer interaction issues in the Internet environment. Specifically, he is interested in user error, user training, user-centered design, and Web usability. Dr. Lazar is the author of the book, *User-Centered Web Development*, to be published by Jones and Bartlett Publishers in January 2001. Dr. Lazar has taught many Information Systems courses, including courses in System Analysis, System Design, Human-Computer Interaction, Web Development, Online Communities, and Database Management. He is interested in integrating community service with courses and research in Information Systems, and Dr. Lazar was named the Towson University Faculty Advisor of the Year in May, 2000.

Wilfried Lemahieu is a post-doctoral researcher at the Katholieke Universiteit Leuven, Belgium. He holds a PhD in Applied Economic Sciences from the K.U.Leuven (1999). Besides hypermedia systems, his research interests include object-relational and object-oriented database systems, distributed object technologies and web-based information systems.

Alf Linney is a Reader in Medical Physics at University College London and head of the Medical Imaging Group. He lectures undergraduates and postgraduates in statistics, medical imaging and image analysis and assessment. His research over the last 20 years has amongst many other disciplines involved computerised planning of maxillo-facial and cranio-plastic surgery, facial analysis and indentification (forensic science), analysis of radiographic images and computer assisted surgery.

Jonas Löwgren is an interaction designer, researcher and teacher with experience from academia and industry. His work mainly addresses interactive visualization, innovative information technology and design theory. He is currently Director of Research at the Interactive animation studio in Eksjö and Professor of Interaction design at Malmö University College, Sweden. More information is available at http://www.animationenshus.eksjo.se/Jonas.Lowgren.

Anthony F. Norcio is a Professor of Information Systems at the University of Maryland Baltimore County. Dr. Norcio is also the Co-Director (with Dr. Marion J. Ball) of the World Health Organization /Pan American Health Organization (PAHO) Collaborating Center for

Health Informatics. Dr. Norcio serves as an external advisor to the PAHO and to the Inter-American Development Bank (IDB) on computing and health informatics. He is an invited member of the PAHO/IDB Health Task Force of The Informatics 2000 Initiative for Latin America and the Caribbean. He also currently serves as a Computer Scientist at the Artificial Intelligence Center of the Naval Research Laboratory; he has also served as the Scientific Advisor to the Mathematical, Computer, and Information Sciences Division of the Office of Naval Research. He regularly participates on planning and program committees for national and international conferences. Dr. Norcio has published dozens of scientific papers in various journals as well as the proceedings of numerous national and international conferences.

Hiroaki Ogata received the BE, ME and PhD degrees in Department of Information Science and Intelligent Systems from Tokushima University, Japan in 1992, 1994 and 1998, respectively. Since 1995, he has been a research associate in Faculty of Engineering, Tokushima University. His current interests are in Computer-Supported Collaborative Work and Learning. He is a member of the Information Processing Society of Japan, The Institute of Electronics, Information and Communication Engineers, the Japan Society for Information and Systems in Education (JSiSE), IEEE, ACM, AAAI, Association for the Advancement of Computing in Education and International Society of Artificial Intelligence in Education. He got the best paper awards from JSiSE in 1998 and from WebNet in 1999, respectively. E-mail: ogata@is.tokushima-u.ac.jp.

Sooyong Park is Assistant Professor of Computer Science at Sogang University. He received his Bachelor of Science Degree in Computer Science from Sogang University, Seoul, in 1986, the Master of Science Degree in Computer Science from the Florida State University, in 1988, and a PhD in Information Technology with a major in Software Engineering from George Mason University in 1995. He has been involved in various large scale system integration projects through C3I Center and Software Systems Engineering Center in GMU and TRW as a research assistant and senior software systems engineer. His research interests include requirements engineering, agent-oriented software engineering, software architecture.

Ronald E. Purser is Associate Professor of Management in the College of Business at San Francisco State University. He is co-author of four books including: *The Self Managing Organization: How Leading Companies Are Transforming the Work of Teams for Real Impact* (The Free Press, 1998), *The Search Conference* (Jossey-Bass, 1996), *Social Creativity, Volumes 1 & 2* (Hampton Press, 1999).

Mahesh S. Raisinghani, is the founder and CEO of Raisinghani and Associates, a diversified global firm with interests in software consulting and technology options trading. As a faculty member at the Graduate School of Management, University of Dallas, he teaches MBA courses in Information Systems and E-Commerce and serves as the Director of Research for the Center for Applied Information Technology. As a global thought leader on E-Business and Global Information Systems, he has been invited to serve as the local chair of the World Conference on Global Information Technology Management and the track chair for E-Commerce Technologies at the Information Resources Management Association. He has published in numerous leading scholarly and practitioner journals, presented at leading world-level scholarly conferences and has recently published his book

E-Commerce: Opportunities and Challenges. He has been invited to serve as the editor of the special issue of the *Journal of Electronic Commerce Research on Intelligent Agents in E-Commer*ce. Dr. Raisinghani was also selected by the National Science Foundation after a nationwide search to serve as a panelist on the Information Technology Research Panel and the E-Commerce Research Panel for Small Business Innovation. He serves on the editorial review board for leading information systems publications and is included in the millennium edition of *Who's Who in the World, Who's Who Among America's Teachers* and *Who's Who in Information Technology.*

Duska Rosenberg obtained a BA (equiv.) in English Language and Literature with Ethnology as subsidiary subject, University of Zagreb, Croatia; an MA in Linguistics, University of Reading, and a PhD in Computer Science, Brunel University. She is Senior Lecturer in Management Information and Communication Systems at Royal Holloway, University of London. She has international and interdisciplinary working links with research institutions in Europe and the USA and with industrial partners, particularly in the construction industry such as Balfour Beatty - Stent Foundations Ltd., Ove Arup and Partners, DEGW. Her most recent activities include design-oriented research, particularly in the areas of Computer-Supported Cooperative Work and Workplace Studies, specializing in informational requirements of cooperating groups involved in risk decision making. A key theme of her work is the need to develop a sound theoretical base for the study of information and its use in organizational settings. Her projects address issues such as the impact of advanced interactive systems on human cognition and communication in the workplace, in particular, the role of common artefacts and multi-media representations in facilitating teamwork. She has significant experience of multidisciplinary research in the areas related to people and technology at work and substantial knowledge of industry's needs for better communication facilities and services. E-mail at duska@dircon.co.uk.

Lawrence L. Schkade, PhD, CCP, CSP, is Garrett Research Professor of Information Systems, a distinguished appointment by the Regents, The University of Texas System for international scholarship and service. A Ford Foundation Post-doctoral Fellow at the University of Chicago and the University of California at Berkeley, he was also a Ford Foundation Research Fellow, Instituto Tecnologico de Monterrey, Mexico. Dr. Schkade is a Fellow, American Association for the Advancement of Science and a Fellow and Past President, Decision Sciences Institute. He has held faculty appointments at the University of Louisiana-Lafayette, Louisiana State University and The University of Texas at Austin before joining The University of Texas at Arlington. His administrative experience includes service as department chair, Associate Dean and Dean of Business, and Dean of the University Graduate School. Internationally recognized for his research on system theory, human information processing, artificial intelligence, and computer disaster recovery, he has numerous listings include *Who's Who in Finance and Industry, Who's Who in Science and Engineering, Who's Who in the World* and in the 1996 and 2000 editions of *Who's Who Among America's Teachers*. In addition, he is a member of eleven honor societies for scholarship, leadership and research. His current research concerns metrics for organizational communication, electronic commerce, knowledge management and organ transplantation. His many publications, including several books and numerous research articles in more than thirty journals such as: *Administrative Science Quarterly, Applied Intelligence, Behavioral Science, Communications of the ACM, Decision Sciences, Expert Systems, Health Care Management Review, Human Systems Management, Information and Man-*

agement, Journal of the American Medical Association, Journal of Business, Journal of Risk and Insurance, Knowledge-Based Systems, Personnel, Public Welfare, Quarterly Journal of Operations Research, and *Systems Practice.*

John Sillince is Professor of Management Information Systems at Royal Holloway, University of London. He has researched and published in the area of virtual teamwork and the use of technology for enabling collaboration, the social and emotional aspects of computer-mediated communication, effectiveness of face-to-face meetings, and the use of language in managing organisational change. His research focus is argumentation as a means for information systems to enable collaboration in teams. This focus has been motivated by requirements for new forms of remote working together in organizations brought about by globalization of business. He is Project Coordinator for the EU funded 'Internet-based intelligent tool to Support Collaborative Argumentation-based LEarning in secondary schools (SCALE)' and Guest Editor for the forthcoming Special Issue of *Virtual Teamwork* of the *Journal of Information Systems.* j.sillince@rhbnc.ac.uk and http://www.ms.rhbnc.ac.uk/comp-media.htm.

Vijayan Sugumaran is Assistant Professor of MIS in the department of Decision and Information Sciences at Oakland University, Rochester, MI. He received his PhD in Information Technology from George Mason University, Fairfax, Virginia. His research interests are in the areas of: Domain Modeling and Reuse, Component-Based Software Development, Knowledge-Based Systems, Internet Technologies, Intelligent Agents, and E-Commerce applications. His recent publications have appeared (or forthcoming) in *Communications of the ACM, Data Base, Industrial Management and Data Systems, Automated Software Engineering, Expert Systems, Journal of Network and Computer Applications,* and *HEURISTICS: The Journal of Knowledge Engineering & Technology.* He has presented papers at various national and international conferences including the International Conference on Information Systems.

Tony Wright is Professor of Otorhinolaryngology and the Director of the Institute of Laryngology and Otology at University College London. His clinical interests are in middle ear and mastoid surgery and the surgery of acoustic neuromas. His research interests are in medical imaging, surgical microscope technology and stereoscopy in scanning electron microscope imaging. Personal experience of major difficulties during oto-neurosurgical procedures have convinced him of the absolute need for CASPIT. Also having obtained a degree in law, he is fully aware of the implications of replacing surgeons by robots!

Yoneo Yano received BE, ME, and PhD degrees in Communication Engineering from Osaka University, Japan, in 1969, 1971, and 1974, respectively. Since 1974 he has been with the Faculty of Engineering, Tokushima University, Japan. He is currently a Professor in Information Science and Intelligent systems. From 1979 to 1980, he was a visiting Research Associate at the Computer-Based Education Research Lab. University of Illinois, U.S.A. His current interests are in the intelligent CAI, human interface and groupware. He is a member of the IPSJ, IEICE, JSISE, Japan Society for Educational Technology, AACE and IEEE.Currently, he is an Editor in Chief of JSiSE and an Editor of IEICE. E-mail: yano@is.tokushima-u.ac.jp.

Index